HUDSON'S SHAKESPEARE.

ADVERTISEMENT.

the edition under notice the best and most convenient extant. The volumes are of just the proper size for handling, and the notes are at the bottom of each page." — *Boston Morning Post.*

"We know of no better edition of Shakespeare. In its paper, typography, and wood-cuts, the present American edition is quite equal, if not superior, to the English. Great pains have been taken to render the text accurate; and Mr. Hudson has scrupulously eliminated all superfluous and merely speculative matter in the notes." — *The Evening Transcript, Boston.*

"Mr. Hudson has made so judicious a selection from what it was advisable to preserve from previous collections of other plays, that we have nothing but praise to bestow upon his labors. The type, too, is clear and pleasant, and the volumes not too large for the hand or the pocket. — *The Examiner, London.*

"For convenient handling and holding, for clearness and beauty of typography, we prefer this edition of Shakespeare to any other extant."
Washington Republic.

"There is every probability that, as soon as Mr. Hudson's 'Shakespeare' becomes known, as it well deserves to be, in this country, it will meet with no inconsiderable amount of patronage here; for, in addition to what we have already said, the size, the quality of the paper, the excellence of the type, and all the minor accessories, are unquestionably in its favor."
New Quarterly Review, London.

"A most acceptable service will be rendered to the reading world, and to the admirers of Shakespeare in particular, by Mr. Hudson's labors upon this edition of the works of the great dramatist. As editions are so numerous, and discrimination between them not easy to those who have a little leisure, we may do such a service by giving them a brief idea of the merits of the one before us. It is modelled upon the celebrated Chiswick edition, published twenty-six years ago — preserving very nearly the *tout ensemble* of that work, but differing from it most essentially in the text and annotations. The almost multitudinous corruptions which were incorporated in the Chiswick copy — the fruits of successive editorial corrections — so called — of the original text, have been expunged, and the true readings restored. The annotations are frequently entirely new, a necessity arising from the correction of the text. . . . . We have only to add, that the mechanical execution of the work is almost faultless, and that it will probably be completed during the present year." — *Southern Lit Gazette.*

"An edition of Shakespeare, edited so admirably as this — so convenient in its form, so elegant in its execution, and so cheap in its price — will, we hope, have a circulation over the country, corresponding to its great merits."
Graham's Magazine, Philadelphia.

"As a work for schools and families, this edition will be found better adapted than any other we have examined. The volumes are convenient in size, and the printing clear." — *Godey's Lady's Book.*

"The same judicious style of annotation, not excessive, but sufficient for the ordinary reader, which marks the former volumes of this edition, characterizes the two before us. In point of size, goodness of type, portability, &c., this is certainly the best edition of Shakespeare, as a text for reading, now extant in the language." — *Methodist Quarterly Review.*

"It is, of all editions yet published, a favorite one with us, and we have some half dozen or more." — *Hunt's Merchants' Magazine.*

"The introduction to the several plays by the editor, Mr. Hudson, one of the best Shakesperian students and interpreters of the day, are very full, abounding in elegant criticism upon the creations of the poet's genius, and containing appropriate historical notices of the plays. Indeed, the edition is in all respects an excellent one, and notwithstanding the multiplication of copies of Shakespeare, there is ample room for the present issue, as it supplies a place not filled by any previous one." — *Lowell Journal.*

A RECORD

OF

THE BOSTON STAGE.

BY

WILLIAM W. CLAPP, Jr.,
EDITOR OF THE "BOSTON EVENING GAZETTE."

BOSTON AND CAMBRIDGE:
JAMES MUNROE AND COMPANY.
MDCCCLIII.

CAMBRIDGE:
ALLEN AND FARNHAM, PRINTERS.

PREFACE.

THE following pages were originally published in the *Boston Evening Gazette*, and the favor extended to them by the public has induced the writer to present them in a more convenient form, for reference and perusal. Many corrections and considerable additions have been made, since they first appeared; and, by the kindness of friends, many material facts relating to the progress of the Drama have been obtained.

The sources of information from whence the facts have been obtained, were the most authentic; and it has been the writer's endeavor to present to the public an interesting sketch of the progress of the Drama in this city, from the earliest times to the present day. How far he has succeeded, the reader will judge.

BOSTON, 1853.

CONTENTS.

CHAPTER I.

CHAPTER II.

CHAPTER III.

CHAPTER IV.

CHAPTER V.

CHAPTER VII.

CHAPTER VIII.

CHAPTER IX.

CHAPTER X.

CHAPTER XI.

CHAPTER XII.

CHAPTER XIII.

CHAPTER XIV.

CHAPTER XV.

CHAPTER XVI.

CHAPTER XVII.

CHAPTER XVIII.

CHAPTER XIX.

CHAPTER XX.

CHAPTER XXI.

CHAPTER XXII.

CHAPTER XXIII.

CHAPTER XXIV.

CHAPTER XXV.

CHAPTER XXVI.

CHAPTER XXVII.

CHAPTER XXVIII.

CHAPTER XXIX.

CHAPTER XXX.

CHAPTER XXXI.

CHAPTER XXXII.

CHAPTER XXXIII.

CHAPTER XXXIV.

CHAPTER XXXV.

A

RECORD OF THE BOSTON STAGE.

CHAPTER I.

Introductory Remarks. — First Performance in Boston. — Law against Theatricals. — Amateur Theatricals. — Burgoyne's Play. — Attempt made to Repeal the Law against Theatricals. — The Exhibition Room in Board Alley. — Opening Bill. — "Moral Lectures." — Trouble at the Theatre. — Arrest of Harper, and Trial in Faneuil Hall. — Death of Governor Hancock. — Charles Stuart Powell and his "Evening Brush for Rubbing off the Rust of Care." — First American Play. — Origin of the Federal Street Theatre. — A Curious Pamphlet.

THE introduction of the Drama into the United States dates back to the year 1749, and it flourished to some extent at the South before it found a "local habitation and a name" in Massachusetts. The colonial authorities of this State were opposed to theatrical amusements. They had but a very imperfect idea of their bearing, and in their ignorance deemed the theatre the abode of a species of devil, who, if allowed once to exist, would speedily make converts. The first allusion to the subject is made by Increase Mather in

1686. In a preface to his "Testimony against profane and superstitious customs," he says: "There is much discourse now of beginning Stage Plays in New England;" but we have no account that any representations were actually given, and it is generally conceded that the first public dramatic performance in this city was Otway's "Orphan, or Unhappy Marriage," which was produced at the Coffee House in State street, by two young Englishmen, assisted by some volunteer comrades from the town. Such an innovation was looked upon with horror. The more puritanical at once protested against the proceedings, and in the month of March, 1750, the General Court of Massachusetts passed the following act:—

An Act to Prevent Stage-Plays, and other Theatrical Entertainments.

For preventing and avoiding the many and great mischiefs which arise from public stage-plays, interludes, and other theatrical entertainments, which not only occasion great and unnecessary expenses, and discourage industry and frugality, but likewise tend generally to increase immorality, impiety, and a contempt of religion.

SECTION 1.—Be it enacted by the Lieutenant Governor, Council, and House of Representatives, that from and after the publication of this act, no person or persons whosoever shall or may, for his or their gain, or for any price or valuable consideration, let or suffer to be used and improved, any house, room, or place whatsoever, for acting or carrying on any stage-plays, interludes, or other theatrical entertainments, on pain of forfeiting and paying for each and every day or time such house, room, or place shall be let, used, or improved, contrary to this act, twenty pounds.

SECTION 2.—And be it further enacted, that if at any time or times whatsoever, from and after the publication of this act, any person or persons shall be present, as an actor or spectator of any stage-play, interlude, or theatrical entertainment in any house, room, or place where a greater number of persons than twenty shall be assembled together, every such person shall forfeit and pay, for every time he or they shall be present as aforesaid, five pounds. The for feitures and penalties aforesaid to be one half to his Majesty for the use of the Government, the other half to him or them that shall inform or sue for the same; and the aforesaid forfeitures and penalties may likewise be recovered by presentment of the grand jury, in which case the whole of the forfeitures shall be to his Majesty for the use of this Government.

A law so stringent had the desired effect. Private theatricals were clandestinely given, however, and efforts were made to effect its repeal. In 1767, says Bradford in his History of Massachusetts, attempts were made to permit theatrical exhibitions, and to repeal the laws before made against them. The proposal this year (some unsuccessful efforts having been previously made to repeal the old laws) was equally vain; a majority of the people were opposed to such exhibitions and entertainments. They considered them as calculated rather to corrupt than to improve the heart. They said: "They claimed, indeed, to be innocent amusements; but they believed them the means of disseminating licentious maxims, and tending to immorality of conduct."

In 1775, the British army in Boston received a powerful reinforcement from England under Generals Howe, Clinton, and Burgoyne. General John Burgoyne was a dramatic author, and in the year 1774, the "Maid of the Oaks," a very indifferent composition from his pen was performed at Drury Lane. On his arrival in this country, to relieve the tedium of head quarters, he produced his second drama, called the "Blockade of Boston." The English army at the time was beleaguered in the city by the American militia; and this piece was written with a view of inspiring his men with due contempt for the enemy, and performed in Faneuil Hall. One of the programmes read as follows: —

On Saturday next, will be performed by a society of ladies and gentlemen, at Faneuil Hall, the "Tragedy of Zara." The expense of the house being paid, the overplus will be applied to the benefit of the widows and children of the soldiers. Pit one dollar; gallery quarter of a dollar. Doors to be opened at five, and begin precisely at six o'clock. — *Vivant Rex et Regina.*

Burgoyne's play was probably frequently played, for the military are proverbially fond of the stage, and many actors, who have become oraments to the profession, can date their first appearance at the theatre of the barracks. It is related, that during one performance of the "Blockade of Boston," probably in March, 1776, prior to the evacuation of the city, a very curious scene occurred. In one of its merriest scenes, a sergeant, without his hat, and in the wildest confusion, suddenly rushed on the stage, and shouted in a voice of thunder, "the rebels — the rebels — they're attacking the Neck!" which the audience supposing to be a part of the piece, applauded very loudly, being struck with the soldier's highly natural acting. A few minutes afterwards the beating of drums served to break the illusion, and the scampering off of the actors, put an end to the play.

The prohibitory law was reënacted in 1784, and though theatres were in full success in New York and Philadelphia, no attempt was made in this city to establish one till the 5th of June, 1790, when Hallam and Henry presented a petition to the Legislature, praying for leave "to open a theatre in Boston under proper regulations;" but the petition was not considered. The leading residents of Boston, many of whom were above the vulgar prejudices of the day, in regard to theatrical representations, and who possessed a taste for refined pleasures, in the autumn of 1791, brought this subject by a special warrant before the town meeting. An attempt was made to postpone any consideration of the subject, but a majority were in favor of it, and instructions were adopted at an adjourned meeting, requested the representatives to the general court, to effect a repeal of the law, the instructions stating that, "A theatre, where the actions of great and virtuous men are represented, under every possible embellishment which genius and eloquence can give, will not only afford a rational and innocent amusement, but essentially advance the interests of private and political virtue; will have a tendency to polish the manners and habits of society, to disseminate the social affections, and to improve and refine the literary taste of our rising republic."

Shortly after the opening of the legislature in January, 1792, Mr. Tudor, one of the representatives from Boston, brought the subject up. "After stating the reasons," says Mr. Buckingham in the New England Magazine, "which had induced him thus early to rise, he read the law prohibiting theatrical entertainments, and moved that a committee be appointed to consider the expediency of bringing in a bill to repeal it. No person rose to speak on the motion; the question was called for, and decided in the negative, 47 to 69. On the speaker's declaring the vote in the negative, Mr. Gardner, of Hallowell, moved for a reconsideration. His motion was advocated by Messrs. Widgery, Beck, and Jarvis. The question of reconsideration was finally carried, 71 to 33, and the subject was committed to Messrs. Gardiner, Greenleaf, Hichborn, Bowers, Flagg, Washburn, and Kingley. A remonstrance against the repeal had been presented to the House, by sundry inhabitants of Boston, and was referred to the same committee. Mr. Gardiner on the 20th, reported verbally, that it was inexpedient to repeal the law. He remarked that the committee consisted of seven members, that two were decidedly against the repeal, that two others had voted against it, but acknowledged that they were not perfectly acquainted with the whole nature and tendency of stage-plays; and that himself and the other two members were in favor of repealing it. On the 25th, the report of the committee was called up as the order of the day. Mr. Tudor opposed the acceptance of it, and Mr. Gardiner followed in an elaborate speech of several hours duration in opposition to the report. Dr. Jarvis, and others, advocated the same opinion. There was no reply — but when the question was taken, the law was sustained by accepting the report, 99 to 44."

The friends of the drama, however, were determined to encourage theatricals, and probably thought that the only way to show their opponents the folly of their course was to present them with an opportunity for enlightenment. A committee composed of Joseph Russell, Esq., General Henry Jackson, Joseph Barrell, Dr. Jarvis, and Joseph Russell, Jr., built at their own expense in Board Alley, now Hawley street, (originally a path through a pasture made by the worshippers at Trinity Church, who resided in King street, — and called Board Alley from the fact that it was subsequently boarded over,) a theatre, in every thing but the name, and call it the "New Exhibition Room." It was capable of holding five hundred persons. On the 10th of August, 1792, it was opened under the management of Mr. J. Harper. The following is the opening bill: —

NEW EXHIBITION ROOM.

BOARD ALLEY.

Feats of Activity.

This Evening, the 10th of August, will be exhibited Dancing on the Tight Rope by Monsieurs Placide and Martin. Mons. Placide will dance a Hornpipe on a Tight Rope, play the Violin in various attitudes, and jump over a cane backwards and forwards.

INTRODUCTORY ADDRESS

BY MR. HARPER.

SINGING

BY MR. WOOLS.

Various feats of tumbling, by Mons. Placide and Martine, who will make somersetts backwards and forwards over a Table, Chair, &c.

Mons. Martin will exhibit several Feats on the Slack Rope.

In the course of the Evening's Entertainments, will be delivered

THE GALLERY OF PORTRAITS,

OR

THE WORLD AS IT GOES,

BY MR. HARPER.

The whole to conclude with a Dancing Ballet, called

THE BIRD CATCHER.

With the Minuet de la Cour, and the Gavot,

BY MONS. AND MADAME PLACIDE.

☞ Doors to be opened at seven o'clock, and the exhibition to begin precisely at half after seven.

☞ Tickets at 6s. First Seats, 4-6 Second Seats, and 3s. Third Seats, may be had at the Post Office, at J. Leverell's, Marlborough street, and at B. Russell's Printing Office, State street, of whom the first seats may be taken from the hours of 10 till 1, A. M., and from 3 till 5, P. M., on Exhibition Days.

N. B. — Ladies and Gentlemen are requested to order their servants to set down and take up with their horses' heads towards Summer street.

The performances were similar to the above for some time, and the writers in the papers stated that the promised influence upon the morals of the community was not so great as anticipated, and expressed the opinion that the tight rope applied to the *legs* is not so effectual, to refine the *morals* of the people, as the old fashioned way of applying it to the *neck*, practised in other countries.

The tight rope dancing, however, was soon superseded by plays, given under the title of Moral Lectures. Garrick's farce of "Lethe" was produced as a satirical lecture called Lethe, or Æsop in the Shades, by Mr. Watts, Mr. and Mrs. Solomon. Otway's "Venice Preserved" was announced as "A Moral lecture in five parts, in which the dreadful effects of conspiracy will be exemplified." The "West Indian," "Poor Soldier," "Rosina," "Love in a Village," "Romeo and Juliet," "Hamlet," were also performed, as moral lectures. The bills, announcing these moral lectures, were written with considerable tact. We have a copy of a bill of "Othello" produced in this disguise at Newport, R. I., similar undoubtedly to those at the Exhibition Room, which is as follows:—

KINGS ARMS TAVERN — NEWPORT — RHODE ISLAND.

On Monday, June 10th, at the Public Room of the above Inn, will be delivered a series of

MORAL DIALOGUES,

IN FIVE PARTS,

Depicting the evil effects of jealousy, and other bad passions, and proving that happiness can only spring from the pursuit of virtue.

Mr. Douglas—will represent a noble and magnanimous Moor,

called Othello, who loves a young lady named Desdemona, and after he has married her, harbors (as in too many cases) the dreadful passion of jealousy.

Of jealousy, our being's bane,
Mark the small cause, and the most dreadful pain.

Mr. Allyn—will depict the character of a specious villain, in the regiment of Othello, who is so base as to hate his commander on mere suspicion, and to impose on his best friend. Of such characters, it is to be feared, there are thousands in the world, and the one in question may present to us a salutary warning.

The man that wrongs his master and his friend,
What can he come to but a shameful end?

Mr. Hallam—will delineate a young and thoughtful officer, who is traduced by Mr. Allyn, and getting drunk, loses his situation and his general's esteem. All young men, whatsoever, take example from Cassio.

The ill effects of drinking would you see?
Be warn'd, and fly from evil company.

Mr. Morris—will represent an old gentleman, the father of Desdemona, who is not cruel or covetous, but is foolish enough to dislike the noble Moor, his son-in-law, because his face is not white, forgetting that we all spring from one root. Such prejudices are very numerous, and very wrong.

Fathers beware what sense and love ye lack,
'Tis crime, not color, makes the being black.

Mr. Quelch—will depict a fool, who wishes to become a knave, and trusting to one, gets killed by him. Such is the friendship of rogues—take heed.

When fools would knaves become, how often you'll
Perceive the knave not wiser than the fool.

Mrs. Morris—will represent a young and virtuous wife, who being wrongfully suspected, gets smothered (in an adjoining room) by her husband.

Reader, attend; and e'er thou goest hence
Let fall a tear to helpless innocence.

Mrs. Douglas—will be her faithful attendant, who will hold out a good example to all servants, male and female, and to all people in subjection.

> Obedience and gratitude
> Are things as rare as they are good.

Various other dialogues, too numerous to mention here, will be delivered at night, all adapted to the improvement of the mind and manners. The whole will be repeated on Wednesday and Saturday. Tickets six shilling each, to be had within. Commencement at seven, conclusion at half-past ten, in order that every spectator may go home at a sober hour, and reflect upon what he has seen before he retires to rest.

> God save the king,
> And long may he sway
> East, north, and south,
> And fair America.

Many have undoubtedly witnessed "Othello," without being aware of the many moral lessons it inculcates. At the Board Alley Theatre on the 5th of October was presented, "A Moral Lecture announced in five parts," wherein, (says the bill,) the pernicious tendency of libertinism will be exemplified in the "Tragical History of George Barnwell, or the London Merchant."

> Learn to be wise, by others harm,
> And ye shall do full will. — Lillo.

Delivered by Messrs. Harper, Morris, Watt, Murrey, Solomons, Redfield, Miss Smith, Mrs. Solomon, and Mrs. Gray.

The company consisted of Mons. Placide, Mr. Woods, Mr. and Mrs. Morris, Mr. and Mrs. Solomon, Messrs. Robert, Adams, Watts, Jones, Redfield, Tucker, Kenny, Murray, Powell, Mrs. Gray, Miss Smith, Miss Chapman, and the performances had some claims to the character of intellectual entertainments. The opponents of theatricals were struck with terror, and many gave vent to their indignation at this open and bold example of disrespect for the laws, through the columns of the newspapers. A writer in the Chronicle, Nov. 22d, indignant not only that foreigners,—most of the actors being English,—should palm themselves on a republican people, but also with "tales of love between my Lord and Lady, or Sir Charles and his Maid" in this land of liberty and equality,—thus versifies:—

"Bostonians
Shall a lawless Bandittis, faces,
The refuge of a degenerate people
Pass unnoticed, and be suffered
To triumph over the opinions
And the long, well established maxims
Of our venerable ancestors?
Shall vile minions, from a foreign land
Affect to treat with open, marked contempt
The mild influence of our government
In the prevention of those evils
Which experience and well known prudence
Long since stampt by the slow finger of time
With wisdom and success?
What insult is not to be awaited
From men, who, regardless of their honor
Trample upon our laws—our sacred rights,—
When the history of whose lives would put
Modesty and every kindred virtue
To the blush!"

Soon after the opening of the theatre, the Supreme Judicial Court was in session in Boston, and the matter was laid before the Grand Jury, but they did not return a bill of presentment; and as informers were less inclined to do the small work of pseudo reformers than they are now-a-days, the manager enjoyed a feeling of security, and was congratulating himself upon his excellent business; for the little box was crowded nightly, when an event occurred which temporarily checked the fortunes of the drama.

Just after the first act of the play had been performed, on the 5th of December, 1792, the sheriff, in pursuance of a warrant from their Honors, Justice Greenleaf and Barrett, to apprehend sundry persons, said to be infractors of the law against theatrical entertainments, executed his duty so far as Mr. Harper was concerned, being obliged to return *non inventus* on others included in the warrant. The audience finding themselves baulked, were uproarious. Governor Hancock was always a bitter opponent of the theatre, and, supposing that the arrest was made at his instigation, the spectators leaped on to the stage, tore down the arms of the State which decorated a tablet, and trod under foot a portrait of Hancock, which hung in front of the stage box.

Judge Tudor exhorted the audience to be orderly, and several gentlemen immediately came forward and became bound for the appearance of Harper; and at the request of the manager, the audience quietly withdrew, receiving their entrance money.

We have heard another version of this affair, which implicates one Mr. Jerry Allen, who was the sheriff at the time. It is said, that after Allen had done his duty, and taken several gentlemen as surety for Harper's appearance, that he was induced, by a few of his private friends with whom he was on good terms, to take a seat and witness the rest of the performances, which he did, greatly to the amusement of those present. Sheriff Allen was a fine specimen of a bachelor, who loved his fish dinners on Saturdays, and rarely partook of them, unless surrounded at his residence by a dozen or more choice spirits, whose judgment upon wines and dainties, was not to be disputed. We are inclined to believe, however, from information in our possession, that the play did not proceed, and that sheriff Allen executed his duty with becoming dignity, and retired from the theatre with due respect for his office.

The examination was held in "Faneuil Hall," which was thought most proper to proceed to business in, as his Honor Justice Greenleaf's official chamber would not admit the numerous spectators who waited with anxious expectation the result of this *important inquiry.* Attorney Sullivan read a special order from Governor Hancock. O. G. Otis, counsel for Harper, objected to the legality of the warrant, as contrary to the fourteenth article of the Declaration of Rights, which requires that no warrant shall be issued except upon complaints made on oath. Mr. Tudor, also, of his council, supported Mr. Otis, which point was combated by Mr. Sullivan. The justices acceded, and the defendant was discharged amid loud applause. A few days after this transaction, the legislature, owing to the prevalence of the small pox in Boston, met at Concord, when Governor Hancock made allusion to "an open insult upon the laws and government of the Commonwealth," and recommended a more rigid enforcement of them for the future.

It does not appear that any further prosecution was made, although the law was to remain in force till 1797. Governor Hancock was at the time in very feeble health, and died the following October. The law became a dead letter, and was subsequently repealed.

Before the completion of the Exhibition Room, Charles Stuart Powell arrived in Boston, and gave public entertainments. The following is his advertisement:—

At Concert Hall, on Monday, August 13th, ('92,) Wednesday, 15th, and Friday, 17th, will be presented, for the first time here, by Mr. Powell, from the Theatre Royal, Covent Garden, a favorite Pasticcio, called "THE EVENING BRUSH, *for rubbing off the Rust of Care.*"

The Chief Subjects of Laughter: Modern Spouters, Stage Candidates, Tragedy Tailors, Wooden Actors, Butchers in Heroics, Buffoons in Blank Verse, Bagglers, and Blunderers, &c.

Laughter, with reason,
Is surely no treason,
Proportion of grace can have no cause to blush;
And the sons of true merit
No grudge can inherit,
To see rank impostors exposed by the Brush.

With a contrasted set of original Songs; particularly the Tragicomedy of Human Life; the Roman Veteran, or Date Obolum Bellisario; the Golden Days of Good Queen Bess, &c. The whole to conclude with a Whimsical Transformation, or Humorous Dwarf Dance. Tickets half a dollar, &c.

Mr. Powell appeared at the Exhibition Room, and gave his "Brush," and his name will frequently appear in subsequent chapters. At the Board Alley Theatre, the "Contrast," a comedy in five acts, the first American play ever produced by a regular company of comedians, was performed. It was written by Royal Tyler, Esq., of Vermont, and originally produced on the 16th of April, 1786, in New York. It was quite a popular piece, and, in 1790, was published by subscription. The Board Alley Theatre was in full operation till the middle of June, 1793. On the 14th, Mr. Powell gave his "Brush," and in the advertisement regrets he cannot present a farce, as the company have left town. He concludes by saying: —

> "The public may rest assured, this will be positively and definitely the last night of performing this season, as the house will be taken down on Saturday."

The Board Alley Theatre proved so successful, and met with such encouragement, that it was determined to erect another, on a larger and better scale. An association was formed, on the joint stock principle, comprising the liberal and wealthy citizens of Boston, and Messrs. Perez Morton, Joseph Russell, Samuel Brown, Charles Bulfinch, and Henry Jackson, were the trustees, who took measures for building the Boston Theatre, which was in process of erection during the year 1793.

After the destruction of the Board Alley Theatre, entertainments were given at Mr. Bryant's Hall. One of these must have been of a unique character, judging from the announcement, which promises that —

> "Master Henry, from London, will walk on his belly in the shape of a camel. Master Manly will balance his whole body on the edge of a candle-stick, without the assistance of hand or foot. He will pick up two pins with his eyes, and a dollar at the same time with his mouth; rolls like a whale in the sea."

Entertainments of a more refined character, were soon provided for the citizens at the Boston Theatre. In the year 1792, a pamphlet was published in this city by Young & Etheridge, Market Square, with the following title: "Effects of the Stage on the Manners of the People; and the Propriety of Encouraging and Establishing a Virtuous Theatre: By a Bostonian." The copy-right is taken out by William Haliburton, of the

District of Massachusetts, and the contents are worthy of a passing notice, if from their singularity only. The author states, that "as the theatre is once more become the theme of general conversation, and the minds of many appear to be filled and agitated with the subject, it will not be improper to throw together a few observations on the Stage." The author then states his ideas, and in the course of his remarks, says:—

"If only a theatre were wanting, a semicircle would be the most commodious form; but as other, and greater advantages are intended, it would come cheaper, appear more beautiful, be more commodious, useful and durable in the form of a fourteen-sided figure.

"The building should be surrounded with a piazza, whose pillars, at twelve feet distance, should help support a grand dome or roof, and add dignity to the whole figure; so contrived as to admit the light and let out the heated air; the whole body of the building to be furnished with windows, posited so as to be seen in the spaces between the surrounding pillars, also a small seat or bench, attached to the building, and carried from door to door, for the convenience of sitting under the piazza; a narrow coach road to surround the whole, lamps on every corner pillar, and, *if it could be obtained*, a garden of twenty, twenty-five, or thirty feet width, laid round the coach road, from gate to gate, stocked with beautiful flowers and aromatic herbs; which will serve to regale several senses at once. Thus the piazza would become one of the most healthy and delightful walks in the world, and the gentlemen and ladies would be there sheltered from rain.

"Full half the building being reserved for the theatre, a thirty feet passage gives ascent at each end to *large* stair-cases, communicating with the several apartments and galleries, the said passage ornamented by three noble arches with pendant lamps. The first floor on one side, will accommodate the whole legislative assembly, in separate chambers, (with convenient offices and committee rooms adjoining,) where they may deliberate free from the noise of carriages, &c.

"Some will object to the legislature sitting in such a building! It is asked, would they object to sitting and deliberating in a temple or place of worship? No, such places are intended to make men good!

This also is intended to suppress vice, and advance virtue; and serves likewise to make men better, and more virtuous.

"Moreover this costs nothing; will be equally or more commodious than any other building they can erect or purchase; and the assembly will be actually at the distance of sixty feet from the theatre, with no less than three intervening walls of brick. Exhibitions are only in the night time, the assembly sits but seldom and rarely in the night; but any inconvenience on that score may be obviated, by sitting down the company at a distance, or even preventing exhibitions on such nights.

"The *second floor* may be an assembly room, handsomely decorated for the gentlemen and ladies, and serve also the purpose of a noble large dining-room, when celebrating the great events of the nation, accommodated by with-drawing-rooms, as on the floor below. The third story will serve for a military hall, and other purposes. That part of the building devoted to the theatre, will save to the town the great expense of building a hall for town meetings, being very capacious, lightsome and excellently fitted for such use; the galleries will be so constructed, that the feeblest voice below, will be very audible, and distinctly heard in those galleries.

"It is designed to have a lower floor that will contain two thousand spectators, and three galleries to contain fifteen hundred, fifteen hundred, and twelve hundred spectators in five distinctions of seats inclusive of the pit; the prices thus: one shilling, eighteen pence, two shillings, two and sixpence, and three shillings — or, may be varied as prudence shall suggest; total price of the several seats, including the pit, is ten shillings, which, divided by five, gives two shillings as the average price of tickets; multiplied by six thousand, give two thousand dollars for one night of a full theatre; out of which deduct the proportionate share of the annual sum due for principal on the building and the interest, the proportion of salaries, payments to authors, and other incidental expenses, and there will remain a large sum, to be applied to promoting manufactures, employing the able, and maintaining the helpless poor. If the legislature of Massachusetts established such a theatre, and take proper measures to procure persons for actors who are really excellent in their way, and make the most wholesome regulations for the government thereof, its effects on the manners of the people, must be truly astonishing. History will undoubtedly mark an era so favorable to the intellectual powers of man, in this western world. Not only the governors of the State, but all the members of that patriotic assembly, will be recorded as promoters of a design so grand and so beneficial. The first actors and managers, will be also eternized; and the history of the stage will ever after have a conspicuous place in the History of America."

He also proposed to give free admission as a reward of merit to poor citizens who conducted themselves well. The ideas of the author were in advance of the times, however, and his plans were not listened to.

CHAPTER II.

Opening of the Boston Theatre. — Description of the Building. — First Bill. — Snelling Powell. — Mrs. Powell. — The Prize Prologue. — The Early Critics of Boston. — Col. J. S. Tyler's Management. — The New York Company. — Hodgkinson and Hallam. — First Performance of Macbeth. — Death of Joseph Russell. — Anecdotes of Cleveland, and "King Kenny." — Biographical Sketch of John Hodgkinson. — The Introduction of various Customs. — Respect of the Managers for Religion, &c., &c.

THE opening of the Boston Theatre, in Federal street, marks an era in the history of the drama of this city. The change in public opinion, which at that time took place, was the dawn of that spirit of liberality which has since infused itself into our local institutions. It gave an impetus to theatrical representations by allowing temples to be dedicated to Thalia, and Melopemene, and fostered a taste for this innocent and instructive amusement, which has been cultivated, wherever civilization has shed its illumined rays of wisdom, by men of purity, intellect, and genius. The establishment of a theatre on a firm basis, — the most respectable citizens being among its stockholders, — was regarded "as the triumph of taste and liberal feeling over bigotry and prejudice;" and the record of Boston theatricals commences with the opening of its doors on the 3d of February, 1794, under the management of Messrs. Charles Stuart Powell, (who visited England, in 1793, to procure the company,) and Baker, assisted by the trustees, who retained a controlling power over the affairs. The theatre in those days was considered a fine specimen of architecture and creditable to the architect, Mr. Bulfinch. It is alluded to as a lofty and spacious edifice, substantially built of brick, with stone facias, imposts, &c. It was one hundred and forty feet long, sixty-one feet wide, and forty feet high. The entrances to the different parts of the house were distinct, and at the time the opponents of the theatre made strong use of this fact, alleging that by affording a special door to that portion of the house, usually the resort of the vile of both sexes, a premium on vice was offered. In the front there was a projecting arcade, which enabled carriages to land company under cover. The interior of the building was tastefully decorated. The stage opening was thirty-one feet wide, ornamented on each side by two columns, and between them a stage door and projecting iron balcony. Over the columns a cornice and a balustrade were carried across the opening; above was painted a flow of crimson drapery, and the arms of the Union and of the State of Massachusetts, blended with emblems, tragic and comic. A ribbon depending from the arms, bore the motto, "All the world's a stage." At the end of the building a noble and elegant dancing room was constructed. This was fifty-eight feet long, thirty-six wide, and twenty-six high, richly ornamented with Corinthian columns and pilasters. There were also spacious card and tea rooms, and kitchens with proper conveniences.

The performances on the opening night were as follows:—

NEW THEATRE.

Mr. Powell takes this opportunity of acquainting the Ladies and Gentlemen of Boston, and its vicinity, that the new and elegant THEATRE will open

THIS EVENING

With the truly Republican Tragedy of

GUSTAVUS VASA;

THE DELIVERER OF HIS COUNTRY.

All the characters (being the first time they were ever performed by the present company) will be personated by Messrs. Baker, Jones, Collins, Nelson, Bartlett, Powell, S. Powell, and Kenny; Miss Harrison, Mrs. Jones, Mrs. Baker, and the Child by Miss Cordelia Powell, being her first appearance on any stage.

To which will be added an Entertainment, called

MODERN ANTIQUES;

OR, THE MERRY MOURNERS.

Mr. and Mrs. Cockletop, by Mr. Jones and Miss Baker. The other characters, by Messrs. S. Powell, Collins, Nelson, Baker, &c., Mrs. Jones, Mrs. Baker, and Mrs. Collins.

As we shall ever wish to give what we conceive to be the most harmonic to the soul, and congenial to the general sentiments of our brethren of the land we live in, the following distribution of the music will precede the drawing up of the curtain:

YANKEE DOODLE.

Grand Battle Overture in Henry IV.

General Washington's March.

The prefatory Address, by Mr. C. Powell, between the Acts.

A Grand Symphony by Signor Charles Stametz; Grand Overture by Signor Vanhall; Grand Symphony by Signor Haydn; do. by Charles Ditters.

☞ Box one dollar; PIT 3s. 9; GALLERY one quarter of a dollar.

The doors will be opened at five, and the curtain drawn up precisely at six o'clock.

Among the actors above enumerated the name of Snelling Powell occurs. He was born in Camarthen, Wales, and commenced his theatrical career at an early age. His father was a manager of a theatre, and had a respectable company and circuit. Mr. Powell, at an early period of his life, devoted his attention to printing, and when he came to America, in 1793, with his brother, Charles Stuart Powell, he brought with him considerable printing apparatus, which he used in printing the programmes of the theatre. His name will occur frequently in this record. In 1794, Mr. Snelling Powell married Miss Elizabeth Harrison, who also came out under the auspices of Mr. C. S. Powell. This lady was born in Maraison, the county of Cornwall, in the year 1774, and was first cousin to Rev. Henry Martin, an eminent divine. Miss Harrison, previous to her visit to this country, appeared before George the Third, by command; and she had also frequent opportunities of performing the second characters to the queen of tragedy, Mrs. Siddons, who was so much pleased with her acting, that she obtained permission for Miss Harrison to accompany her through a circuit of the provincial theatres. She was the original in this city, as will be seen, of many characters which still retain a position among the favorite theatrical representations of the day; and her impersonations of Shakspeare's heroines entitle her to a rank among the highest in her profession. Mrs. Powell died in December, 1843. Charles Stuart Powell, (noticed in our last chapter in connection with the Brush,) formerly of the Theatre Royal, Covent

Garden, was the first manager of the Federal Street Theatre.

A gold medal was offered for the best written prologue, and the prize was unanimously adjudged to Thomas Paine, then only eighteen years of age, who afterwards took the name of his father, Robert Treat Paine, by leave of the legislature. This production was delivered by C. S. Powell in the character of Apollo, and was highly creditable to the poet's genius.

The theatre was crowded on the opening night. It would not have been possible to have selected from the whole catalogue of English plays one which would have been more appropriate to the occasion than "Gustavus Vasa," a tragedy by H. Brooke, written in 1739, but which, on account of its political sentiments, (admirably adapted, however, to this locality, corresponding as it did with the opinions of a great majority of the citizens,) was prohibited to be played, even after it had been rehearsed at Drury Lane. The author, however, was not injured by the prohibition; for on publishing the book by subscription, he cleared a thousand pounds.

The theatre was well patronized, entertainments being given three evenings each week; and in order to conciliate the more rigid inhabitants, it was announced that on no account would the evenings fall upon those devoted to religious services, which were held in Rev. Dr. Belknap's church in the same street. The custom was then introduced, which prevailed for many years, of allowing the audience to call upon the orchestra for such pieces of music as suited the popular taste; and though popularity was in a measure obtained by allowing the members of both political parties to hear their favorite airs, oftentimes indicative of party spirit, which then ran high, it was the source of much confusion. In Philadelphia, about the same time, a riot occurred, owing to the orchestra refusing to respond to the call; seats were broken, and the play terminated. No difficulty of this kind, however, occurred, though Powell and Baker quarrelled; and the latter, with his wife, withdrew from the company after a few months, and gave Dramatic Olios at Concert Hall. The season closed on the fourth of July, 1794.

The second season commenced Dec. 15, 1794, Mr. C. S. Powell as manager. Mrs. Pownall (who died in 1796) was engaged. She was a singer of considerable ability, and gained great applause in opera divertisements. On the opening night the bills announced that a comedy written by Shakspeare, entitled "As You Like It," and "Rosina," would be performed.

The company consisted of C. S. Powell and wife, Snelling Powell and wife, Jones and wife, Collins and wife, Hughes and wife, Bartlett, Taylor, Kenny, Heelyer, Hipworth, Villiers, Mrs. Heelyer (afterwards Mrs. Graupner), Miss Harrison, &c. &c. Mr. Taylor was a new face, and gained great credit as *Octavian* in the "Mountaineers." He returned to England subsequently, and died. The company was not a strong one, if we can judge by the criticisms which appeared in the journals. One critic, after slaughtering the male members, states that it is with pain he is called upon to censure the fairer part "of our species," and alluding to an actress, he mildly informs the reader that she has neither face, nor voice, nor form, nor action, in short, no one talent for the profession she has usurped.

"When to enforce some very tender part,
The right hand sleeps by instinct on the heart;
Her soul, of every other thought bereft,
Seems anxious only where to place the left."

The season, which terminated June 19th, 1795, resulted in Mr. C. S. Powell becoming a bankrupt, though he was guaranteed for the services of himself, wife, and daughter, from the proprietors, twenty pounds per week. During the summer interval, Mrs. Pownall gave an occasional concert in the theatre; and the Assembly Hall was used for dancing parties.

Col. J. S. Tyler, a gentleman interested in theatricals, was solicited at this time to assume the responsibility of the management by the trustees; and, more from a desire to advance the cause of the drama than from any pecuniary motives, he consented to take charge of the business, and at once made arrangements with Messrs. Hallam and Hodgkinson to bring on the New York company to Boston; and having engaged a portion of the former company, the whole formed a very effective and numerous corps, comprising, as the regular Boston company, Snelling Powell and wife, Harper and wife, Chambers and wife, Hughes and wife, Baker and wife and daughter, Taylor, Villiers, Kenny, and Mrs. Pick. The company from New York consisted of Hodgkinson and wife, Hallam and wife, Tyler and wife, Hamilton and wife, Johnson and wife, Cleveland and wife, King and wife, Martin Premore, &c., &c.

A brilliant and profitable season was anticipated; and certainly so strong a band merited success. The proprietors were sanguine; but, seeing the impossibility of accomplishing much at the old prices, they were raised, as will be seen by the following advertisement inserted in the newspapers of the day:

TO THE PUBLIC.

From a consideration of the enormous expense which the present Manager of the Boston Theatre is subject to, by having engaged a company of thirty-eight persons for the ensuing season, several of whom are confessedly in the first line of excellence, together with a more numerous orchestra, and preparations of several splendid pantomimes.

The proprietors have unanimously, upon mature deliberation, been compelled to adopt the following prices, the same as at the principal theatres on the continent, viz:

Boxes, one dollar.

Pit and Slips, three quarters of a dollar.

Gallery, half a dollar,

assuring the public, that at the reduced prices adopted heretofore, a full audience every night of performance, would not be more than barely adequate to the expense.

From so numerous a company, every species of theatric exhibition may be expected, and is assured to the public by the manager. Boston may now rival, nay, outvie any other theatre on the continent. To a liberal and discerning public this statement is given, and the proprietors presume, on their cheerful acquiescence, to a measure absolutely necessary to the support of their favorite amusement.

By order of the Trustees,

Jos. Russell, *Secretary.*

Boston, Oct. 22, 1795.

The third season accordingly commenced on the 2d of November, 1795, under Colonel Tyler's management, the title of colonel having been acquired as commander of the Cadets. Mr. John Hodgkinson assisted him as stage manager. The public was partial to Mr. Tyler on account of his being an American, and it was anticipated that he would adopt, as he did, a liberal system, which it was thought would stimulate the dormant genius of our countrymen, and reduce the dependence then placed upon foreign talent. The success of the theatre was great; and we find in the "*Federal Orrery*," a poetical address which was "intended to have been spoken by Col. J. S. Tyler at the opening of the theatre." It is quite lengthy, and though not delivered, is sufficiently interesting to warrant an extract:—

"Let mirth within these walls your souls employ,
Like brothers worship at this shrine of joy;
Let Feds and Antis to our temples come,
And all unite firm *Federalists in Fun;*
Let austere politics one hour flee,
And join in free *Democracy of glee!*"

This was conciliating, to say the least, especially as men then carried their political feelings into the very inner circle of social life, oftentimes severing social ties on this account, and looking upon a political opponent as we should be apt to regard an escaped thief or marauder. Another passage is at once personal and biographical. The manager is supposed to raise his eyes to the gallery, and address the following to the upper row of censors:—

"Luff up my hearties! cheer each drooping box,
The good *ship*—Theatre—is *on the stocks*,
Her *ways* are *greased*—her *after blocks away*,
Then jump her, *jump her*, if you'd give her way.
In me, her captain, know me for your friend,
Your townsman,—town born, town bred—at north end;
Let British lords their haughty birth declare,
I boast of being born in—*Old North Square.*
Then heave ahead, doff hats, and now or never
Come give us three huzzas—NORTH END FOREVER."

The New York company was comprised of Mr. Hodgkinson, an actor of great repute, and Mr. Hallam and others who were excellent in their way; the Boston company included Mr. and Mrs. S. Powell and other favorites. There was considerable trouble between the members of the House of York and the House of Boston, and at times serious results were apprehended; but Mr. Tyler with tact was enabled to conciliate the parties, and outwardly at least there was appearance of harmony. The "Provoked Husband," "School for Scandal," and "Richard III." were brought out; and Dec. 21, 1795, "Macbeth" was performed for the *first time* in this city. *Macbeth*, Mr. Hodgkinson; *Macduff*, Mr. Hallam; *Lady Macbeth*, Mrs. S. Powell. The critics of the day notice the performances very favorably, and demand that Shakspeare's acting plays should be produced, in order to cultivate a taste for the legitimate drama. In November, this year, Mr. Joseph Russell, the active treasurer of the stockholders of this theatre, died. In him the profession lost a warm admirer, who had done good service in promoting a taste for the drama.

Mr. and Mrs. Cleveland were members of the company this season. Mr. Cleveland was a good actor, and very prepossessing in his personal appearance, gifted also with an agreeable address. He was the apologist of the theatre. If an actor was sick, no one could state to the public the substitution of another with so much grace; if a play was not ready on the night announced, no one could lay the case before the audience with such a certainty of having the piece proposed in its place so warmly applauded — in fact, he had a peculiar knack for making apologies, and rarely did he retire from the execution of this, to him agreeable task, without receiving a round of applause. On one evening he was performing "Romeo." The play had reached the fifth act, and the noble Montague lay dead, the fair Juliet weeping over him. At this point the Old South bell began to toll out alarming peals, and with such vehemence did the bell-puller do his work, that the audience began to fear that even the theatre was in flames, and some movement occurred in the dress circle. Poor Cleveland, dead as Romeo, but still alive as the Apologist, could not resist the ruling passion. He immediately, in the midst of Juliet's lamentations, set up and said: "*Ladies and Gentlemen, I beg you not to be alarmed. It is only the Old South bell, I assure you,*" and before the fair Capulet had time to recover from her astonishment, Romeo again lay dead before her.

Kenny was also a member this season. He was more familiarly known as King Kenny, from the fact, that he always did the kingly parts. He was an eccentric fellow, and sometimes guilty of altering Shakspeare, when he was not perfect in his part. Snelling Powell, who was not only a good actor, but an excellent critic, stood at the wing, and heard Kenny deliver some speeches which it would have defied any one to find in the bard's works. As he came off Powell said: "My heavens, Kenny, what is all that stuff you've been talking?" "Shakspeare slightly altered so that the audience would understand it," replied Kenny, without a smile crossing his kingly face. "Anthony Pasquin," whose real name was Williams, had the entree to the green room, and one evening while there, Kenny, dressed in his regal robes, and having the air of royalty itself, strutted in. Pasquin was a high tory, and glancing at Kenny he said: "They may talk about republicanism, as much as they please; but you, Kenny, I consider the only real republican in this country. Kenny, a little toryish himself, quickly retorted, "How so?" "Why," said Pasquin, "you *murder* all the kings." His offended majesty strutted off indignant at the attack, and was soon giving his wholesale orders on the stage.

The company of Hallam and Hodgkinson closed their performances on the 20th of January, 1796, and returned to New York, where they opened in the following February.

We have alluded to Mr. John Hodgkinson, the first actor who visited the Western world in possession of a transatlantic reputation as a man of considerable ability. He was born about 1765. His career as a son of Thespis commenced, like many others, in a quiet cellar, fitted up by juveniles, for the purpose of dramatic entertainments on a very limited scale; the taste for the stage having been acquired by visiting the exhibitions of strolling players. His parents kept a public house in Manchester, England; and John, when a boy, aided them in their laborious duties by discharging the offices of pot-boy, though while quite young he was bound out as apprentice to a silk weaver. The interests of his masters were, however, secondary to his own inclinations, which led him to cultivate his talents as a violinist, and secretly to manage a small company who spouted plays under his direction. Discovered in his subterranean retreat by his master, and routed from his adopted leadership, he resolved, being then about fifteen years of age, to start in the world on his own account; and with a crown in his pocket, the gift of two gentlemen who had been pleased with his execution on the fiddle, he set out from Manchester for Bristol, where he dropped his real name, Meadowcraft, and assumed the more homely one of Hodgkinson. On the road, Hodgkinson fell in with a wagoner, whose object it was at first to return the runaway apprentice to his home, but was dissuaded from the idea by the songs he favored him with. So pleased was he with Hodgkinson, that on arrival in Bristol he introduced him to the landlord of the inn at which he put up, and on his recommendation was cordially received and entertained for some time without charge. Soon after his arrival the theatre was announced to be opened by the company just returned from Bath, and John laid his plans to obtain an introduction to the manager. There was a long passage leading to the stage door, and for the first two days in the forenoons he stood at the outside; but becoming impatient he took his station in the passage, and, with his cap under his arm, sought to conciliate those who passed in and out by obsequious bows, omitting, however, to salute one elderly gentleman, who was too repulsive and forbidding for our hero to honor with such attentions, but who in reality was the kind-hearted Keasberry, the manager of the company. John, however, though not the possessor of a fortune, resolved if he could not be a participator behind the scenes he would at least be a spectator, and a large share of his crown piece, though all his worldly fortune, speedily went in obtaining admittance to the gallery. At the expiration of five days, the watchful sentinel was honored by a word from Keasberry, and plainly told him that he wished to become an actor. He was conducted in upon the stage, and after rehearsal the manager announced that he had an individual who desired to be an actor. "What can you do?" asked the manager.

"If I can do nothing else I can snuff candles, or deliver a message, or do any thing that young lads can do."

"You can, indeed?"

"Yes, sir; and I can do more—I can play the fiddle, and sing a good song."

"A song, song!" shouted the members of the company, who collecting round were ready to enjoy a little fun at the new comer's expense, and who were not backward in their jibes and remarks.

"Give him a fiddle as he calls it," said Keasberry.

Hodgkinson took the fiddle, and pitching upon the finale, at the end of the first act of the Padlock, he played it and sung it to the astonishment of all. The smile of derision on the faces of the actors changed to a smile of approval.

"Can you sing with orchestral accompaniment?" asked the manager.

"I'll try," said John, and he succeeded so admirably that he requested the orchestra to play, "Oh, dry those Tears."

At this request the company again smiled, as if they thought his vanity was carrying him too far.

"Try him, by all means, try him," said Mr. K.

He sang it so well, that their surprise was now raised to astonishment; and at the conclusion, Mr. K., patting him on the head, said—

"My boy, you'll never be a candle snuffer. For the present, however, you may carry a letter, or something more, perhaps."

John was soon enrolled a member of the company, and was quite efficient in carrying letters, singing in the chorus, &c. He was extremely assiduous, and was aided by the prompter, who directed him what works to peruse, and so far as he was able made amends for the defects of his early education. In a short time he joined the company of the eccentric James Whiteley, manager of the extensive midland circuit, and was afterwards with Whitlock and Munden, and, during a provincial tour made by Mrs. Siddons, was appointed to perform the principal characters in every play. Hodgkinson, with all his abilities, was peculiarly susceptible to the tender passion; and coördinate with the rise of his fame and fortune, therefore, was the growth of the evils which were fated to endanger the one and make shipwreck of the other; and his professional success and his gallantries, running parallel to each other, like two wheels of a gig, left their marks on every road he travelled in the north of England, and involved him in considerable difficulty. The offer of Henry to visit this country in 1792, was accepted; and with a Miss Brett, whom he made his legal wife on landing in America, he left Bath. Mrs. Hodgkinson was an actress of considerable merit, but inferior to her husband, who was good in whatever he attempted, though his *forte* was comedy. This desire to be everything, actor, author, and manager, was a serious injury to him. He soon became a manager; and in this city and other places, he was at the head of various establishments. A better stage manager probably never existed. He was posted up in all the details, and could if necessary jump into the orchestra and take the lead. His ability, however, as a financier, was wanting. He wrote a play, called "The Man of Fortitude," and several minor pieces. He was a handsome man, and possessed a remarkably retentive memory, and would read over a new part of twenty lengths, (a length is forty lines,) and lay it aside until the night before he was going to play it, attending the rehearsals meantime; then sit up late to *study* it, and the next morning repeat every word, and prompt others. Hodgkinson, as we have seen, was connected with the early history of the drama in this city, and will again figure in this record. He died near Washington, on the 12th of September, 1805; and as it was feared that his demise was caused by the yellow fever, he was wrapped in a blanket by negroes, and conveyed to an obscure burial ground on the Baltimore road. The following appeared in a Boston paper soon after his death. The author's allusion to Hodgkinson sleeping with the "wise and just," is more fanciful, perhaps, than true: —

EPITAPH

ON JOHN HODGKINSON,

The Celebrated Comedian.

Written at the Request of his theatrical friends, by Anthony Pasquin, Esq.

Shrin'd, mid the ashes of the wise and just,
Here Roscius sleeps in his primæval dust!
That tongue is mute which charmed a polish'd age,
Gave zest to wit, and dignity to rage, —
Those eyes no more, will issue lambent fires,
Nor Taste refine the tide of his desires!
Th' obedient Passions hail'd his mimic sway,

The Muses breath'd their influence in his lay—
With pond'rous apothegm and attic jest,
He smote the Demons of the guilty breast;
Bade virtue consecrate what Science saw,
And nerv'd the system of our moral law.
Though Death has triumph'd, Destiny has giv'n
His fame to Honor, and his soul to Heav'n.

CHAPTER III.

Success of the Theatre under the Boston Company.—Pit Tickets Counterfeited.—Management of J. B. Williamson.—A new Theatre talked of.—Proposals for building the Haymarket.—The Inducements held out by C. S. Powell.—Legerdemain.—Arrival of Mr. and Mrs. G. L. Barrett.—Mrs. Whitlock.—Mrs. Rowson.—Opening of the Haymarket.—First Appearance of Mr. Dickson.—Biographical Sketch of Mr. Dickson, &c.—Jealousy of the Rivals.—John Burk.—His play of Bunker Hill.—Anecdotes of the Play.—John Adams, Critique.—Proposed Launch of the Frigate Constitution, and a Managerial Coup de Theatre.—A Patriotic Song.—Destruction of the Federal Street Theatre by Fire.—Mr. Dearborn's Rooms.—Bowen's Columbian Museum.—An American Vauxhall.—Proposals made by the Fanatics.—Wisdom of the "Solid men of Boston."

THE theatre, after the departure of the New York company, was dependent entirely upon the Boston company, and the business was fair. On the 25th of January, "Othello" was brought out. Mr. J. B. Williamson, then just arrived in the country from the Theatre Royal, Covent Garden, made his first appearance in America, as *Othello*, and it was called a good piece of acting. Mrs. Powell, who always adorned the boards sustained the part of *Desdemona.* On the same evening, Mrs. Williamsom, formerly Miss Fontenelle, appeared as *Little Pickle* in the "Spoiled Child," and it was pronounced "unquestionably the most brilliant and astonishing display of theatrical genius ever exhibited to an American audience."

Col. Tyler was successful as a manager, so far as keeping order before and behind the scenes. He encountered naturally many vexations, and not the least of these, was the counterfeiting his pit tickets. The tickets were so like the real ones that it was almost impossible to detect the false from the genuine, and the cheat was only discovered when the house was made up, exhibiting a great discrepancy between the cash received and the tickets taken. A reward of thirty dollars was offered for the perpetrator of this forgery, which put an effectual stop to further proceedings. In April, Mr. Tyler voluntarily resigned the management, and Mr. J. B. Williamson was appointed to succeed him by the trustees. He carried the theatre through the season, which closed May 16th, 1796.

During the early part of this year, Mr. C. S. Powell gave entertainments at Concert Hall, and revived "The Evening Brush." At this time political excitement between the two parties, then denominated Federal and Jacobin, ran high and furious, and it was believed by many, and not without reason, that the Federal Street was managed by those opposed to the Jacobins, and that the trustees, who were all of the federal school of politics, had upheld and justified the manager in the introduction of pieces, tending to provoke the resentments and animosities of their political opponents. This idea was encouraged by the French Consul and others; and Charles Stuart Powell, taking advantage of this condition of affairs, issued his proposals for building a new theatre, to be called the Haymarket. He stated that it could be erected for $12,000, which he proposed to raise by subscription, and to divide the stock into sixty shares, at $200 per share.

Among other inducements he held out, was the promise of a benefit every season for the widows and orphans, which "he doubts not will be a stimulus for the manager of the other house to do the same; by which means, both ends meeting, it will amount to a considerable sum, and draw on each party the blessings of the indigent, and make their theatrical pursuits not subversive, but subservient to a laudable purpose." Every subscriber was to be guaranteed a season ticket during life, even though he sold his share, "provided said share is sold to Charles Stuart Powell." He proposed to take the theatre on a lease of fourteen years, at an annual rent of $1,200. He concludes his proposals by saying: —

> "The following arrangements shall be made for the ease and convenience and general satisfaction of our fellow citizens. The pit shall be spacious, so as to be able to admit them at 3s. The galleries on the same extensive plan. The first gallery 2s. 3d.; where our citizens may go with their wives, or into the pit, as in Europe. The upper gallery, 1s. 6d. These prices never to be altered."

A meeting of Powell's friends was held in Concert Hall, and the stock was immediately taken up. The Boston mechanics were not partial to the Federal Street, and favored the project. Daniel Messenger, Mr. Homer, and others, took stock, and those who were not able to pay the money, also subscribed for shares, and paid in labor, furnishing the material for constructing the building. The site selected was near the corner of Tremont and Boylston streets, where now stand a block of brick houses, painted white.

During the summer the Federal Street was occasionally opened for exhibitions and minor entertainments. Then, as now, foreign seigniors indulged in legerdemain, and optical illusions were sought after; for we read that Seignior Falconi gave a choice entertainment there. The advertisement states that the Learned Swan, an early edition of "Macallister's Peacock," will appear, "the whole to conclude with the appearance of the 'Ghost of the celebrated Charlotte Corde,' as when in the last act of stabbing Marat. She will appear a luminous body, enveloped in darkness, as large as life, and every feature distinguishable for the space of three or four minutes."

The summer vacation was one of considerable activity. The new house was approaching completion; the manager, C. S. Powell, was on a visit to Europe to beat up recruits. The Federal Street was undergoing a thorough cleanliness, and a confidential messenger had also crossed the Atlantic to engage talent for this house; and from time to time, notices were given through the journals of this or that acquisition to the old or new theatre.

The arrival of actors tended to keep up an excitement. Among the first to arrive, were Mr. and Mrs. Giles L. Barrett, parents of George H. Barrett, Esq., familiarly known as "Gentleman George," who at that time was being instructed in the first principles of declamation. Mr. Giles L. Barrett and his lady had a good reputation in England as actors, and their advent to the new Haymarket was deemed a great acquisition. Mrs. Barrett was a pupil of Macklin's, and made her debut as *Portia* in London. Arriving several months prior to the opening of the new theatre, Mr. Barrett, to relieve the tedium, and for pecuniary emolument, — the hoarding of money never having been characteristic with the family, — gave lessons in fencing and in the manly art of self-defence. Several of his pupils are still living in this city. One of our most eminent surgeons first gave exercise to his muscles under Barrett, and is probably indebted to that early training for the admirable manner in which he is able to execute the most difficult surgical operation with such skill and muscular power. Mr. Barrett was a perfect gentleman, somewhat vain, perhaps, as men of superior capabilities are apt to be, but therefore pardonable. A good anecdote is related of him. He announced a sparring exhibition, and, in order to give *eclat* to the affair, procured the assistance of a Jew, — a powerful person, who had some skill as a boxer, — whose name was Isaacs. On the night of the exhibition, Mr. Isaacs stood up as a sort of a butt, receiving Barrett's blows without flinching. "This blow," said Barrett, "is often used by the celebrated Mendosa;" and then, by way of illustration, he would fall back and tap Mr. Isaacs on the skull. "This blow is that of another great boxer," continued Mr. Barrett, and Mr. Isaacs's eye would receive a rap. Before the illustrations were through of the various styles of the noted champions of the ring, Mr. Isaacs's knowledge-box was in rather a confused state, and as the tutor was proceeding to illustrate still farther, Mr. Isaacs remonstrated: "It ish all vare foine, Monsieur Barrett; but show de gentleman de blow of Isaacs."

After going through the series Mr. Barrett said: "Now, gentlemen, I will show you the favorite blow of Mr. Isaacs."

"No, sare," exclaimed Isaacs, "he vil show de blow hisself;" and without more ado, he walked into Mr. Barrett with the fury of a Hyer, and completely throwing him off his guard, would have beat him from the stage, had not Barrett called for quarter. Isaacs granted it, and turning to the audience, said, "Dat ish Mr. Isaacs's blow."

The season at the Federal Street commenced September 15, 1796, when the "Dramatist" was produced. The part of *Vapid* was played by Mr. Chalmers, an English actor, who, it is said, left England on account of the jealousy which Lewis, the comedian, entertained towards him. He was a gentlemanly, high-minded man, and a good actor, receiving his £50 per night. Chalmers was a member of the stock for several seasons, and was held in high estimation by the citizens. His appearance was soon followed by that of the celebrated Mrs. Whitlock, as *Isabella*, in the "Fatal Marriage." Mrs. Whitlock was sister to Mrs. Siddons, John Kemble, Stephen Kemble, and the veteran Charles Kemble, and was born at Warrington, Lancashire, April 2, 1761. She was a striking and pleasing resemblance of her sister, possessing a full share of her noble air and elocutionary powers, with more amusing powers of conversation. As Miss Elizabeth Kemble, she acted some time at Drury Lane, till she married Charles Edward Whitlock, (a descendant of the great lawyer Whitelock,) who was manager at the time of the Theatre Royal, at Newcastle-upon-Tyne. She was the support and ornament of his company, and came out with her husband to America in 1793, through inducements held out by Hodgkinson. Mr. Whitlock was even then past the meridian of life, and dependent upon his wife's attractions. Of her powers as an actress, a Boston critic remarked:—

"Many votaries of the tragic muse, in their attempt to personate the leading characters of the drama, have discovered more ambition than talent; and in some instances, not destitute of merit, the momentary display of partial excellence has been blemished by some outrage of sentiment,—

'Which sham'd the noblest beauty that they ow'd.'

But Mrs. Whitlock never violates the unity of characters by departing from the dramatic personages she assumes. There is less of the *theatrical imposture*, and more of the *educated mind;* less of the mockery of sensibility, and more of the discrimination of taste in her performances, than, perhaps, in strictness, the scenes of imitative life demand."

Mrs. Whitlock had the honor of playing before George Washington, in Philadelphia. That great man was by no means a stoic at the sight of tragedy; but he hated to be seen weeping, and always wiped the tears with his handkerchief hastily from his face.

Bates appeared as *Justice Woodcock*, in the opera, "Love in a Village," and *Sharp*, in the "Lying Valet." The company always included Mr. Jones, a great favorite, Mr. and Mrs. Rowson, and others. The mention of Mrs. Rowson will recall to the memory of more than one Boston matron, pleasant reminiscences of their early school days. Mr. Joseph T. Buckingham, in his late work, "Personal Memoirs," thus alludes to this lady: —

"Mrs. Susanna Rowson was an acceptable and highly-valued correspondent of the Galaxy. Her contributions were chiefly of a religious and devotional character, and usually signed with her initials; "S. R." She was the daughter of William Haswell, an officer in the British Navy, and, in 1786, was married to William Rowson, a leader of the band attached to the royal guards in London. Mr. and Mrs. Rowson were engaged by Mr. Wignell, the manager of the Philadelphia Theatre, and arrived in this country in 1793. Before she left England, Mrs. Rowson had been engaged in some of the provincial theatres, and was an agreeable singer and performer in the musical after-pieces. She had also written some novels, and a few critical papers, which introduced her to the favorable notice of several distinguished characters among the nobility. The most popular of her works was 'Charlotte Temple, a Tale of Truth,' over which thousands have 'sighed and wept, sighed and wept, and sighed again,' which had the most extensive sale of any work of the kind that had then been published in this country, — twenty-five thousand copies having been sold in a few years. While employed on the stage, in Wignell's company, she found time to employ her pen to advantage. She wrote a novel, called 'Trials of the Heart,' the 'Volunteers,' a farce, founded on the Whiskey Insurrection in Pennsylvania, another called 'The Female Patriot,' and a drama, called 'Slaves in Algiers.' This couple came to Boston in 1796, and performed one season at the Federal Street Theatre; and during that season, Mrs. Rowson wrote a comedy, called 'Americans in England,' which was performed for her benefit, and her last appearance on the stage. At the close of her engagement, she opened a school for young ladies, and afterwards removed to Medford, where her academy and boarding-house were thronged with pupils from every quarter. Her institution was afterwards removed to Newton, and again to Boston. While occupied in this laborious profession, she wrote a novel called 'Reuben and Rachel,' which I remember to have read and admired when I was an apprentice. She published a dictionary, a geography, and, I believe, some other elementary books for the benefit of her pupils. Mrs. Rowson was singularly fitted for the office of a teacher. Her industry and intelligence were great, and her knowledge and skill in household economy was almost unparalleled. Such were her accomplishments, her refined and moral principles, and her pious and charitable dispositions, that her friends were numerous, and her pupils represented the most respectable families in the community. Many of them are now to be seen in the refined and polished circles of the capital of New England. She died in March, 1824, respected, beloved, and regretted by all who knew her."

The old theatre was a favorite resort for the residents of the city and neighboring towns. The audiences were more careful of their dress than those of modern days, and the ladies, especially, paid that attention to their toilets, which is now only bestowed when a visit to Almacks or to the Opera is anticipated. A marshal of ceremonies was in attendance to escort ladies to their seats; and a degree of ceremony observed, of which Bostonians had a faint counterpart when the gentlemanly ushers, under Le Grand Smith, conducted them to their places at Jenny Lind's concerts in 1850. The Old Theatre, as it was called, to distinguish it from the Haymarket, — then known as the New Theatre, — flourished singly and alone; but ere many months elapsed it had a formidable competitor for public favor, and a rivalry commenced, which, with short intervals, has ever since existed between two or more places of theatrical entertainment in this city.

On the 26th of December, 1796, the Haymarket opened. It was an immense wooden pile, proudly overtopping every other building in the metropolis. It had three tiers of boxes, a gallery, a pit, drawing-room, &c. The company was strong and notable, from the fact that it introduced to an American public several who have since made Boston their home, and are closely identified with the subsequent theatrical history of this city, while many, who have been, and still are favorites on the stage, can trace their genealogy back to members of this corps. The company embraced Mr. and Mrs. G. L. Barrett, Mr. and Mrs. Simpson, three Miss Westrays, (daughters of Mrs. Simpson, by a former marriage,) and a *corps de ballet*, among whom were Francisquy, Val, Legé, and their ladies. The opening play was Mrs. Cowley's "Belle's Stratagem," with the following cast:—*Doricourt*, S. Powell; *Sir George Touchwood*, Marriot; *Flutter*, C. Powell; *Saville*, J. H. Dickson, (first appearance in public;) *Courtall*, Taylor; *Villars*, a young American; *Hardy*, Simson, (first appearance;) *Letitia Hardy*, Mrs. S. Powell; *Lady Frances*, Mrs. Hughes; *Miss Ogle*, Miss Harrison, (afterwards Mrs. Dickson;) *Mrs. Rackett*, Mrs. Simpson, (first appearance). Mrs. Marriot, and others, were also attached to the theatre. The play was entirely successful. Mr. Simson made a hit as *Hardy*, and at once established himself as a favorite, and others were equally well received. Mr. Powell delivered an address, written by himself, which was highly applauded. This fortunate opening was followed by the appearance of Mr. G. L. Barrett, as *Ranger*, in the "Suspicious Husband," (Dec. 28th,) Mr. Williamson, (from Covent Garden,) as *Tom Tug*, in the "Waterman," (Dec. 30th,) and Mrs. G. L. Barrett's impersonation of *Mrs. Beverley*, in Moore's tragedy of the "Gamester," first acted at Drury Lane in 1753, (Jan. 2, 1797,) all of whom appeared for the first time in America, and proved great cards. The name of Mr. Dickson will undoubtedly recall to many of our elderly readers the palmy days of Old Drury,—those da y when Bernard, Dickson, Mrs. Powell, and others, performed to houses crowded from pit to gallery with the fashion, the beauty, and the talent of our city, — when the Perkinses, the Parkmans, the Sullivans, had their boxes, and the dress circle presented a sight, seen of later days but too seldom.

The hand of time rested lightly on Mr. Dickson, and preserved him to a ripe old age, rich in that reverence of friends, which a life of worth and integrity gained for him. Mr. Dickson died on Friday morning, April 1st, 1853.

For a few days previous to his death he had been unusually cheerful, taking great interest in matters which of later years had possessed but little attraction, and his friends were anticipating many years of enjoyment in communion with a mind richly endowed with natural gifts, and possessing in an eminent degree, for a man of his age, marked and peculiar powers of retention. His associations in early life had enabled him in many matters to obtain a correct knowledge of events, while his intimacy with almost every man of local distinction during his lifetime, opened for him a store of historical and biographical reminiscences, which gave to his conversation an unstudied attractiveness. In social intimacy with those who were his cotemporaries, he dwelt with pleasure upon the past. He duplicated, as it were, his earlier years of enjoyment. To the young and inquiring he never withheld anything that might be conducive to their interest, and in more than one instance, at great personal inconvenience, imparted information of value, which otherwise would have passed unrecorded. Mr. Dickson is known to us as manager, actor, and merchant, and in each of these callings he acquired distinction. He was born in London in the year 1774, and at the age of twenty-one came to Philadelphia, where he had an uncle. His stay there was brief. At a dinner of a few friends he made some remarks, and quoted so aptly from Shakspeare, delivering the passages with such accuracy, that his companions declared him admirably qualified for the theatrical profession. Prior to his coming to this country, he had associated with members of the profession, and had acquired some little knowledge of declamation; but his education in a mercantile house had been pursued with the idea of becoming a merchant. To this training, and a perfect knowledge of accounts, may be partly attributed his success in after life. In 1796, Mr. Charles S. Powell, who had then contracted for the erection of the Haymarket Theatre in this city, visited Philadelphia for the purpose of securing a company, and engaged Mr. Dickson and a Mr. Trenchard to do the minor business of the theatre. The youthful Thespians made the passage to this city in a vessel. It was Mr. Trenchard's first experience of a sea life, but he subsequently became a sailor, and at the time of his death was a commander in the American navy. On their arrival, they took lodgings with Mr. Dearborn, then the principal of a young ladies' school, located in what is now known as Theatre Alley. It was customary to close the quarter with declamations and private theatricals; and it was under such auspices that Mr. Dickson first trod the boards, wearing on the occasion the garments borrowed of a militia officer. He had at this time changed his name for family considerations, and called himself Dickenson; but in after years, the more certainly to render his legal title to property secure, he assumed his real name, by authority of the legislature, and became naturalized. The Haymarket Theatre, as we have stated, was opened on the 26th of December, 1796, when "Belle's Stratagem" was performed, *Saville*, by Mr. Dickson, his first appearance in public; *Letitia Hardy*, Mrs. S. Powell; and *Miss Ogle*, by Miss Harrison, sister to the last named lady, and afterwards Mrs. Dickson. He gave at that time but little promise of the possession of histrionic talents; but he was attentive to his business, and his study being remarkably rapid, he was highly valuable to the management, who termed him his "sheet anchor," being ready at a short notice to supply a deficiency to the best of his ability. The theatre under John Hodgkinson was not remarkably successful, and for a short time Mr. Dickson was connected with Mr. Trenchard (who did not carry out his intention of adopting the stage) in business. This was brief; for when the Boston Theatre was rebuilt in 1798, after its destruction by fire in February of the same year, Mr. Dickson, under Hodgkinson, became attached to it in the capacity of prompter and deputy manager; and to his charge was intrusted the general superintendence of affairs. Mr. Dickson, when first offered the post, refused it; but Hodgkinson assured him that he could learn more in one year by holding the prompt book, than he could by acting seven,—a remark which was fully realized by the recipient of this valuable hint. He occasionally went on, when necessity required it; and his adoption of a particular line of business, that of leading old men, was the result of mere accident. Mr. Bates, who was cast for *Sir Oliver Oldstock,* in "He Would be a Soldier," was taken sick. He sent for Mr. Dickson in the morning, and begged of him to fill the part; but his natural modesty at once compelled him, from attempting to give satisfaction in a character which Mr. Bates had made his own. The case was one that required immediate decision, and from a spirit of accommodation Mr. Dickson consented; and his success was unequivocal. During the season of 1802 and 1803, he appeared as *Sir Anthony Absolute,* and for years he was the sole impersonator of this character on the Boston boards. His acting displayed the most accurate and critical nicety both in conception and rendition, while his attention to the propriety of dress, and the delivery of the language, gave him at once a powerful hold upon public patronage. His benefit for many years was honored by the attendance of the *elite,* who appreciated the worth of the man and the talent of the actor, and resulted always in the receipts exceeding a thousand dollars.

In 1806, Mr. Dickson became joint lessee of the Boston Theatre with Snelling Powell and John Bernard, under whose auspices the theatre did a most flourishing business. He gave to the "Forty Thieves," at the time of its production, a powerful impetus, by his impersonation of *Mustapha,* and through his exertions, the play was put on the stage in a style of unparalleled magnificence. As manager, he visited England during his summer vacations, (and during his life crossed the ocean upwards of forty times,) to engage talent, and brought to this country many of the most popular favorites of the day. With Cooper, he was instrumental in inducing the great George Frederick Cooke to visit America. The Duffs and others came out under his protection; we may truly say protection, for his friendship was cautiously bestowed, but once given, it knew no limit. After Bernard's retirement, the firm was Powell & Dickson; subsequently Powell, Dickson, & Duff; and still later, after the death of Mr. Powell, in 1821, he was connected with Mrs. Powell & Kilner, and only retired when Kilner & Finn became the lessees. His retirement from the active duties of his profession took place many years prior to his release of the management; for on the 14th of April, 1817, he took his leave of the public, appearing as *Cosey*, in "Town and Country." He appeared, however, twice after this, on the occasion of Mrs. Powell's benefits; his last appearance on any stage was on the 14th of May, 1821, when he appeared as *Sir Robert Bramble*, in the "Poor Gentleman," *Will Steady*, in "The Purse," and *Tag*, in the "Spoiled Child."

When Mr. Dickson first came into the management, there was existing a bitter feeling against theatres and theatrical representations. The hostility was not confined to the ignorant; but many families were so deeply imbued with puritanical ideas, that they never ventured beneath the roof of a playhouse. To conciliate this class, required not only good judgment, but a personal example; and in a very few years, those who had been bitter opponents became warm friends, when they perceived that men of industry and character were engaged in the management. The esteem in which Mr. Dickson was held, contributed materially to the establishment of the drama on a firm foundation, not only in this city, but in Providence, Newport, Portsmouth, &c., where the company, during the summer, gave representations. Under his auspices, the theatre became a charitable institution, dispensing of its receipts to the poor and the unfortunate. There is scarcely a contemporary society but received aid from some benefit given at the old theatre, and the proceeds of all premiums on great attractions were freely distributed among the deserving. The money thus distributed was not confined to any locality; for the residents of Savannah, Geo., and of Portsmouth, N. H., when their cities were laid in ruins by fire, received most generous aid. Upwards of six hundred dollars were sent to the latter place; and in acknowledgment of it, a committee tendered their heartiest thanks for the exercise, as they truly remarked, of "that benevolence so congenial to gentlemen of your profession." Mr. Dickson, cherishing sentiments of respect for the religious rites of society, often at loss to himself, closed his theatre on days of public fast and church days, deeming it a duty he owed to society and the cause of good morals.

We have spoken of Mr. Dickson in his public capacity. After his retirement from the active duties of the profession, he was, till the time of his death, engaged in business. His youthful habits of economy procured for him the basis of an ample competence, laboriously and honestly accumulated. His body was followed to the grave by many of his fellow citizens. Honest in his dealings with all, scrupulously exact in his intercourse with his fellow men, possessing a generous heart

4

and liberal ideas, he departed, having fulfilled an honorable mission.

In thus paying a brief tribute to one who so long swayed the fortunes of the drama, we have anticipated some events which will necessarily form a portion of this record; but the reader will pardon both the digression and repetition.

The three Miss Westrays, who were members of the Haymarket company, will be recollected by many of our elderly readers, and perhaps remind them of their early days of gallantry — for these young ladies had many admirers. Miss E. Westray was afterwards the celebrated Mrs. Darly, who, to personal beauty and grace, united a delicacy that interested, and a naiveté that fascinated. More than one susceptible heart acknowledged the power of her charms, and after her marriage, the jealous husband took forcible means to decrease the number. Another of the Miss Westrays married Mr. Wood, and the third was married to Mr. Villiers, and, subsequently, Mr. Twaits.

The prosperity of the Haymarket stimulated the actors at the old theatre to exert all their energies, though the contest for superiority was against fearful odds. The most intense jealousy existed between the stockholders, managers, and others connected with the two establishments, and the stockholders of the Federal Street, being gentlemen of wealth, spared no expense to injure their new competitor. Each shareholder had his night, when he not only paid the whole expenses, but took pride in having a crammed house. Tickets were sold till the demand was answered, when the balance were given away to those persons who would pledge themselves never to enter the Haymarket. Many thus obtained free entrance to the old house during the season. An elderly gentleman informs us that he was a "dead head" under this promise, and for a long time kept it, till his fellow apprentices lauded a play performed at the Haymarket to such a degree that he resolved to have a peep at it. This he did by quietly visiting the gallery of the Haymarket, where he slaked his curiosity and returned home, trusting that he had enjoyed his stolen pleasures, unknown to any one. The next day, however, he was called up by his master, a firm friend and stockholder in the Federal, and severely reprimanded for breaking his faith, and visiting the enemy. On one occasion, John Burk, the editor of the Polar Star and Daily Advertiser, was accused by the Federal Street party of gross partiality, owing to a mistake of the printer in setting up the advertisement giving the wrong evening of performance. Burk was a man who prided himself on his impartiality, and he enters into a lengthy explanation to prove that it was not done with malice *prepense*, but originated entirely through inadvertence. The Federal Street at this time was obliged to reduce its scale of prices to a portion of the house, and adopted the following prices: Pit, fifty cents; Slips and Gallery, twenty-five cents. The "Mountaineers" and other spectacles were produced, and William Charles White, a gentleman of Boston, made his debut before the close, which took place on the 5th of June, 1797.

This ballet corps, consisting of Val, Legé, Audain, Francesquay, and their ladies, was a very fine one.

Monsieur Val was a nobleman by birth, but lost his fortune during the French Revolution. He and the others were gentlemen of fine manners, and true artistes. After their engagement had concluded here, they went south, and thence to St. Domingo, where unfortunately for themselves, they arrived at the time of the insurrection of the negroes. They were imprisoned, and their black captors made them perform occasionally for their own amusement, though they did not exempt them from the general massacre of the whites which followed.

The Haymarket brought out a piece called "Bunker Hill, or, the Death of General Warren," written by John Burk, the editor. As the same piece, or an adaptation, is performed occasionally, we give the first bill: —

HAYMARKET THEATRE.

(*Never Performed.*)

This Evening, February 17, will be presented a Tragedy, entitled the

BATTLE OF BUNKER HILL;

Or, The Death of General Warren.

Written by Mr. Burk.

Gen. Warren, Commander at Bunker Hill, .	Mr. Barrett.
Col. Prescott, Major Generals in the American Army, . .	Mr. S. Powell.
Col. Putnam, Major Generals in the American Army, . .	Mr. Hughes.
Gov. Gage, ...	Mr. Marriott.
Lord Percy, ...	Mr. Williamson.
Gen. Howe, ...	Mr. Dickson.
Col. Harman, ...	Mr. Fawcett.
American Grenadier, ...	Mr. Wilson.

Officers, Soldiers, and attendants by the rest of the Company. And

Col. Abercrombie, in love with and beloved by Elvira, an American lady, captive in Boston, ...	Mr. Taylor.
Anna, attendant on Elvira, ...	Mrs. Hughes.
And Elvira, American captive, ...	Mrs. Barrett.

To conclude with a grand procession in honor of Warren, whose dead body is borne across the stage on a bier — the American army moving slowly to the sound of solemn martial music — young women dressed in white, holding flowers in their hands, each with one hand on the bier, will accompany the procession. At proper intervals, flags will display Republican emblems, and popular devices.

Principal Mourner and Singer, . . . Miss Broadhurst,
who will introduce an original patriotic Elegy, to the much admired tune of Roslin Castle, over the bier of Warren.
Second Singer and Mourner, . . . Mad. Pick.
Third, ... Miss Eliz. Westray.
Fourth, ... Miss Gowen.
Fifth, ... Miss Westray.
Sixth, ... Miss Eleo. Westray.
The Prologue to be spoken by . . . . Mr. Powell.
Scenery incidental to the piece, painted by . Mr. Audain.

American Music only will be played between the Acts.

To which will be added the favorite Musical Entertainment, called

THE PADLOCK.

Vivat Respublica.

At that time it was well received, the British being well peppered, and the "stars and stripes" floating triumphant. It was local in character, and the scene laid in Charlestown and Boston. Mr. Dickson personated *General Howe,* and how acceptably may be judged from the fact, that the author made $2,000 by the play. Mr. Buckingham, in his "Reminiscences of Newpapers," and gentlemen connected with them, alludes to Burk, and states that his paper suddenly departed this life in 1797. Of the tragedy of its author, he says: — "The tragedy had not a particle of merit, except its brevity. It was written in *blank verse,* if a composition having no attribute of poetry could be so called. It was as destitute of plot and distinctness of character as it was of all claim to poetry. Burk afterwards was the editor of a political paper in New York, called the Time Piece, and was arrested on a charge of publishing a libel, contrary to the provisions of the Sedition Law of 1798. The issue of the affair I never knew. About the year 1800, it was reported that he was killed in a duel in one of the Southern States." The literary merits of the piece, according to this, were very few, but the success, we are assured, was great, which does not speak volumes for critical acumen of the early theatre-goers. Dunlap, in his "History of the American Stage," alludes to a History of Virginia, by Burk, as exhibiting talent and learning.

We have heard one or two anecdotes of this piece which are too good to be lost. The company attached to the Boston Theatre, during the summer vacation, generally visited some of the provincial towns. On one occasion, while at Portland, Mr. Dickson appeared in the play as *Colonel Abercrombie*, who, wishing to marry an American lady, is told that he must desert the cause of the British, and embrace the American side. In this dilemma, he soliloquises, exclaiming: "Heavens! that madness should so bereave a man of his senses as to doubt which of the two to choose — love or honor." "It generally does, Mr. Dickson," exclaimed a voice in the pit, which called forth shouts of laughter. The person who had thus given his opinion was Mr. George, for many years an editor in that city — an unfortunate cripple, who was especially licensed, by public consent, to say what he thought, without regard to time or place. On another occasion, an actor came out to announce the play of the following evening: "Ladies and gentlemen," said he, "we thank you for your attendance this evening, and to-morrow night we shall have the honor of presenting you the much admired play of ——;" here the actor's memory proved treacherous — he bungled, and was at a loss what to say, when little George came to his rescue, by exclaiming: "It is no consequence for you to mention it — the bills are sticking up in the lobby." The play of "Bunker Hill" was performed in New York. President Adams, being in the city, was invited to attend, and at the conclusion of the piece he was conducted by the managers and leading actors to his carriage with considerable pomp and show. Mr. Barrett, who had performed *General Warren,* ventured to express the hope that the President had been pleased. "Sir," replied Mr. Adams, "my friend, General Warren, was a scholar and a gentleman, but your author has made him a bully and a blackguard." Mr. Adams's critique was at once concise and correct.

The season at the Haymarket, which closed in June, 1797, was not very prolific in those results so pleasing to managers. Mr. C. S. Powell and Giles L. Barrett had a quarrel; the former attacked the latter through the newspapers — accused him of being a dictator — and the editors promise a reply from Mr. Barrett. A pause of some days' duration occurs, when Mr. Barrett intimates that he does not wish to strike a man when he is down, alluding, probably, to Powell's pecuniary distress, and simply publishes the contract with Powell, as a vindication of his course. Mr. Barrett played one night at the old house prior to its closing. Mr. C. S. Powell gave one of his entertainments, "For Rubbing off the Rust of Care," at the new theatre on the 4th of July, 1797; and Chalmers, Williamson, and Barrett also gave an olio of readings, lectures, recitations and songs, at the Columbian Museum, entitled "Nature in Nubibus, or a Melicosmeotes — an antidote for the spleen."

The Haymarket, although the season closed, was opened for benefits till the 24th of July, 1797, when Mr. Hodgkinson returned to Boston, and assumed the management. Dulnap states that "his receipts on the opening night were only $220. He engaged Mr. and Mrs. C. Powell at $32 per week; Mr. and Mrs. S. Powell, and Miss Harrison at $42; Mr. and Mrs. Simpson, and two Miss Westrays at $50; and Mrs. Pick at $12; in addition to his company, already too large for the time;" and the same authority states, that before the season terminated, his expenses were $1,100 per week.

In September of this year, Hodgkinson accomplished a managerial *coup de theatre*. The frigate Constitution was announced to be launched on the 20th from Ballard & Hart's yard. The President of the United States, John Adams, who was then at Quincy, was to be present; and thousands, even in those days of family vehicles, were expected to flock in to see the "pride of the Columbian navy" glide into the water. Mr. Hodgkinson conceived the idea of dramatising the launch, and in *forty-eight hours* completed a very respectable production. The parts were given out, the scene painter wrought out on canvas a representation of the launch, and for the night of the event it was announced; its attractive features more vividly and glaringly set forth than ever Barnum heralded the advent of any of his novelties. President Adams, the Governor and Lieutenant-Governor of the Commonwealth, and other dignitaries, proceeded to the yard; but the ship only moved about twenty feet, where she remained firm. The papers stated that the contractor was unwilling to risk a second attempt that day from "motives of safety;" and others thought it a wise dispensation of an overruling Providence, for if she had taken to the watery element, thousands of small boats filled with anxious visitors would have been swamped. Another unsuccessful attempt was made subsequently to launch this noble frigate, but it was not until the third trial, 21st of October, 1797, that she finally "walked the waters," where she has since floated with such honor to our country. The launch at the theatre, however, came off on the first night of the proposed launch, and during its performance, the following song was sung by Tyler — no relation to Col. J. S. Tyler:—

I.

"Come, all Columbian sailors here,
Where honest hearts are void of fear,
Who wish in Freedom's cause to steer,
Huzza for the CONSTITUTION.
No frigate stems the watery main
'Gainst which we won't her rights maintain;
We all are staunch
To our favorite Launch,
No pirate but we will make fly,
Prepared to conquer, boys, or die,
Along with the CONSTITUTION.

II.

"We cruise to guard our country's trade
Not other's liberties invade ;
Columbians prize the laws they've made
O' the glorious CONSTITUTION.
Oppression freemen all disdain,
Yet freedom's cause we will maintain

'Gainst all the world,
Our flag's unfurled ;
We fear no power, we know no friend ;
When forced our commerce to defend
With the frigate CONSTITUTION.

III.

" Sweet Girls, when we are far away
We'll still retain hope's cheering ray,
That love's soft ardor will repay
Our toils in the CONSTITUTION.
So now for dangers we prepare
Of honor each to gain his share,
We fearless brave
The dashing wave,
You'll cheer us on as we bid adieu,
With three huzzas to the jolly crew
Of the Federal CONSTITUTION."

The Haymarket closed for the season on the third of November, 1797, with a "Cure for the Heart Ache," for the first time in America. Several benefits, however, subsequently took place. On the 6th of December, 1797, the Federal Street opened, the company comprising Mr. and Mrs. Bates, Mr. and Mrs. Baker, Mr. and Mrs. Barrett, Mr. and Mrs. Harper, Mr. and Mrs. C. Powell and daughter, Mr. and Mrs. S. Powell. On the 22d of January, 1798, Messrs. Barrett and Harper assumed the management, and the play of the "Roman Father" was performed.

During the summer recess the old theatre had been improved, slightly enlarged, and the decorations were new. The season, under Messrs. Barrett and Harper, was very brief, though entirely successful. They paid promptly, and every thing betokened prosperity; the company was a strong one, and the pieces brought out were got up with great care. An event occurred, however, which checked the tide of prosperity.

When Mr. Hodgkinson was in Boston, in 1794, he had two dressing-rooms built in the rear which were heated by stoves. On the afternoon of the 2d of February, 1798, the porter built the fires as usual, and left wood under the stove to dry, which probably ignited; for a few hours afterwards, fire broke out in that portion, and the building fell a prey to the destructive flames. Nothing of consequence was saved, though in the attempt to rescue a portion of his wardrobe, Mr. Barrett was seriously injured by the falling of a door. The brick walls confined the fire to the building, though citizens from Charlestown, Roxbury, Dorchester, and Cambridge were attracted to the spot by the great light, and were "indefatigable in their efforts to suppress the flames." Such was the magnitude of the fire, that an elderly friend informs us that he well remembers when intelligence reached his school, where he was at the time, that the master immediately dismissed the boys, who rushed to the conflagration. The stores were generally closed, the occupants having deserted their ledgers to witness the fire. The cost of the building (including probably the land) was seventy thousand dollars, and only *one share* was covered by insurance; but this did not discourage the proprietors, who at once resolved to rebuild, with all expedition, a more elegant and commodious edifice.

The Haymarket at that time had been leased to Mr. Hodgkinson. Mr. Barrett at once obtained a lease of it for a month, paying ten per cent. on receipts to Hodgkinson; and a series of benefits for the actors who had suffered by the fire, took place. Dramatic olios were also given at Mr. Dearborn's rooms and Bowen's Columbian Museum. Mr. Dearborn's rooms were located in Theatre Alley. This gentleman was an early instructor of youth, and his school-room was the scene of several successful attempts at private theatricals. The school-room extended over that portion of the building afterwards occupied by Mrs. Dunlap.

About this time it was contemplated to lay out a lot of land on the Cambridge side of Charles River bridge, on which there was a handsome grove of trees for an American Vauxhall; but the project fell through.

The opponents of theatricals again rallied, and pretended to see the hand of God in the destruction of the old theatre. Notices at once appeared in the different journals against theatrical entertainments, and an effort was made to revive the law against them. One writer authorizes the editor (Benjamin Russell) of the *Centinel* to state that he will contribute three hundred and forty dollars towards demolishing the Haymarket Theatre, if the legislature will *wisely* direct the same; and another offers to relinquish his share in the Haymarket, on the same conditions, trusting that "the good citizens of Boston will receive the destruction of the old theatre as a serious admonition to encourage the design." The "solid men" of Boston were well aware, however, that a city's prosperity is dependent in a degree upon its public amusements, and wisely declined listening to the gratuitous advice of their opponents.

CHAPTER IV.

Visit of Cooper to Boston. — A Biographical Sketch. — Incidents of his Life. — Anecdotes. — His Death. — The Learned Pig. — Opening of the Federal Street Theatre. — Visit of President Adams to the Theatre. — Debut of Master George Barrett. — Death of Washington. — Observances at the Theatre in Philadelphia. — Obsequies in Boston. — The Monody at the Theatre. — Mr. Whitlock's Management. — Mrs. Jones. — George Barnwell. — Anecdote. — Pizarro. — Row at the Theatre. — The gloomy Days of the Drama.

THE destruction of the theatre was seriously felt by the *corps dramatique*. They were thrown out of employment at a season when the southern theatres could afford them no relief. Several members went to Salem, and gave entertainments. Mrs. Powell appeared at the Columbian Museum, and Mr. Barrett gave fencing lessons, prior to the brief season at the Haymarket, alluded to in the previous chapter.

Hodgkinson in July, 1798, re-opened the Haymarket, and on the 27th Thomas A. Cooper, the tragedian, made his first appearance before a Boston audience as *Hamlet*, a character he had sustained in London with great applause. Mrs. Hodgkinson played *Ophelia*. On the second night of the season, owing partly to the want of attraction, but mainly to the presence of the yellow fever, the house was so thin that Mr. Hodgkinson dismissed the audience.

Thomas Apthorpe Cooper, the son of an Irish surgeon, was born in 1776. His father was an Irish gentleman, and long resided at Harrow on the Hill. He entered the service of the East India Company, and died in their employ. Cooper's mother, visiting Holland, he was left, when about nine years of age, with the celebrated William Godwin, who superintended his education, with the assistance of the celebrated Holcroft. He announced his intention of becoming an actor, and his friends sent him at once to Edinburgh, where Stephen Kemble then was. He was recommended as able to perform Norval, but Kemble at once detected a lack of talent. He finally made his debut in the part of Malcom, and he was hissed before he got through his first effort. Mr. Kemble's verdict was, "Order the treasurer to pay Mr. Cooper five pounds. Mr. Cooper, I have no further service for you." Cooper persevered, however, and before he was nineteen years of age he impersonated Hamlet and Macbeth, and gained the applause of those who had witnessed the veteran skill of Garrick and Kemble. The political tendency of Godwin and Holcroft affected their pupil. The critics did not darkly hint, but directly affirmed that he was a Jacobin, and this had an effect upon his success.

In 1796, Mr. Wignell, the manager of the theatres in Philadelphia and Baltimore, was in London, and made Cooper an offer which he accepted, and arrived at New York on the 16th of October, the same year, whence he proceeded with Wignell to Philadelphia, and there made his first appearance in America in the character of *Macbeth* on the 9th of December. His success, at first, was not great, but he had not then reached the height he afterwards attained; and it is stated by Dunlap that on the night of his first benefit in America he called in the aid of an elephant to fill the house.

Cooper soon after commenced as tarring tour, and visited the leading cities. At one period he was quite indifferent, and rarely correct in his part; but he afterwards recovered from this fit of indolence, and took the eminent position he maintained for many years. Cooper was connected as manager with many theatres during his life. His great coup as manager was the bold stroke he made in England, by which he induced the great George Frederick Cooke to visit this country, which we shall allude to in a sketch of that eminent actor. Mr. Cooper, although an Englishman, became an American by adoption. He made several professional visits to London, and in 1827 appeared at Drury Lane. He was damned by the critics, but their opinions were not the unbiassed expression of honest minds. They intend to rebuke Mr. Cooper, not only for his desertion of England and his remark, that America was the country of his love and adoption, but for kidnapping Cooke, and his supposed enmity to Edmund Kean. Cooper, prior to 1830, had exhibited his talents in sixty-four theatres, and visited every State in the Union. He had performed four thousand five hundred nights and travelled over twenty thousand miles in this country, and frequently he posted in his own vehicle between New York and Philadelphia. Mr. Cooper was twice married, and a son by his first union received an appointment in the navy of the United States.

Cooper received a large amount of money for his services; but he spent it with a prodigality too frequently characteristic of the profession. He lived in the most sumptuous style, and a more tasty equipage than his did not roll through Broadway. His society, when at the zenith of his popularity, was sought for by the most fashionable, and he moved in the best literary circles. The day of misfortune, however, came at last, and he lingered long on the stage after the prestige of his name had departed, obliged so to do from pecuniary considerations. In 1834, Mr. Cooper took a benefit in New York, when Miss Priscilla Cooper, his daughter, made her first appearance. The play was Knowles's "Virginius," and the fact that a daughter, more in hopes of affording a support to an aged parent, than from any predilections for the stage, was to appear, attracted a great house. During the first scene, as well as the second, there was an anxiety to behold the young daughter. This was heightened in a wonderful degree, when *Virginius* (Cooper) said: "Send her to me, Servia" — and every heart beat when *Virginia* (Miss Cooper) came tripping in and stood before her *own* father, saying: "Well, father, what's your will?" the whole house burst forth in one simultaneous shout of approbation, louder and longer than Cooper himself had ever received. It was several moments before he was enabled to reply; and indeed he could not if he would, for both the father and daughter were so overwhelmed that their feelings found utterance in tears. Miss Cooper subsequently played in this city.

His last appearance in this city was at the National Theatre, and to alleviate his want, benefits were given him in the different cities.

Mr. Cooper's second wife was a daughter of James Fairlee Esq., of New York, by whom he had several children, among them Miss Priscilla Cooper, who married Robert Tyler, Esq. a son of President Tyler.

Miss Cooper did the honors of the White House under her father-in-law, and secured for her own father an appointment in the Arsenal near Philadelphia, and subsequently at the Custom House at New York, and he died at Tyler's residence in Bristol, Pennsylvania, (April 21, 1849,) with perfect calmness in the arms of his daughters, Mrs. Tyler and Mrs. Campbell. He lies in the old churchyard at Bristol. His wife and several grand-children are around him.

"Mr. Cooper, in his prime," says a critic, "possessed from nature the primary accomplishments of a pleasing actor; a fine person, a voice of great compass, of most melodious silver tone, and susceptible of the greatest variety of modulation; an eye of the most wonderful expression; and his whole face expressive, at his will, of the deepest terror, or the most exalted complacency, the direst revenge, or the softest pity. His form in anger was that of a demon; his smile in affability that of an angel."

Another writer remarks: "Mr. Cooper has exceeded every actor that ever trod the American boards in personal requisites. His voice, figure, action, and countenance, have never been surpassed; the first in sweetness, fulness, and flexibility; the next in beauty of proportions; the third in ease, propriety, and grace; and the last in tragic expression. In these physical excellences he was more rare than in his judgment, in which, and in the niceties of reading and power of embodying the great characters of Shakspeare, he was not equal to some other actors."

Mr. Joseph T. Buckingham said of Cooper, in 1820: "Macbeth is Mr. Cooper's *chef d'œuvre*. He is perfectly identified with the character. The *dagger scene*, which he plays in a style altogether his own, is one of the sublimest efforts of histrionic genius. The terrible agonies of his mind, which proclaim their existence with 'most miraculous organ,' are too powerful to be long the object of attention. In the latter part of the play, after Macbeth has 'supped full with horrors,' the moral reflections are given with such exquisite beauty and feeling, that we almost forget the crimes of the murder, and pity the wretched victim writhing with the tortures of his own conscience."

Anecdotes of Cooper are numerous. Joe Cowell, in his book, thus notices his first introduction to Cooper:—"A day or two after he addressed me behind the scenes with, 'Mr. Cowell, no one has been civil enough to introduce me to you, therefore I am compelled to do it myself!' and, after paying me some very handsome compliments, ended with inviting me to dine with him; and we have been very intimate ever since; nor do I know, in my large list of acquaintances, a more agreeable companion than Thomas Cooper. During my residence in the Northern States, I was a frequent guest, for a day or two at a time, at his delightful cottage at Bristol, Pennsylvania; where the luxuries attendant upon affluence were so regulated by good taste, that Cooper never appeared to such advantage as when at home. His family was numerous, and very interesting. He used to boast of never allowing his children to cry. 'Sir, when my children were young, and began to cry, I always dashed a glass of water in their face, and that so astonished them that they would leave off; and if they began again, I'd dash another, and keep on increasing the dose till they were entirely cured."

We have alluded to Cooper's improvident manner of living. It is stated that one afternoon he was standing in Broadway with a gentleman, and he noticed a load of hay approaching. "I will bet you," said Cooper, "the value of my benefit to-night, against an equal sum, that I will pull the longest wisp of hay from this load." "Done," said his friend. The wisps were pulled, and Cooper lost. "Ah!" remarked Cooper, with the greatest nonchalance, "I've lost two hours' acting." The benefit netted the winner upwards of $1,200.

Mr. Cooper's performances in this city will be alluded to as we proceed.

The theatre after Cooper's failure was closed for a short time, when it was re-opened with "Jane Shore," but Hodgkinson, whose expenses were $900 per week, called his company together and dismissed them for want of proper encouragement. A portion of the company then visited Newport, where the temporary theatre was lighted by huge tapers, burning in lard.

During that summer, Bostonians were almost entirely deprived of amusements, and were obliged to seek recreation at the Columbian Museum, or patronize an exhibition which then visited the city, of the "Learned Pig" that did every thing but speak. The Federal Street Theatre, however, was rapidly rising, much improved in its interior. The architect, Mr. Bulfinch, had exerted himself to make it superior to any theatre in the Union, and at the time the interior was finished, it was unsurpassed for neatness and chastity of design, by any on this continent. With some few alterations, such as the substitution of the parquette for the pit, and the raising of the stage, changes in the lobby, it remained till pulled down in 1852, the same in general design. On the 29th of October, 1798, Mr. Hodgkinson opened the theatre. The pieces performed were a prelude, called "A First Night's Apology, or All in a Bustle," written by Milne, for the occasion; "Wives as they Were and Maids as they Are;" and the "Purse, or American Sailor's Return." The company was a strong one, and included Whitlock, Chalmers, Simpson, Williamson, Villiers, Kenny, Mrs. Hodgkinson, Mrs. King, and Mr. S. Powell. Mr. Hodgkinson spoke a dedicatory address, written by Mr. Paine, which commenced as follows:—

"Once more, kind patrons of the Thespian art,
Friends to the science of the human heart,
Behold the temple of the Muse aspire
A Phœnix stage, which propagates by fire!

"Each fault rescinded, and each grace renewed,
By magic reared, and with enchantment viewed,
Our dome, new mantled, 'mid its ravaged wall,
Stands, like Antæus, stronger by its fall;
And like Creusa's ghost, in Trojan strife
Its spectre rises larger than its life!"

It was at the opening of the Federal Street by Hodgkinson, that Mr. Dickson became attached to it in the capacity of prompter and deputy manager.

The season was not notable for any decided peculiarity worthy of comment, and it closed in April. The same month, Hodgkinson opened the Haymarket, with many of the old company and several new members. On the 5th of June, President Adams attended the theatre, when Mr. Hodgkinson sang Paine's song of

Adams and Liberty. The receipts during the season, however, were not large, and Hodgkinson closed on the 4th of July, and left Boston never to return.

Mr. G. L. Barrett was the next manager of the Federal Street, and the season commenced October 14th, 1799, when "Laugh when you Can, Be Happy when you May," with other plays was brought out. The leading characters in the comedy were sustained by Barrett, Harper, Whitlock, Kenny, Simpson, Mrs. Whitlock, Mrs. Simpson, Mrs. Harper, Miss E. Westtray, Mrs. Graupner; and the present George Barrett made his first appearance on any stage as the child. Mr. Snelling Powell and Mr. Bates soon after joined the company.

In December of 1799, an event occurred which threw a nation into mourning, and caused a gloom to overspread the land. About the 24th of the month tidings reached Boston that WASHINGTON WAS DEAD. In every part of the country, the obsequies in memory of this great man were observed, and the theatre joined in the public testimony for the loss of America's Hero. In Philadelphia, on the 28th, the theatre, which was literally full to overflowing, displayed a scene calculated to impress the mind with the utmost solemnity and sorrow. The pillars supporting the boxes were encircled with black crape, the chandeliers decorated with the insignia of woe, and the audience, particularly the female part, appeared covered with the badges of mourning. About seven o'clock the band struck up "Washington's March;" after which a dirge was played, when the curtain slowly rising, discovered a tomb in the centre of the stage, in the Grecian style of architecture; in the centre of it was a portrait of the General, encircled by a wreath of oaken leaves; under the portrait, a sword, shield, and helmet, and the colors of the United States. The top was in the form of a pyramid, in the front of which, appeared the American Eagle, weeping tears of blood for the loss of her General, and holding in her beak a scroll, on which was inscribed: "A Nation's Tears." The sides of the stage were decorated with black banners, containing the names of the several States of the Union. January the 10th, 1800, was the day devoted by the citizens of Boston to a public exhibition of that sorrow which preyed on every heart. The bells of the several meeting-houses were tolled at various periods of the day. Services were held in the South Meeting House, consisting of prayer by Rev. Dr. Eckley, a hymn by Rev. J. S. Gardiner, a eulogy by Hon. George R. Minot, and appropriate music. The theatre, when the news of Washington's death was received, *remained closed during the week*, but on the evening of the public ceremonies it was opened, and a monody, according to the following notice, was delivered after the plays: —

A MONODY,
ON THE DEATH OF
GENERAL WASHINGTON.
By Mrs. Barrett,
In the character of the
GENIUS OF AMERICA
Weeping over the tomb of her beloved HERO.

With a solemn March of Officers, Drums, Fifes, Band of Music — Soldiers with Arms and colors reversed, forming a Grand *Processional Dirge.* After the recital, Military Honors will take place over the Monument of the departed, but never to be forgotten

SAVIOUR OF HIS COUNTRY.

N. B. — The theatre will be hung with black, and every tribute of respect due to the melancholy occasion properly attended to.

The monody was the production of John Lathrop, Esq. Mrs. Barrett's figure, manner, attitude, and pathetic voice, were finely adapted to convey the sentiments and feelings of its author. We append this production: —

"Hung be the heavens in black, with pallid gleam,
Portentous moon, effuse thy specter'd beam!
Earth! wrap'd in sable shrouds, in solemn state,
Expressive, *muse* thy loss, and mourn thy fate —
A nation's tears o'er worth *divine* are shed,
For god-like, matchless WASHINGTON, is dead —
Afflicted nature looks, but looks in vain,
Among her sons to find his like again;
The drooping Muses to their grove retire,
And breezes sigh thro' each neglected lyre,
While holy Freedom views with sad dismay,
Thy victory, death! thy most-triumphant day! —
Her saviour gone, ah! whither shall she fly?
Where turn her steps, or rest her anxious eye?

" *Columbia's* genius to her tomb repairs,
Deep — deep the gloom, her brow majestic wears!
Fix'd to the sacred spot the mourner stands,
And views with frenzied glare her martial bands;
Recalls that form, which long before them strode
With soul and force, and motion like a God —
And sees that sword, which, when a foe was nigh,
Flam'd like Jove's lightning darting thro' the sky.

"See where yon hardy veteran weeps his friend;
Well may the soldier o'er the hero bend,
Cold is that heart, whose patriotic fire,
Could coward hosts with dauntless rage inspire,
Nerve the weak arm, a conqueror's sword to wield,
And bid VICTORIA *thunder* o'er the field —
Ah! he who oft our firm battalions led —
To fame — to freedom — WASHINGTON IS DEAD.

"From realms of glory, sainted spirit deign,
To guard and guide Columbia's grateful train,
Still in the Senate, be thy wisdom found,
Still may thy virtues in our lives abound —
Thou art not lost while pensive memory pays,
To thy long services, her willing praise.
Each mighty deed a bright example shines,
Exalts the mind and every sense refines.
Tutor'd by thee, ingenuous youth aspires
To place his name among yon starry fires,
Follows the track thy feet with zeal pursu'd
And heart devoted to the public good.

"Behold the Chief! — sublime he mounts on high —
What light unusual spreads along the sky?
From East to West the gates of heaven unfold: —
Now blaze immortal thrones with gems and gold,
Angels approach to pay him honors due —
Impervious splendors hide him from our view
Oh! radiant saint! our guardian God — ADIEU."

The grief which prevailed throughout the community at this irreparable loss, was detrimental to theatrical performances, and though Mr. Barrett managed the theatre with industry and tact, the expenses exceeded the receipts. He had during a visit to New York become involved in debt, which he endeavored to pay by his earnings in Boston, and these with other causes, brought the season to an early close, on the 28th of April, when Mr. Barrett took a benefit, and Mrs. Cowley's "Bold Stroke for a Husband" was first introduced to a Boston audience.

In the summer of 1800, Mr. C. E. Whitlock engaged the theatre, and at once set out for England in search of attractions, but he was not very successful. He returned and commenced the campaign on the 27th of October, with "Speed the Plough" and "Rosina."

His company comprised several old favorites, and the most noted new one, whose name has come down to us, was Mrs. Jones, who proved a valuable acquisition to the company. She was one of three daughters of a respectable physician in London, by the name of Granger, who, dying while she was young, left her in the care of a mother and grandmother, Mrs. Booth of Drury Lane. His circumstances at his death not being flourishing, the grandmother took this daughter under her own care and introduced her, at an early age, as a singer at the theatre where she was herself engaged. Miss Granger was married to Mr. Jones a short time previous to her embarking for America. In ballad and pathetic style of music, she was unrivalled, and in comedy and farce, she was equally good. Mrs. Jones, after leaving Boston, performed at the South; and in 1806, maintained her four children by her exertions in New York, her husband having separated from her. She died in New York on the 11th of November, 1806, aged twenty-four, leaving four young orphans. In her private relations, Mrs. Jones is highly spoken of, and though the object of public admiration, "she bore her *faculties so meekly*, that the lowest underling of the theatre was more presuming than she."

At this time the custom was imported from England of presenting "George Barnwell," once or twice during each season, and its moral effect is alluded to in the *Boston Gazette* of that day. It is related on good authority, that when Mr. Ross performed the character of *George Barnwell* in England, in the year 1752, the son of an eminent merchant was so struck with certain resemblances to his own perilous situation, (arising from the arts of a real *Millwood*,) that his agitation brought on a dangerous illness, in the course of which he confessed his error, was forgiven by his father, and was furnished with the means of repairing the pecuniary wrongs he had privately done his employer. Mr. Ross says, "Though I never knew his name, or saw him to my knowledge, I had for nine or ten years, at my benefit, a note sealed up with ten guineas and these words: 'A tribute of gratitude from one who was highly obliged, and saved from ruin, by witnessing Mr. Ross's performance of *George Barnwell*.'" The anecdote must convince the most rigid moralists that the stage at times inculcates lessons of high morality, and the mirror which it holds up is not always devoid of effect.

Mr. Whitlock brought out this season, "Pizarro in Peru, or the Death of Rolla." He put it on the stage in an admirable style, new scenery painted by Mr. Bromley, scenic artist from Drury Lane, new dresses, and for the first time in Boston, the original music. It had a long and successful run. In the month of March the theatre was the scene of a political row, which caused considerable excitement. A comic opera called the "Lock and Key," was brought out in which *Cheerly*, Mr. Story, gave a song commemorating the bravery of the English tars, as displayed in the engagement of the Aratheusa with a French frigate. "It did not," says a critic, "in reality contain any thing offensive to an American ear, unless it be derogatory to consider ourselves the descendants of a brave nation." The song was encored, and repeated with general applause and partial hisses, which by the lively jealousy of party spirit, then dominant, was construed into mutual insult. The first night was only a first rehearsal; the second night more clamor occurred, and on the third night the heroes of the sock became passive spectators and the audience the principle actors, and presented a medley entertainment in its finished state, so far as disorder can approximate to perfection. The attempt to stop the song, was ineffectual; for the friends of the theatre prevailed. The following appeared in the *Boston Gazette*, and contains personal allusions to the actors before the scenes: —

SCENE,

THE FEDERAL STREET THEATRE.

The man of leather high his station took,
Whence gods above the scenes below o'erlook;
The spotless lawyer, and his comrades sit
Amidst the motley critics of the pit —
While Galen bold a *safe position* chose
To feel amid the storm *secure* repose.
In front, in flank, and rear the softer sex
The friend of freedom and France protects,
Around their myrmidons, a patriot band,
For noise and mischief ripe attentive stand —
Soon as the odious verse assails the ear,
Soon as the feats of British tars they hear —
A *sullen* murmur thro' their ranks resounds,
A *goose-like hiss*, the obnoxious passage drowns.
With rage and *grog* inflam'd the patriots rise,
And horrid oaths and curses rend the skies.
But ah ! in vain ! the friends of France oppose,
For federal fingers *greet* each patriot nose.
Though slow to wrath, the *sons of order* move
When roused — impetuous — firm — resistless prove,
With honest fire their clubs and weapons wield,
Their battered foes inglorious quit the field.

In May the theatre closed with "Macbeth," — *Mac-*

beth, Rutley; *Banquo,* Mr. Whitlock; *Lady Macbeth,* Mrs. Whitlock; with the whole of the original airs and choruses of Matthew Lock, got up under the direction of Mr. Graupner.

The season resulted in a loss of four thousand dollars to Mr. Whitlock. Thus far the theatre had proved but a sorry speculation for managers; all had either become bankrupt, or left it poorer than they entered it. A brighter day, however, was coming, and the succeeding chapters will delineate a more pleasing picture of early theatricals in this city. All honor, however, is due to those who struggled manfully against the tide which opposed them, and through whose efforts the drama finally attained a firm position.

CHAPTER V.

Tragedy in real Life. — Powell and Harper's Management. — Mr. Cromwell. — Success of the Theatre. — Munroe and Francis. — Edition of Shakspeare. — Closing of the Haymarket. — Its destruction. — Mrs. Darley. — Mr. Dickson's Sir Anthony Absolute. — Mr. John Bernard. — A brief Sketch.— Death of Hamilton. — Fox. — Cooper's first appearance at the Boston Theatre. — "Cooper or No Play." — Row at the Theatre. — The Benefit Season. — Mr. Bernard's return to England. — Non arrival of the Vessel. — Master Loring. — Hon. Mrs. Twistleton. — Mr. Caulfield. — S. P. Q. A. — The Columbian Museum, &c. &c.

In the summer of 1801 a tragedy in real life excited the attention of the citizens of Boston, and for a time entirely engrossed public attention. We allude to the murder of Miss Fales, by Jason Fairbanks. The trial was the great topic of the day, and various opinions were entertained of the guilt of the accused, whom it will be remembered gave information of the murder of Miss Fales, stating that she took her own life. He was found guilty, and on the 10th of September, by a warrant from authority, was removed from the Boston jail to the line of the county of Norfolk, where he was received by the sheriff of Norfolk, attended by the Roxbury troop of horse, and conveyed to the jail in Dedham, from whence he was conducted, under the escort of a detachment of one hundred of a volunteer guard of the inhabitants of Dedham, to the place of execution on the common, where he was hung between two and three o'clock. He did not confess the deed, though attempts were made by several clergymen to induce him to acknowledge his guilt, but maintained a stoical indifference.

On the 30th of November, 1801, the Federal Street opened under Messrs. Powell & Harper, with a fair company. Mrs. Snelling Powell and Mrs. Whitlock were of the company, and Mr. Cromwell made his debut.

Mr. Cromwell was an American by birth, and had appeared in New York. He went to England and played at Drury Lane. One of the journals made the rather equivocal remark, that "this Cromwell is no Pretender." Like actors of modern days, he procured the insertion of favorable puffs in the London papers, and upon these false representations he was engaged by the managers of the Boston Theatre, but they found that the article was not up to invoice value.

The managers were enabled to pay their bills, but did not accumulate a fortune. The season closed in June, but the theatre was opened on the fourth of July. The Haymarket was opened during this and subsequent years for a few evenings by strolling companies, but it paid the proprietors so poorly, that it was offered for sale. Boston could not then support two theatres — and even *now,* two regular and legitimate houses of theatrical representation, find it any thing but easy work to fill their coffers.

During the summer of 1802, Messrs. Munroe & Francis published a 12mo. edition of Shakspeare's Works, the first edition ever issued in this city. It was published in numbers, and sold at fifty cents. The notes were rewritten and condensed by Mr. Munroe from an English edition, and subsequently adopted by several publishers. The plays were set up in type, and an edition of about three thousand copies worked on a hand press. The publishers, we are happy to say, were repaid for their arduous labors, and the firm was only dissolved in 1853, by the death of David Francis, which occurred on the 20th of March. He died respected by the residents of a city whose early literature he was instrumental in forming.

The opening of Federal Street, on the 27th of October, 1802, by Snelling Powell, brings us to a period of theatrical prosperity previously unknown. For four years from this date, Mr. Snelling Powell was the sole manager, and by perseverance, tact, and talent, he was enabled at the close of each season to issue the following agreeable document:—

☞ All persons having demands on the theatre, are requested to send their accounts to the manager for settlement on Saturday noon.

Mr. Powell was thus the *first successful manager of a theatre in Boston.* He adopted a straightforward course, and honorably kept his engagements, and by offering to the public entertainments worthy of patronage, "conjured back into the boxes," to borrow an expression of a critic of those days, "the long absent taste and beauty of Boston." Early in March, 1803, the Haymarket Theatre was sold at auction, under condition that the materials be removed within sixty days. The land was subsequently disposed of. This gave a clear field to the old theatre, and the lovers of the chaste and regular drama found in Mr. Powell one who only required encouragement to serve the public most faithfully. It would perhaps prove uninteresting to follow in detail, season after season, the success of this theatre during the four years it was solely under Mr. Powell's management, but we will allude to such events as may serve to illustrate the progress of the drama, or interest from association the elderly reader. The company of 1802 and 1803, included Messrs. Harper, Taylor, Barrett, Begnall, Kenny, Wilmot, Mr. and Mrs. Dickson, Mrs. Harper, Mrs. Powell, and the charming Mrs. Darley, formerly Miss E. Westray, who first appeared at the Haymarket, and her husband. It was during this season that Mr. Dickson first astonished the critics, and delighted the audiences by giving proof of histrionic talent, which many were surprised to see evinced by one who, although a very clever actor and a general favorite, had been content to appear only in minor parts, eliciting applause merely for a truly comic and original style of acting. On the 31st of December, 1802, the play of the "Rivals" was revived, after a lapse of four years, and Mr. Dickson sustained *Sir Anthony Absolute* with such marked effect, that for years he was the sole impersonator of this character, which, though often attempted, is rarely portrayed to the satisfaction of the critical.

The season of 1803 and 1804 witnessed the re-appearance of Mrs. Jones, after an absence of four years, who again resumed her enviable position as a Boston favorite; and Mr. Henry Whitlock, son of the celebrated Mrs. Whitlock, then only sixteen years of age, made his first appearance as *Young Norval.* The critics pronounced him "a rough diamond who wants the assistance of the lapidary." Mr. John Bernard, subsequently manager of the theatre, also made his appearance this season, and proved a very valuable accession. His wife, Mrs. Bernard appeared, but did not possess any great claims to distinction. Mr. Bernard was a discriminating actor in the presentment of "many colored life," excelling more particularly in the comic. Many comedians are too much in the habit of dashing the *pound brush*, and all they aim to throw upon the canvas is a dazzling confusion of the primary colors, without extermixture, gradation, or lineament. It was not so with the designs of Mr. Bernard; his, if not the pencil of Titian, was at least that of Hogarth. His father was lieutenant in the English navy, and Bernard, who was born at Portsmouth, England, in 1756, first received that applause which prompted him to adopt the stage as a profession, when performing "Hamlet" at an exhibition given by the pupils of an academy. He performed in several theatres in England, and was a popular actor at the Theatre Royal, Covent Garden, London, where he performed light comedy, fops, etc., and after the decease of the celebrated Edwin, he succeeded him in many of his principal parts. In the summer of 1797, he visited America under the auspices of Mr. Wignell, making his bow before an American audience at the Greenwich Street Theatre, New York.

During the summer of 1804, the theatre remained closed, excepting the usual performances given on election day, and on the 4th of July. On the 26th of July, in this year, the citizens of Boston paid a tribute of respect to Alexander Hamilton, whose death was consequent on the duel between that great and good man, and Aaron Burr. The details of this duel, forced upon Hamilton, are familiar to all. His death was regarded as a public affliction, and in all the principal cities obsequies in his honor were observed. In this city, at an early hour, the vessels in the harbor displayed their colors at half mast, the public offices were closed, and outward demonstration marked the sincerity of inward grief. At noon a very large and respectable procession, under escort of the Independent Corps of Cadets, moved from the State House to the Chapel, where the Hon. Harrison Gray Otis delivered an eulogy on the deceased, in which he gave a biographical sketch of his character, and paid a just tribute to his worth.

The season of 1804 and 1805 commenced in October. Mr. Fox from the southern theatres was the only new face, but the receipts of the first week were greater than were ever before received for the same period of time. Mr. Fox was originally an engraver in Philadelphia. He had a great impediment in his speech, and stuttered so badly, that when he first made application for an engagement he was laughed at. They gave him a trial, however, and on the stage there was not the least hesitation or peculiarity. He was a versatile, pleasant actor, good in tragedy, comedy, or comic opera.

In the month of March, 1805, Mr. Cooper, then recently returned from Europe, arrived in Boston. The benefit season had commenced, and Mr. Powell was bound in the articles of agreement with his stock company, not to employ any extraneous aid, and therefore no opening was offered. His friends remonstrated, but the stock stated that their expenses would be so materially increased, that their benefits, which in these days were harvests indeed, would be seriously impaired, and announced their determination to hold Mr. Powell to his contract. The manager desired to engage Mr. Cooper, in accordance with the wishes of the public, but both his pecuniary interest and his honor were against the arrangement. Thus placed between two fires, it was a difficult question to decide what course to pursue; for within the theatre there was a cry of "We do n't want him," and outside, "We must have him."

Thus the matter stood, and the curtain went up. Mr. Cooper occupied a prominent position in the dress circle apparently determined to appear before the public, if not allowed on the stage. The play passed off, and, as usual, the benefit of the next night was announced. At this, Mr. Cooper's friends, scattered in different parts of the house, shouted out, "Cooper or no play;" and "Cooper or no play" was reiterated from all parts of the house. Mr. Dickson, who was on the stage at the time, singled out one of Mr. Cooper's friends, who was foremost in creating the disturbance, and, pointing to him, said: "Very well, Mr. ——, no play then." The following day rumors were current that the house would be packed by Cooper's friends, who determined to carry out their threat of "no play," and taking the advice of several distinguished friends of the theatre, who were anxious to avoid a riot at any sacrifice, the house was closed, and the money refunded to purchasers of tickets. Mr. Cooper, somewhat chagrined, probably, at the serious aspect of affairs, and the unjustifiable attempt to force the management to an engagement, which certainly would prove unprofitable to the actors, intimated a desire to consult with the parties. The place of meeting was at Julian's; and Mr. Powell, Mr. Dickson, and Mr. Cooper there sat down, and over a chop, perhaps a glass of port, which, "full of bounty, prompts the open hand," made a satisfactory arrangement. Mr. Cooper was very liberal in his terms. Taking the list of benefits to come off, he said, "There, I will play gratuitously for this one and that one, for they are sure of a full house without me, and how much will these actors probably receive, Mr. Dickson?"

"A hundred dollars is about the average."

"Well, then, replied Cooper, "I will share with them, after they have received their hundred dollars."

All parties being satisfied, Mr. Cooper made his first appearance at the Boston Theatre on the 11th of March, as *Hamlet; Ophelia,* Mrs. Jones; *Queen,* Mrs. Powell. The theatre was crowded, and it was the general opinion that the histrionic powers of "our Roscius," as he was termed, America having been the scene of his earliest success, were much improved and ripened by his transatlantic excursion. The benefits this season were very large, and the following statement of receipts will sufficiently evince the praiseworthy manner in which the Bostonians then supported those who contributed to their amusement and instruction: Snelling Powell, $1,100; Bernard, $1,050; Fox, $900; Wilson, 900; Chalmers, $800; Dickson 1,050; Jones, $850; Bignall, $700; Sauberes, $750; Kenny, $800; Cooper, 1,050; Barnes, $700; Mrs. Powell, $1,163; Mrs. Dickson, $850; Mrs. Bernard, $750; Mrs. Jones, $950; Miss Bates, $700. The above were eighteen successive benefits. The theatre was calculated to contain, by admeasurement, eleven hundred dollars, though on some occasions the receipts had been as high $1,400.

Cooper's visit, however, to England had not resulted in that triumph which was anticipated. At the time, (1803,) Kemble had retired from Drury Lane Theatre, on account of declining health, and was on a tour to the continent of Europe, and Cooper was invited to fill his place. His performances were received with much applause, but the people there having formed their taste on the model of Cooke and Kemble, or from his real inferiority to these gentlemen, did not consider him equal to their favorites. During his engagement in Boston, he performed *Douglass*, *Richard III.*, *Octavian* in the "Mountaineers," *Pierre*, *Zanga* in the "Revenge," *Osmond*, in the "Castle Spectre," (a part in which Mr. Hodgkinson had been very successful,) *Othello* and *Rolla* for his benefit. The Boston critics were much pleased with his "Othello," "Hamlet," and "Zanga," and he was then esteemed second to no one who had trod the Boston boards, though his faults were freely discussed, and the correctness of his readings often called in question.

The last season of the sole management of Mr. Powell commenced in October, 1805, with "Speed the Plough," and the expenses of the theatre greatly exceeded any previous season. On the 15th of November the "Honeymoon" was performed, for the first time in Boston:—*Duke Aranza*, Cooper; *Juliana*, Mrs. Powell;— and during this season Cooper brought out "Coriolanus" for his benefit. The orphans of Hodgkinson received a benefit at the theatre, which was but one of the many kind acts that marked Mr. Powell's managerial career.

In the summer of 1806, Mr. Bernard visited England, for the purpose of obtaining accessions to the Boston Theatre. On his arrival out, he found the London managers on the alert to embellish their respective theatres with all the genius and attraction of the profession; and so anxious were they, that they did not confine their researches to the boards of England, Scotland, and Ireland, but offers were made to several

English actors, then in America. Mr. Bernard was not very successful in beating up recruits. He, however, enlisted Mr. Caulfield from Drury Lane, Mrs. Stanley, (Hon. Mrs. Twistleton,) from Covent Garden, Signor Cipriani, ballet master, from Saddler's Wells, and a singer by the name of Vining, with whom he set sail for Boston in the schooner Neutrality, Capt. Sprague, of Duxbury. The theatre was announced to open on the 13th of October, under the joint management of Powell, Bernard, and Dickson, and as intelligence had been received of Mr. Bernard's departure from Bristol, he was anxiously expected to give *eclat*, with the aid of the new faces, to the opening of the house. But his partners were doomed to disappointment, for the schooner Neutrality did not come to port, and on the 13th of October the season commenced with "Speed the Plough." Mr. and Mrs. Poe, (parents of Edgar A. Poe, the poet,) from the South, made their appearance, and Master Loring made his debut as *Richard* to a cash receipt of $855.87 1-2. Nearly two weeks was passed by the friends of Mr. Bernard, in fear lest the schooner might have been swamped or foundered; but, on the 25th of October, the Neutrality, after a passage of *fifty-three* days, arrived, and on the the 27th, Mr. Bernard appeared as *Nipperkin*, when he was most warmly welcomed. Mrs. Stanley was a lady-like actress, and gave great satisfaction. She was Hon. Mrs. Twistleton. Mr. Caulfield appeared as *Sir Edward Mortimer*, and was pronounced a classical performer.

Caulfield was quite a wit at times. Over each of the stage doors at the theatre were placed the initials, S. P. Q. A. (Senatus Populus, &c.). An actor, looking up one day, endeavored to arrive at some clue to their meaning, but being unable to do so, he turned to Caulfield, and asked for his version. "Oh," said Caulfield, glancing at what he had perhaps never noticed before, "do n't you know what they stand for?" "No, I do not," rejoined the applicant. "Well," said Caulfield, "S. P. Q. A. means that Snelling Powell Quizzes All."

We have alluded in this record to the Columbian Museum, which was commenced in Boston by the exhibition of a few specimens of waxwork, at the American Coffee House, opposite the Bunch-of-Grapes, in State street. The proprietor was Mr. Daniel Bowen, whose collection received very handsome notice in the papers of June, 1791. It was soon removed to the hall over the new school-house, near the Rev. Mr. West's meeting. Additions of natural and artificial curiosities, paintings, &c., were constantly made to the collection till 1795, when it assumed the name of *Columbian Museum*, and it was established at the head of the mall, (on the corner of Broomfield's Lane,) in the longest, and perhaps the most elegant hall in the United States. This establishment rose in value and in public estimation, and became a fashionable resort, till January 15, 1803, when it was destroyed by fire. The liberality of the public, and the aid of private friends, enabled Mr. Bowen to commence another Museum, at the corner of Milk and Oliver streets, in the succeeding May. In 1806, Mr. Bowen, in connection with Mr. William M. S. Doyle, erected a costly brick edifice, five stories high, on the lot north of the Chapel burial-ground, and removed the collection, which had now become splendid, to that place, which was opened for company on Thanksgiving evening, Nov. 27th. On the 15th of January, 1807, the Museum again took fire, from the explosion of a preparation which Mr. Martin used in his exhibition of the Phantasmagoria, then occupying the upper hall, and all the valuable curiosities were destroyed. After the fire had subsided, a very melancholy catastrophe occurred. A great part of the south wall of the Museum fell into the Chapel burying-ground, killing six young men and wounding several others. The proprietors of the Museum, however, were not wholly disheartened. With some encouragement from the public, they rebuilt the house to the height of two stories, and opened it on the 2d of June, 1807. Mr. Bowen some time after removed from Boston, and Mr. Doyle continued the sole manager until the collection was sold to the proprietors of the New England Museum, (January 1, 1825).

CHAPTER VI.

Mr. James Fennell. — Mr. C. S. Powell. — Benefit for the Lunatic Asylum. — Readings from Shakspeare. — Mr. Webster. — Mr. Twaits. — Appearance of the celebrated Mrs. Warren (Miss Brunton). — Biographical Sketch. — Mr. Cooper. — Harwood. — A Joint Engagement. — Criticisms of Robert Treat Paine. — Remarks upon Mr. Cooper and Mr. Fennell's Acting. — A touch at pseudo-critics. — The Embargo, etc., etc.

The season of 1806–7, is notable on account of the appearance of Mr. Fennell, who, when he arrived in Boston, had just concluded an engagement of thirteen nights in Philadelphia, where the receipts had been $13,000, then pronounced to be "the greatest instance of patronage ever given to the American Drama." Fennell's engagement was not a successful one. His performance of *Lear* was the only attractive part which the Bostonians honored.

Mr. C. S. Powell, the former manager of the Haymarket, appeared this season. For many years he was connected with theatricals in Halifax, under the patronage of the Duke of Kent. Mr. Powell died in Halifax in 1810.

A night was devoted by the trustees, to a benefit to assist the fund then raising in behalf of a lunatic hospital. The benefit was an entire failure; the project at that time being viewed with an unfavorable eye by the public. The trustees of the old theatre always reserved one night, the receipts of which were given to the poor of the town.

After the close of the season, Fennell gave readings from Shakspeare, with remarks, at the Exchange Coffee House — the first Shaksperian readings in this city, since so popular, of which we find record.

The season of 1807–8 introduced to the public Mr. Webster, a singer of considerable repute, who, unfortunately for his fame and his pocket, subsequently became a party to some disgraceful proceedings, and was obliged to take French leave of Boston. Mr. Twaits, who married Mrs. Villiers, formerly Miss Eliza Westray, appeared. He was born on the 25th of April, 1781, and was brought to this country by Mr. Wood, who found him in Birmingham, England.

Dunlap says that "neither his style of playing, nor his face or person was like any other individual then on or off the stage. Short and thin, yet appearing broad, muscular yet meagre, a large head, with stiff, stubborn carroty hair, long colorless face, prominent hooked nose, projecting large hazel eyes, thin lips, and large mouth, which could be twisted into a variety of expression, and which combining with his other features, eminently served the purpose of the comic muse." His voice was powerful, and his queer humor, made him a great favorite with convivialists, as with lovers of comedy. Mr. Twaits was extremely popular as a low comedian, but like many others in that line, fancied that tragedy was his *forte*. He attempted *Lear* and *Richard III.*, and performed them beyond the expectation of the audience. It has been said, and with much truth, that actors are the poorest judges of their own talent. The celebrated Liston acted *Octavian*, and similar characters at Newcastle before he appeared in London, where he became the most popular low comedy-man of the day. Mr. Finn was also impressed that tragedy was his line; but of this more in the appropriate place. Mr. Twaits was manager of the Richmond theatre at the time of the great fire.

On the 20th of November, 1807, Mrs. Warren, celebrated in theatrical annals as Miss Brunton, made her first appearance in this city as *Belvidera*. Mrs. Warren's fame and superior talent were not generally known here, and there being no actor of eminence to support her, the first night was but indifferent, under the circumstances. The frequenters of the theatre soon sounded her praises, and her acting became known and duly appreciated by the public. On Monday, Nov. 30th, she performed *Elvira* in "Pizarro" to a large and fashionable audience. Mr. Fennell was engaged for her next two nights, and appeared as *Horatio* to her *Calista* in the "Fair Penitent," and as *Romeo* to Mrs. Warren's *Juliet*, (her great London part,) and on both of these occasions the theatre was crowded. She played seven nights, and with her benefit received one thousand six hundred dollars. Miss Brunton was the daughter of John Brunton, a manager and actor, who maintained a respectable rank in England. It was not until she had attained her fifteenth year that she gave any evidence of the possession of histrionic genius, her earlier days having been passed in the repose of retired life, far from the scenes of her father's labors; her mother, contenting herself with qualifying her daughter to be like herself, a good wife and mother. Mrs. Brunton was the preceptress of her own children, and the father was more than astonished, when one day, by desire of her mother, the daughter recited some select passages in his presence. Though not gifted with that dignity of stature suited to the embodiment of tragic parts, the father, who had battled hard to obtain the means of subsistence for his family, saw that a mine of wealth had long been concealed in his own family, under modesty and reserve, and at once determined to encourage the talent which had lain dormant, and bring his daughter before the public. Without any stage practice, without the advantage of studying in other actresses what to do or what to avoid, having very rarely seen the interior of the theatre, she was announced, while she yet fell short by two months of sixteen years of age, to appear at her father's benefit in Bath as *Euphrasia.* Mr. Meyler wrote a prologue for the occasion, and some kind friends were evil disposed enough to predict the failure of the young lady, stating that her youth and smallness of stature were insurmountable obstacles to her personating the Grecian daughter. The night arrived. More hearts than one trembled for the result, and the anxiety of the parent exceeded the fear of the debutante. Though the trepidation inseparable from such an effort diminished her powers at first, the sweetness of her voice struck every ear like a charm; the applause that followed invigorated her spirits so far, that in the reciprocation of a speech or two more, her fine, clear articulation struck the audience with surprise, and when more assured by their loud approbation, she came to the speech:—

> "Melanthon, how I loved, the gods who saw
> Each secret image that my fancy formed, etc."

she seemed to pour forth her whole heart and soul in the words, and emitted such a blaze as filled the house with rapture and astonishment. Brunton on the same evening played the aged father, and the meeting on the boards of father and child was the signal for applause, only equalled in modern times by the parallel cases of Kemble and his daughter, and Cooper and his daughter. Miss Brunton rose at once in public estimation, and augmented her reputation by performing *Horatia* in the "Roman Father," and *Palmyra* in "Mahomet," and in less than a month the fame of this prodigy reached every town and city of Great Britain and Ireland. The London managers were at once on the *qui vive* for such a star; and on the 17th of Oct., 1785, Miss Brunton made her first appearance at Covent Garden Theatre in the character of *Horatia.* The London critics stamped the coin as pure metal, and her success was immense. Whenever her name was announced, a crowded house was in attendance, and great was the regret of all, when it was announced that she was about to marry Mr. Robert Merry, a gentleman of literary attainments, and would retire from the stage. This step was taken, not in accordance with her own desires, for she was an actress *con amore,* but to propitiate the favor of Mr. Merry's family, who affected to be wounded at his marrying an actress. At the conclusion of her engagement in 1792, she was married to Mr. Merry, and left for Paris, where, with Mr. Fennell, it was their intention to give English readings, as M. Le Texier had been very successful in giving French readings in London. The convulsions in France prevented the execution of this plan; and after a three months' visit they returned to England, and lived in retirement until 1796, when Merry, who was a *bon vivant,* found that his reduced fortunes required immediate aid; and Mrs. Merry most willingly accepted an engagement with Wignell for Philadelphia, and sailed for New York, which they reached, in twenty-one days' passage, on the 19th of October, 1796. In the same vessel, Thomas A. Cooper and Mr. William Warren came passengers. Mrs. Merry made her first appearance in America in Philadelphia, on the 5th of December, 1796, as *Juliet*; Moreton being her *Romeo.* Her talent was appreciated in this country, and in the large cities she became the favorite of the day. Mr. Merry died at Baltimore in 1798. Mrs. Merry remained a widow till 1803, when she married Mr. Wignell, who died in seven weeks after their marriage. On the 15th of August, 1806, she married Mr. William Warren, her fellow passenger on her outward passage, and for near two years they lived together in ease and felicity. Mr. Warren being obliged to attend his company to their customary summer stations, prepared for his departure, and at her earnest solicitation, though she was daily expecting her accouchement, took his wife with him. They reached Alexandria, and she was there taken in travail; and though appearances and her lusty health promised a safe deliverance, she was seized with epileptic fits and died. Dunlap in his history, in recording her death, says: "The year 1808 was rendered remarkable in theatrical history, wherever the English language is spoken, by the death of Mrs. Anne Warren, in the thirty-eighth year of her age, and in the full possession of all those eminent qualifications which rendered her, as a tragedian, only second to Mrs. Siddons."

On the 25th of January, 1808, Mr. Cooper appeared as *Richard III.*, and followed in *Hamlet*, etc. Harwood appeared each night in the afterpiece. This was the first season that Cooper may be said to have failed; and notwithstanding he had the aid of Harwood, who was an excellent comedian, he did not attract. The result was that an engagement was made with Fennell; and they acted *Jaffier* and *Pierre*, *Othello* and *Iago*, *Horatio* and *Lothario* in the "Fair Penitent."

This joint engagement was one of the most exciting on record, and created the greatest enthusiasm not only in this city, but throughout the country. Every one was anxious to hear the result of their success. The tragedy of "Venice Preserved" was brought out; *Jaffier*, Fennell; *Pierre*, Cooper; *Belvidera*, Mrs. Stanley.

"Venice Preserved" was written by Thomas Otway, who was born in 1651. It was first acted in 1682. Few, perhaps, while witnessing the performance of this play,— moved to sympathy by the sufferings of *Belvidera*, or touched with pity by the sensitive and affectionate nature of *Jaffier*,—reflect upon the fate of its author, who died in 1685, it being stated, that the immediate cause of his death was hastily swallowing, after a long fast, a piece of bread which charity had supplied:—

> "O glorious trade! for wit's a trade,
> Where men are ruined more than made!
> Let crazy Lee, neglected Gay,
> The shabby Otway, Dryden gray,
> Those tuneful servants of the Nine,
> (Not that I blend their names with mine,)
> Repeat their lives, their works, their fame,
> And teach the world some useful shame."

Robert Treat Paine, then *the* theatrical critic of Boston, thus alludes to this engagement. In an article upon "Venice Preserved," he says:—

> "Messrs. Cooper and Fennell were the rival candidates for the wreath of Thespian victory; and the combined effect of their talents was very powerfully assisted by the *Belvidera* of Mrs. Stanley. In this, as in all contentions of a similar nature, the spirit of party was on the alert; a divided sentiment prevailed, which was wholly repugnant to impartiality of judgment. * * * In the natural gifts and requisites of an actor, Mr. Cooper has never had a competitor on the American stage, and in good sooth, it must be said, that 'speech famed' Fennell has gathered much lore at the feet of Cratippus. Mr. Fennell, who prides himself on his scholastic 'vis et venustas et ordo verborum,' acquired on this occasion no distinction beyond his antagonist in the severer graces of eloquence; although, in some

brilliant moments of personation, he went beyond any former effort of his own. We feel a reluctance to speak of Mr. Cooper's *Pierre* in contrast to Mr. Fennell's *Jaffier* from this very sufficient reason, that, in this disposition of the parts, nature has pronounced her inhibition against the one, and has given her amplest commission to the other. Every actor has peculiar habitudes of gesticulation, speech, and expression; in all these, Cooper is moulded and fashioned into *Pierre;* and beyond these, which are great and striking endowments, he is eminently happy in transfusing the soul of his author into the character of his action. We do not believe this bold, ingenuous, generous, affectionate rebel, was ever personated with more propriety, fire, or discrimination, on the boards of London. In the scene with conspirators, after the discovery of Renault's lecherous breach of trust, it may be truly said, he

'Lurched all swords of the garlands.'"

The same critic, alluding to Fennell's and Cooper's impersonation of *Iago*, says:—

"In the part of *Iago* our unequivocal preference went along with Mr. Cooper, *per totum agmen.* In correctness, or force of reading, we scarcely know to whom the balance would incline. But one or two diversities of emphasis occurred, and none of interpretation. The differences were immaterial, and only such as the incidental lapses of performance might occasion. For the distinctions were all of manner in the personation of character, in its varieties of address to the other persons of the drama, with whom it was necessarily intermingled. Here, indeed, the merit of the representation belongs most eminently to Mr. Cooper. In the conduct of the scenes his subtle honesty to *Othello*, his imposing assurance to *Roderigo*, and his deadly malignity in soliloquy, were more deeply imbued with discrimation, 'form and pressure.' The colors were applied with a bolder pencil, and the lines were traced with a stronger character. Nature has denied to Mr. Fennell the use of such powerful means, as Mr. Cooper can employ prodigally, without exhausting them. In the economy of the stage art and situation, Mr. Cooper was wonderfully superior. Yet, if we drop the curtain, and consider the exhibition as a mere didactic example of recitation, Mr. Fennell does not halt behind his antagonist."

In the course of our reading, we have never met

with criticisms upon theatricals more in accordance with good taste than those from the pen of Mr. Paine. He wrote according to his honest convictions, and we learn, from private sources of information, that he knew not "a Tyrian from a Trojan," when in the exercise of this duty. He possessed a great love for the drama, could apply the rod with scorching effect, or bestow the meed of praise when due, without disgusting the recipient by a lavish profusion of unmerited eulogium.

The following passage may be read with profit even in these enlightened days. It hits off a class, who, lacking critical acumen, are ever ready to ascribe personal motives or private pique to that person who independently expresses an unbiased opinion, which may not accord with their own: —

"Mr. Cooper could not swell his fine melodious voice to the 'top of its compass' without a responsive thunder from the house; nor could Mr. Fennell extend his 'many a rood of limb' in two gigantic strides from one stage door to the other, but the most learned 'million' beat their palms with ecstasy and exclaimed: '*What an admirable* READER.' We have not indulged this vein of sarcasm to ridicule the exertion of eminent talents, which has so justly 'earned its chronicle,' but to expose to merited contempt that fashionable affection, that most excellent foppery of taste, which has of late usurped the balance and the rod of criticism among our full grown babes of learning, who have suddenly become commentators in playing, by going to school at thirty to learn their mother tongue, and have formed an intimate acquaintance with authors, by spelling their names on labels at the backs of their volumes! Without knowing the distinction in terms between pronunciation, emphasis, and reflection, yet with the aid of a little effrontery in a side box, and a well-committed rosary of words, which they use in succession without choice or connection, they acquire a frothy reputation for classical wisdom, which at once gives tone and circulation to their opinions, throughout the wide range of the shallow profundity of polite life!

What a facility of literary education! Why, it were a device worth the experiment, if a patent might be obtained for it; the market women in the public streets of Athens repeated lines from Homer, while they sold apples and filberts; then wherefore should not the disciple of a tailor and a frizeur make as good a commentator of a beau, as the perusal of Malone, Johnson, or Walker? The process, too, would prevent a great many fruitless headaches, would keep down the price of calfskin, and would save the expense and trouble of learning to read. What a crop of connoisseurs should we have; they would grow up, like the dragon's teeth, and destroy themselves for the amusement of their wits! This, then, will be the very millennium of letters, when taste shall be reduced under the dominion of fashion, and

'The fop, the flirt, the pedant, and the dunce
Start up, (God bless us!) critics all at once.'"

Owing to the embargo, this was one of the most unproductive seasons the theatre ever experienced, but the actors never left on a Saturday without receiving their full due.

We have alluded to Mr. James Fennell. He came over to this country during the year 1792. His reputation as an actor was not fully known on this side of the Atlantic; as a rattle-brain spendthrift, he was very much better known. In the early part of his life, Fennell studied the law, but he soon spurned the intricacy of the path, and under the name of Cambray, offered himself to the managers of the Edinburgh Theatre, and in 1787 made his first appearance as *Othello*. Until the day of his death, this was his favorite character. Under the assumed name of Cambray, he played with some success in the various provincial cities. The increasing fame of Mr. Fennell induced the managers of the Edinburgh Theatre to wish his return to their stage, where he proceeded and played there some time with approbation, till one evening, being announced to perform the character of *Jaffier*, and the gentleman who had formerly represented it (Mr. Wood) was fixed for *Pierre;* but enraged at the exchange, though the characters have ever been deemed equally good, Mr. Wood complained of the injustice of the manager to his friends. An apology was demanded from the manager, and a law case ensued. Mr. Fennell quitted the stage in that city with indignation, and played a short time at York, and in 1789, appeared at Covent Garden, London, but without the expected success. He afterwards engaged in a periodical publication, the Theatrical Guardian, and produced a comedy, entitled "Lindel and Clara, or a Trip to Gibraltar," which has been frequently performed, and was printed in 1791. He visited Paris, where he lived like "my lord Anglais," and supported a hotel in great style, at the expense of all who trusted to his specious manner and fine appearance. Fennell was a remarkably handsome figure, above six feet in height; his features, not handsome, were expressive, and over which he had a wonderful command. Thomas A. Cooper, the tragedian, used to say, when perceiving Fennell's approach, "Here come *two yards of a very proper man.*" In Philadelphia his style of living was extravagant. He was the idol for the time of the town, the companion of all the dissipated limbs of aristocracy, who have caused the ruin of more actors by their flattery and friendship (?) than they ever contributed dollars to the treasury of all the theatres in the United States. He performed in all the theatres in this country, and possessing great ingenuity, erected salt works on a new model of his own, which failed him. In the year 1800, he was oppressed by poverty and debt, and in 1802 he was imprisoned for debt, etc. At last he became so reduced and besotted that a Mrs. Brown, in Philadelphia, with whom he resided, was under the necessity of turning him out of the house. For several days nothing was heard of him. One night, after she had retired to rest, she awoke by a noise in the street; raising the window to ascertain the cause, she was answered by Fennell begging admission:

"You cannot come in here, Mr. Fennell, indeed you cannot."

"I am a wanderer, madam, an outcast, homeless, pennyless."

"I cannot help you, Mr. Fennell; you know how you behaved before."

"I remember nothing, Mrs. Brown, but that I am wretched, sick, and helpless."

"All this I admit, Mr. Fennell, but why not go somewhere else?"

"I have no friend but you; then do —

'Pity the sorrows of a poor old man
Whose trembling limbs have borne him to your door,
Whose days are dwindled to the shortest span,
Oh! give relief and heaven will bless your store.' "

This appeal induced the old woman to throw out the latch string.

Mr. Fennell, when the decay of fortune and consequent shyness of *professed* friends had reduced him to a *summer* suit in the midst of *winter*, was presented by Mr. Leigh Waring with a surtout. The tragedian instantly produced the following neat effervescence of genius and gratitude: —

"Dear Sir, your surtout
Is a present to suit,
While fortune to me is so sparing,
It's been worn it is true
But your kindness makes new
What can ne'er lose its value from *Waring*."

About the year 1804, Mr. Fennell retired for a time from the stage, and established salt works on an original plan, near New London, Connecticut, which eventually ruined him. Mr. Fennell was a gentleman of fine classical attainments, and at one time kept an Academy at the Barrell House, Charlestown. Mr. Fennell wrote a work entitled "An Apology for my Life."

CHAPTER VII.

John Howard Payne. — Mr. and Mrs. Darley. — Mr. and Mrs. Claude. — William Charles White. — First Production of Forty Thieves. — Mr. and Mrs. Duff. — Mr. and Mrs. Samuel Drake. — Anecdote of Morse. — George Frederick Cook's First Appearance in Boston. — A Biographical Sketch. — His Last Appearance on any Stage at Providence, etc., etc.

On the 3d of April, 1809, John Howard Payne, then only seventeen years of age, made his first appearance at the Boston Theatre in the part of *Young Norval*, and was justly considered a histrionic wonder. Though not a finished artist he possessed a vivid genius, and his readings united classical correctness to truth of feeling. During this engagement he appeared as *Romeo*,

Selim, *Tancrede*, *Hamlet*, etc., in all of which he was not only considered excellent, but the term included excellence as an actor, not as a mere boy. His first appearance attracted an audience of $745.62, and at his benefit when he played *Hamlet*, there was $987.37 in. He received for six nights $800.

Master Payne was born in New York, on the 9th of June, 1792, and his parents removed to this city when he was quite young. It was here that he acquired a taste for theatrical representation, and early in life at private theatricals was the star *par eminence*. When thirteen years of age, he was sent to New York and placed in a counting-house; but the dry details of business were unsuited to his temperament, which soon found an appropriate sphere of action in publishing a weekly paper, called the Thespian Mirror. It was a respectable, though crude attempt of the future author and actor. He made his first appearance at New York on the 26th of February, 1809, and after visiting Boston, made a tour of the northern and southern theatres with great success. He visited England, and on the 4th of June, 1813, made his debut at Drury Lane Theatre, London, and though styled the "American Roscius," was received with great applause. After visiting the English provincial theatres and Ireland, he retired from the stage for several years, and devoted his attention to literary pursuits. In 1826–7, Mr. Paine edited in London the Opera Glass. Mr. Payne, during his early theatrical career in this country, besides the characters already mentioned, appeared as *Octavian*, *Rolla*, *Romeo*, *Zaphna*, *Frederick* in "Lovers' Vows," etc. Nature bestowed upon him a countenance of no common order, and though there was, when young, a roundness and fairness, which but faintly express strong turbulent emotions, or display the furious passions, these defects were supplied by an eye which glowed with animation and intelligence. A more extraordinary mixture of softness and intelligence were never associated in a human countenance, and his face was a true index of his heart. In general his action was elegant, his attitudes bold and striking, and his most prominent defects were those of pronunciation. Mr. Payne's contributions to the stage are "Brutus," which is still occasionally performed. He is also the author of "The Lancers," "Oswali of Athens," "Peter Smink, or Which is the Miller," "Proclamation," "Richelieu," "Therese," "'T was I," "King Charles the Second, or the Merry Monarch," "Clari," and other pieces. Mr. Payne's name, however, will ever be associated in the minds of all lovers of melody, with that simple yet soul trusting poem, "Home, sweet Home," of which he is the author. Mr. Payne held the office of United States consul at Tunis, and died there on the 10th of April, 1852. We cannot do the reader a greater favor than by giving the following article upon Mr. Payne, which was contributed to the Evening Gazette in May 1, 1852, by one of his schoolmates. It was written by a gentleman of the finest literary attainments.

"There are many subscribers to the Gazette who are old enough, as well as myself, to remember something of the brilliant boyhood and youth of Mr. John Howard Payne, whose death at Tunis, where he was consul for the United States, has just been chronicled in the newspapers.

"He was an example of precocious talent, the like of which I doubt whether this country has produced, and the object of an admiration such as I have never known to be bestowed on any other young person.

"My acquaintance with him dates so far back as the autumn of 1804, when I was put to the 'Berry Street Academy,' as his father's boarding school in the street crossing from Atkinson to Federal Street was called. He belonged to a family of genius. A sister, who died in early womanhood in 1818, was especially admired for rare endowments and accomplishments. In the family, as pupils, were several young ladies, who have since done great honor to their training. Miss Sedgwick was one of them. Howard Payne, as he was called, a boy then of twelve years of age, used to figure on training days as the captain of the 'Boston Federal Band,' a military company, completely uniformed and equipped, so as to be in its blue and white an exact miniature of Sargent's company, the 'Boston Light Infantry.' I recollect that on one occasion the 'Boston Federal Band' took station on the left of one of the regiments at a review on the common.

"Young Payne was a perfect Cupid in his beauty, and his sweet voice, self-possessed yet modest manners, wit, vivacity, and premature wisdom, made him a most engaging prodigy. At this time he was publishing a little weekly paper, of four pages quarto, called 'The Fly.' His father had diligently cultivated his talent for elocution, and he was the star of the exhibitions which we used to have at the Berry Street Academy, where a mimic theatre was got up, with stage, curtain, and pit, and in all but dresses and properties we flattered ourselves that we rivalled the regular practitioners in the Federal Street Theatre across the way. I have not forgotten how he frightened me one night, when in my best Sunday clothes I had been soliloquizing as *Old Roque, Floranthe's Follower*, and at the proper time he rushed in and collared me, in the rags and tatters of Octavian, which, without concert with me, he had borrowed of Mr. Powell. I have faced fiercer onsets since, but none I think which more tempted me to turn my back and disappear.

"About this time young Betty, as the *Young Roscius*, was making a great noise in England by his personations of Hamlet, Romeo, Tancred, Selim, Zaphna, Frederic, Norval, Octavian, and so on; and our booksellers' shop-windows were full of prints representing his attitudes in this or that dramatic exigency. This was the spark for which the tinder of young Payne's scenic ambition was all ready. Themistocles could not sleep for thinking of the trophies of Miltiades; waking, Payne thought, and sleeping, he dreamed of the laurels of Betty. He studied, recited, and attitudinized, and the vision of weeping boxes and shouting gallery and pit filled his mind.

"Among his pieces of fugitive poetry at this time, some of your ancient readers may remember a 'New Year's Ode,' and an 'Elegy on the Irish starveling boy, poet Dermody.' As to the highest inspiration of poetry, that is another thing; but in respect to exact selection of words, to perfect taste and finish, and grace of versification, those pieces are not to be exceeded.

"Payne was placed in a counting-room in New York, I believe, in 1805. Presently there appeared, from week to week, a sheet entitled the 'Thespian Mirror,' containing criticisms on theatrical performances. They were so bright and judicious as to attract attention and curiosity. William Coleman, then editor of the Evening Post, took pains to trace out the author, and to his astonishment found him a boy of fifteen. He introduced him to his friends, and Payne became all the rage in the fashionable New York circles. Irving, Paulding, and Verplanck, (a trio then becoming famous by Salmagundi,) Fay, (father of the diplomatist of our day,) Blauvelt, and Brevoort, were among those whose flattering notice he attracted. Having gracefully borne his part, as not only the Cynthius of the minute, but of the season, he and his friends assented to the proposal of a New York gentleman, by the name of Seaman, to be at the expense of his education at college, and to Schenectady he went for that purpose.

"But to remand a young man from public celebrity into studious college retirement, is not much easier than to bring about the recent scheme of some of our Congressional Solons, of remanding California into a territorial State. Payne had tasted the cup of applause too young, and perhaps it was scarcely in nature not to crave more; the notice of the great, and the smiles of the fair, were not for a boy easy to turn his back upon. He had scarcely got to his place of work at Schenectady before the 'Pastime,' a weekly magazine of eight octavo pages, opened a new communication with the public. An old file which we have just looked up, shows the first number to have been issued in February, 1807. In the seclusion of a then inland Calvinistic college the seductions of the drama still pursued him, and sock and buskin made their prints all along the pages of the 'Pastime.'

"At length, in 1808, the ruling passion burst through all restraint, and he came home to Boston to make his preparations for the stage, A generous motive, of an impulse of filial duty, excused to him, and perhaps concealed from him, the force of the prompting of his own taste and ambition. His father had fallen into unprosperous circumstances, from which his now advancing age did not afford a prospect of relief. I was still a member of the family, and shared Howard's room, along with the office of prompter and critic, while he 'ran through each mode of the lyre,' the diapason of histrionic passion. At the same time he conducted the 'Boston Mirror,' for Oliver & Munroe, the latter since editor of the Baltimore Patriot.

"His first appearance on the boards was at the Park Theatre, New York, in the month of February, 1809. He played in Betty's range of characters with immense success. He then came to Boston, where an equal enthusiasm greeted him. It followed him to Philadelphia, Baltimore, and other Southern theatres. The many-headed was entranced, and adepts considered his performances not only astonishing for his years, but essentially in a high style of art. His large early earnings were said to have been devoted to the relief of his father's embarrassments.

"His dramatic career was perhaps at no stage more brilliant than at the beginning. I have an impression that, as he enlarged his range of characters, he studied them with less care. His success in Boston in 1811 and 1812, was not equal to that of his first appearance.

He had wearied of his profession at that time, and said that nothing detained him in it but the want of some other means of livelihood. In the spring of that year he embarked for England to try his fortune in that country. The war was then just coming on, and popular prejudice, which is nowhere more savage than in play-house pits and galleries, told against the young American. Some one got up a story that he was a son of Thomas Paine. These disadvantages were too much for him; and after having forced his way to a second or third night at Drury Lane, he withdrew.

"He acquired the friendship of some Englishmen of distinction, and in particular, formed an intimacy with Counsellor Phillips. He went the round of the provincial theatres, but after awhile was led to turn his professional talent and experience into another channel, that of translating French *vaudevilles* and other pieces, and adapting them to the English stage. In this way he composed the 'Merry Monarch,' 'Theresa, the Orphan of Geneva,' 'Clari,' and other little comedies better known to your theatrical readers than to me. In these, his charming poetical talent came into play. For one of them he wrote the sweet song of 'Sweet Home,' for which he told me he received fifty pounds, while the musical composer had five hundred pounds. The tragedy of 'Brutus' was a more original work, more sustained, and of more pretension. Parts of it, I believe, are but a *cento* from earlier and more famous writers. But those which are in every sense his own, are among the best of the piece.

"War, distance, and different pursuits suspended my intimacy with him from 1812 to 1825, when arriving in Paris, I immediately sought him out with the impatience with which one seeks those who have been another self in childhood. I found him sharing the lodgings of Washington Irving, (who, I believe, was just then in Spain,) and engaged in the service of one of the great London theatres, in watching for the purpose just mentioned, the new pieces brought out in those of Paris. It was delightful to find him as little changed since our parting, as it was possible for the lapse of more than thirteen years to leave a man. During that time (still a boy when he had exiled himself) he had been absent from home and friends; he had been loose upon the world; he had been living about London and Paris green-rooms. But he had retained all the freshness and simplicity he had carried away. The glorification and caresses of early times had not spoiled him for rational satisfactions and a modest self-estimate. The world had sometimes gone hard with him, but it had done nothing in the way of making him acrid and morose, The man was as gentle, unhackneyed, sincere, and sanguine as the boy.

"He returned to this country in 1831, and in the following winter a benefit was arranged for him by some of his old friends at the Tremont Theatre.

"He made his home in New York, with an attached younger brother, who had risen to eminence as a practitioner of law in that city. He sent out proposals for a magazine on a scale of such magnificence and costliness that the scheme did not succeed. At this time he consulted me respecting the publication of a 'Life of the Saviour,' which he had prepared in the manner of a harmony of the four Gospels. It was beautifully executed, on the common theory of the three years duration of the ministry of Jesus. But the recent publication of Mr. Ware's admirable work with the same title, had pre-occupied the market. He became interested in the affairs of the Cherokees, at the time of their troubles, and was for awhile actively employed with John Ross, in his own country and at Washington. At one time he was arrested and carried off by a party of Georgia militia, on whom he took good-natured but exemplary vengeance by a history of their exploit in the newspapers. He had a taste for hazardous adventure. Before leaving America, he had been one of the party which defended Hanson's printing office in Baltimore, and which was afterwards attacked by the mob, who killed one or two, in the jail where they had been lodged for their protection.

"In 1841 he was one of the most welcome and frequent *habitués* of the Presidential mansion. In the summer of that year he received from President Tyler the appointment of Consul at Tunis. As I sat with him at his table that evening, he pointed to his full sized portrait hanging by, representing him in the character of Zaphna, in the dress which we both remembered to have first worn in that part. He said he had the dress still, and asked me how I thought it would do for him to wear it at his presentation to the Bey. But he made no joke of his official business. He did it very thoroughly and ably. I have looked over his letter books, and I do not believe the government has often had agents who have better filled their place. I remember the books, too, as a feast to the eye. His hand-writing was beautiful. Indeed, in whatever belonged to him, from verses to furniture, from the choice expression of a letter to the folding of the sheet that bore it, there was a rare governing elegance and taste.

"Mr. Polk's administration recalled him from the consulate at Tunis. He was re-appointed to it last year by Mr. Webster, and at that post, it seems, has now closed his life. Many mourn him. The fascination of his early brilliancy has left its record on many minds. The tidings of his departure touch many hearts with very tender memories. Always buoyant, full of resource, rich in the stores of a varied and peculiar experience, his society had always a singular attraction. Always busy about something, he always kept his mind cheerful and wide awake. His abilities did not fulfil their early promise. His faculties were never disciplined by the healthy toil of exact study, nor was his knowledge enlarged by methodical and various acquisitions from books. But, if he did not assimulate or amass in the way necessary for a higher eminence than he attained, so quick a mind with such opportunities could not fail to collect a great deal of what was profitable and pleasant for immediate use; his grace of expression from boyhood to age, combining remarkably the exactness of art with the ease of nature, had a singular charm; and I presume a collection of his letters might be made which would take a high rank in that department of composition. But what I like most to think of is, that a life begun in some respects so unpropitiously should have passed to its end so blamelessly and so happily. To be the spoiled child of public enthusiasm, and not be a ruined man — to lose the huzzas that have cheered one on to the threshold of life and not become a *blazé* or a misanthrope,—to be made drunk with admiration in the feebleness of one's teens, and not wake to a chronic imbecility or spleen, bespeaks the presence of elements of a noble nature.

"The following lines, addressed by him to Miss Mayo, of Virginia, now Mrs. General Scott, I set down from memory. They were written, I believe, in 1813 or 1814:—

'Last night, while restless on my bed,
  I waited for the dawn of morrow,
Soft slumbers eased my aching head,
  And soothed in fairy dreams my sorrow.

'I stood in that serene retreat
  Which smiles in spite of stormy weather,
Where flowers and virtues clustering meet,
  And cheeks and roses blush together.

'When soon twelve sylph-like forms, I dream'ed,
  Successive on my vision darted,
And still the latest comer seemed
  Fairer than she who just departed.

'But one there was, whose azure eye
  A melting holy lustre lighted,
Which censured while it waked, the sigh,
  And chid the feelings it excited.

'"Mortal," a mystic speaker said,
  "In these the sister months discover ;
Select from these the brightest maid,
  Prove to the brightest maid a lover'

'I heard, and felt no longer free,
  From all the rest I gladly sever,
And in perennial joy with thee,
  Dear May-O! could abide forever.'"

On the 18th of September, Mrs. Darley, formerly Miss Westray, re-appeared as Helen Worrett in the comedy of "Man and Wife." Mr. Darley made his first appearance before a Boston audience as *Paul* in "Paul and Virginia," and at once established his fame as a vocalist, and in the opinion of the critics was pronounced the best who had then appeared in Boston. His Frenchmen were also good, and his fine manly face gave him superiority to most who represented the second gentleman of the drama.

Mr. and Mrs. Claude appeared. Claude married Mrs. Hogg, who possessed a good figure, sung well, and was a very respectable actress. Claude was only fair as an actor. He gained some repute for his representation of "Tekeli" the first season of that piece at the Federal Street. He was occasionally rather loose in his habits, but subsequently became serious, studied theology, and preached in Boston once or twice during a visit he made here.

An American play by William Charles White, Esq., entitled "The Clergyman's Daughter" was brought out. The play was formed in some respects upon the "Gamester," and was quite successful.

At this time the taste of our citizens for spectacles, began to evince itself. "Tekeli," brought out in 1809, had proved successful, and the managers announced as in preparation "The Forty Thieves," that much admired play, at once the delight of the juveniles, and a favorite with children of an older growth. In order to bring it out with fine effect, the theatre was closed for ten days, and on the 12th of March, 1810, the grand spectacle was produced, in a style of magnificence, we are assured by those who saw it, which has never been equalled since. The leading characters were personated as follows: *Ali Baba*, Mr. Bernard; *Ganem*, Darley; *Mustapha*, (the cobler) Dickson; *Selim*, Adams; *Cassim*, Johnson; *Abdallah*, Claude; *Hassarac*, Mills; 1*st Robber*, Barnes; *Arcobrand*, Robinson; *War*, Parsons; *Famine*, Stowell; *Fraud*, Sumes; *Rapine*, Allen; *Morgiana*, Mrs. Darley; *Cagia*, Mrs. Mills; *Zaide*, Mrs. Simpson; *Ardenelle*, Mrs. Turner; *Attendant on the Faerie*, Mrs. Graupner; *Gossamer*, Miss Worrall; *Zelie*, Mrs. Claude.

When this piece was produced, the managers were about two thousand dollars out of pocket on the business of the season, but it proved the "open sesame" to the purses of the public, and so great was the attraction that people were refused admittance on several evenings, every inch of room being occupied long before the curtain went up. Books of the performance were sold at twelve and a half cents, and the managers not only retrieved the losses made in the earlier months of the season, but divided some three thousand dollars clean profit over and above all expenses. The receipts of the first night were nine hundred and eight dollars and thirty-seven cents, and the amount received for nine successive performances was six thousand six hundred and forty-seven dollars and twelve cents. The play had a good run for many seasons.

Fennell, who was then editing a magazine here, called "Something edited by Nemo Nobody," composed the following epigram on the play: —

"The Beggar's Opera they say,
(Sure fashion is a witch;)
Made Rich, the manager, be gay,
And Gay, the author, rich.

"So *here* aspiring honesty
No patronage receives;
While thick as bees the public fly
To help the Forty Thieves.

"'Tis well our managerial clan
The public taste have hit;
For had they not, this season's plan
Had left the biters bit.

"No more counts Powell what it cost —
His cheeks with rapture burn;
What forty *honest* souls had *lost*
His Forty *Thieves* return."

Mr. Dwyer appeared during this season.

The season of 1810–11 brought before the Boston public Mr. and Mrs. Duff. They were engaged by Mr. Dickson in England. Mr. Duff was an Irishman by birth, and with his wife had performed in Dublin. Mr. Duff made his first appearance as *Gossamer*, in "Laugh when you Can;" his forte was in genteel and sprightly comedy. In Philadelphia he was a great favorite, and, on one occasion, exhibited the versatility of his powers by performing *Macbeth* and *Diddler* on the same evening. His second benefit in that city yielded $1,574. Mr. Duff was subsequently manager of the Federal Street Theatre, and died in Philadelphia in April, 1831.

Mrs. Duff made her first appearance as *Juliet* to her husband's *Romeo*. A more beautiful woman had not trod the stage, and so far as the making up, and *personal* was concerned, it was admitted that a more gentle

Juliet, or one possessing so black an eye, had not appeared; but the "spirit" seemed wanting. Her style was indifferent, and lacked both power and conception, and her best friends lost all hopes of her ever assuming a position. Mr. Duff had his faults, and among them a love of jovial company, which threatened to check his prosperity as an actor. Stimulated by necessity, and fearful, perhaps, that she might at any moment be thrown upon her own resources, Mrs. Duff brightened up, and though for years she had been content to toil and travel as a third rate actress, she suddenly, as if touched by a magic wand, threw off the languor of indifference, and exhibited the true fire of genius. The change was sudden, but it proved permanent, as many who recollect her *Belvidera*, *Juliet*, etc., at the Tremont can testify. Mrs. Duff was formerly a Miss Dyke, and sister to Tom Moore's first wife, and we have seen it stated that the poet's song commencing —

"Mary, I believe thee true,"

was addressed to Mrs. Mary Duff. After her husband's death this lady contracted a very singular marriage with Charles Young. She met this gentleman, then superannuated, in Broadway, New York, who saluted her with the courtesies of the day, and begged permission to escort her to her lodgings. As they were walking along very quietly, Mr. Young, after a few moments of mental abstraction, said: "Mrs. Duff, you are a widow and I am a widower; suppose we step into the office of a magistrate and get married."

"With all my heart," replied Mrs. Duff, and so said so done, and Mr. Charles Young was legally wedded to

Mrs. Mary Duff. Prior to the ceremonial it was agreed that the marriage should not be consummated till the lapse of six weeks, and in the meantime Mrs. Duff was to go by her former name, in order that she might secure professional preferment. Thus far matters worked well, but Mr. Young wishing at the end of a few days to take his wife to his home, called on the lady and found her gone to Philadelphia. Mrs. Duff avowed that she had perpetrated the act of matrimony under the influence of mental hallucination, produced by sorrow and illness, in connection with potations of opium, and never acknowledged Mr. Young as her husband. Mrs. Duff is still living. We shall have occasion to allude to her impersonation frequently in this record. She made a visit to England, after she had attained to popularity here, but with no marked success.

Mr. and Mrs. Samuel Drake and daughter also appeared this season. Mr. Drake became one of the pioneers of the drama in the West, and the first of a family which has ever followed the profession. Miss Julia Dean, the most promising American actress of the present day, is the daughter of Miss Julia Drake, who died in the bright meridian of her theatrical glory, and Mr. Samuel Drake is her grandfather, who is still living in Kentucky. Mr. Entwistle, Vining, etc., were members of the stock. It was also about this time that Mr. Morse, a law student,. encouraged by Mr. Cooper's commendations, first attracted attention as an actor, but the sanguine hopes of his friends and the public were not realized as he increased in years. In the last war with Great Britain, Morse, who had played *General Warren*, in the melo-drama of "Bunker Hill," made application to General Hull and General Dearborn for a commission, which at that time it was easy to obtain. "What commission would you like, Mr. Morse?" asked General Hull. "Why," replied Morse, "I should like a pretty good one; I should like a Captain's commission." "That is a very modest request," said General Dearborn, "for one who can play the General as well as he can." He entered the service, served during the war, and has since died.

On the 3d of January, 1811, GEORGE FREDERICK COOKE, one of the greatest actors of his day, then recently arrived from England, made his appearance at the Boston Theatre, and as his name will ever be associated with the brightest and most distinguished in the theatrical callender, we will give a brief biographical sketch of his career:

George Frederick Cooke was born at Westminster, England, on the 17th of April, 1756. His father, a dashing officer, died while he was young, leaving his mother in straitened circumstances. His mother did not long survive his father, and after her death, Cooke was apprenticed to Mr. John Taylor, a respectable printer of Berwick. His attention was chiefly engrossed by getting up private theatricals, and he paid but little attention to types or ink. For several years he was a rolling stone, wandering here and there. Visiting London, he saw Macklin and Garrick perform, and in the spring of 1776, first faced an audience at Brentford, in the character of *Dumont*, in the tragedy of "Jane Shore." For two years he was a member of a strolling company, and though he gained experience he gained little else. In the spring of 1778, Mr.

Cooke made his debut in London, and whether it was not the season, or that he lacked talent, we know not, but he made at that time no decided impression. He performed with Mrs. Siddons at several of the provincial theatres, but already he had contracted habits of dissipation and drunkenness, which he was only temporarily free from during a life brought to a premature close by brutal self-indulgence. In 1794, then thirty-eight years of age, having been seventeen years a player, he made his first appearance in Dublin as *Othello*. He was connected with the theatre here a year, when, in a fit of desperation, he enlisted as a private, in a regiment destined for the West Indies, but a fit of sickness prevented his embarking with his regiment, and through the aid of friends, after remaining some time in service, he obtained his discharge, and appeared again at Manchester, and was greeted with the most enthusiastic applause. Shortly after, he again disappeared from the theatrical world, and it is a matter of uncertainty where he passed twenty months, though, when under the influence of liquor, he asserted, that during this period he was in the British navy, which attempted to subjugate the United States. In 1794, Cooke married Miss Daniels, an actress, who soon forsook her lord, when on a visit to Dublin, and returned to England, and the marriage was afterwards declared null and void by legal authority. For two years Cooke remained in Ireland, leading a life of dissipation, performing when able, and disappointing the public when physically unable to appear. In 1800, Mr. Cooke was offered an engagement at Covent Garden, and for a time he rose above the debasing habits he had contracted, and on the 31st of October, appeared as *Richard III.*, astonishing a London audience by his genius. In some characters of tragedy he was thought by many even superior to John Philip Kemble, who till then held undisputed sway in the tragic theatrical world. His great success at this time was in *Shylock*, in *Iago*, and in the *Man of the World.* In these he did not fear, and had no occasion to fear any competition in his own times, and his fame would have been established and his fortune made, had he not taken, on the 18th of April, 1801, the first of those *strange liberties* with the public, that afterwards became insulting and insufferable.

When Cooper returned to England in 1803, Cooke had again contracted the habit of drinking to excess. On one occasion, after having passed a day with Cooper, he attempted to perform, but the hisses were loud and strong, and, overcome by the fumes of wine, he walked up the stage. Mr. Johnstone, who was playing *Sir Calaghan*, addressing the audience in full brogue, said: "Ladies and gentlemen — Mr. Cooke *says* he *can't spake.*" Mr. Cooke was a member of Covent Garden with Mr. Kemble and Mrs. Siddons, and on one occasion, when he was to perform *Pizarro* to Mr. Kemble's *Rolla*, and Mrs. Siddons's *Elvira*, he was so *indisposed* that after a few ineffectual attempts to proceed, he made an effort to address the audience, and began — pressing his hand upon his cheek, and making a lamentable face: "*Ladies and gentlemen: my old complaint — my old complaint.*" This was irresistible, and the laughter so instantaneous that he retired. Once playing *Shylock*, when intoxicated, he was much hissed;

two nights after, he was advertised for *Richard*, but did not appear at all. On his next performance he was received with much disapprobation, when he turned to Claremont, and said, "On Monday I was drunk, but appeared, and they did n't like that; on Wednesday I was drunk, so I did n't appear, and they do n't like that. What the devil would they have?" Once, at Glasgow, Rich, of Edinburgh, had occasion to make an apology for Cooke's being unable to act, and it was to a tragic tone, suiting the action to the word: "Ladies and gentlemen — Mr. Cooke, I am grieved to say, has been taken with the *bowl* complaint," alluding to George Frederick's predilections for the punch-bowl. In the summer of 1802, Cooke played *Glenalvon*, to Master Betty's *Young Norval.* Master Betty was one of those wonderful cases of precociousness which from time to time astonish the theatrical public. His success was immense throughout England, Ireland, and Scotland, and no prodigy since has ever created such a furore. Cooke lost cast by playing with the pigmy, but he was obliged to do so, being entirely dependent upon his earnings for support. In 1808, Miss Lamb, with whom he became acquainted in Edinburgh, arrived in London as Mrs. Cooke.

Our limits will not allow us to enter into any lengthy details respecting the stratagem used by T. A. Cooper, then manager with Price of the New York theatre, for inducing Cooke to visit America. It was in 1800, that Cooper, then in Liverpool, England, met with Cooke, who still continued his course of dissipation. They met, and Cooper, not expecting to induce the great tragedian to go across the water, asked him if he knew of any good actors that he could engage? Cooke replied that he himself might be induced to go, and Cooper, after consulting with Dickson of the Federal Street Theatre, then in London, wrote him in August from London, offering him twenty-five guineas a week for ten months to play at New York, Boston, Philadelphia, and Baltimore, a benefit at each place, and twenty-five cents a mile for travelling expenses between the above-mentioned places; his passage over the Atlantic being paid by Mr. Cooper. To this Mr. Cooke made no reply, and all negotiations were for the time ended, till Mr. Cooper again met Mr. Cooke at Prescott, then just recovering from one of his "semi-occasional sprees." He accepted the offer, and Mr. Cooper, aware that if Mr. Cooke's departure were known, it would be prevented, at once resolved to carry him to a friend's house, near Liverpool. Here, in a state of inebriety, he remained over night, and was conducted thence in a carriage and four to the place of departure. On their alighting, says Mr. Dunlap, in his "Life of Cooke," from which we gather many particulars for this condensed biographical sketch, Mr. Cooper addressed Cooke, offering him his choice, either the barge or the coach. He persisted in his intention of going, and he was rowed on board the Columbia, Captain Hazard, which set sail on the 4th of October, 1810. Even after he was on board, he was only prevented from again being taken on shore by bribing the custom-house officers, owing to some informality in his name being omitted in the passenger list at the custom-house.

Cooke's arrival in America, which marks an era in

the dramatic world of this country, was a fact that could scarcely obtain credence. Many were inclined to believe that it was an impostor, and he was actually playing in New York, before the residents of Boston and Philadelphia were aware of his advent. The passage, which had been one of abstinence, had physically improved him, and on the 21st of November, 1810, he made his first appearance on the American stage, in the character of *Richard the Third,* before an audience of three thousand two hundred people. Mr. Cooke was then in the fifty-fifth year of his age, but he never, perhaps, had performed better in his life, and his success was immense. There was $1,820 in the house, and, till he disappointed the public on the night of his benefit in his usual way, the receipts invariably exceeded a thousand dollars per night. During the seventeen nights he played in New York, the money received by the manager was $21,578.

On the 3d of January, 1811, Mr. Cooke made his appearance at the Boston Theatre in *Richard the Third,* with the following *cast:* "*Duke of Buckingham,* Mr. Entwistle; *Earl of Richmond,* Mr. Duff; *Prince Edward,* (first appearance,) Master Drake; *Lord Mayor,* Mr. Dickson; *Queen Margaret,* Mrs. Powell; *Lady Anne,* Mrs. Duff; *Duchess of York,* Mrs. Drake. During this visit to Boston he sat to Stuart for his portrait, and was engaged in several rows, the consequence of his old habit. The result of this engagement, however, was as follows:—

January	3d,	Richard, . . .	$881 50
"	4th,	"	739 87 1-2
"	7th,	Man of the World, . .	887 75

January,	9th,	Merchant of Venice, . .	979 37 1-2
"	10th,	Douglass and Love a la Mode,	764 00
"	11th,	Man of the World, . .	614 12
"	14th,	Merchant of Venice, . .	825 75
"	16th,	Othello, ...	841 75
"	17th,	Merchant of Venice, . .	624 87 1 4
"	18th,	Macbeth, (Mr. Cooke's clear night, ...	1,008 12 1-2
"	21st,	1st part of Henry IV., . .	867 50
"	22d,	Othello, ...	1,115 25
"	24th,	1st part of Henry IV., . .	665 37 1-2
		Richard III., ...	915 62

The house had not been so crowded for six years, and, as will be seen, the receipts were great, when we consider the capacity of the house. Price (Cooke being paid a salary) received for this engagement $3,640 68. While in Boston, it is said that at a private party, he was asked what was the most beautiful passage he had ever read. "Mr. Cooke replied: "St. Paul's Defence at the Tribunal of King Agrippa," and calling for the Bible he read it. Our informant states it was certainly the most exquisite piece of reading he ever listened to. The subsequent visits of Mr. Cooke to this city we shall allude to in this record according to their data, and will briefly close this sketch. Cooke, after this, visits Philadelphia, and while there sat for his portrait to Sully. The portrait is in the possession of the Academy. It represented him in *Richard*. He performed sixteen nights in Philadelphia, and the total receipts were $17,360 32. He also appeared in Baltimore, performing with Mr. Cooper, and was married to Mrs. Behn, in New York, on the 20th of June. After performing several engagements in the principal northern cities, he visited Providence, R. I., with the

Boston company, and on the 31st of July, 1812, performed *Sir Giles Overreach* to a house, the receipts of which were $285, — *his last appearance on any stage.* He returned to New York, and on the 26th of September, 1812, the great tragedian breathed his last, aged fifty-seven years and five months! Mr. Cooke had frequently announced his intention of returning to England, but his career was terminated through the brutal indulgence of his love of drink, and his genius and talents crushed by the blighting effect of that demon who obtains oftentimes the strongest hold over those who are the most brilliant in intellect.

Those who recollect Mr. Cooke, speak of him in terms of the highest praise; but no evidence to substantiate his claims is necessary, for the man who could descend from the pride of *Glenalvon* to the sycophancy of *Sir Pertinax,* who could assume the gentlemanly part with the unmanly conduct of *Stukely,* and abandon it for the imposing boldness of *Pierre* — who could display the violent transitions of *Richard,* or the unwilling gradations of *Macbeth,* must have been the possessor of a range of talent as great as its power was eminent. We are told, that a transient view of this wonderful performer off the stage, impressed an observer with the idea that he could not be an actor. He possessed a frame neither lofty nor graceful, neither strong nor symmetrical; a face not peculiarly flexible, although irradiated by an eye of piercing brightness; a manner rather inelegant, and so peculiar that it appeared incapable of change or adaptation to variety of character, and the absolute destitution of voice, (for all his conversation was in a kind of whisper,) were circumstances which would seem incompatible with versatility of dramatic exhibition. Such is a description of an actor who was pronounced to be "the true disciple of the bard who dipped his pen in the heart." In the Boston Museum there is a wax figure of Mr. Cooke in the dress in which Cooke performed.

CHAPTER VIII.

Cooke's Last Engagement in Boston.—Entwistle and Cooke *hors du combat.*—The Burning of the Richmond Theatre.—The War of 1812, and its Effects on Theatricals.—Cooke in Providence.—Anecdotes.—The Play of "A New Way to Pay Old Debts.—Commemoration at the Boston Theatre of the Capture of the Guerriere by the Constitution.—Mr. and Miss Holman.—Sketch of Holman.—"Timour the Tartar."—Commemoration of Perry's Victory on Lake Erie.—Great Fire at Portsmouth, and Benefit.—Visit of Commodore Perry to the Theatre.—Anecdote of McKenzie.—Visit of Commodore Stuart to the Theatre, etc., etc.

THE theatre, during the vacation previous to the season of 1811–12, was refitted. A new stage was built, new decorations provided, and lamps of American manufacture, of a peculiar structure, were introduced. On Monday, the 30th of December, Mr. Cooke was announced to appear and play his farewell engagement, prior to his departure for Europe, having at that time engaged his passage on board a ship which was to sail from this port to England, but owing to a five days' gale in Long Island Sound, he was detained, and did not open till the next night. The receipts of this engagement were:—

Tuesday,	Richard III., ...	$761 37
Wednesday,	Venice Preserved, ...	593 87
Friday,	Man of the World, . . .	811 00
Monday, (Jan. 6, 1812,)	Henry IV., . .	703 62
Wednesday,	" " . . .	838 87
Thursday,	Wheel of Fortune, . . .	736 50
Friday,	Venice Preserved, and Love a la Mode,	854 25

On this night Mr. Cooke had a return of the *bowl* complaint, and the disease proved contagious, for Entwistle was also taken with it, and the habit clung to him till death. It is stated that Entwistle committed suicide in New Orleans. He took a dose of poison, and then went to his room, where, with a bottle of brandy at his side, and a cigar in his mouth, he awaited the certain coming of death, and was found in this position after the fatal drug had done its work. Both were so badly afflicted in the evening that they could not retain control of their *understandings*, and were obliged to give up before the afterpiece was concluded. The audience hissed, and Cooke retired in disgust — his kind friends stating that his weakness was owing to exposure on board the packet on his passage from New York. He did not act again until Monday, the 20th, when he was received very coldly, and as it will be seen the houses fell off:—

Monday, (Jan. 20th,)	Merchant of Venice, . .	$470 50
Wednesday,	New Way to Pay Old Debts, . .	417 62
Thursday,	Revenge, ...	520 12
Friday,	Richard, ...	704 75
Monday,	Macbeth, ...	609 50

Tuesday,	New Way to Pay Old Debts, . .	451 50
Wednesday,	Revenge, ...	365 37
Friday,	Lear, ...	557 00
Monday,	Othello, ...	376 25
Wednesday,	Merchant of Venice, ...	658 37
Thursday,	Lear, ...	573 75
Friday,	Macbeth, (Benefit,)	696 25

Mr. Cooke received for his share of this engagement of nineteen nights, $3,200.

The memorable conflagration of the Richmond (Va.) Theatre, causing its entire destruction, and the immense loss of life, which occurred on the 26th of December, 1811, just previous to Cooke's second visit to this city, must claim a passing note. Mr. Cooke was, in a measure, the cause of this sad catastrophe. The theatre would have been closed several weeks previous, but Mr. Cooke was engaged to appear there and it was kept open, when the eccentric tragedian, though a carriage was in waiting at New York to transport him thither, took a fancy that he would visit Boston, and thus disappointed them. On the night of the destruction of this theatre a new play and pantomime was advertised for the benefit of Mr. Placide, and the entertainments attracted an audience of seven hundred. The play and the first act of the pantomime went off — the second act had begun, when from some mismanagement of the lights, a portion of the scenery took fire, and sparks fell upon the stage. A portion of the audience conceived this to be a part of the performances, while others started, but were reassured when it was announced from the stage that there was no danger. But the flames spread more rapidly than the performers could detach the scenery, and finding all attempts fruitless, it was announced that the house was on fire. Those in the pit and gallery succeeded in making their escape, but those in the boxes became panic-struck, and rushed for the stairway, which was very narrow, and was almost instantaneously blocked up with human beings. One or two in the rush were thrown into the pit, and from thence found easy exit. In two minutes after the alarm was given, the whole audience were enveloped in hot, scorching smoke and flame. The lights were extinguished by the black smothering vapor. Those who had gained the outside implored the sufferers to leap from the windows, and many did so, though they were severely injured. The alarm soon became known in the city, and mothers and fathers, relatives and friends, at once repaired to the spot to seek out sons and daughters, parents and relations. But who can picture the distress of those, who, unable to gain the windows or afraid to leap from them, were pent up in the long narrow passages, suffocating by the smoke, or writhing in agony in the flames? Several, who emerged from the building, were so much scorched that they perished, while many others were crushed under foot after getting outside of the door. But we will not dwell upon a scene of such destruction, nor relate instances of peculiar grief. Seventy-one persons in all were either suffocated or burnt to death that night. On the 27th, business was suspended in Richmond, banks and stores were closed, and a law was passed prohibiting amusements of every kind for the term of four months. The following Wednesday was set apart for a day of humiliation and prayer, and in many of the cities of the Union religious services were holden, while the citizens were mourning for thirty days.

Before the close of the season of 1813, Master John Howard Payne again appeared at the Federal Street Theatre with success.

The formal declaration of war with Great Britain, made by the United States on the 18th of June, 1812, caused by British excesses in violating the American flag on the great highway of nations, the impressment of American seamen, and other harassing measures adopted by England, threatened to dim the prospects of theatrical operations. In times of great excitement, the public mind is too occupied to pay much attention to the stage, and consequently in seasons of political contest, or time of war, the theatre is apt to be deserted.

In the summer vacation of 1812, Messrs. Powell and Dickson engaged Cooke to appear in Providence, prior to his intended departure for England. On the 13th of July the great actor commenced an engagement at Providence, where he opened as *Shylock*. He was remarkably steady and regular in his habits, never once failed to perform when announced, and some nights it was thought that he acted better than he had ever done in Boston. On one occasion, Cooke, to oblige his friend Colonel Blodgett, of Providence, consented to play *Falstaff*, which is a somewhat arduous undertaking in the heat of summer. Just prior to the rising of the curtain, a heavy thunder-shower occurred, and very few had gathered to witness the performance. Mr. Cooke looked at the empty benches, and then addressing the manager, said, "What shall we do? postpone the play?" "Oh no; that is not according to the rule of the Boston Theatre; we always play, good houses or poor houses," was the reply. "Why," said Cooke, "there are not twenty dollars in." "The Boston Theatre has been opened, and the whole performance given, when there were only nine dollars in the house," replied the manager. "Well, then, we will play," said Cooke. Before the curtain went up, the single public hack, which Providence then possessed, had made repeated calls at the theatre, delivering its closely-packed occupants, till the house was well filled. Cooke's engagement concluded, as we stated with *Sir Giles Overreach*, his last performance on any stage.

The play of "A New Way to Pay Old Debts" will ever be memorable, from the fact that the great Cooke closed his theatrical career with the impersonation of *Sir Giles*. This drama has been considered one of the finest of the ancient stage, and possesses so many features of merit, that it has retained its position among the popular acting dramas for upwards of two hundred years. The author, Philip Massinger, was an unfortunate poet, whose life was spent in obscurity and poverty, and who dying in 1640, almost unknown, was buried with no other inscription than the melancholy note in the parish register of Bankside, Southwick, "Philip Massinger, *a stranger*." He wrote a great number of pieces, of which eighteen have been preserved. The "Virgin Martyr," the "Bondman," the "Fatal Dowry," the "City Madam," and the "New Way to Pay Old Debts," are the best known of his productions. In the production of the "Virgin Martyr" he was assisted by Decker, who had considerable poetical enthusiasm, which enabled him to beautify many scenes, and supply Massinger's deficiency in this respect. The "Fatal Dowry" was also the joint production of Massinger and Nathaniel Field, and in connection with Middleton, Rowley, he produced "The Old Law." The comedy of "A New Way to Pay Old Debts" was produced prior to the year 1633, when it was first printed in quarto: the title-page stating it to have been "oft acted at the Phoenix in Drurie-lane, by the queen's majesty's servants." The scene is laid in the country near Nottingham, and the time of its action may be supposed to occupy about five days. The powerful character of *Sir Giles Overreach*, is shown by Gifford to have been probably copied from nature, together with the parts of *Justice Greedy* and *Marrall;* the originals being called Sir Giles Mompesson, one Michel, a poor mean justice, and his clerk. About 1621, Jame I. had granted to the two former a patent for the manufacture of gold and silver lace, which they perverted by adulterating the metals "with copper, and sophistical materials," which produced the most deadly effects. "Sir Giles," continues Wilson, in his Life and Reign of James I., "had fortune enough in the country to make him happy, if that sphere could have contained him; but the vulgar and universal error of satiety, with present enjoyments, made him too big for a rusticall condition; and when he came to Court, he was too little for that; so that some novelty must be taken up to set him in equilibrio to the place he was in, no matter what it was, let it be never so pestilent and mischievous to others, he cared not, so he benefited by it."

Massinger had not (remarks Charles Lamb) the higher requisites of his art in any thing like the degree in which they were possessed by Ford, Webster, Tourneur, Heywood, and others. He never shakes or disturbs the mind with grief. He is read with composure and placid delight. He wrote with that equability of all the passions, which made his English style the purest and most free from violent metaphors and harsh constructions, of any of the dramatists who were his contemporaries.

Henderson appeared as *Sir Giles*, at Covent Garden in 1781. J. P. Kemble also sustained the part with very considerable talent; but perhaps Edmund Kean first performed it with absolute perfection, at Drury Lane, January 12, 1816. He acted it in his very best style: he kept close to the character, and indulged himself in few or none of those freaks or relaxations of manner, into which he occasionally broke in his other parts, and injured their integrity. His performance was vigorous, true, uniform, and complete; and the conclusion was as terrific as any thing that has been seen upon the stage. It threw ladies in the side boxes into hysterics, and Lord Byron himself into a "convulsion fit." One veteran actress was so overpowered, by the last dying speech, that she absolutely fainted upon the stage. Kean performed *Sir Giles* seventeen nights before the 9th of March.

Of later years, Booth and Brooke have both performed this part with marked vigor, and though both lacked voice, their impersonations have commanded the admiration of those who remember the performances of Cooke and Kean. Booth excelled in the scene where *Sir Giles* communicates to *Lovel* his ambitious aspirations, and his desire to have his daughter right honorable. Brooke was truly great in the last scene, which is regarded, we believe, by all, as the finest display of histrionic genius witnessed in modern times upon the Boston stage.

The regular season at the Boston Theatre commenced on the 28th of September. The prices of admission were, boxes, $1 ; green boxes, 75 cents ; pit, 50 cents ; gallery, 37 1-2 cents. Among the new comers were Mr. Warring, from England, Mr. Spiller, and Mrs. Wheatley, from London and Bath, Mr. and Mrs. Chas. Young, from New York. In the early days of the theatre, every public event of sufficient importance was immediately dramatized, and during the progress of the war, the spirit was kept up by the frequent production of pieces in honor of our naval victories. On the 19th of August the capture of the British frigate Guerriere, under the command of Captain Dacres, by the American frigate Constitution, commanded by Captain Hull, took place off the Grand Bank of Newfoundland. Intelligence of the result reached Boston in the evening, during one of Cooper's engagements. Although a Briton born, Mr. Cooper rejoiced in the success of his adopted country, and suggested to the manager that the audience should be informed of the victory. Mr. Powell, who was a naturalized citizen, announced the capture to the audience. There was a perfect hurricane of enthusiasm ; the National Air was called for and repeated again and again amid prolonged applause. The news was received by the public with every manifestation of delight, and on the 2d of October, a patriotic effusion, entitled "the Constitution and

Guerriere" was brought out at the theatre. The principal characters were sustained by Messrs. Dickson, Entwistle, Drake, Roberston, Spiller, Young, Warring, Miss Dellinger, etc. In the course of the entertainment the following scenery, incidents, etc., occurred:

SCENE 1st. State street. *Huzza for the Constitution.* SCENE 3d. Cabin of the ship. Song, *A Cruising we will go.* Duett, *Conquer, or die.* The Guerriere is seen through the cabin window under sail — orders are given to clear the ship for action, and scene changes to *a view of the ocean.* The Guerriere is seen under easy sail and the Constitution in chase. The action commences — the mizzenmast of the Guerriere goes by the board — the action continues and the Guerriere loses her foremast and mainmast — fires a gun to the leeward and surrenders to the Constitution. SCENE last. State street. American officers, sailors, and marines enter with American colors, and the piece concluded with a song and chorus, called the "Good Ship Columbia."

After an absence of ten years, half of which had been spent in England, the celebrated Mrs. Whitlock reappeared, opening as *Isabella.* She performed eight nights, and received $581.43. During her absence she had ample opportunity of constant critical scrutiny, and returned much improved as an actress. Mr. Whitlock also appeared. He was thought to be one of the best actors in America in his particular line, the father in tragedy and serious comedy.

On the 2d of January, Mr. Holman, with his daughter, Miss Holman, afterwards Mrs. Gilfert, appeared. They had been performing in New York and Philadelphia with great success. Miss Holman made her first appearance on the following Wednesday as *Lady Townley*, in which she was eminently successful. She also played *Belvidera* to her father's *Jaffier*, and *Calista*, in the " Fair Penitent," to her father's *Horatio*.

Mr. Joseph G. Holman was of very respectable family, having descended from Sir John Holman, Baronet. He received the rudiments of his education under Dr. Barrow, London, who in order to improve his pupils in oratory, had theatrical exhibitions during the Christmas holidays. In the year 1778, at one of these private theatrical entertainments, which have ever been fruitful in developing histrionic talent, young Hoffman performed the part of *Hamlet*, and was so successful that soon after he embraced the profession, though intended for the Church. He made his first appearance on the public stage in the character of *Romeo* at Covent Garden Theatre, in 1784. His *debut* was not remarkable. He possessed a fair share of talents, nothing more; but aware of his imperfections, he studied hard to amend them, and rose rapidly to the first rank as a tragedian. He afterwards visited Dublin and Edinburgh, and met with but partial success. In 1798, he married the youngest daughter of the Hon. and Rev. Frederick Hamilton, who died in 1810.

He returned to London in 1812, and appeared at the Summer Theatre, in the Haymarket, several nights, in *Jaffier* to his daughter's *Belvidera*. He was also at the same time engaging performers for the theatre at Charleston, which proved an unprofitable speculation, and there he took the prevalent fever. He returned to New York and died at Rockaway, Long Island, of apoplexy, on the 24th of August, 1817, in his fifty-third year. Mr. Holman married Miss Lattimer two days previous to his death.

Mr. Holman possessed a considerable transatlantic reputation, having maintained a powerful rivalship with Kemble, and there were critics who pronounced him even superior to that great actor, in *Hamlet*, in which part he opened in Boston. He was distinguished as a gentleman and a scholar, having contributed to the dramatic literature of the day, and by the urbanity of his manners and force of his talents, greatly exalted the character of his profession. While in America he attempted to enlarge the dramatic taste in Albany, but like others who have attempted the same fruitless task, the city even now (1852) boasting only an apology for a theatre, he reaped but meagre pecuniary reward. The father and daughter performed eighteen nights to genteel and fashionable houses in this city, and received for their joint services $2,150.

The principal of Mr. Holman's writings for the stage were "Abroad and at Home," "The Red Cross Knights," "The Votary of Wealth," "What a Blunder," "Love gives the Alarm," and the "Gazette Extraordinary."

Mr. Cooper made his annual visit and opened in *Macbeth* to $534.50; he acted ten nights. The theatre was, as usual during his engagement, well attended. He received for his services $1,878.62. The theatre was closed during the season, to give time for the preparation of "Timour the Tartar," which was performed on the 15th of March to $779.12, and was acted six successive nights to good houses, and occasionally during the rest of the season. Mr. Dwyer made an engagement for six nights, but failed in attraction.

On the 9th of April, the crew of the United States Frigate Constitution attended the theatre, on which occasion it was brilliantly illuminated.

During the summer of 1813, the unfortunate engagement between the Chesapeake and Shannon, which occurred June 1st, occupied the attention of the citizens, to the exclusion of all other matters.

The proprietors of the theatre gave the interior of the building a refitting. The entire front of the stage, pilasters, balconies, etc., were newly painted and richly ornamented. On the outside of the green curtain was a full length figure of the "Tragic Muse," and on the other side of the stage the "Comic Muse" was seen. Shortly after the opening of the theatre, which occurred on the 4th of October, 1813, on which occasion we notice the accession of Mr. McFarland, an able delineator of Irish character, Mr. Hughes, Mr. Stockwell, father to the present scenic artist, Sam. B. Stockwell, another piece in commemoration of a naval victory was celebrated at the theatre by the production of a play called "Heroes of the Lake, or the Glorious Tenth of September," written to commemorate the brilliant victory of the youthful Perry, who then only twenty-eight years of age, had achieved the famous victory on Lake Erie, memorable in our annals, and associated in our recollections with his laconic announcement to General Harrison, "We have met the enemy, and they are ours." The piece had a temporary popularity, and fully answered the ends for which it was written. It was in December of this year that the third great fire, which had occurred within eleven years, destroying almost the town of Portsmouth, N. H., took place. The ground burnt over was nearly fifteen acres in extent, and over a hundred dwelling-houses, sixty-four public buildings besides shops, etc., were destroyed. Aid in extinguishing the fire was even rendered by residents of Newburyport. The managers of the Boston Theatre, with their customary generosity, at once offered a benefit to help the sufferers, which resulted in obtaining the handsome sum of $632.00. After a short season, during which Cooper and Mr. and Miss Holman re-appeared, the theatre closed, but re-opened again on the 9th of May, when Commodore Perry, the hero of Lake Erie, visited the city, and an appropriate performance was given, consisting of the "Sailor's Daughter," (Cumberlands's comedy,) "Naval Fete," "Patriotic Songs," etc. It was on the occasion of Perry's visit to Boston, that the citizens tendered him a public dinner. He was escorted to the hall by the Rangers, Winslow Blues, New England Guards, and Boston Light Infantry, commanded respectively by Capts. Rice, Parker, and Sullivan, and Lieut. King, all under the command of Col. Sargent of the B. L. I. At the dinner, odes, written by Charles Sprague, John Lathrop, Jr., and John Pierpoint, were delivered. Commodore Perry was shown every civility, and a handsome service of plate was presented to him.

In March, 1814, Alexander Eustapheve, Esq., produced his play of "Alexis," which was well received and performed three nights, the last being for the author's benefit. Mrs. Powell and Mrs. Darley sustained the principal female characters.

The season of 1814–15 was not remarkable for any very noted feature. Mr. McKenzie, Mr. and Mrs. Bray, Mr. Savage, Mr. W. Jones, and Mr. Fennell, Jr., were among the new performers. Mr. McKenzie, a Scotchman by birth, was a very good actor in heavy tragedy. *Michael Ducis* in "Adelgitha," and similar characters were suited to his talent. Like many others, he was too fond of putting an enemy into his mouth, and was more than once discharged for indulging in this vice. Confined to his room, owing to his indulgence, he sent for a physician, who seeing his condition, wrote as a receipt, "Water — use it freely." McKenzie, glancing at it, exclaimed, "Why, Doctor, water will be the death of me," and sure enough it was, for the last that was seen of him alive, was walking towards the Back Bay, where his body was found after he had been missing several day. The theatre was beautifully fitted up, and was pronounced superior to any theatre in the United States. The treaty of peace, at Ghent, made on the 24th of December, 1814, and ratified by the President on the 18th of February, 1815, was celebrated in Boston on the 22d of the same month. At the theatre the stage was elegantly decorated with transparencies, emblems, mottoes, etc. Songs were sung commemorating the event, among which was "Wreaths for the Chieftain we Honor," written by L. M. Sargent, Esq., the music composed by Mr. Bray. A triple Allemande with flags, then a popular dance, was given by Mr. Jones, Mrs. Bray, and Miss Stockwell. The latter lady will be better known when we mention that Miss Stockwell is now Mrs. George H. Barrett, who has delighted the audiences at the Museum and National Theatre of late years.

On Easter Monday, in 1815, "The Ethiop, or the Child of the Desert," was brought out for the first time. The scenic artist, Worrall, had exerted himself, and produced some scenes which, from the description, we doubt if they have been equalled in our city. The play had a good run, and gave way to Mr. Bibby, an amateur actor from New York, where he had been successful in acting imitations of Cooke, to such a degree of perfection, that it was difficult to believe the great actor was not on the stage. His *Richard* was admirable.

The return of the Constitution frigate to Boston, called forth another of those productions, which, written at short notice, generally filled the treasury. Captain Stewart was escorted to his hotel by the Independent Boston Fusileers and Winslow Blues, and in the evening visited the theatre, when "The Sailor's Return, or Constitution safe in Port," was performed. These pieces had little incident, and less connecting plot, but consisted of songs and dances, interspersed with patriotic dialogues, calculated to thrill the heart of all "true Americans." Of course they took well.

CHAPTER IX.

Early Circuses. — Pepin & Breschard. — Anecdote. — Mrs. Mestayer. — Gas Lights. — Mrs. Moore. — Mrs. Williams. — Guy Mannering.— Mr. Pelby.— Frederick Brown. — Hilson. — Charles Incledon.— Several Anecdotes of him. — His last Song. — Mr. Phillips. — Mrs. Powell. — Early Criticisms. — Puffery, etc., etc.

In the month of July, 1815, Mr. J. H. Shaffer announced a grand concert at Vauxhall, Washington Garden.

We have not in this record alluded to the various circuses, and other minor entertainments which were given. The first regular circus of which we find any note was established by Messrs. Pepin & Breschard, in Charlestown, in 1809. These persons were Frenchmen, and the number and splendor and training of their stud, were a perpetual source of admiration and wonder. Pepin, the leader, is described as one who was deserving of his great name, and the account says: —

"Whether on foot or on horseback, he showed the port of a king. No Pepin of France that ever rode into Paris with his doughty Austrasians, could have claimed greater homage than our martial equestrian as he brought up the rear of his glittering troop, he himself in the costume of a Gallic field-marshal. Pepin differed, however, from his royal precursors in one great respect — he had rather more brains; and both in ruling his state and staving off revolutions, showed a firmness and skill that grander heads might have copied. It is with his dignity, however, that I am chiefly concerned; his sustaining belief in the paramount importance of his own noble art, which, as illustrated in an occurrence I have already referred to, I may be allowed to append.

"Pepin on one occasion had sent his troop on to Boston for a summer's campaign, he remaining at New York to complete other arrangements; but some misfortune occurring, which required his presence, he set off on horseback to join his confederates. Unluckily, however, he reached a town in Connecticut on Saturday night, and of course was told he must rest all the following day. He started at this order, and could only ascribe it to the most pitiable ignorance of himself and his object. These good people were not aware that he was required to reach Boston for the Monday's performance; that the circus could not possibly open without him; to yield, therefore, was not only a wrong to the public, but a gross disrespect to his own proper dignity. Accordingly, next morning, arrayed in his regimentals, he took his horse from the stable, (finding no one else would,) and paying his bill, continued his journey. A few miles were managed in perfect security, but among the buildings he passed, at length towered a meeting-house, and the clatter of his gallop drawing the deacons to the door, he was summoned to alight in no faltering tones; but the right royal Pepin's was no soul for submission. Scarcely viewing the 'Imbeciles,' he only answered so far as to wave them away with a calm air of contempt. The deacons, enraged, ran at once to their steeds, and king Pepin soon found that these people could ride. Confiding, however, in the power of his horse, he smiled, as he believed, at their impotent fury; but our hero had to learn that it takes much to wear out a Connecticut poney, especially with a deacon and a cudgel above him; and the consequence was, that after a pretty sharp chase, his majesty of the saw-dust was fairly run down and gripped by a set of as resolute muscles as ever outraged the robes of unfortunate station. He was captured; but still had an unconquered soul that coverted his fall into a species of triumph. He succumbed after the style of a Boufflers or Villars. Extending his sword to his captors, with a graceful wave of his hat — 'Messieurs,' he exclaimed, '*La fortune de la guerre — c'est le votre voila,*' which the deacons replied to with a very natural stare, and a 'guess we don't want to fight you, you wild wicked crittur — come back to meetin'. Upon which, turning his horse southward, they led him off at full trot, and, on reaching the chapel, conducted their prisoner to a conspicuous seat, where, whilst the pastor enlarged upon the guilt he had committed, king Pepin received the fixed stare of the assembly, as their unrestrained homage to overthrow dignity!"

Equestrian performances had also been given at various other places, at the Washington Gardens, and at one of these establishments at the bottom of the Common. Mrs. Mestayer, in 1815, astonished the citizens by dancing on the wire, she being the first lady that trusted herself in this city upon so brittle a foundation. Among other exhibitions which received attention from their peculiarity, the following notice taken from the Gazette of November 30, 1815, gives an account. We copy it as it appears: —

The Gas-Lights which are to be exhibited at the Boylston Museum this evening, (Thanksgiving,) will be an interesting curiosity to those who are unacquainted with chemistry, as the lights will be burnt upwards of one hundred feet from the reservoir which contains the gas, without the aid of tallow, oil, or wick. We understand that the streets of the city of London are lighted with this gas in various directions for upwards of fifteen miles.

Such an announcement cannot fail to cause a smile. The editor in assuring his readers that neither "tallow, oil, or wick," were used, undoubtedly excited the imagination of his readers. But in those days, the erection of gasometers, and the use of gas were not known, and the theatres then did not appear as now like so many illuminated palaces, but were lighted by oil, and dimly lighted at that. It was, we believe, in 1815, that Covent Garden Theatre in London was first lighted by gas.

In 1816, two actresses of merit made their appearance. Mrs. Moore, formerly Mrs. Woodham, who has many descendants, highly respected in society, still living in this city, was an interesting actress, and her *Lady Teazle* was an admirable impersonation. The second lady was Mrs. Williams from the Theatre Royal, Drury Lane, who was a versatile performer, and whether considered as an actress, a dancer, or a singer, was ranked in the first class. A critic of those days thus pays Mrs. Williams a well-turned compliment: "She displays the manners of the English drama with genuine French vivacity. Thalia presided at her birth, and study and art have only been the handmaids of nature."

Mr. McMurtrie also appeared, and the Boston Theatre held undisputed reign, where (to borrow again from a critic) the cautious guardian of female innocence may safely conduct his charge to the enjoyment of scenes which excite the glow of pleasure that is unmingled with the blush of shame; and where the rigid moralist may acknowledge the injustice of his inhibition of those scenes where a Powell and a Moore officiate at truth and nature's altar, and adorn it with the garlands of taste.

Prior to the opening of the theatre, in the fall of 816, the interior had been refitted. The first night was honored by the presence of His Excellency, the Governor, Commander-in-Chief, and the General of the Brigades with his Aids. The plays were "He Would be a Soldier, or the Captain pro tem," and "The Boarding House, or five hours at Brighton." On the 9th of October, of this year, a play which still holds its place on the catalogue of the acting plays of the present day, and which has immortalized at least one actress of our own times, was brought out. We allude to "Guy Mannering"—*Dominie Sampson*, Mr. Dickson; *Julia Mannering*, Mrs. Moore; *Meg Merrilies*, Mrs. Powell. The piece had been popular at Covent Garden, and from the cast, a full house was in attendance, composed of the fashion of the town. Mrs. Powell as *Meg* was truly "great," and Dickson's *Dominie Sampson*, says our informant, was "prodigious." Mrs. Powell made a more classic character of it than Miss Cushman does, though at the time some there were, who accused her of faults which we have seen alleged against Miss Cushman's conception of the part.

During this season Mr. William Pelby was among

the stock. He was acting in minor parts, and though never a great actor, was afterwards as we shall see, closely connected with theatricals in this city, both as a manager and actor. Mr. Pelby, we believe, came from the western part of New York State.

Mr. Bernard, after an absence of several years, re-appeared, and was warmly welcomed. He continued a member of the company several years, and like an old oak the more majestic, the more it is beaten by the storms of adversity, he appeared more vigorous and lively in mental powers, the nearer he approached to the declivity of age. Mrs. Mortimer, Mr. Blanchard, Mr. Drummond, Mr. Hilson also appeared during this season.

Another actor, who subsequently created some noise both here and in Montreal, came out from Liverpool, the scene of his greatest triumphs. Mr. Fred. Brown, son of D. L. Brown, of high repute as an artist, and brother to a lady, who until removed by death, adorned for many years a circle of admiring friends in this city, made his appearance and performed with Mrs. J. Barnes, who had then just come from New York. Mrs. Barnes was an actress of great merit. Her *Juliet*, and *Mrs. Haller*, were excellent performances. Miss Johnson, afterwards Mrs. Hilson, appeared about this time in the "Child of Nature;" she was quite pretty, but forcibly weak. West's company of Equestrians, from London, Edinburgh, New York, and Philadelphia, brought out "Timour the Tartar" this year, with great success.

On the 14th of April, 1817, Mr. Dickson took his leave of the stage, appearing as *Cosey* in "Town and

Country, or What I call Comfortable." Mr. Dickson did not, however, retire from the management, but for many years continued to direct the affairs of the theatre with that skill and tact which enabled him to meet the wishes of the lovers of the drama, and to give satisfaction to members of the profession.

The season of 1817–18 commenced in October, the theatre being under the joint management of Powell, Dickson, and Duff, the company comprising Mr. Bernard, Mr. and Mrs. Drummond, Mr. and Mrs. Wheatley, Mr. Adamson, (low comedian,) Mr. and Mrs. Duff, etc.

Among the "stars" from across the ocean, was Mr. Incledon, a singer of great merit, who drew well.

Incledon was rather a vain fellow, and it is related, that on one occasion in England, he was dining in company with several of the nobility, at the residence of a brother actor, and, after the cloth had been removed, the Duke of Sussex called on Mr. Price for the song of the "Thorn," one of Incledon's favorite pieces. Incledon took great affront, and his indiscretion knew no bounds. It was monstrous to call upon another to sing the "Thorn" when Charley Incledon was in the room. The duke perceived his mortification, and, anxious to make amends for his own incautiousness, invited him to favor the company with one of his beautiful ballads. Incledon, stung to the quick, resolutely declined, alleging hoarseness and incapacity. He then turned to his host, Mr. R., and, in spite of importunities to the contrary, thus addressed him: "Now, Ned, music, do you see, is all a humbug. It's all dead and gone; there's nothing now but your Jews, (referring to Braham,) with their 'Love among the Roses,' and affectation and nonsense. Good singing has gone by — it 's dead and buried, and there 's nothing like it — nothing worthy of the name — talent is very rare ; you 're a man of talent, and so am I. To tell you the truth, Ned, there never were but three who knew any thing about music ; all the rest were humbugs." "And who were they ?" says Mr. R. "Why, the first," replies Incledon, "was the great God above, that made us all ; the second was Dr. Jackson, my master of Exeter ; — and the third was myself."

An anecdote is related of Cooke and Incledon. The former was one evening very merry at a tavern, when Incledon, coming in, was requested by our great tragedian to sing "The Storm," but, it being late, he refused, and retired to bed. Irritated at this, Cooke determined to be revenged ; and, after musing for a few minutes, asked the waiters if they knew the man who had just been sitting in the same box with him. They replied, it was Mr. Incledon. "No such thing !" exclaimed Cooke ; "'tis some vile impostor, for he has stolen my watch and notes, and I insist on an officer being sent for, that we may search him." Remonstrance was fruitless ; so at length the guardian of the night was summoned, and they all ascended to Incledon's chamber, with Cooke at their head. Incledon, roused from his first nap, asked what they wanted. Cooke insisted that he was the man who had the notes, at the same time observing, "If it is really Incledon, he can sing 'The Storm.' Let him do so, and I shall be convinced of my error." Incledon now perceiving the drift of the joke, without further preface, addressing himself to Cooke, struck up "Cease, rude Boreas;" and having concluded, Cooke acknowledged his identity, and the party left him to his repose.

Another anecdote is related, of which Incledon is a party. Pope, the tragedian, had a great love for the good things of this life. Amid many other sayings, one of his was to the effect that he knew of but one crime that a man could commit, and that was peppering a rump-steak. When Incledon returned from America, he met his old friend Pope, and, after mutual congratulations, the latter exclaimed, "Well, Charles, and how do they feed?" "Immortally," replied Incledon, "the very poetry of eating and drinking, my dear Pope, in all things but one — they put no oil on their salads." "No oil to their salads!" reiterated the horror-stricken tragedian. "Why did we make peace with them?"

Incledon was quite eccentric. On one occasion, he and Mathews were travelling, on a very fine summer's day, on the outside of a stage-coach, soon after the death of Incledon's first wife, to whom he had been warmly attached. A very consumptive-looking man sat near him, about whom Incledon's humane heart made him feel an interest; and he frequently spoke to him, inquired into his history, and found that the poor man was going home to his friends to be nursed. Incledon, when the coach stopped, addressed the poor invalid, for the last time, as follows: "My good man, we're going to leave you. It's my opinion, my poor fellow, that you're *bespoke;* you're now, I take it, as good as ready money to the undertaker. In fact, you're *booked;* so there's a seven-shilling piece for you, my good man; — and, if you see my dear, sainted Jane, pray tell her you saw me, and that I'm well!" The poor creature stared, and took the money with an humble bow, but made no reply to this extraordinary address, which he doubtless supposed to come from a lunatic.

The last song Incledon ever sang was in the kitchen of a country tavern in England. He had attended the glee club, but declined singing, and left the room rather depressed in spirits, and, accidentally on his way out, strolled into the kitchen, where, recovering his spirits, and gathering the servants around, he sang them the "Farewell, my trim-built Wherry!" in his usual brilliant style; scarcely had he finished it, however, when he relapsed into his previous gloom, quitted the house, and not many days after died.

We have not alluded to every appearance of Mr. Cooper, in these articles. For many years he paid Boston annual visits, and was always greeted with good houses. In 1818, he played a most excellent engagement, and his *Hamlet* to Mrs. Wheatley's *Ophelia* was never done better. For ten nights he received $2120.75. Mr. Bray also made quite a part out of the *Grave-Digger*.

Early in 1818, Mr. Phillips, a vocal performer, made his debut before a Boston audience, in the "Devil's Bridge." Our citizens had not then become very familiar with the lyric drama, and were pleased with Phillips, whose chief excellence did not consist in the tone or compass of his voice, so much as his skilful management of it.

An anecdote is related of Phillips, that when in this city, on the first night of his engagement, after he had executed two or three songs, apparently to the satisfaction, though not much to the astonishment, of the audience, he addressed a note to some of his musical friends in the boxes, informing them, that he was displeased with his reception; that he was accustomed to be *encored* wherever he went, and that, unless a more general degree of applause was bestowed upon him, he should be unable to acquit himself to the approbation of the public. During the songs which succeeded, Mr. Phillips had no reason to complain for want of encomium. He received in this city for eleven nights about $2500. Mr. Phillips was killed on the 27th of October, 1841, in England, by a railroad accident on the Grand Junction Railroad.

The annual benefits of the actors, in those days, were in reality *benefits*. That of Mrs. Powell was always honored by a full house, and so highly was she esteemed, that the following, on the occasion of her benefit, taken from the newspapers of the day, only expresses the truth: "Mrs. Powell has been with us even from her childish days. She has been fostered by the smiles of our fathers, and is the companion of our sisters and our wives. She is an ornament to society, and her character is an illustration of the maxim of Solomon, that 'a virtuous woman is a crown to her husband.'"

We have before alluded to this lady as an actress, but equally in the home circle was she noted for those admirable qualities of heart, which rendered her an exemplary mother and friend. Her benefits often amounted to $1000, so highly was she esteemed.

The severity with which the press formerly alluded to actors deficient in their parts, or devoid of histrionic talent, will strike any, who look through the journals, with astonishment. The writers upon theatricals in 1818 well understood — if we can judge from the following abstract — that fulsome praise was an injury to the stage and to the profession; that the lash well applied was, in fact, required to correct abuses, and to give to actors a healthy stimulus to praiseworthy exertion. They did not then call over the stock-roll, and exhaust the vocabulary of laudatory words and phrases, but tinctured their remarks with discretion. The following is perhaps a shade too bitter, but still it 's far better than the puffs which now issue from the "box-office," and are paid for at so much the line: —

"To Mr. Harding 'from the English theatres,' who made his first appearance in 'Henry,' we have a word or two to say — not in malice, but in kindness. He is advised to apply immediately at the intelligence office, or consult the advertising papers for some employment. In such a town as this, where occupations are so numerous, the calls for labor so frequent, and the compensation so liberal, he can certainly turn his hand to something more honorable and profitable to himself, and less offensive to others, than that which he has chosen. If, however, having rubbed his back against the scenes, it is condemned to itch forever after, we beseech him, if he is movable, to remove hence, and return to the 'English theatres;' where having arrived, let him speak of us as we are. * * * The audience which endured him for a whole evening, can never be requested to give any further of their kindness to inexperience and awkwardness, ignorance and folly."

"Aladdin, or the Wonderful Lamp," was brought

out towards the close of the season; the scenery of the piece was new and splendid. J. H. Payne's "Accusation" was also produced. A detachment of the company went to Portsmouth, N. H., during the summer season.

CHAPTER X.

The Season of 1818–19. — First appearance of Mr. James W. Wallack in Boston. — A Sketch of his Life. — Mr. and Mrs. Bartley. — Their troubles in Connecticut. — Anecdote of Mrs. Bartley. — Mr. John N. Bernard. — Dykes. — Cooper. — Mr. Fred. Brown. — Jos. T. Buckingham. — Robert Manners. — Philo-Dramatic Society. — Introduction of Camels.

The season of 1818–19 commenced in September, under flattering auspices. The "Honeymoon" and the "Bee Hive" were the opening pieces, in which Mrs. Powell, Mr. Duff, Mr. and Mrs. Green, Mr. Bray, Mrs. Barnes, Mr. and Mrs. Williams, and Mr. Arthur Keen, the vocalist, appeared. A new drop-curtain, painted by Worrall, giving a view of Boston, taken from South Boston Bridge, was much admired. The Exchange Coffee House was destroyed by fire on the evening of November 3, this year, and one or two of the actors suffered by loss of wardrobe, etc.

On the 30th of November, Mr. James W. Wallack opened as *Rolla*. His London reputation was considerable, and New York had endorsed him. He played Hamlet, Coriolanus, Richard, etc. There was a difference of opinion respecting his talents. He was too melodramatic to please those who remembered Hodgkinson, Cooper, and Cooke, and the critics asserted that he wanted both simplicity and nature, though his *Hamlet* was favorably received. Wallack was, however, popular both on the stage and off, and he was honored by full houses.

Mr. Wallack was born at Hercules Buildings, Lambeth, (London,) on the 24th of August, 1794. His parents intended him for the navy, and at an early age he received his appointment as midshipman; but, irresistibly attracted by the profession of which his father had been a distinguished member, he soon renounced the "cocked hat and dirk," and became one of a number of young aspirants, called "The Academicals." It was during one of their performances that the great Richard Brinsley Sheridan was struck with the promise displayed in the impersonation of young Wallack, and, in consequence, procured for him, at the age of twelve, an engagement at Drury Lane Theatre, where, for some years after, his precocious talents continued to be remarked and appreciated. He was but eighteen when we find him playing *Laertes* to Elliston's *Hamlet.* This was on the occasion of the opening of the new Theatre Royal, Drury Lane, the old theatre having been completely destroyed by fire. From this period he continued a member of the Drury Company, playing, with Edmund Kean, *Macduff*, *Edgar*, *Richmond*, *Iago*, etc.; a position of responsibility which, in such an establishment, at so early an age, we believe to be unparalleled. His marriage with the daughter of the celebrated Mr. John Johnstone, better known as "Irish Johnstone," took place in 1817, and his departure, on his first visit to the United States, followed immediately. He made his first appearance in New York, in "Macbeth," at the old Park Theatre, to a house crowded to the ceiling, and his success was instantaneous and decided. In 1819 his eldest son, Mr. Lester Wallack, was born, and may thus be said to be the first comedian introduced by his father to New York. Mr. Wallack returned to England early in 1820, and appeared at Drury Lane as *Hamlet*, *Macbeth*, *Othello*, etc. In 1822 he again visited America, and played a most brilliant engagement in New York. Thence he departed for Philadelphia, and during that journey it was that, by the breaking down of the stage, a compound fracture of the leg incapacitated him for business for the space of eighteen months. When he had sufficiently recovered from this terrible check to his labors and his triumphs, he again departed for England, leaving his wardrobe in New York, having determined to act nowhere after his accident, until his reappearance in America. When he *did* make his bow at the Park Theatre, some short time afterwards, it was in the character of Captain Bertram, an old sailor *on crutches*. The large audience assembled to give him welcome, though delighted as usual at the beauty of the acting, felt a mixed sensation of regret to think that the favorite artist was forever deprived of the free use of his limbs. The expression of surprise and enthusiasm may be imagined, when, in the *second* piece — "My Aunt" — he stepped upon the stage as *Dick Dashall*, with the elasticity and firmness of tread that had been wont to distinguish him during his earliest engagements. Since then, Mr. Wallack has been a constant and welcome visitor to our shores, and his popularity would seem to increase with each succeeding visit. In Boston, he has ever been a most especial favorite, no better proof of which could be adduced than the fact, that when he played here, some six years ago, it was the *fourth* engagement in eleven months, each one of which was most brilliant and successful. Mr. Wallack, in 1852, became manager of what was formerly the Lyceum Theatre, New York. His own reappearance, with all the pristine vigor of former years, has been a triumph of the most flattering nature, and his theatre is in the full tide of successful operation.

Wallack was succeeded by Mr. and Mrs. Bartley, who came out from Liverpool in the preceding November, and had met in the southern cities with great support. The Bostonians, however, even forty years ago, were not disposed to accept, as up to standard value, every coin bearing the impression of New York critics, and Mr. and Mrs. Bartley were not so well received here as elsewhere. They had the mortification of playing to very fashionable and thin houses, and they were feted by the most wealthy and intelligent of our citizens. Mr. Bartley was a native of Bath, England. He made his debut as the *Page* in the "Purse." He gradually acquired confidence, and the summer of 1800 found him at Margate, then the grand resort of the English nobility. While performing there, the celebrated Mrs. Jordan went from London, where she commenced her performances with *Rosalind*, and was so much struck with Mr. Bartley's *Orlando*, that, at the conclusion of one of his speeches, she exclaimed "Bravo!" loud enough to be heard by the audience. That "bravo" was the first stone of his future fame in England, for shortly after he was called to London, through Mrs. Jordan's influence, and appeared at Drury Lane as *Richard III.*, *Sir Anthony Absolute*, *Shylock*, and other leading parts both in tragedy and comedy. In 1814 he married Miss Smith, considered in England, both before and after her return to England, an actress of considerable ability in tragedy. After having acquired celebrity in the provincial theatres, she was engaged to appear at Covent Garden, London. She was engaged, says her biographer, at eighteen pounds per week for the first season, nineteen for the second, and twenty for the third. After the managers had made the engagement, they seem to have recollected that Mrs. Siddons belonged to their company; and as it would be rather ridiculous to have *two* Lady Macbeths on *one* evening, and the part being in the possession of Mrs. Siddons would preclude Miss Smith from playing it at all, whether she had merit or not, they soon made the discovery that Miss Smith must play subordinate characters or receive her salary for doing nothing. Accordingly, when her first appearance came to be talked of, and she fully expected to be brought out in some first-rate tragic heroine, she was informed she must make her debut in *Lady Townley* in the comedy of "The Provoked Husband:" to this, however, she decidedly objected, as it gave no scope for the display of tragic powers. She at length agreed to perform the character, on condition of being allowed to recite Collins' "Ode on the Passions" between the play and the farce. This met its objection in turn; Mr. John Kemble, the then acting manager, declared it impossible; it was so irregular, it could not be thought of; but Miss Smith had too much regard for her own fame, to suffer herself to be talked out of what was rational, by people who could understand infinitely better the fitting of a harlequin's jacket than the engagement of a tragic actress, and refused to play without it. The comedy passed off languidly, with but little applause, but *the Ode* fully redeemed any unfavorable opinions the audience might have hitherto formed of Miss Smith.

It was not until recently that the "blue law" of Connecticut against theatres and circuses was repealed. Mr. and Mrs. Bartley had a practical example of its workings, when in this country. It happened as they were going their first journey from New York to Boston, that they halted to breakfast at the principal hotel in Hartford. It was soon known that they were in the city, and, before Mr. Bartley had finished his meal, the landlord informed him, that several gentlemen were in an adjoining room, and requested to speak with him. Mr. Bartley waited upon them, and they explained to him, that the fame which had attended Mrs. Bartley in New York made them most anxious to have an opportunity of witnessing her talents in Hartford; that they had no theatre, but a tolerably large assembly-room, which they would fill, if she would engage to give readings or recitations. It was soon agreed that she should do so, on her return from Boston. The night was fixed, and the room crowded to excess. Her readings from Milton and Shakspeare were highly approved, and she promised to repeat them, on her way to Boston, at her next visit. The inhabitants of Hartford apprised themselves of the period of her next engagement at

Boston, and wrote to Mr. Bartley, requesting him to add his quota to the promised evening's entertainment at Hartford. This was acceded to; but no sooner was the announcement made, than the rigid and puritanical part of the community set up an outcry against these repeated innovations, and Mr. Ebenezer Huntington, (the attorney-general of the State,) resolved to put into execution a dormant act of the legislature, against the performances. In the meantime, Mr. and Mr. Bartley (wholly unconscious of what had been threatened) arrived, and were received as warmly as ever. The hour of performance having approached, the room was again crowded, and all was on the eve of commencement, when a letter addressed to the landlord of the hotel in which the assembly-room was situated, came from Ebenezer Huntington, stating that if Mr. and Mrs. Bartley proceeded in their unlawful practices, he would prosecute them under the existing law of the State. The contents of this letter were concealed from Mr. Bartley, and the performance went off with great *eclat.*

Shortly after Mr. and Mrs. Bartley had retired to rest that night, the myrmidons of Ebenezer came with a writ, to serve it on the unconscious offenders. The singularity of the proceedings, together with the indelicacy of selecting the hour of midnight as the proper period for the execution of the process, aroused the indignation of several gentlemen, who were still in the hotel, and they gave their personal securities to produce Mr. Bartley the next day, or to answer the consequences, at the same time depositing five hundred dollars to meet the expenses of the suit. A tremendous fall of snow rendered the roads impassable on the following day, and Mr. and Mrs. Bartley were consequently detained. Still the whole transaction was carefully kept from their knowledge; but some legal persons, who interested themselves greatly in the matter, and differing as to the construction of the law from the attorney-general, put the question in a train of judicial hearing, and were adventurous enough to invite Mr. and Mrs. Bartley to repeat the entertainments that evening, as the weather was so unfavorable to the prosecution of their journey to Boston. They were still unconscious of what had happened; and it was not until after some grave argumentation in a court of justice, and a decision favorable to the accused, that Mrs. Bartley was made acquainted with all that had occurred, by the gentlemen who had so spiritedly defended the prosecution, at their own risk.

Mrs. Bartley and her husband, prior to their return to England, gave readings at Concert Hall, in this city, and also appeared at the theatre, but with poor success. Mr. Bartley is still living, and has, within a few years, given readings before Queen Victoria. His final retirement from the stage took place in February, 1853.

Mrs. Bartley's talents, even in her own opinion, were not duly appreciated in this city; and, mortified that with her great talents, great person, and great voice, she could not obtain the favor of the public, remarked, in the green-room, that as turkeys were so abundant, the American standard should be changed, and a turkey substituted for the eagle. Mrs. Powell dryly replied, that, by the same rule, the British lion should give place to a donkey, as asses were the most numerous class of animals in Great Britain.

Mrs. Powell's benefit took place in April, when Mr. Dickson reappeared, — his last performance but one on the stage.

In the summer of this year, a new brick amphitheatre was opened at the Washington Gardens. Mr. Bernard was the director, and Mr. Betterton, Mr. Jones, and Mrs. Wheatley, were the principal performers. The entertainment comprised songs, addresses, and recitations, and short vaudevilles were given. After this season, Mr. Bernard returned to England, where he died on the 29th of November, 1828, in very reduced circumstances.

The regular season commenced in October, when Mrs. Young made her debut as *Miss Blanford.* She had been performing in Canada. Her face and figure were interesting, and her performances characterized by much vivacity and archness. Mr. Dykes, who married Miss Brailsford, of this city, was a member of the company this year, and also Mr. and Mrs. Fred. Brown. Among the most notable plays brought forward, was that of "Brutus," by John Howard Payne. *Brutus,* Brown ; *Titus,* Williams, an actor of unwearied industry, who dressed well, and succeeded in obtaining the approbation of the public. Master Edward and Miss Caroline Clark, two liliputian singers, served to fill up the interlude between the farces. Wallack again appeared this season, and was shortly after followed by Cooper — his superior as an actor — but who, from the frequency of his visits, had become too well known; and coming as he did so soon after Wallack, who being of late importation it was more fashionable to admire, the houses were so slim, that the engagement was mortifying to himself and friends.

The season was varied by a little episode, not unusual in the history of the drama, in which the press and the stage figured. Mr. Fred. Brown was not inclined to play second to either Cooper or Wallack, and he, therefore, during the engagement of these gentlemen, absented himself, and on other occasions, when cast to what he considered an inferior part, walked through it with perfect indifference. The audience hissed him, and determined that he should play what he was wanted for; and from little the matter grew till it assumed a serious appearance. Mr. J. T. Buckingham had accused Brown of using expressions disrespectful to a Boston audience, and, on the evening of December 3d, the editor was confronted with the actor, and the result was such that the managers, fearful of a row, allowed Mr. Brown to depart for Montreal. Mr. Buckingham stated the case in the *Galaxy*, in which he gave his opponent a severe drubbing.

Early in 1820, Mrs. Barnes played *Hamlet*, and played it well too. A wicked wag contributed the following to a paper: —

ON MRS. BARNES' "HAMLET."

Strange, Mrs. Barnes so much bewitches,
Because, forsooth, she wears the breeches;
Strange, that so many husbands roam
To *see* — what they *endure* at home.

There are many who recollect Mr. George Manners, the English consul at this port. It was during the year that he brought out a comedy, called "Reformation," which was successful. Mr. Manners was of the school of "fine old English gentlemen." He was consul at the port of Boston from 1817 until 1835, when he removed to Canada, and devoted himself to agricultural pursuits till his death, which occurred at Coburg, Canada West, on the 18th of February, 1853. The year is farther notable, from the fact, that it was the first upon which performances were given five evenings in the week, at the Old Theatre. Another innovation was also made this year — that of giving theatrical entertainments on Thanksgiving evening. The managers did not take this step without due consideration. They thought that *after the divine services of the day were over*, there was no impropriety in gladdening the hearts of many, who had no social firesides to gather round, though the theatre was invariably closed on fast days.

In the summer of this year, a society, composed of young men, organized the Philo Dramatic Society, and gave occasional entertainments at the Amphitheatre, Washington Garden. The primary purposes of the society were improvement in declamation, reading, and recitation, the expenses being defrayed by an annual assessment. No professional actor was permitted to take any part in the performances. Of the origin of this society, John Preston, Esq., gives us the following account: — "The first idea originated with James Ellison, who resided in South street, and was first bookkeeper in the Boston Bank at that time. Mr. Ellison did not like to be active in the concern for two reasons;

he had a large family, and was connected with a financial institution; but he gave *us* the benefit of his services as a more than clever poet. He was a remarkably strong lover of the drama, and his able criticisms on theatricals can be found in the Boston Gazette of that day, which at the time was partly under the control of John Russell. Mr. Ellison was the author of a number of successful dramatic pieces that were all in print at that time. I, at this moment, recollect only one by its title; it was 'The Siege of Tripoli.' I remember seeing Duff play *Aben Hamet*, the principal character in it; of this I am not very certain however. Ellison had drawn this *Aben Hamet* to represent Napoleon as a tyrant. He furnished us almost every night we played, with an original prologue or epilogue. He asked me to name the idea of getting up a "Philo Dramatic Society" to Josiah Spurr, Thayer, Charles Kupfer, Whittaker, and probably others that I do not now remember. I did so. They all agreed to be present, provided a meeting of that kind should be called. Kupfer and myself put in the first advertisement, I think in the Evening Gazette, calling that meeting. It was more fully attended than we had expected; but they all wanted to be *paying* members, not *active*. Mr. Ellison was there, but declined taking any office, although he was more potentially influential to the society than all its officers combined. We made J. T. Buckingham, president; Whittaker, vice president; and Spurr, secretary. Mr. Thayer, who subsequently became a professional actor, was the most active member."

The amphitheatre was so arranged that it could be used for a circus. A rhymer thus alluded to the gardens, in 1819:—

"Bostonians are charmed with various feats,
At John H. Shaffer's splendid *garden* treats,
Where West is manager, and justly draws
A host of auditors and great applause,
By showing Yeomen riding upside down,
Where Godean proved the wonder of the town,
Where * * * * is retailed by the single glass,
And Doctor Preston gave his Oxide Gass."

The "Bride of Abydos" was produced. It was a dull and tedious play, and the only redeeming feature was the brilliant and expensive scenery. The reappearance on the Boston stage of Mrs. Drummond, (Mrs. Barrett,) who had much improved during her absence south, was noticed in congratulatory terms by the Press. She was a most fascinating actress. Cooper appeared again this season, and brought out "Virginius." The season, however, was not a successful one to the managers. Duff, Brown, and Bray put forth their strength in vain. Cooper became "as a guest, who tarries too long;" and camels from Arabia, introduced in "Blue Beard," though *powerful* attractions, did not *draw.*

CHAPTER XI.

A Sketch of the Life of Edmund Kean. — His Early Days. — First Appearance on the Stage. — Miss Tisdale. — His Performances in the Ring. — Anecdotes. — Appearance in London. — Marriage. — Leo, or the Gipsy. — His Family. — Kean — and Arnold. — Charles Kean, etc., etc.

The year 1820 witnessed the arrival on our shores of a great actor, one ripe in his powers, and in the very heyday of his prosperity — Edmund Kean — who was born November 4, 1787. The parentage of this eminent actor is involved in some degree of mystery. He himself, at one time, affected to believe that the old Duke of Norfolk knew more about it than anybody else. His mother, however, was the daughter of George Saville Carey, an actor, dramatist, lyrist, and lecturer of considerable repute in his day, and her husband, Kean's father, also named Edmund, was, at one time, an apprentice to a surveyor, but died as a copying clerk in an attorney's office. Kean was almost entirely neglected in his infancy, so much so that at one time it was found necessary to use bracing-irons to bring his limbs — deformed by his attempts to imitate his companions — back to their natural shape. His mother, being connected with the theatre, Kean had free *entree* behind the scenes, where he almost lived. His first appearance before the public, was when the opera of "Cymon" was produced, which is thus recorded by Michael Kelly, in his reminiscences: — "Before the piece was brought out, I had a number of children brought me, that I might choose a Cupid. One struck me with a fine pair of black eyes, who seemed by his looks and gestures most anxious to be chosen as the little god of love. I chose him, and little did I then imagine, that my little Cupid would eventually become a great actor; the then little urchin was neither more nor less than Edmund Kean." The little urchin continued to serve in the theatre, and when John Philip Kemble conceived the idea of introducing infant imps around the witches' cauldon in "Macbeth," Kean was among them, and seems to have entertained a suspicion of the mummery of the whole affair, as he continued to trip up the heels of some of his fellow-phantoms. Kemble, as may well be imagined, was excessively annoyed, whilst Kean appeased his offended dignity by the readiness with which he begged the manager "to consider that *he had never appeared in tragedy before.*" At a very early age, Kean gave promise of his future ability as an actor. His perceptions of the beauties of the different plays were very good, and even in his sixth year, his recitation of the tent-scene in "Richard III." was marked by a judicious spirit, and a clear conception of every passage. Kean grew up, apparently, without any motherly care; he was ignorant of the first rudiments of education, and he repaid the kindness of some friends who placed him at school, by "taking French leave," and entering the merchant service as a cabin-boy. He sailed from Madeira, where he was taken sick, and after remaining several months in a hospital, worked his passage home, where he arrived pennyless, homeless, almost houseless, and for aught he knew, friendless. Miss Tisdale, of Drury

Lane Theatre, whom he had from his infancy been taught to regard as an aunt, in connection with Mrs. Price, another aunt, sent him once more to school, but the irksome inflictions of scholastic severity were too fatiguing, and again taking to heels, he joined the show establishments of Richardson & Saunders, and became, under scientific tuition, an expert tumbler in the ring, and a most daring equestrian. When at Bristol, on one occasion, while exhibiting some extraordinary exploit in the circus, he lost his equipoise, and, falling on the sharp boards that formed the ring, fractured both legs. The consequences of the accident were always discernible. He continued this life of vagabondage for some time, though in every vicissitude, his predilections for Shakspeare and the regular drama abated not one jot, and thanks to Miss Tisdale, he was finally induced to accept a situation in a small theatre in Yorkshire, where he acquitted himself — though still a boy — in many of the leading characters of tragedy, with considerable success, and in such a way as to give promise of becoming eventually, if not a very great, at least a very clever actor. Kean had many years of severe probation to pass through, but he struggled on, gaining slowly in reputation. He became a member of a "commonwealth," which, as in later days, proved a state of common poverty. The circuit he was on, was in the immediate vicinity of London, and oftentimes he found himself as poor as a pauper; for the tragedian, who afterwards obtained his £100 per night, at one period actually *lived*, or rather existed, on the sum of *three shillings and sixpence;* and at one time, in the town of Croyden, he was so reduced, that a bundle of clothes received from Miss Tidswell, were sold to pay for food, or to use Kean's words, "for better security, my *aunt's* parcel was consigned to the charge of 'my *uncle.*'"

In this same town of Croyden, where Kean had experienced the effects of a short purse, it was, that shortly after, Kean, by one of the happiest retorts on theatrical record, evinced the consciousness of his own mental power, and triumphantly repelled the ignorant and invidious attack of the "cant of criticism." He was announced for *Alexander the Great*, and the triumphal car, in which the hero was drawn in mimic procession, had just reached the centre of the stage, when, as it passed in "slow and solemn state" by the foot-lights, some supercilious coxcomb in the stage-box, exclaimed, with a sneer, "Alexander the *Great!* Alexander the *Little!*" Kean, with an admirable presence of mind, turned his head deliberately round without altering his position, and fixing his eyes with a look of ineffable scorn upon the self-sufficient sneerer, replied, "Yes! but with a *great soul!*" The spirit of the actor roused the audience to a just sense of the insult that had so unworthily been offered to him, and whilst they applauded the promptitude and manliness of the retort, his mortified assailant slunk away from the scene of his opponent's triumph.

To follow Kean in his provincial tours, would be neither interesting nor of value, so far as it might affect a just appreciation of the man. As opportunity presented itself he improved himself in fencing, music, dancing, and singing, and had the honor, in Belfast, of performing with Mrs. Siddons, who predicted his future success. He visited Birmingham, and other principal cities, and while in Scotland, he was summoned by his aunt to repair at once to London, where she had procured him an engagement at the Haymarket Theatre. He lost no time in obeying the summons, which he looked upon as the result of his provincial and northern exploits; and confirmed in this notion by observing the play of "The Mountaineer" placarded as the opening performance at the Haymarket, he paused in joyous expectation of seeing his own name announced as *Octavian*—the fame of his representation of that character having, he flattered himself, reached the metropolitan managers. But who shall describe his disappointment and mortification, when he discovered that Mr. Rae was to enact the hero of the piece; whilst, nearly at the fag-end of the *dramatis personæ*, he read:—

GANEM, ... By Mr. Kean.
(*His First Appearance at this Theatre.*)

Kean, however, did his duty to the manager and the public, and by the touching delivery of some half-dozen words, uttered in the act of kneeling to *Bulcasim Muley*, he aroused the sympathies of the whole house, who rewarded the unlooked-for burst of energy and feeling by three distinct rounds of applause.

Finding that no advantageous opening could be made at the Haymarket, Kean determined to apply to John Philip Kemble, then manager at Covent Garden, but his reception was so chilling that he returned to his post and patiently fagged through the season. The next season Kean became a member of Mr. Watson's company, and while at Cheltenham, married Miss Chambers, who was then playing the heroines. The marriage proved an unhappy one, and brought with it nothing but disappointment and enduring wretchedness. Kean was then only twenty years of age, and he was soon convinced, that so far as money was concerned, instead of realizing the golden dream in which he indulged, he had entailed upon himself the additional expenses of an establishment befitting a married man. He was deceived, but the deception was all his own, for his wife was no party whatever to his self-delusion. Dissatisfied with himself, he sought for solace in dissolute and dissipated society, which proved so destructive to his fame towards the latter part of his life.

At the close of his second season, in that district, Kean joined the Swansea company, then managed by Mr. Cherry. At this time, he achieved a succession of triumphs as *Sir Giles Overreach*, *Reuben Glenroy*, and as *Luke*, in "Riches." In *Richard*, in *Octavian*, *Shylock*, and many other characters, Kean was not less eminently successful. By a strange coincidence — never equalled in the annals of the stage — it happened that James Sheridan Knowles was, at that time, also a member of Cherry's company; and at Waterford, he produced for his own benefit, his first acted drama. It was a musical piece, entitled "Leo; or, The Gipsy," abounding with passages of pure poetry, and with descriptions and imagery worthy of the author of the "Hunchback," "Virginius," etc. Kean played the hero with much applause. But, to render the coincidence still more extraordinary, on that same season, and a few nights after Knowles' successful essay, Kean, too, added the character of a dramatist to that of a tragedian, by producing a melodrama, of which the dialogues, songs, and music, were of his own composition. The melodrama was afterwards sent to Miss Tisdale through the post-office; the postage, however, amounting to nearly three pounds, she declined purchasing such an unanticipated gratification at so dear a rate, and it was returned to the dead letter office, where it was doubtless committed to the flames. Though he had, as occasion required, disported during the season, as first tragedian, low comedian, principal vocalist, ballet-master, comic singer, and harlequin, the most singular effort of his eccentricity was reserved for the evening announced as the benefit of Mrs. Kean, who appeared as *Elivina* in the tragedy of "Percy;" Kean himself enacting *Douglass*, which he followed by singing a comic song between the play and farce; and closed the evening's entertainment as *Champanze*, the monkey, in "Perouse!"

Kean's movements were erratic — now here and now there — often penniless, and frequently degrading his profession by his personal dissipation. Kean, while at Guernsey, neglected the opportunities of cultivating an intimacy with members of a higher grade of society, and sought that of smugglers, and so low down did he get that the company left him there, in an almost desperate condition, and he was forced to give an evening's entertainment of recitations, to obtain the means of leaving the island. It was while at St. Pierre, that on the night of Kean's benefit, his "first-born" Howard, appeared as the infant *Achilles*, in a ballet of action, got up for the occasion, and entitled "Chiron and

Achilles," in which Kean himself personified *Chiron.* Howard was then about five years old, and as fine and interesting a boy as ever gladdened the heart of a parent.

Kean passed through the vicissitudes incidental to a man of his temperament and profession, but his reputation was constantly on the increase, and the autumn of 1813 found him performing at Dorchester, where he was barely able to maintain his wife and two children, Howard and Charles. The houses were very slim, and Kean did not exert himself; and, one evening, after he had played but indifferently, he was addressed by a gentleman, who introduced himself as Mr. Arnold, who, at repeated solicitations of Dr. Drury, had been despatched by the committee of Drury Lane Theatre, then at the lowest possible ebb. Mr. Arnold invited Kean to breakfast with him the next day. Kean went home in an agony of despair: "I have ruined myself forever," said he to his wife, "Arnold has been in the house these two nights. I have been playing carelessly and gagging; for who can play to such houses?" His wife's judicious reply was, "It is fortunate for you, you were ignorant of his presence, or you would certainly have overacted your part." After a sleepless night Kean met Arnold; the conference was brief, an offer was made and accepted for his appearance at Drury Lane. Two days after this unexpected turn in his affairs — this brightening of the horizon, which chased away the gloomy clouds which heretofore had dimmed the future — his beloved Howard had died. The child — by "many a pang endeared," as we have stated — was one to gladden the heart of a parent.

There was a singular beauty and expression in every feature of his fair face — an intellectual joyousness and spirit in his bright eyes. His early death carried sorrow to his parent's heart, and deprived the world, perhaps, of one who might have filled his father's place, without inheriting his father's vices.

Kean met on his arrival in London the troubles incidental to an actor, but patiently did he encounter them — checking the promptings of his proud heart. The great day arrived; it was the 26th of January, 1814. To one it was to decide his future life, for upon his success depended all. The audience was a very thin one. After having greeted the new *Shylock* with the customary reception, all was painfully silent until the passage was reached, where *Shylock* says: —

> "The man is, notwithstanding, sufficient; — three thousand ducats; — I think I may take this bond.
>
> "*Bassanio.* — Be assured you may.
>
> "*Shylock.* — I *will* be assured I may; and that I may be assured I will bethink me," etc., etc.

"I *will* be assured" was a new point — it moved the audience; and "then," as Kean expressed it, "then, indeed, I felt, I knew, I had them with me!" Approbation ripened into enthusiasm; the few who had come there were startled, for though his voice was harsh, his style new, his action abrupt and angular, there was the inspiration of genius in the look, the tone, the bearing of the hard, unbending Jew, which was too powerful to escape their notice. That night was the starting-post of the course upon which he was destined to run his splendid race. For a period of nineteen years did Kean pursue an extraordinary career — to allude to the events of which, or to convey an idea of his talents, is a task we shall not attempt, aware of our total inability to do justice to the man, in the space we have allotted to this sketch. With the genius to have been more than a Garrick in his art, he had the follies and passions at times to reduce him almost beneath a Cooke in his habits.

One scene in his life, we cannot, in closing this outline of Kean's life, omit, as it introduces one who is still living, and who has himself filled no minor place in the theatrical world. Edmund Kean, aware of the caprice of public favor, had determined to discountenance his son, the present Charles Kean, from embracing that profession in which he himself had risen to such eminence, and, through the interest of his friend, Lord Essex, procured for him an appointment as cadet in the service of the East India Company. But when Kean imagined that every arrangement was completed, he found his son's anxiety for the welfare of his mother so great, and his apprehension so strong, lest, by any reverse of his father's prospects, she might be exposed to misfortune or suffering during his absence from Europe, that he had resolved, firmly and immovably, to remain in England, and seek for reputation and wealth on the stage. It was not for some years, and, indeed, until in consequence of some misunderstanding with the lessee of Drury Lane Theatre, that he withdrew from that theatre, and hastily concluded an engagement with M. Laporte at Covent Garden, that he ever became so far reconciled to his son's adoption of the profession as to consent to appear in the same play, or even on the same boards with him. But Laporte, rightly estimating the attraction that the appearance of father and son, as the representatives of two such characters as *Othello* and *Iago* would prove, rendered that condition the *sine qua non* of the arrangement. They were accordingly announced for the 25th of March, 1833, and a house crowded in every part justified the most sanguine anticipations of their success. "The scene in which the Moor appeared, followed by 'mine ancient,' can never be forgotten," observes an eye-witness, "by those who beheld it." The applause was tumultuous — the spirit of enthusiasm pervaded all — and never, perhaps, were the generous sympathies of an audience more displayed than at that moment. It was a spectacle never to be forgotten, to see the great tragedian, the only *Othello* of the modern stage, leading forward that son, — attesting, with a father's pride, their perfect reconciliation, — enjoying the paternal triumph which his success at so early an age could not fail to excite in such a heart as Kean's, — presenting him to those from whose hand he had himself won the meed of high renown, as a worthy competitor for the garland of dramatic fame which they had conferred upon him, whenever the hand of time should snatch it from his own brow. But, if all hearts beat high with joy and exultation in that scene, what were the sensations with which, after the delivery of the passage in which Kean breathed, in tones of soul-subduing pathos, the anguish — the all but mortal agony of an o'ercharged heart — giving its last sigh of desolation and despair to the wreck of all its hopes, of all its happiness — the last "farewell" to the hero's ambition, to the soldier's glory, to the husband's cherished bliss, to the human weakness, the sympathies and the affections of the man — the mournful melody of his voice coming over the spirit like the desolate moaning of the blast that precedes the thunder-storm — he faltered forth the words, "Othello's occupation 's gone!" and sank almost exhausted on the arm of his son. A sudden and a saddening conviction smote every heart, that the last effort of the tragedian was then made, and that the stage had lost its brightest ornament. Upon Mr. Charles Kean devolved the melancholy but filial duty of bearing his exhausted father from the field of his former triumphs, and from the eyes of those whom he had so often moved to admiration, to wonder, to enthusiasm, to pity, and to tears. Mr. Kean was removed to his house at Richmond, where every attention was paid, but in vain. He lingered until twenty minutes past nine o'clock in the morning of Wednesday, the 15th of May, 1833, when he tranquilly expired.

In person, Mr. Kean was scarcely of the middle height, and was accordingly deficient in the dignity of deportment requisite for certain characters, as that of the noble Roman, Coriolanus. His features, though not sufficiently regular to be termed handsome, were capable of almost illimitable expression; his eyes, as it were, played with the passions in the very spirit of mastery; his voice in the undertones boomed with melancholy music, and in sudden transitions, abounded with fine, meteor-like effect; and although, as we have said, he was not of dignified stature, he walked the stage with ease and self-possession attainable only by true genius. We have not alluded, in the above, to many incidents in Kean's life, which mark his "evil hours." Plays were often omitted or changed through his caprice, and while intoxicated, he has insulted audiences of the highest respectability. On one occasion while in Glasgow, the fourth act of a play — to favor Mr. Kean, who had been too free in the indulgence of his social qualities in the afternoon — was shortened. The audience deemed this an unwarrantable innovation, and after the manager had come forward, and vainly endeavored to restore peace, Mr. Kean appeared and motioned to be heard. Silence being obtained, he, with a look of ineffable disdain, turned up his countenance to the galleries, and addressed the gods with — "What is *your* pleasure, *gentlemen?*" As these gentlemen had commenced the uproar, and as the way in which Mr. Kean expressed this address was so laconic, it had an instantaneous effect on those of the *lower regions*, and they completely outdid the celestial inhabitants in their turn with their shouts of applause. Mr. Kean, however, gave a careless, inanimate, and uninteresting representation, and lost cast there as elsewhere, by his neglect of that courtesy which the public can demand of an actor, as their right, and the omission of which justly merits the severest reprobation. Other instances might be given of Kean's short-comings, one or more of which we shall have occasion to allude to as local events.

CHAPTER XII.

Kean's First Appearance in Boston. — The Rush for Tickets. — The Premiums given to Charitable Societies. — Kean's Receipts. — Mr. Thayer. — Master Ayling. — The Sea Serpent. — Death of Mr. Bray. — Death of Snelling Powell. — Last Appearance of Mr. Dickson. — Kean's Return to Boston. — His Troubles. — The Eccentric Kemble. — Squibs at Kean, etc. etc.

THE announcement that Kean was to appear in Boston created an excitement quite equalling — when we take into consideration the population of the city — that caused by the notice of Jenny Lind's approach to our shores. Mr. Kean had already passed through the principal cities of the Union, and had everywhere been received with the greatest applause. The New York journals had vied with each other in their adulation, and his firm friend, the late M. M. Noah, then editor of the *Advocate*, was his warm eulogist, and subsequent to his troubles became his apologist. Mr. Kean, "from the Theatre Royal, Drury Lane," was announced for eight nights — performances on Monday, Tuesday, Thursday, and Friday evenings. The rush for tickets for the opening night, was great — people employing men to procure "boxes," though only one "box" was sold to one person; but after the first night, the tickets were sold at auction, and, with a generosity characteristic of Messrs. Powell and Dickson, the premiums were given to various charitable institutions. We have before us a letter to the managers from Lewis Tappan, Esq., acknowledging a donation of $90 for the Society for Employing the Poor; another, from Ann G. Southack, in behalf of the Methodist Female Sewing Society. The following was also sent to the managers: —

At the Quarterly Meeting of the Managers of the Boston Dispensary, held on Friday, April 13, 1821.

Present — His Honor William Phillips, Joseph Tilden, Edward Tuckerman, S. H. Walley, Samuel Snelling, Edward Phillips, Gideon Snow, T. A. Dexter, Esqs., and Rev. Henry Ware.

It was Voted, That the thanks of this board be presented to the managers of the Boston Theatre, for their liberal donation of the premium money, accruing from the sale of box tickets, on the twenty-fourth day of February, 1821.

It was Voted, That the secretary be a committee to communicate to the managers of the Boston Theatre, the preceding vote.

A true copy from the Record.

Attest: THOMAS A. DEXTER,
Secretary.

There was scarcely a society in the city, without regard to any sectarian feeling, but were the recipients of a portion of the funds thus generously given.

Mr. Kean opened, on the 12th of February, 1821, in "Richard." The house was crowded, and continued to be throughout his engagement; for the Kean fever broke out and raged without cessation. His acting was the all-engrossing topic of fashionable discussion, and Kean himself became the lion of the day. His engagement was for nine nights. He shared with the managers after $1000 per week, and had a clear benefit; and the engagement resulted in his adding to his treasury the neat sum of $3302.68. So great was the rush to see him, that he was re-engaged for six nights more at £50 per night and clear benefit, which gave him $2151.58. The last night of his re-engagement the premiums on the tickets amounted to $640, and though thousands of dollars were thus paid, the managers only reserved $500, which offset sundry extra expenses incurred to better accommodate the public.

During Kean's visit, he appeared as *Lear*, *Hamlet*, *Brutus*, in Payne's play, and other leading characters, performing several of his great parts as he only could perform. On his closing night after the tragedy, he was called before the curtain, and the cry was universal for him to prolong his stay. Mr. Kean expressed his gratitude for the marked attention which had been shown him by the public and by many distinguished persons, and regretted that engagements at the South prevented him from re-engaging at that time; but should any circumstances arise which he could avail himself of, to revisit what he was pleased to style the "literary emporium of the New World," he should certainly embrace it with heartfelt satisfaction.

Mr. Thayer — a gentleman who first appeared as *Young Norval* before the Philo Dramatic Society — appeared this season, and Master Ayling made his appearance as a singer. On the 4th of April, 1831, Mrs. and Miss Pelby (afterwards Mrs. Anderson) took a benefit, when Miss Pelby gave a new garland dance. The sea serpent afforded, at this time, the subject of a piece, entitled the "Sea Serpent, or Harlequin in Gloucester," which was brought out for Mr. Bray's benefit. Mr. Bray appeared, we believe, but a few times after this benefit, which took place in the spring of 1821. He was then taken sick, and his disease — a complication of disorders — baffled the skill of the faculty of this city, and as a last resort, he was induced to visit his native land, in the hopes of finding health on England's shores. He left America, where he had resided for seventeen years, in the spring of 1822, and reached Leeds, England, in June, but he died two days after, at the house of his sister, Miss Bray, the day on which he completed his fortieth year. His eldest son accompanied him on his trip. As a professor of the drama, Mr. Bray was the delight of those who witnessed the exhibition of his talents. He possessed considerable talents both as an author and a musical composer; and as a private individual, no man was ever more highly or more deservedly respected.

The theatre, this year, sustained an irreparable loss in the death of Snelling Powell — the first successful Boston manager — who died on the 8th of April, 1821, aged sixty-three. As a manager, he was highly esteemed; as an actor and a gentleman, appreciated by our citizens. Towards the latter part of his life, he played but seldom. The celebrated John Hodgkinson pronounced his personations of such parts as *Lissardo,* and *Spatterdash* to be the neatest he had seen in America, and his *Romeo, Richmond, Barnwell,* and similar characters, were always respectable and often excellent.

Though born — as we have stated in an earlier chapter — in a foreign land, he had passed nearly half of a longer life than is usually allotted to man, in this city, and had imbibed a respect for our institutions. To quote from an obituary notice: — "It was the native land of his children, it was endeared to him as the scene of many friendships and associations; it was here that he had found friends, a home, and a country; it was here that he had prepared a tomb. He had seen something of the vicissitudes of life. When he arrived in Boston, violent prejudices existed against the establishment of a theatre; players were viewed by some of the narrow-minded bigots of that period as hardly entitled to the common privileges of humanity, and even the more liberal almost dreaded contamination from their approach. Mr. Powell was prudent enough to pursue a course of upright and gentlemanly conduct, and he was fortunate enough to conciliate, by that course, the refined and the liberal, and if he could not win the favor of the uncandid and uncharitable, he did at least disarm their enmity of some portion of its malignity, and soften the obstinacy of the ignorant. It is not too much to attribute to the private worth and respectability of Mr. and Mrs. Powell, the credit of having dissipated much of the prejudice which characterized our puritanic townsmen in 1795. They have at least proved that actors do not *necessarily* belong to the inferior ranks of society; for they have been examples of industry and prudence, rising from a depressed condition to affluence and respectability."

Mr. Powell was a much-esteemed member of the masonic fraternity. He was one of the original petitioners for the charters of Columbian Lodge, and St. Paul's R. A. Chapter, and had repeatedly held the office of master in the Lodge. His generosity had there often been tried and never found wanting. His funeral was attended by a large number of those who had been his friends, and respected him, not only for his excellent taste in catering for public amusements, but for those sterling qualities, which marked him as an honest man — the noblest work of God. He was buried under Trinity Church. At his demise, Mrs. Powell became interested in the management of the theatre, with Messrs. Dickson and Duff, and on the 14th of May, she took her benefit, but owing to her recent domestic affliction did not appear. Mr. James A. Dickson volunteered, and appeared as *Sir Robert Bramble*, in the "Poor Gentleman," as *Will Steady*, in "The Purse," and *Tag*, in the "Spoiled Child," — *his last appearance on any stage.*

In the early part of May, 1821, Kean — having concluded his engagements at the South, and most of the theatres being closed for the season — signified his intention of visiting Boston. Mr. Dickson wrote to him and endeavored to dissuade him from the idea, as it was the dull season and many were out of town, and urged him to postpone his visit till fall, — Kean having then announced his intention of remaining a twelvemonth. To this Mr. Kean would not listen, as he felt assured he could draw at any season. He accordingly came and opened as *Lear* on the 23d of May, to a fair house. The second night he appeared as *Jaffier*, to a slim house, and on Friday, the 25th, he was announced for "Richard III." Kean went to the theatre at the usual time, and was much chagrined to find only a very few present, and, instead of performing his duty of dressing, walked round, stating that he should not play to bare walls. The time for the curtain to rise having arrived, Kean was solicited by the managers to prepare, but walking to the front, and taking a view of the house — which was quite thin — he declared it would be impossible for him to play. Mr. Dickson urged him to perform that night, and keep good faith with the public, offering to release him from his engagement; but Kean refused, and extending his hand, invited the manager to take a parting drink, as it was his intention to leave Boston early the next day. Mr. Kean then left for his hotel, and he had been absent but a short time, when the boxes filled up, and there was a fair house. Mr. Dickson sent word to Kean that Col. Perkins and other distinguished citizens had come in, and requested him to return, as the house was as good as some that Cooke had played to; but he was inexorable, and declined. Among the audience considerable impatience was manifested, in consequence of the unusual delay in the time of the rising of the curtain, and about ten minutes before eight o'clock, Mr. Duff went in front and addressed the assembly. He stated it was with extreme regret and embarrassment, he was under the necessity of declaring that Mr. Kean, after repeated importunities to the contrary, had positively refused to perform that night, and he was preparing to leave town. Mr. Duff then expressed a wish that the audience would decide whether the performances should go on without the aid of Kean. This was answered by loud affirmatives from all parts of the house; and Mr. Duff remarked in conclusion, that those who desired it, could have their money returned on application at the box-office. On the rising of the curtain, there was another call for the manager, and the performers were directed to leave the stage. Mr. Duff again appeared, and asked the pleasure of the audience. He was requested to state the reasons of Mr. Kean's refusal to play, to which he replied, it was for the want of patronage. There were a few disposed to stop the play; others insisted that an eccentric individual, named Kemble,* who had been giving readings and imitations of Kean should appear, but order was soon restored, and the play proceeded — Brown sustaining the part of *Richard*. Early the next morning, Kean left in a private carriage, and proceeded to a neighboring town, where he awaited the arrival of the mail stage.

There was a feeling of general indignation at this unmanly and miserable retreat. He had come against the expressed wishes of the management, and he was bound according to every principle of honor and usage, to stand the hazard of the die. The newspapers of the day were severe in their remarks. In one appeared the following: —

ONE CENT REWARD!

RUN away from the "Literary Emporium of the New World," a stage-player, calling himself KEAN. He may be easily recognized by his misshapen trunk, his coxcomical, cockney manners, and his bladder actions. His face is as white as his own froth, and his eyes are as dark as indigo. All persons are cautioned against harboring the aforesaid vagrant, as the undersigned pays no more debts of his contracting, after this date. As he has violated his pledged faith to me, I deem it my duty thus to put my neighbors on their guard against him. PETER PUBLIC.

Another journal — the Galaxy, opposed to Kean and his acting — inserted the annexed: —

* Kemble visited Cambridge to give his readings, but before he arrived the students broke the benches and windows, and amused themselves in true collegian style. Mr. Kemble shortly after reached the hall, and looking round, said he came there to amuse the students, but as they had succeeded so much better, in amusing themselves, it would be superfluous for him to proceed.

THE TWO MURDERS.

"When Cain the first foul murderer, as we're told,
His righteous brother slew in days of old,
God drove him forth and damned him with a stain,
That all might know the guilty wretch again.

"But modern Kean — that vagrant cockney wight
Who murders sense and nature every night,
Forestalls *his* doom, *runs off* — crack-pated elf,
Proves *fool* as well as knave, and *damns* himself."

The feeling against Kean was not confined to Boston. In New York there was considerable talk upon the subject. Soon after his arrival in that city he published the following letter: —

TO THE EDITOR OF THE NEW YORK NATIONAL ADVOCATE.

1st June, 1821.

"Sir, — As I have yet some months to remain in this country, it is my earnest wish to preserve the good opinion of those friends who have so generously and nobly manifested their approbation of my character and talents. As the servant of the public, I am aware that I am amenable to public opinion and censure; and if the public voice declare that I have been in error, I am ready to apologize with all due submission. But, sir, is it not extraordinary, that the offence with which I am charged took place at Boston, with the concurrence of the managers; with the approbation of friends, with whom I afterward spent the evening — gentlemen of fortune and literary acquirements; and that I should not hear any dissatisfacton expressed until I arrived in this city? I passed the following morning at Boston tranquilly; and on my arrival at New York, murmurs of disapprobation were heard, which appeared to me like an overwhelming *avalanche* at the termination of a brilliant harvest.

"At an immoderate expense, and with all that additional cost which falls to the lot of a stranger, I repaired to Boston to fulfil my engagements. Had I been acquainted with the customs of the country, I should have made different arrangements; but my advisers never intimated to me that the theatres were only visited during certain months of the year; that when curiosity had subsided, dramatic talent was not in estimation. I never could or would believe that the arts in this country were only encouraged periodically, or that there could be any season in which Shakspeare was diminished in value; but as I am now initiated in these mysteries, I shall hereafter profit by my experience.

"Sir, I live by my professional exertions. Innumerable family claims are satisfied by each month's disbursements—I cannot afford to give those talents away. I had performed two of my principal characters, without hopes of remuneration in that town, where my efforts had, two months before, contributed largely to augment the public charities. I repeat, I had acted two characters to the very extent of my abilities without profit. On looking through the curtain, at seven o'clock, on the night I was to represent *Richard the Third*, (that character which has been the foundation of my fame and fortune,) I counted twenty persons in front of the theatre. I then decided, hastily, if you please, that it was better to husband my resources for a more favorable season, and, in this decision, no disrespect was contemplated to the audience, slender as it was. The managers apparently concurred with me, deplored the unfortunate state of the times, and we parted in perfect harmony and confidence.

"It was my intention to leave America on the close of my southern engagements. I now think it my duty to return again to Boston, and in person vindicate my cause at the season when those who most patronize the theatre are assembled. The public have treated me with the greatest liberality, and I shall ever acknowledge its favors with pride and gratitude. At the latest hour I shall remember those friends by whom I have been encircled, and whose amity and confidence I am convinced I have not forfeited. But I may be permitted to say, that the present hostility is not the voice of the public; it is that spirit of detraction ever attendant on little minds—a spirit which watches for its prey, and seizes upon transient and accidental occurrences to defame and destroy. That respectable presses in this country should have been influenced by such feelings, and denounce with such acrimony and bitterness, is to me extraordinary. 'There is something in it more than natural, if philosophy could find it out.'

"I understand some gentlemen have asserted that I have acted to equally bad houses in England. I lament that they are driven to such extremities; or, rather, that they should compel me to declare that their assertions are untrue. The present existence of the first theatre in Europe, is founded on the abilities which they affect to despise. The provincial managers of England, Scotland, and Ireland, have thankfully rewarded my efforts by sums equal to what I receive from my friend, Mr. Price, the worthy and efficient manager of the theatre in this city. For the first three years of a career unprecedented in dramatic annals, I was in receipt of double that sum in every theatre in which I acted, and even, allowing a trifling diminution in the space of seven years, what am I to think of a city in which I have been received with equal enthusiasm, and witness a total desertion in the space of three months? But the public say I was too precipitate, — that I should have performed that evening, and then closed my engagement. Granted. Our feelings frequently mar our better judgments, and from trifling causes lead to results which we subsequently regret. The error was venal, for who is exempt from error? But all unprejudiced people will, I trust, take into consideration the unprofitable labor of acting *Richard the Third* to a solitary few, who subsequently acknowledged themselves perfectly contented with the gentleman who represented the character.

"I am now convinced that the fine weather was my chief enemy, and shall again resume my station in the Boston Theatre before I return to England.

"I beg leave, sir, to submit this 'round unvarnished tale' to the consideration and decision of the public; and I have too exalted an opinion of their justice and liberality not to anticipate a verdict in my favor. EDMUND KEAN."

This called forth the following: —

TO THE PUBLIC.

"The managers of the Boston Theatre, having suffered not only severe mortification, from the disappointment experienced by the public, but a heavy pecuniary loss, from Mr. Kean's non-fulfilment of his engagement with them, indulged the hope that they should not, in addition, be accused of 'concurring in any *offence* to the public;' Mr. Kean's statement, however, re-published in the Boston paper of to-day, has reduced them to the unpleasant alternative of either by silence admitting the truth of that statement, or of publicly disavowing it. They, therefore, respectfully state, that Mr. Kean's refusal to perform the part of *Richard the Third*, was not only without their concurrence, but met from them all the opposition in their power, which they thought decorous and gentlemanly. This course was dictated by a sense of duty that they owed to the patrons of the drama, and when they add, that he was not to receive any specific sum for his services, but was to share the receipts of the eight nights, if they exceeded a certain agreed sum, and to have the ninth night clear for his benefit, it will appear evident, that *interest* as well as *duty* would prevent them from concurring.

"The managers submit this statement in duty to the public and themselves, not from any hostility to Mr. Kean.

J. A. Dickson,
John Duff.

"*Boston Theatre, June* 4, 1821."

Mr. Kean, previous to his first letter, addressed the following to Mr. Dickson : —

"My Dear Sir, — I much regret the occasion of my abrupt departure, but you must feel with me that my professional reputation must not be trifled with. An indifferent house to such plays as "Venice Preserved," etc., *however well acted*, may be found in the catalogue of histrionic events, but a total desertion of the public to that character which has been the foundation of my fame and fortune, requires a greater portion of philosophy than I am master of. I must lament to find that curiosity alone was the incitement of the apparent enthusiasm that attended my efforts on the first engagement. I had vainly conceived the *talent* not the *novelty* had attracted. Be kind enough to pay into Mr. Tileston's hands my portion of the first night's receipts. I am dear Sir,

Yours, etc.,
Edmund Kean."

The above bears no date, and as will be seen bears marks of a slight repentance for his hasty act. The italics are Mr. Kean's.

A second letter soon followed the first; — the public feeling had increased in New York, and a riot, if Kean played, was feared : —

MR. KEAN'S FAREWELL TO AMERICA.

[*From the New York National Advocate of June 8th.*]

"Sir, — As I find it impossible for individual efforts to stem the torrent of opposition with which I have to contend, and as I likewise consider it inconsistent with my feelings and character to make additional apologies, I have resolved to return to my native country, and beg leave to offer to the public my thanks for that portion of favor bestowed on me, and respectfully bid them farewell.

"Had I been aware of the enormity of the offence which has excited so much indignation, I certainly should not have permitted my feelings to interfere with my interest.

"The 'very head and front of my offending' amounts to this: an actor, honored, patronized by his native country, and enjoying a high rank in the drama, withheld his services under the impression that they were not duly appreciated; and so much do I fear the fraility of my nature, that it is not improbable, under the same circumstances, I might be tempted to act in the same manner. I therefore think it proper to leave the theatre open to such compeers, whose interests it may be to study the customs, and not offend them by my presence any longer.

"Before I left England, I was apprized how powerful an agent the press was in a free country, and I was admonished to be patient under the lashes that awaited me; and, at a great sacrifice of feeling, I have submitted to their unparalleled severity and injustice. I was too proud to complain, and suffered in silence; but I have no hesitation in saying, that the conduct I pursued was that which every man of reputation would pursue under the same circumstances, in that country where Shakspeare was born and Garrick had acted.

"Again, I disclaim any intention of offending; and although every natural domestic tie, as well as the public love, await me on my own shores, it is with reluctance and regret I leave my friends in America.

EDMUND KEAN."

This appeared June 8th, the day after Kean sailed in the Martha for Liverpool, and the subsequent day a third letter was published in the Advocate. It was addressed to M. M. Noah, Esq., the Editor: —

"OFF SANDY HOOK, June, 1821.

"DEAR SIR, — Impress upon the public mind that I do not leave America but with the most sincere impressions of admiration and respect; and though I have temporarily yielded to the torrent of hostility, which I was too proud to contend against, still, on the termination of my Drury Lane engagement, I shall return again to share the favor of those friends, whom I shall ever rank foremost in my affections, in whatever climate fortune may dispose me.

EDMUND KEAN."

It was during this visit to America that Mr. Kean caused the body of Cooke to be disinterred, and removed to an eligible spot in St. Paul's church-yard, near the corner of Broadway and Vesey streets. The monument over the remains is in marble, and consists of a square pedestal on two steps surmounted by an urn, from the top of which a flame issues. The inscription on the tomb, which was furnished by Dr. Francis, who superintended the removal of the remains, is as follows: —

"*Erected to the Memory of* GEORGE FREDERICK COOKE, *by Edmund Kean, of the Theatre Royal, Drury Lane*, 1821.

'Three kingdoms claim his birth,
Both hemispheres pronounce his worth.'"

The Boston Theatre soon after closed. The company visited Portland during the summer, and Mrs. Powell released the theatre for three years.

CHAPTER XIII.

The Act of Incorporation. — Tom Kilner. — Labasse. — Samuel Woodworth. — Boston a City. — Booth's First Appearance in Boston. — Biographical Sketch of Booth. — Remarks on his Acting. — Appearance of Miss Elizabeth Powell. — George Barrett. — Announcement of Mr. Finn's Appearance. — A Biographical Sketch of Henry J. Finn, etc. etc.

THE business of the theatre had, previous to this year, been managed by the trustees of the theatre, but it was found so inconvenient to carry out the joint-stock principle, that an act of incorporation was applied for, which was granted by the legislature, on the 16th of June, 1821.

The theatre for the season of 1821–2 opened on the 19th of September, under the acting management of Messrs. Kilner & Clarke. The house had been repainted, and a large audience was assembled to witness the "Foundling of the Forest," in which Messrs. Duff, Thayer, Clarke, Moreland, Perkins, J. Mills Brown (first appearance in Boston), with Mrs. Drummond, Mrs. Parker, Mrs. Barnes, and Mrs. Powell appeared. Mr. Spear, formerly of the Washington Gardens, also appeared this season. On the 28th of September, Kilner made his first appearance before a Boston audience as *Sir Anthony Absolute*, his wife appearing as *Lucy*. They were warmly received, and time justified the prediction then made, that they were great acquisitions to the company. Mr. Kilner is still living in Ohio. Mr. Cooper played an engagement, and Mr. Hilson, Mrs.

J. Barnes, and Mrs. Holman, a singer of merit, with Phillips, who was here in 1813, were among the stars. Mrs. Holman and Phillips did well, and the receipts on the last night of Mrs. H.'s engagement, when she took her benefit, amounted to $806. During the season, "La Belle Peruvienne," a ballet, was produced under the direction of Monsieur Labasse, and Samuel Woodworth, the author of the "Moss-covered Bucket," brought out a play entitled "The Deed of Gift," which, however, met with a poor reception, and was almost immediately shelved. In 1822, the act of the legislature was passed conferring upon Boston the name and privileges of a city; and on Monday, April 8th, the first city election took place, which resulted in no choice. On this evening Mr. Duff took his benefit, but the adherents of Quincy and Otis were too much occupied to attend the drama, and the result was any thing but gratifying to the beneficiary. On the second trial, the Hon. John Phillips was chosen mayor, and the political excitement had had time to die away, when the advent of Junius Brutus Booth was announced. The first appearance of this great actor in Boston, where for so many years he has attracted those most conversant with the different schools of acting, and has delighted elsewhere the most critical audiences in the world by his masterly impersonations, occurred on the 6th of May, 1822. He made his appearance as *Richard*, a character which he is identified with wherever he has performed. His acting then received the applause of a Boston audience; and up to his last appearance in this city prior to his death, he retained the position he so eminently deserved. During his first engagement, he performed *Sir Edward Mortimer*, *Sir Giles Overreach*, *Octavian*, and for his benefit *Hamlet*, which drew an eight-hundred-dollar house. There was a chasteness in Booth's earlier delineations, which never failed to command approbation. His voice, which latterly had lost its mellow tones, was most musical, and though as *Richard* he had at the time of his death no equal on the stage, his impersonation had lost the vigor of his more youthful days. Booth's acting always evinced genius. Like Edmund Kean, there was inspiration in his embodiment of Shakspearian characters, and even when the words were lost to the hearing, the eye needed no vocal interpreter, for Booth, more than any actor we have ever seen, possessed the power of combining a meaning in every gesture, and a silent glance was equivalent to a delivered sentence. As a soliloquist, Booth excelled. With many actors, all soliloquies seem like so many title-pages to the succeeding acts, but Booth avoided all strains after startling points, and gave to such passages, both in "Hamlet" and "Richard," an interest without destroying the unity of the play. The part of *Richard*, it has been remarked, is beyond all others variegated, and consequently favorable to a judicious performer. Booth's acting in the scene with *Lady Anne*, and the tent scene in the "Richard," was unequalled by any performance of modern days; and though there are portions of the *Apostate* and *Sir Giles Overreach* which command admiration, his master-piece, we think, was that portion where *Richard* starts out of his dream and exclaims, "Give me another horse!" etc. The intensity of his acting, the admirable conception of the part, and the delineation of remorse, hatred, and repentance, which alternately harrow the soul of the hypocrite and murderer, rendered this scene the best, if not the very best, in all Booth's range of character.

A brief biographical sketch of this actor may not be inappropriate. Booth was said to be a descendant of the celebrated Barton Booth, the greatest English actor of ancient times, but this fact seems not to be well authenticated. His father was an attorney, his mother lineally descended from the celebrated John Wilkes. The elder Booth, a warm admirer of the writings of Junius, named his son (who was born at St. Pancras, near London, on the 1st of May, 1796,) after the object of his admiration, adding thereto that of Brutus, over which signature the illustrious incognito sometimes wrote. In his younger days, he was remarkable for his love of drawing and painting, the pursuit of which studies, however, he soon abandoned, and entered the navy as a midshipman. His father's opposition to such a life induced him to commence printing, which he gave up for the law. But Themis had few charms for him, and he applied himself to sculpture, from which he soon turned to his final profession, the stage. His debut was at a *cow-house* in Pancras street, Tottenham-court-road, as *Frank Rochdale*, in "John Bull." Here he played *Buckingham*, and on one occasion read *Collooney*, in the "Irishman in London." He soon joined a strolling company, and made his regular debut at Peckham on the 13th of September, 1813, as *Campillo*, in the "Honey Moon." With this company he performed at Ostend, Amsterdam, Antwerp, Brussels, and Ghent. At Brussels he made a hit as *Megrine.*

Here he was married. After some difficulty he succeeded in obtaining an engagement at Covent Garden, and in October, 1813, played for the first time in London, enacting *Sylvius* in "As You Like It." When at Covent Garden, before the brilliancy of his talent had dazzled all eyes, it is recorded that the celebrated Miss Sarah Booth, the leading actress, and a great favorite by reason of her great personal beauty as well as dramatic ability, requested him to add an "*e*" to avoid being mistaken as her relative. The riots at Covent Garden in 1817, of which Booth was the cause, are too familiar to need notice here. Leaving this theatre, he played the "Lear of Private Life" at the Coburg, which he left for Drury Lane. In 1820 he had a rencontre with "Il Diavolo Antonio," and soon after he left for America. His debut in America took place at Richmond, on July 13th, 1821, as *Richard.* On the 5th of October he opened in the same part in New York. In 1825 he left his farm at Bel-Air, Maryland, whither he had sojourned for some months, and returned to England, opening at Drury Lane as *Brutus.* His visit was of short duration, and he again crossed the water. During his first visit to New Orleans, he appeared as *Oresté* in Racine's "Andromaque," at the French theatre, and the purity of his accent perfectly electrified the Frenchmen, who crowded the house on the evening in question. Shortly after this singular freak, he passed some time at the "Hermitage," by invitation of Gen. Jackson. In September, 1831, Mrs. Booth, one of the most beautiful women of her day, first trod the boards at the Holiday street, Baltimore, as *Rosalie Somers* to her husband's *Reuben Glenroy.* This lady remained but a short time on the stage, yet gained an enviable reputation for her impersonation of the above part and of *Susan Ashfield.* On one occasion, in Baltimore, Booth appeared as the *second actor* to Charles Kean's *Hamlet,* and at the conclusion of the soliloquy, "Thoughts black," etc., the audience rose *en masse,* and cheered him to the echo. On October 27th, 1832, Booth played *Old Norval* to the *Young Norval* of Wm. Warren, the favorite comedian of this city, it being the debut of that gentleman. In 1836, Mr. Booth, for the last time, visited his native country, where he remained nearly a year, returning thence to the land of his adoption. Since then his career is well known. Probably no actor ever gave rise to more of anecdote, both mythical and recital, than Mr. Booth. His numerous eccentricities would fill a volume. "*The Actor, or A Peep behind the Curtain: Being Passages in the Lives of Booth and some of his Contemporaries,*" published in New York in 1846, gives the best life of the gifted tragedian we have yet met with. Mr. Booth's last appearance in this city was at the Museum, as *Richard,* on October 31st, 1851.

Mr. Booth subsequently visited California, where he was very successful, and then returned to play his last drama on the boards of the St. Charles, New Orleans. His last appearance on the stage was on Friday, Nov. 19th, as *Mortimer* and *John Lump.* Mr. De Bar, (a connection of Mr. Booth,) was the *Sampson,* and Mark Smith the *Winterton* of the evening. The *Picayune* says of the occasion: — "The St. Charles Theatre was crowded last evening for the benefit of this veteran performer. Many ladies graced the dress circle with their presence. * * * * Mr. Booth appeared in his favorite character of *Mortimer*. To say that he enacted it in a style that delighted every one, would be speaking without exaggeration. Indeed every successful performance during his two brief engagements appeared to show Mr. Booth's powers to better advantage, and the regret is general that he should stay so short a time with us. Talent like that he possesses is so rare now-a-days, when respectable mediocrity is the chief qualification of the American stage, that we cannot make up our minds to part with Mr. Booth until we have at least seen all the faces of the jewel of dramatic genius, whose brilliancy has illumined his name not only for the present generation, but for posterity. Mr. Booth was called out after the play, and again after the farce, — the famous one of the Review. Public curiosity was much excited to see him in a part so opposite to the tragic character he had represented in the early part of the evening, and it was difficult to recognize in the stupid, awkward Yorkshire clown, *John Lump*, the form, and face, and voice, that moved the audience in *Shylock*, *Bertram*, and such powerful characters."

While in New Orleans, Mr. Booth contracted a violent cold, which greatly enfeebled him. He took passage on the steamer J. S. Chenoweth, intending to return home, but on the 30th of November, 1852, at noon, while on the Mississippi, he died, his disease having turned into consumption of the bowels. For three days before his death he had become speechless. On the 11th of December, his burial took place at Baltimore, from his residence in North Exeter street, and was attended by the relatives of the deceased, the Baltimore Dramatic Association, who were very numerously represented, the various members of the Baltimore orchestras, and a large number of personal friends. The train proceeded to the Baltimore cemetery, where Vollandt's band performed an appropriate and impressive dirge, composed for the occasion.

Mr. Booth's claims to authorship rest solely upon "Ugolino," one of the best productions of the modern stage, a work possessing great poetry of diction and nervousness of style. It was originally written for Mr. and Mrs. Henry Wallack, who first produced it at the Chesnut St., April 20th, 1825, sustaining the principal characters of *Ugolino* and *Angelica*. Mr. John R. Scott has, we believe, of late years, possessed the right of representing it, and it was performed with success at the Howard during the season of 1849–50, the hero and heroine being delineated by Scott and Mrs. J. B. Booth, Jr. This play is published, easily accessible, and worthy a place in every library. The following lines will serve as an extract; they are simple, yet extremely beautiful: —

> "Let us part,
> Since part we must, like brothers and like friends,
> Who bent on travel, thus dividing stray,
> As Fortune or as Fancy leads the way, —
> Far off, yet not forgotten, though apart,
> Dwelling together in each other's heart."

Mr. Booth has had, we think, three children. The first was a daughter to whom he was much attached. The news of her death reached New York on a certain day, on the evening of which he was "up" for *Richard*.

Careful of his reputation and distressed by his affliction, he was in great anguish, not knowing how to avoid the performance, when he accidentally met Mr. Forest. On being told of his affliction, Mr. Forest immediately offered to perform the part, though he had not played it for some years. This little act of unsolicited kindness speaks volumes for the warm heart of the actor. Mr. Booth's eldest son, J. B., Jr., now in California, is well known here. His debut occurred at the old National in the season of 1840–41, as *Tressel* in "Richard III." Edwin Thomas Booth, now also in California, made a successful debut in the same part at the Museum, Sept. 10th, 1849.

At the close of the season, the company as usual left for some of the neighboring cities. A portion visited Portland, where on the 16th of August, 1822, Miss Elizabeth Powell, (afterwards Mrs. Finn,) daughter of Snelling Powell, made her debut in the part of *Julianna* in the "Honey Moon." The season of 1822–3 commenced on the 16th of September, and the opening night introduced to a Boston public Mr. George Barrett, more familiarly known as "Gentleman George," who, after an absence of many years, returned to the "boards," where he first made his bow to an audience, when quite a boy. Mrs. Warring this season made her first appearance in America, and on the first night, recited Collins's Ode, on the Passions. Mr. Barrett's excellent acting is still so fresh in the remembrance of many, that any allusions to his qualifications are almost useless. At the time he made his reappearance, he was probably the best comedian on the American stage. Mr. Barrett subsequently married Mrs. Drummond, who, at his first benefit in Boston, appeared as *Jesse Oakland*, to Barrett's *Young Rapid*, in "A Cure for the Heart-Ache." In later years, Mr. Barrett was connected with the Tremont Theatre, and recently with the Broadway Theatre, N. Y. In 1850 he made a tour of the United States with his daughter, Miss Georgiana Barrett, (now Mrs. Warren,) and in 1852–3 was stage-manager of the theatre at Charleston, S. C.

On the 16th of October, 1822, the "Child of Nature" was brought out for the purpose of bringing forward Miss Elizabeth Powell, who appeared during the season in many parts, and gradually succeeded in overcoming that timidity which was the chief fault in her acting. Her *Hester* in "To Marry or not to Marry," and *Zorayda* to Finn's *Octavian*, were above mediocrity.

Miss P. was the only child of the Powell family who had an inclination for the stage, and adopted the profession against the wishes of her friends.

In the newspapers of the day, an announcement appeared, which we copy. It appeared in the papers of 1822:—

"☞ MR. FINN, the Tragedian, is shortly expected. Due notice will be given of his appearance in this city."

Henry James Finn, one of the most popular actors that ever made Boston his home, was born in Cape Breton, Sidney, about the year 1785. His father was at one time in the British Navy, but retiring from the service, he came when the subject of this sketch was quite a child to New York. Finn evinced no decided predilections for the stage till 1804–5, when he obtained an *entreé* behind the scenes at the Park Theatre, and soon enlisted as volunteer to the "property man," deriving an ample equivalent for any hard work he might do, by being allowed to make his appearance on the stage to deliver a letter, or in some other minor capacity. He devoted his evenings to this recreation, during the day serving in the office of Thomas Phœnix, Esq., as copying clerk, having received the rudiments of an education at the academy at Hackensack. His employer, however, soon ascertained the chosen spot of his clerk's nightly retreat, and, fearing that it might lead to evil, requested Mr. Stephen Price, then manager, to forbid any farther visits. The manager did as he was requested, and the door being closed on him, he was obliged to seek other sources of amusement, for his pecuniary affairs prevented his ingress to the front of the house. His father dying, it devolved upon Finn to support his mother, a task which he fulfilled during his life with filial obedience and solicitude. It was about this time that Finn and his mother embarked for Europe, in the hopes of bettering their condition through the influence of his father's relatives, but on their arrival in London, they could find no near relations, and Finn was obliged to teach school. His earnings were barely sufficient to purchase bread with, and he experienced the sufferings which many have undergone in London, and which stimulated him to make exertions which finally led to his adoption of the profession. After many struggles with misfortune, he left the metropolis one morning, without even taking a farewell of his mother. Unacquainted with the roads, he wandered on until dark, when coming to a village where a strolling company had put up, he soon ingratiated himself into their good graces, and was regaled with part of their cheer. On proceeding to the barn where the performances were to take place, Finn discovered that the little knowledge he had picked up in the paint-room of the Park Theatre could be put into requisition, and immediately, with the aid of a little red and yellow ochre, chalk, size, and whiting, he re-touched the scenery, and much improved the general effect. The discovery of a pure vein of golden ore would not be more acceptable to a party of miners, than was Finn's talent to this wandering company. He was immediately pressed into the service, and thus humbly commenced his career as an actor. His first earnings were sent to his mother, and during the time he travelled, her welfare was the subject of his most tender care. Finn after this returned to America, and, we believe, made his first appearance as actor on the stage in New York. In 1818 he visited Savannah, where he made a good hit. He appeared in December of that year as *Mercutio*, *Donald* in "The Falls of Clyde," and in January, 1819, performed the *Stranger* in Kotsebue's play for his benefit to a crowded house. He subsequently returned to Savannah, and in 1820 was associate editor and publisher with J. K. Tefft, of the *Savannah Georgian*, a daily paper, which bears evidence of Finn's ready pen, literary taste, and pure morality. He wrote at this time a series of articles, entitled "The Moralist," which appeared every Saturday. They are of a serious cast, yet written in an attractive vein. Finn, in the year 1821, was again in London, where he subsisted by the aid of his pencil as a miniature painter, making trips to the large provincial theatres, and it was Mr. Finn's original intention to become an artist. About this time Finn attached himself to the Surrey Theatre as leading melo-dramatic tragedian, but the manager becoming insolvent, Finn's demands on the treasury were not paid, and he returned to America, and on the 28th of October, 1822, made his first appearance at the Federal Street, in the part of *Richard.* Shortly after his arrival here, he received praise for his personation of *Mark Antony*, and performed with general acceptance *Othello* to Cooper's *Iago*, *Pythias* to Cooper's *Damon*, George Barrett appearing as *Cassio*, Mrs. Henry as *Desdemona*, Mrs. Warring as *Emilia* in the former, and Charnock appeared as *Dionysius*, Mrs. Powell as *Hermion*, and Mrs. Henry as *Calanthe*, in the latter. Those who recollect Mr. Finn only as *Paul Pry*, *Lord Ogilby*, *Monsieur Jaques*, *Dr. Pangloss*, *Bob Logic*, *Billy Black*, *Beau Shatterley*, *Mawworm*, in which he had no equal in his day, may smile to think of one who is associated in the memory as the laughing son of Momus, assuming so tragic a part; but the assumption was not a caricature, and had he preceded Cooke, Cooper, and Kean, he would have been encouraged to pursue this line of characters. Indeed, his reading of Hamlet, in the opinion of many, challenged comparison with that of the most famed tragedians, and even as late as 1836 he performed *Richard* in Philadelphia to the acceptation of those who are critical in such matters. Mr. Finn was engaged as a permanent actor at a salary of $25 per week, and, as will be seen, performed second to Cooper, Forest, Macready, and others. He subsequently was manager of the theatre in conjunction with Kilner, and afterwards a member of the stock at the Tremont. His poetical contributions on festive occasions were numerous and exceedingly witty, though the wit of many of his conundrums was lost —

> "——— unless you print his face."

He invariably kept the public in a continual roar by his mirth-provoking sallies, but in private he was very sedate ; and to see him quietly seated in the Athenæum, his favorite place of resort, no one would imagine that the spare man with eyes so intent upon some foreign Review, was he who at night as *Billy Black* would keep the audience "laughing in *tiers*."

Finn, in 1829, gave entertainments similar to Mathew's "At Home," in Portland, and was very successful. He had the faculty for this species of entertainment ; and when he exercised it either at the table of a friend or in public, his stories and songs were irresistible. Finn, in the latter part of his life, "starred" it with great success, retiring in the summer to his cottage at Newport, to pass the warm months with his family. He accumulated considerable money by his professional services, a portion of which, however, was lost in unfortunate speculations in 1835–6.

The fate of Mr. Finn is too well known to require any lengthy notice. He was a passenger on board the Lexington, which was burnt on Long Island Sound, on the night of the 13th of January, 1840. Universal was the regret expressed throughout the country at his loss, and the sympathy of his many friends was extended towards his family. He left a widow (who is still living in this city) and five children, two of whom have made their appearance on the stage. Our "Record" will contain farther notice of Mr. Finn, relative to his connection with theatricals in this city.

CHAPTER XIV.

Charles Mathews in Boston. — His First Appearance. — Sketch of His Life. — Anecdotes. — His Libel Suit. — Arthur Keene. — Adams. — "Coleridge's Remorse." — Booth, "No New York Managers Here." — The City Theatre. — Joe Cowell's Troupe. — "Tom and Jerry" brought out. — The "Shakspeare Jubilee." — The Prize Ode. — Report of the Committee. — Presentation of the Pitcher to Charles Sprague.

In the month of December, 1822, Charles Mathews arrived in this city. He was born June 28, 1776, in the Strand, London, where his father was a respectable bookseller. It was a boast of Mathews, that the great David Garrick, on one occasion, while at his father's bookstore, took him in his arms. He received at the Merchant Tailors' School a good common education, and afterwards, while an apprentice to his father, had opportunities of gleaning knowledge from the various books which passed through his hands, and early pronounced an inclination for the profession he subsequently adopted, by singling out for perusal "Bell's British Theatre," "The Beauties of the Dramatist," etc., in preference to those of a more serious cast. He soon thirsted for an opportunity to distinguish himself on the stage, and an opportunity presented itself. Hearing that "hard by there were spirits at work," he made it a point to initiate himself into their good graces, and under the pretence of improving his French, he repaired nightly to a kind lady, who gave evening lessons to a few select pupils, who in return complimented her by bringing out a play. In a small room, in the Strand, over a pastry-cook's shop, Mathews appeared in the part of *Phœnix* to Elliston's *Pyrrhus*—a name which will not occur in our local record of dramatic events in Boston, but who was intimately connected with theatricals in Europe for many years. At the time of Mathews' first juvenile effort, he had not seen the interior of a theatre, and it was not till 1790 that he paid a stolen visit—his parents being strictly opposed to all such entertainments—when "The Orphan" and the farce of "Retaliation" were presented. The future course of his life was shaped by this event; the dry details of business, the tedious duties of an apprentice were neglected, and the counter of his father's store was the rostrum upon which he gave—for the especial benefit of his fellow clerks—imitations of what he had seen at the theatre.

In September, 1792, Mathews and a young friend equally stage-struck, heard that for ten guineas, the manager at Richmond, near London, would allow them to indulge in their *penchant* for the stage; and in the early part of this month, having paid for that honor, Mathews appeared as *Richmond*, in "Richard the Third," and *Bowkitt* in "The Son-in-Law"—with what success may be judged from a notice in the paper, that he "did not disgrace the company he performed with." His father, finding his son's mind fixed upon the stage, one day addressed him thus: "Charles, there are your indentures, and there are twenty guineas; I do not approve of the stage, but I will not oppose your wishes. At any time hereafter, should you feel inclined to an honest calling, there are twenty guineas more if you send for them; and your father's house is open to you." The second twenty guineas Mathews never claimed.

There is a great similarity in the lives of all actors — the same hard toil to perform — the same aspirations — the same disappointments. Where one rises to any thing like respectability in the profession a score or more retire from the stage, or settle down as second or third-rates in some stock company. Others, with genius, falter in their career, listen to the fulsome adulations of friends, and are lost, while the laurel wreath is only awarded to those who patiently labor on, devoting their energies and mind to study and acting. Mathews, after leaving his father's house, went to Canterbury, where he played *Old Doiley* and *Lingo*, and thence to Dublin, where, after a feverish existence of eighteen months, being cast to parts unsuited to his talents, and being honored on one occasion by "*a groan for the long lobster who played Beaufort*," he started for Bristol. Contrary winds, however, drove the vessel to Swansea, where he joined Mr. Masterman's company, and continued for three years to act all his favorite parts with considerable success. On the 16th of May, 1803, he appeared at the Haymarket, London, as *Jubal* in "The Jew," and *Lingo*, and from that time to his death, was a great favorite on the stage of the metropolis. Mathews, however, was more successful in his entertainments than as an actor. He possessed a peculiar power of copying the minds of persons of whom he gave imitations, and his greatest efforts were produced by imaging conversations between men which had never taken place, but in which he depicted with a master-hand their minds, characters, and dispositions. This power, added to a copious store of anecdote, the quickest possible perception of the ridiculous, an unequalled talent for singing comic songs of a species which he himself originated, rendered his "evenings" very popular; and his "Mail-Coach Adventures," "Trip to Paris," "At Home," etc., etc., always drew crowds. On the 6th of September, 1822, Mathews arrived at New York, where he was extremely well received, as well as in Philadelphia. His appearance in Boston will form a portion of our local record. On his return to England, he brought out his "Trip to America," which, at the time, was the subject of considerable remark, it being alleged that he had attempted to burlesque the Americans, who had received him so kindly. This he denied, and much was published on the subject, and on his return to New York, in 1834, there was a determination not to allow him to appear. Placards were posted round the streets inviting hostility, and trouble was anticipated. The curtain at the Park Theatre, however, on the 13th of October, 1834, went up, to a house crowded from pit to dome. When he appeared a most tremendous shout greeted him, and the applause long continued. Silence being obtained, he addressed the audience in a strain of eloquence.

He thanked them for their warm and generous reception of him, and asked: was it possible, if he was guilty, that he would have thus come here to face them? No. "I am *not acting now!*" said Mr. Mathews, with great feeling, — which had an electric effect. After the performance of *Monsieur Tonson*, etc., he was called out, and thanking the audience for the reception, stated, that to prove that he had not done injustice to America, he would, with their permission, take occasion to act before them his whole "Trip to America," *verbatim et literatim.* This he did; and the verdict was, not guilty, to the various charges which had been made against him. While in America, Mr. Mathews was present at a dinner given in Philadelphia in compliment to Mr. Sheridan Knowles, who availed himself of that opportunity to testify to Mr. Mathews' uniform admiration — expressed when abroad, of the citizens of this country. Mathews' visit to Boston, in December, 1834, and January, 1835, was the last. He was quite sick while here and confined to his room; his sufferings being alleviated, however, by the kind attention of Mr. Manners, the English consul at that time, by Mrs. Eliot, the Thorndikes, and other families, and it happened that *his last attendance at church* was at the Trinity Church in this city, where he went to hear the preaching of Dr. Wainwright, who, though he did not attend the theatre, was a friend to the comedian. Mr. Mathews returned to New York, where he performed a short engagement, taking his farewell benefit on the 11th of February, 1835, which was his last appearance on any stage. On the 18th of the same month, in company with Mrs. Mathews, he sailed from New

York, and after a voyage of nineteen days, reached Liverpool in exceedingly feeble health. He was removed to the house of a friend near Devonport, and thence to Plymouth, where he expired on the 28th of June, 1835, quitting this world on the fifty-ninth anniversary of his birth. The immediate cause of his death was water on the chest.

Mr. Mathews was married twice. His first wife was Mrs. E. K. Strong, who died in 1802. His second wife (and mother of the present C. J. Mathews) was Miss Jackson, an actress. During his life, he enjoyed the friendship of such men as Sir Walter Scott, Byron, Moore, Rogers, and was with John Kemble, and the veteran Braham, received as a guest by George the Fourth. Kean alone excepted — he made more money than any performer of his day, though he did not die a wealthy man. His body was interred in St. Andrew's Church, Plymouth, and a great number of persons distinguished for rank and respectability, attended the funeral. A handsome monument was subsequently erected in the vestibule of the church, bearing the following inscription by Horace Smith: —

"All England mourned when her comedian died,
A public loss that ne'er might be supplied;
For who could hope such various gifts to find,
All rare and excellent in one combined?
The private virtues that adorned his breast,
Crowds of admiring friends with tears confessed.
Only to thee, O God! the grief was known
Of those who reared this monumental stone!
The son and widow, who, with bosoms torn,
The best of fathers and of husbands mourn.
Of all this public, social, private wo
Here lies the cause, — CHARLES MATHEWS sleeps below."

The memoirs of Charles Mathews, in four volumes, were published in England in 1839. Mathews commenced his first engagement in Boston, on the 26th of December, 1822. The terms were to share after $1,500 for five nights, the sixth to take a benefit at $300 charges. It was renewed for seven nights, share after $300 per night. The managers gave £50 for the fourteenth night, and shared after $300 on the fifteenth and sixteenth nights, and the seventeenth night — his benefit — he paid $300 charges. The tickets were sold at auction, and $500 of the premium went to the management, the rest being distributed among charitable societies.

Mathews opened as *Goldfinch* and *Tonson*, two of his best parts, and his reception was great. His style was original, and it had the great charm of novelty. His "Trip to Paris" drew crowded houses, heavy premiums being paid for tickets; and though the cold was intense, the water freezing in the pitcher in Mathew's room so thick that he could not break it with the leg of a chair, people came from Salem in open sleighs to attend the performances. On the last night of his engagement, which resulted in his amassing $4605.97, Mathews was honored by a call before the curtain, which he answered by a speech.

After the close of the engagement, Mathews gave his "Trip to Paris" in Boylston Hall, ostensibly to meet the wants of those holy puritans, who would not visit the theatre to see an entertainment which they patronized in a hall. Mr. Buckingham (then editor of the *Galaxy*) alluded to this fact in strong language, and also attacked Mr. Mathews' entertainments as low and vulgar, and Mr. Mathews commenced a suit against the editor, setting his damages at $10,000. Like thousands of other suits, brought in a moment of petulance and ill humor, or when suffering under the deserved censure of an independent press, it never came to trial.

Mr. Wallack appeared, and the theatre closed on the 28th of April with Mrs. Powell's benefit, on which occasion an address in defence of the stage was recited by the beneficiary.

During an after-season, Mrs. C. Powell, widow of Charles Powell, the first manager of the Haymarket, arrived in town from Halifax, where with her husband she had long resided, under the patronage of the Duke of York, and received a benefit at the theatre, her daughter making her appearance.

The season of 1823–4 is notable on many accounts. It commenced on the 15th of September; Mr. Keene, then the best professional male singer in America, appearing as *Henry Bertram* in "Guy Mannering." Mr. Adams appeared in tragedy, and Mr. Pelby, who had returned from a successful southern tour as a star, made his reappearance. Cooper paid his annual visit, and brought out Coleridge's "Remorse." Booth, who had increased in reputation, was warmly received, and on the last night of a very brief engagement, he was called out, and — the idea having gone abroad that his engagement was shortened through the influence of Price, the New York manager, who wished Mrs. Holman and Mr. Pearman to appear — a demand was made for him to play one more night, which was mingled with shouts of "No New York managers here!" Booth retired to consult with the managers, and then reappeared, promising acquiescence to the request, but for some unknown reason he did not reappear. The public, believing that it was through Price's influence that they were deprived of a favorite, patronized his proteges but sparingly.

Since the demolition of the Haymarket Theatre till 1823, the Boston Theatre had little to contend against. In 1823, however, the amphitheatre at Washington Gardens was dignified by the name of the City Theatre, and in December of that year, Joe Cowell arrived in town with an equestrian and comedy company combined. Of the male performers were Cowell, Tatnall, Yeaman, Roberts, Hiney, Roper, Ramage, Gales, Lawson, Hughes, Dinneford, Parker, Johnson, Austin, and Lee; part of whom were attached to the ring, and part to the stage. Of the females there were Mesdames Tatnall, Robertston, Stevenson, Parker, etc., and additions were afterwards made. Plays were brought out in a highly respectable manner. To offset the attractions at the City Theatre, Mr. Blanchard's company of rope-dancers, etc., were engaged at the Boston Theatre, and Mrs. Blanchard for some nights continued to ascend on the tight-rope from the back part of the stage to the gallery, delighting crowded audiences.

The popular play of "Tom and Jerry" was brought out at the City Theatre, for *the first time in Boston*, on the 19th of December, 1823, and on the 22d it was produced at the Boston Theatre.

Corinthian Tom, ... Barrett.
Logic, ... Finn.
Squire Hartshorn, ... Kilner.
Jerry, ... Brown.
Kate, ... Mrs. Warren,
Sue, ... Mrs. Henry.
Jane, ... Miss W. Clarke.

The amusements of the city appeared rather oddly contrived, but we presume the managers were of opinion, that

> "The drama's laws the drama's patrons give,
> For those who live to please must please to live."

This decline of the drama at the Boston Theatre was only temporary, for immediately after, Cooper and Conway were engaged, and played together in "Venice Preserved," "Othello," and other tragedies of like order. The following advertisement appeared in all the papers shortly after the opening of the theatre: —

NOTICE!

The Managers of the Boston Theatre having made preparations for exhibiting, in the course of the ensuing winter, a Pageant, in *commemoration of Shakspeare*, in which will be represented his principal dramatic characters, with appropriate Dialogue, and the original Music as performed in the Shakspeare Jubilee at Drury Lane, propose to give a GOLD MEDAL, of the value of FIFTY DOLLARS, for the best ODE or POEM which shall be offered, to be recited on the occasion. It is desirable that the composition should not be less than *fifty* nor more than *one hundred lines* in length. The Medal shall be awarded by a Committee of ten gentlemen, to be hereafter nominated for that purpose; and that no partiality or personal predilection may influence the decision, every piece offered for the prize must be accompanied by a sealed paper, containing the name and residence of the author, none of which seals will be broken, except that belonging to the successful piece. Communications must be addressed (*post-paid* if by mail) to "The Managers of the Theatre, Boston," previous to the first day of December next.

Boston, Sept. 19, 1823.

The offering of prizes for poems, at that time, created a great excitement among the *literati*, and the most gifted poets in the country entered the lists. The committee was composed of our best scholars, and their favorable verdict was of great value. The public partook of this feeling, and a local pride was excited, lest some resident of another city might gain the prize. The committee on this occasion consisted of Warren Dutton, Andrew Ritchie, Theodore Lyman, Jr., Washington Allston, George Ticknor, Alexander Townsend, Henry Cabot, Franklin Dexter, Jared Sparks, and W. H. Prescott, Esqrs. Their position in society, and the reputation of many of them in the literary world, augmented the public interest, and stimulated the poets of the country to use their best exertions — all anxious for a favorable judgment from such a body of critics. The decision was awaited for with impatience, and the following is the report of the committee: —

"The gentlemen who were requested by the Manager of the Boston Theatre to examine the merits of the several poems written on the occasion of the approaching Jubilee in honor of Shakspeare, and to decide which is entitled to the Medal proposed, are of opinion that this honor should be awarded to Mr. Charles Sprague, as the author of the poem marked No. 22.

"The gentlemen, however, owe it to the author of a poem entitled "Shakspeare's Triumph," to say, that its intrinsic merit is so great, and it is so well adapted to recitation, that they consider it entitled to high commendation, and they cannot but express their wish that the author would allow it to be recited on the stage.

W. Dutton,
A. Ritchie.

In behalf of the Committee."

The report was received by the public with every manifestation of pleasure, and we need not add that the merits of the piece still command the attention of scholars.

Mr. Sprague having been the recipient of a Medal

for his Prize Address, on the opening of the new Park Theatre in New York, in 1821, and also a Cup from the managers of the Chesnut St. Theatre, Philadelphia, in December, 1822, for a similar effort, the managers of the Boston Theatre substituted a Silver Pitcher in the place of the Medal which was offered; and in compliment to the author, for this trio of successful poems, Mr. Dickson caused to be engraved thereon an appropriate quotation from "Macbeth" —

"Thrice to Thine."

The poem "Skakspeare's Triumph," alluded to in the report, was from the pen of a distinguished clergyman of this city. The Prize Poem and other addresses were published in a volume.

CHAPTER XV.

The Shakspeare Jubilee. — Compliment to the Author of the Prize Ode. — Conway. — Visit of Lafayette to Boston. — Ebenezer Bailey, Esq. — Bunker Hill Monument. — Enterprise of Newspapers. — City Theatre. — Kean Announced to Appear. — His Troubles in England. — His First Card. — First Appearance in New York. — His Apology to the Boston Public. — Preliminaries. — The Great Kean Riot, etc., etc.

We alluded, in the last chapter, to the "Shakspeare Jubilee." Worrall, the scenic artist, employed his pencil with fine effect. The design of the managers was, after showing Shakspeare's house at Stratford-upon-Avon, to present a procession of the most celebrated characters in his acting plays; the tragedies preceded by the tragic muse with her appropriate emblems in a chariot drawn by *fiends*; and the comedies in a car drawn by *satyrs*, and surrounded by youth, frolic, and good humor. In illustration of the genius of the great poet of human nature, a selection of scenes was made and represented by different performers. A magnificent hall, occupying nearly the whole stage, formed the scene for the representation of the beauties, and the approach of the personages of each production as it occurred in the order of procession was made known by the advance of a banner, displaying the name of the play to be illustrated. The "Prize Ode," written by Charles Sprague, Esq., was intended to be pronounced at the termination of the procession, when all the characters that had appeared, the tragic muse in her chariot, the comic muse in her car, the various banners, and all the "pride, pomp, and circumstance" of scenic show should be collected to give effect to the occasion. In consequence, however, of the protracted length of the scenes from the different tragedies, the audience became impatient, and the pronunciation of the Ode by Mr. Finn, occurred between the display of the tragic and comic diversions. The acting was highly creditable to the talents of Finn, Barrett, Kilner, etc.

The "Jubilee" was repeated on several occasions, after being curtailed and altered, and invariably attracted a large and highly gratified audience. The Ode by Mr. Sprague was appreciated, and is still read with pleasure. At a dinner given to Mr. Sprague, shortly after, he paid a flattering compliment to Mr. Finn, who recited the Ode with fine effect. Prefacing his sentiment by stating that the motto annexed to the Prize Ode was "Airy Nothing," he continued: "The power of recitation that gave to airy nothing a local habitation and a name."

Among the earliest efforts of Mr. Finn, he brought out a piece, called "Boston Bay, or Dumb Shows *v.* Shakspeare."

On the 25th of February, Conway performed *Hamlet*, and followed as *Coriolanus*, *Lord Townly*, etc. A critic of those days, remarked "that the person and face of Mr. Conway are not peculiarly fitted for the stage, the first is rather too large and the other too round and inflexible, reminding us continually of Fennell, whom Mr. Conway also resembles, both in the tone of his voice and his excellent reading of Shakspeare. His voice, however, has far more compass, and is deeper and clearer than that of Fennell. Conway belongs to the Kemble school, with a slight touch of Kean, and we are free to say, we have never seen a *Hamlet* so well read, or more feelingly performed, nor a *Coriolanus* so brilliant in fine points. This excellence is unaccompanied by trick and extravagance too frequently resorted to, to give effect to mere declamation and high-sounding words." Towards the close of Conway's engagement, Cooper appeared in connection with him.

As an actor, Mr. William Conway stood high; his impersonation of whatever he undertook invariably elicited applause. He was born in London, and was educated for the law; but adopted the profession and made his first appearance at the Haymarket Theatre, London. He was subsequently at Drury Lane, and owing to a law-suit with Elliston, he lost his property, and disgusted with his fate in England, he turned his attention to America, and arrived here in the latter part of 1823. Mr. Cooper found in him a rival of no small abilities. Mr. Conway visited the western and southern cities, and, in 1826, announced his intention of retiring from the stage. In the summer of 1827, he visited Newport, R. I., which was a favorite resort, and in a secluded place, adjacent to the ocean, he shut himself out from the world, and confined himself to books, and it is said, was deeply engaged in theology, preparatory to his taking holy orders. He appeared careworn and troubled, and led the life of a hermit. Early in 1828, he took passage for Savannah, Georgia, from New York, and having arrived off the bar of Charleston, S. C., he seized an opportunity when captain and passengers were at tea, and threw himself into the sea. The efforts made to save him were unsuccessful.

About the time that he took passage for Savannah, the following pathetic poem, from his pen, appeared in a New York paper:—

THE FAREWELL.

"A wanderer, doomed to dwell
On foreign shores a solitary man,
To home's lov'd scenes lamenting thus began
The parting sad farewell!

"I leave my happy home,
The streams and meadows I have loved so long,
And the fair city with its joyous throng,
O'er the rude waves to roam.

"Farewell thou valued *one*,
Thou guide and friend of my departed years,
Thou mother of my youth, why gush thy tears,
In blessing of thy son?

"Farewell! Oh, never more
Shall thy dim eyes behold thy wayward child;
Nay, mother, do not thus with accents wild
Thy bitter fate deplore.

"Father, to thee I bow,
Asking thy blessing with this warm embrace;
Chide not the unmanly tears upon my face,
The paleness on my brow.

"Alas! how shall I part
From thee, my father, and not wet my cheek
With tears that tell of love and speak
The sadness of my heart?

"But ye, that wonder so
With uprais'd eyes to see your brother weep,
Soon shall those little lids, seal'd up in sleep,
Forget a brother's woe.

"And thou, whom next I love
To the 'dear kindred blood' that fills my veins,
Farewell to thee — augments all other pains
That I in parting prove.

"But see! the white sails swell!
Ah! blest companions of my early youth,
Dear object of my fondest love and truth,
Sweet home, and friends, farewell.
CONWAY."

During the summer of 1824, Lafayette, the "nation's guest," visited Boston, and received the most cordial reception; and after his departure for the South the theatre opened. The company comprised Finn, Kilner, Young, Brown, Williams, Clark, Fielding Charnock, E. H. Conway, Johnson, Bernard, Spear, Spooner, Tyron, etc.; and Mrs. Powell, Mrs. Henry, Miss Powell, Miss Placide, Mrs. Barnes, Mrs. Kilner, Miss Deblin, Miss Clarke, Mrs. Clarke, etc.

Mr. C. Young had previously appeared at this theatre; Mr. Williams came from Philadelphia; Miss Placide from New Orleans. Mr. E. H. Conway had been ballet-master at the Surrey Theatre, and Miss Deblin was his pupil.

The "star" engagements of this season were those of Miss Kelly, Cooper, Pelby, and Burroughs. Miss Kelly's benefit attracted a thousand-dollar house. Mrs. Burke, the singer before alluded to, a native of New York State, appeared, much improved as a vocalist.

Mr. Finn, this year, brought out an original piece, dedicated to Hon. Daniel Webster. It was a national drama, entitled "Montgomery, or the Falls of Montmorenci," and was very popular.

On the 22d of February, 1825, the theatre was opened in honor of the anniversary of Washington's birth-day. The managers, to commemorate the event, offered a prize for an appropriate ode. Messrs. George Blake, John Pierpont, James T. Austin, Chas. Sprague, John Everett, Franklin Dexter, and N. L. Frothingham, were a committee to decide upon the merits of the contributions, and they unanimously awarded it to Ebenezer Bailey, Esq., for many years the popular principal of the Young Ladies' High School. The house was filled, and Mr. Finn gave the recitation with his usual excellence.

Cooper, during the engagement this year, brought out "Caius Gracchus" for the first time. Mr. and Mrs. J. Barnes returned to Boston from Europe, and were performing an engagement on the 7th of April, when the great fire in Broad street occurred.

At the Washington Gardens, the theatre was occupied by an equestrian company, and the "Cataract of the Ganges" was brought out.

The theatre closed early in the spring, but re-opened when Lafayette re-visited Boston in June. On the 17th of June, 1825, the corner-stone of Bunker Hill Monument was laid in presence of the distinguished stranger, and Hon. Daniel Webster then delivered his great address. The enterprise of newspaper publishers had not then reached the height it has attained in more modern days, and extracts only were published. The address was, however, printed, and three thousand five hundred copies in pamphlet form, were sold in three days. On Monday, June 20, Lafayette attended the Boston Theatre, when "Charles the Second" was performed, and a new drop-scene by Worrall, appropriate to the occasion, was produced. The dinner, given to Lafayette by the Massachusetts Mechanic Association, at which Samuel Perkins, Esq., presided, during this visit, was a notable event. Odes and poems were given or sung by John Everett, H. J. Finn, and Williamson.

Prior to the opening of the Boston Theatre for the season of 1825–6, the interior was re-painted and decorated, and the stage extended and improved. The company was composed of Finn, Kilner, Reed, Johnson, Edgar, Williamson, Brown, Pelby; Mrs. Pelby, Miss McBride, Mrs. Powell, etc. Miss McBride,—afterwards quite popular at the Tremont,—made her first appearance as *Miss Hardcastle*, on the 16th of September.

At the City Theatre there was quite a good company; Mr. Burroughs, Mrs. Warring, Mr. and Mrs. Fisher, and Phillips, gave the theatre a dramatic importance. In the month of October, Cooper brought out "William Tell," for the first time in Boston. Frederick Brown, who had, during an absence of several years, divided his time between Montreal and Charleston, S. C., returned. The debilitating effects of a southern climate were apparent, and his acting had not the force which formerly characterized it.

On the 5th of December, 1825, "Venice Preserved" was brought out at the Boston with Cooper as *Pierre*, Conway as *Jaffier*, and Mrs. J. Barnes as *Belvidera*, and never probably was the play better performed in this city. The combination of such an array of talent attracted great houses, and their benefits were immense. Conway's benefit was on Monday evening, Dec. 19, 1825, and marks the commencement of an interesting period in the history of theatricals in this city. The play was "Othello," in which Cooper and Mrs. Barnes exerted themselves to their utmost, and received the loudest plaudits for their efforts. At the close of the play it was announced that Mr. Kean was engaged, and would appear for four nights, on Wednesday, Thursday, Friday, and Monday next. The announcement was received with tokens of approbation and disapprobation, but it was thought that the approvers were in the majority. Kean's return to this country was of a peculiar nature. It was during the interval between his two visits to America, that Kean lost his position in England both as an actor and a man; and, for these causes, and a desire to replenish his exhausted coffers, he was induced to risk a second visit. Kean had become so negligent, and performed *Othello* and *Richard* so disgracefully as to be hissed repeatedly in the course of the performance, and it was not till 1822, when Mr. Young appeared at Drury Lane, that Kean, who, for years had been without a competitor, was aroused from his lethargy. For a time he improved, and his temporary reform was more than counterbalanced by his subsequent descent. Kean's attachments to the fair sex were numerous, and it is said that he had a *circular* which he despatched to the successive objects of his affection, which must have been couched in irresistible terms, for his conquests were frequent. The most disgraceful *liason* was that with Mrs. Alderman Cox, which was brought to public notice through the legal measures resorted to by the injured husband. The trial came off on the 17th of January, 1825. A mass of correspondence was brought forward, and the crime proved, and the result was a verdict for £800. The trial created a great sensation, and the town and the press were about equally divided on the subject, and though Kean's downfall, dated from this trial, there were those who regarded the whole matter as a piece of persecution, inasmuch as Alderman Cox was in the constant habit of taking his wife behind the scenes, and was cognizant of her visiting Kean's dressing-room. Kean's great mistake at this time, was the boldness and audacity with which he braved public censure, and by attempting to play, claiming public applause on the very heel of one of the most profligate displays ever made public. The people were so exasperated, that when he appeared at Drury Lane, they would not allow him to be heard, and though Elliston, the manager, shook hands with him on the stage, and Kean made an exculpatory speech, it availed him nothing. In the course of time, he regained in some degree, the ear of the public; but he failed in reinstating himself in his old position, and therefore paid a second visit to America.

Kean arrived in New York in the fall of 1825. His loss of position and fortune had affected his health, and his once proud spirit was humbled. Shortly after his arrival in New York, he published the following humiliating card:—

To the Editors of the New York Gazette,

SIRS, — With oppressed feelings, heart-rending to my friends, and triumphant to my enemies, I make an appeal to that country famed for hospitality to the stranger, and mercy to the conquered. Allow me to say, sirs, whatever are my offences, I disclaim all intention of offering any thing in the shape of disrespect towards the inhabitants of New York; they received me from the first with an enthusiasm, grateful *in those hours* to my pride, *in the present* to my memory. I cannot recall to my mind any act or thought, that did not prompt me to an unfeigned acknowledgment of their favors as a public, and profound admiration of the private worth of those circles in which I had the honor to move.

That I have committed an error, appears too evident from the all-decisive voice of the public; but surely it is but justice to the delinquent, (whatever may be his enormities,) to be allowed to make reparation where the offences were committed. My misunderstandings took place in Boston. To Boston I shall assuredly go, to apologize for my indiscretions.

I visit this country now, under different feelings and auspices than on a former occasion. Then I was an ambitious man, and the proud representative of Shakspeare's heroes. The spark of ambition is extinct; and I merely ask a shelter in which to close my professional and mortal career. I give the weapon into the hands of my enemies; if they are brave, they will not turn it against the defenceless.

EDMUND KEAN.

Washington Hall, Nov. 15th, 1825.

Of Kean's first appearance in New York, various accounts were contained in the papers of the day. The house was crowded, and the friends and enemies of Kean were nearly equally divided, though the former carried the day. A newspaper partial to Kean remarks, that "when the curtain was drawn up, a peal of applause rose which resembled more the roar of the ocean than any thing else we ever heard, and in a few minutes after the mimic *Richard* himself appearing, the hisses blended themselves with the applauding, which continued without a moment's cessation for the space of twenty minutes. The hissings, however, were completely drowned in the applause. Mr. Kean made an attempt to speak, but it was impossible to be heard, for whenever the multitude of his friends stopped their shouting, his enemies immediately set theirs a going. A few persons in the slips and third tier kept hallooing out, "off!"—"off!"—"Kean be off!" In one of the boxes of the first tier, a single gentleman, we presume he was, with more than a usual portion of lungs, still kept up the hissing, but the rest of the audience in the box getting tired of it, rose up to a man and put him snugly out into the lobby, there to hiss as much as he pleased.

At no one time was there more than one fourth of the house against him, and many are of opinion that the number of his enemies was far less—at least they diminished toward the conclusion. The hissing characters were noted to be nearly all strangers, and the audience hallooed frequently, "*Put the Bostonians out!*" — "*away with the noisy Bostonians!*" — "*away with Buckingham!*" — (alluding to Mr. Jos. T. Buckingham, the editor, who had been among the leading opponents of Kean since his contempt of a Boston audience,) — "*off with his head!*" — and such like exclamations. When the play was concluded, the curtain fell amidst reiterated shouts of applause, and Mr. Lee, in announcing Mr. Kean's next appearance on Wednesday evening, in the character of *Othello*, was cheered to the very skies."

Encouraged by this reception, which on the whole was more favorable than might have been expected, and relying upon the general acceptance of Kean's humble apology, the Boston managers made an engagement, which was announced as we have stated on the night of Conway's benefit.

Kean arrived in Boston on Tuesday evening, and put up at the Exchange Coffee House; and on Wednesday, December 21, '25, the following card appeared in the morning papers: —

To the Editor,

SIR, — I take the liberty of informing the citizens of Boston, (through the medium of your journal,) of my arrival, in confidence that liberality and forbearance will gain the ascendancy over prejudice and cruelty. That I have suffered for my errors, my loss of fame and fortune is too melancholy an illustration. Acting from the impulse of irritation, I certainly was disrespectful to the Boston public; calm deliberation convinces me I was wrong. The first step toward the Throne of Mercy is confession — the hope we are taught, forgiveness. Man must not expect more than those attributes which we offer to God.

EDMUND KEAN.

Exchange Coffee House.

This apology was received by some with contempt, and by others was deemed an ample atonement for past indiscretions, and during the day was the leading topic of conversation. The newspapers generally advised those opposed to Kean, to show their resentment by keeping away from the theatre; but during the day, it was whispered here and there, that Kean would not be allowed to play, and early in the afternoon of Wednesday, Dec. 21, 1825, Kean being announced for *Richard*, the street in front of the theatre was filled with boys, who evinced a disposition to treat Shakspeare's representative with little regard. All the tickets were sold the day previous, and on the opening of the doors in the evening, every part of the house was soon crammed with males, not a female being present. The excitement inside the house was very evident, and the vociferation of those present commenced so soon as the house was packed. Outside there was a vast accumulation of people, attracted by curiosity, and evincing a disposition for a row. Mr. Finn, one of the managers, soon appeared in front of the curtain. He was received with great uproar, chiefly from the gallery and third row —the boxes being principally occupied by the stockholders of the theatre, and friends to Mr. Kean, who were in favor of Kean's performing. Finn announced Mr. Kean's intention to make an apology, but his voice was drowned in the shouts of the discontented; and though an attempt was made to quiet the uproar by the orchestra performing, it was no evidence in this instance, that

"Music the fiercest grief can charm,
And fate's severest rage disarm."

Mr. Kean appeared immediately afterwards upon the stage, dressed in his every day clothes, and in a very penitent and humble manner seemed to ask forgiveness of the public, and to be desirous of making atonement by an apology. But the wild commotion of the theatrical elements so completely astonished him, that he said not a word. He was pale and dejected, but was assailed by cries of — "off" — "off" — pelted with nuts, pieces of cake, a bottle of offensive drugs, and other missiles. He was encouraged also with cries of "silence" — "hear Kean" — etc. Having been fairly pelted from the stage, Mr. Kilner, dressed for *King Henry*, came forward, and after consultation with those in the stage box, was heard to say, "Mr. Kean wishes to make an apology — an humble apology from his heart and soul; but he will not do it at the risk of his life." Cries of — "off" — "off" — and — "his hypocritical heart" — was the response. One or two gentlemen in the boxes attempted to speak, but they were not heard; but those in the boxes giving some encouragement that the apology might be heard, Kean made his second appearance. No intermission of the uproar took place, and he retired to the green-room, where, it is said, he wept like a child.

Finding it impossible to be heard, the managers then held a written communication with the audience, and a placard was exhibited on which was written, "MR. KEAN DECLINES PLAYING," which was received with laughter. A second placard then asked the question: "SHALL THE PLAY GO ON WITHOUT HIM?" This was answered in such an equivocal manner, that the managers thought they might as well retain the receipts of the house, and the tragedy began; but the vociferations prevented it from being heard. After the first act had been performed in dumb show, Mr. Finn, who was dressed as *Richard*, in answer to repeated calls for Kean, stated that he had left the theatre, and the curtain was dropped.

In the meantime, the mob without had become excited to phrenzy, and made several assaults upon the house; and the audience within began to think not so much of Kean as of their own preservation from danger. The rabble began to assail the lamps, the windows, and the entrances to the boxes, gallery, and pit. A large party succeeded in making a lodgment in the lower lobbies, after having been repulsed. The few police officers present were soon overpowered, but the gentlemen of the boxes maintained their ground manfully for some time. Mr. Kean having left the house, it was difficult to divine the objects of the assailants. The occupants of the pit made a retreat by the stage over the orchestra.

The audience who were in the second tier of boxes found themselves in a most trying situation. The fierce conflict with brick-bats, clubs, etc., at the stairs and doors, effectually shut out their means of retreat, and they were compelled to await in anxiety, and witness the increasing outrages, and approach of the immense mob without, expecting every instant when the internal resistance would be cloven down, and the thronging rabble precipitate them into the pit, or maim them with deadly missiles, or crush them to death in the lobbies. The sense of confinement, joined to the apprehension of fire, rendered their sensations painful beyond description.

In this fearful juncture, the formidable height of the windows did not prevent them from being used as a mode of escape. One person swung himself out of a window, about twenty-five feet from the ground, and upon a thin, narrow board, made his descent about twelve feet on to the frail roof of a small tenement. He was afterwards followed by hundreds.

The rabble without, aided by friends within, were finally enabled to take possession, and they had it all their own way; most of the occupants of the boxes having made their escape, by the windows or over the stage. Windows, chandeliers, seats, box-doors, became objects of wanton destruction; but several citizens, who took possession of the stage, protected the scenery, at the hazard of life and limb, from molestation, and perhaps from fire.

The pit was the scene of several severe tustles; and though an awkward place for a fight, many came to blows, and were more or less injured. During the riot, Mr. Justice Whitman read the riot act twice, advanced to the front of the stage, and attempted to address the rioters, but without effect; as he was unable to carry into execution the provisions of the law, from the small number of civil and police officers collected. Those who were present, with the sheriff, aided by the citizens, exerted themselves to prevent the rioters from entering the house, and to arrest those who were in it, but with little success; and several in the discharge of this duty were injured by the stones and other missiles hurled from the darkness, but none materially. A few citizens with a magistrate, in execution of the law, proceeded to the upper parts of the house, and immediately dispersed a gang there engaged in the destruction; which was found to consist principally of strangers and mischievous boys.

The theatre was damaged to the extent of about $800, and, in the opinion of many present, the riot might have been prevented by the timely arrest of some dozen leading rowdies. Those opposed to Mr. Kean had not anticipated such a result; the extent of their plan was to prevent Mr. Kean's acting, and when this was accomplished they were satisfied; but they had kindled the spirit, and it vented itself in this most disgraceful riot. The police at that time, if the few who were qualified to protect life and property are entitled to so dignified an appellative, were not organized — and an unorganized body can do but little in quelling a disturbance. The following was issued: —

A CARD.

The managers of the Boston Theatre return their sincere and thankful gratitude to those gentlemen who, at personal risk of their lives, so kindly and promptly afforded protection to their property behind the curtain, from the violence and illegal attacks of a mob, that forcibly entered the theatre on Wednesday evening last, and committed an unprecedented outrage by breaking the chandeliers, box-doors, windows, etc., and destroying other property to a large amount. Legal measures have been taken to bring the offenders to punishment. In the meantime, every exertion will be used to repair the extensive damage, and they hope they shall be enabled to announce the re-opening of the theatre on Monday, Dec. 26, with the domestic tragedy of "George Barnwell."

Mayor Quincy was not present at the riot. It has been supposed that he adopted the principle, that they who put a firebrand into the theatre must bear the consequences. The mayor, however, had power only as a

"Justice of the Peace;" and Justice Whitman being already on the ground, he refused personally to interfere. The board of aldermen immediately took occasion from this transaction to pass an order, "that all theatrical exhibitions or public shows, which hereafter may be licensed by the board, shall be liable to be revoked or suspended, notwithstanding the terms of such license, whenever, in the opinion of the mayor and aldermen for the time being, the same shall be necessary to preserve order and decorum, and to prevent the interruption of peace and quiet;" and the following remarks in the mayor's inaugural address are supposed to have had reference to the same: "If a case has occurred, or should hereafter occur, in which any person should, in defiance of the moral sense and general feeling of the public, adopt any measures which would naturally and almost unavoidably lead to disorder and disturbance, they could not reasonably invoke the aid of the authorities of the city government, so long as the invited evil was confined to themselves only; but it is a question of very serious moment, with the inhabitants of a city so distinguished for its religious and moral character, whether farther checks ought not to be provided to prevent that which has been merely tolerated, from becoming the source of disturbances, of danger, and of disgrace, to the citizens and their government."

The managers, by employing a large number of workmen, were able to accomplish the task of re-fitting the theatre; and on Monday evening, the moral play of "George Barnwell," with "Rumfustian," and the "Forty Thieves," were produced to a good house.

Mr. Kean escaped from the theatre before the riot

reached its height, by passing through Mrs. Powell's house, in Theatre Alley, which, adjoining the theatre, had a door to communicate with it. We have heard that Kean slept that night at the "Lamb Tavern," and left the next day; but we believe the most authentic account is that we have received from "Tim Divol," who for years drove a hack for Niles, and who, early in 1853, was found drowned near Charlestown bridge. He drove Kean and Kilner to Brighton, where the former took the stage from Boston for Worcester. Kean soon after appeared at Albany, Montreal, Philadelphia, and Baltimore. At the latter place there was an attempt at a riot, whether to show resentment for the insult offered a Boston public, or to reprove Kean for his immorality, we do not know. His friends, however, anticipating trouble, displayed a banner when the shouting commenced, requesting those in his favor to remain silent, which had the effect of singling out the evil disposed, who soon saw their weakness, and desisted from further attempts to imitate the mobocratic and disgraceful feats of the Boston rowdies. Many may perhaps think that the coloring we have given to this affair is favorable to Kean; but time has softened the asperities even of Kean's most inveterate enemies, and though he was guilty of unpardonable insolence towards the public, the retaliation was unbecoming an enlightened community. Had the affair terminated with driving Kean from the stage, we should acquiesce in the verdict; but scenes of violence have no apology, especially when the innocent, as in this case, suffered more that the guilty.

Miss Kelly came after the Kean riot, and was succeeded by Hamblin, formerly the manager of the Bowery Theatre, New York. Mr. and Mrs. George Barrett also appeared, and "Cherry and Fair Star" was brought out this season for the first time. Cooper and Mr. and Mrs. J. Barnes were also here, but the houses were not remarkable; and the effect of the Kean riot had not worn off when the theatre closed.

CHAPTER XVI.

The City Theatre. — Mælzel's Automaton Chess Player. — Mrs. Pelby. — Williamson. — Mrs. Hamblin. — Forest. — Macready. — Macready's First Appearance in Boston. — Tickets at Auction. — Paul Pry. — First Appearance of Edwin Forest. — Receipts. — A Sketch of Edwin Forest, etc. etc.

In the summer of 1826, the citizens were supplied with amusement at the City Theatre, formerly the Washington, where Mr. Stimpson with an equestrian and dramatic company, composed of Messrs. Ricker, Whitaker, Laforest, Mrs. Godey, Mrs. Benjamin, Mr. and Mrs. Eberle, and Mr. Richards, gave entertainments. Mælzel's Automaton Chess Player at Julien Hall, puzzled the *quid nuncs* — the discovery not then being made of the real automaton inside, who, on a cry of "fire!" started by some wag, made a rapid exit from his limited quarters.

The season at the old house commenced September 25th. Mr. and Mrs. Blake were annou .ced to appear, but owing to some caprice, did not make their appearance, and a Mr. Stanley was substituted; he was a very good actor in genteel comedy. Kilner did not appear during the early part of the season, having broken his leg. Mrs. Papanti and Mr. Brown were added to the company. Mr. Pelby made his first appearance after his return from Europe, and a critical remark then made gives an accurate idea of his abilities. "His voice," says a newspaper, "is not good; and we have to regret, that by this fault of nature, his talents as an actor, which are of no ordinary cast, can never be duly appreciated."

Williamson played *Count Belino*, in the "Devil's Bridge," to Mrs. Papanti's *Rosalvini*. The lady was pronounced of a higher order as a vocalist than any that had appeared for many years.

Mrs. Hamblin, wife of Tom Hamblin, appeared in October, 1826, and was an interesting actress. This season was marked by the first appearance before a Boston audience of two persons, whose career have been among the most prosperous ever recorded in theatrical annals, and for many years have been the representatives of the American and English stage. We allude to Forrest and Macready.

The latter, then fresh from Europe, made his first appearance in Boston, on Monday, October 30, 1826, in the character of *Virginius*, to a crowded and fashionable house. Hon. Daniel Webster was present, and on his entering, was received with cheers. Macready performed during his engagement, *Macbeth*, *Damon*, *William Tell*, *Hamlet*, and repeated *Virginius* and other characters.

The demand for tickets was very great, and speculators reaped a rich harvest. The managers endeavored to put a stop to it, but their efforts proving futile, they adopted the only satisfactory course — that of selling at auction — in Merchants' Hall. The premium received on the sale of tickets for his benefit, was $392.50, and during the whole time, about $1000. Mr. Macready was indisposed one evening, during the engagement, and did not play. On his last night, he was called out, and announced that before he returned to Europe, he should have the pleasure of re-visiting Boston. Mr. Cooper followed immediately upon Macready's heels, and appeared in the same range of characters, supported by Mrs. Gilfert.

In December, Mr. Finn brought out "Paul Pry" with the following cast: — *Col. Hardy*, Kilner; *Frank Hardy*, Mr. Williamson; *Harry Stanley*, Stanley; and *Paul Pry*, Mr. Finn; — one of his best impersonations. *Mrs. Subtle*, Mrs. Barnes; *Eliza*, Mrs. Papanti; *Maria*, Miss McBride; *Phœbe*, Mrs. Pelby. The piece took well, owing to Mr. Finn's inexhaustible fund of humor, and had a good run. "Aboun Hassan," a dull piece, was produced; and "The Lady of the Lake" dramatized by Mr. Cambridge. A Bostonian made his appearance as *Rolla*.

On the 5th of February, 1827, Mr. Edwin Forrest made his first appearance in Boston, opening in his great part of *Damon*, Mr. Finn appearing as *Pythias*. Mr. Forrest also appeared as *William Tell*, *Sir Edward Mortimer*, *Othello*, *Lear*, *Richard the Third*, and on the 23d inst., performed *Rolla*, a character eminently his own. At that time he gave glorious promise of his subsequent splendid career. Every one was pleased with his style, and he was pronounced the Kemble of the country.

The receipts during this engagement, were as follows: —

1827.	Feb.	5th,	Monday,	Damon,	$341 50
"	"	7th,	Wednesday,	Wm. Tell,	457 75
"	"	9th,	Friday,	Iron Chest,	526 50
"	"	12th,	Monday,	Othello,	412 00
"	"	14th,	Wednesday,	Lear,	405 50
"	"	16th,	Friday,	Wm. Tell,	408 00
"	"	19th,	Monday,	Richard III., (Forrest's Benefit,)	945 00
"	"	21st,	Wednesday,	Damon,	453 75
"	"	23d,	Friday,	Pizarro,	760 00
		Total,			$4,710 00

More than a century has now elapsed since the first theatrical representation in this country was given, by a band of English actors in Virginia, and during that long period of time, the histrionic art in this country has flourished, we regret to say, not by the representations of native actors or native productions, but its most efficient supporters have been of English parentage, and the most popular plays of foreign emanation. We may, perhaps, claim the pride which a father has in an adopted son, in the person of Cooper, whose youthful efforts first met encouragement in this country, and whose genius was developed by generous patronage here; — and to Booth we feel bound by that tie of kindred, which the stranger feels in the exiled, who, cast off and persecuted at home, is warmed into life, and receives fresh impulses under a more genial sky; — but

16

in Cooke and Kean, the two brightest stars which have visited our theatrical firmament, and a host of others who have wandered to our shores — some to become its adopted citizens, and some to gather the golden plaudits, and then return to the land of their birth — we take no pride, save that which is reflected from the act of encouraging talent irrespective of nation.

It is true, that now and then an actor has sprung up, who gave promise of a brilliant future, but whose career has either been shortened by death ere the fulfilment of our hopes was attained, or who fell a victim to extra vagant applause or vicious habits, ere the Thespian wreath graced his brow; but we have no lengthy catalogue of actors to point to, as the proud pillars of the American drama. There is, however, one who stands out prominent as the great American star, who is to this country what Talma is to France — what Garrick is to England — the noblest representative of his nation's drama — aye, we may say, more the creator of our national drama — for Edwin Forrest has done more, individually, than all the theatres in the country combined, to draw forth and reward the talents of native dramatists. Edwin Forrest was born on the 9th of March, 1806, in George street, Philadelphia, and early in life was the member of a company of amateur actors, who gave private entertainments to their friends in the old Apollo in South street, which they hired on special occasions. He was at one time in the counting-house of J. R. Baker & Son, German Importers, but his mercantile habits were not remarkably exemplary, owing to his love of the drama. His first a[p]pearance in public was in 1818, when he played

Norval at the Tivoli Garden. On the 27th of November, 1820, he made his second appearance in that character, at the Walnut Street Theatre, and played *Octavian* for his benefit, January 6, 1821. Mr. Forrest was warmly applauded by his friends, but young as he then was, he became fully conscious of the necessity of self-dependence, and resolved to apply himself thoroughly to his profession. Having an opportunity to visit the western theatres, he accepted an engagement in 1822, which was with Messrs. Collins & Jones in Cincinnati, where he played the subordinate characters, by which he gradually qualified himself for that proud position he at present maintains. We have seen it stated, that Forrest, while at the West, played the character of a negro dandy, and that he at one time entertained a serious idea of joining a circus company. If this is true, the more does it reflect to his credit. The elder Kean *was* at one time an equestrian performer, but we do not know that it ever detracted from the pleasure of witnessing his masterly performances, or that the fact that Mr. Forrest was willing to oblige a manager or to gratify himself, or by necessity "blacked up" for a part, ever rendered his *Othello* less effective, or his *Richelieu* less imposing. After an absence of several years, he returned to the North, and fulfilled a successful engagement at the Albany Theatre, then under the management of the eccentric Charles Gilfert, whose powers of persuasion were so strong, that he could always prevail upon the sheriff to go bail for him after arresting him. In the summer of 1826, Mr. Forrest visited his native city, and from that time rapidly rose in his profession. Mr. Forrest appeared subsequently in Washington and in New York, where a paper remarked: —

"Endowed with a versatility of powers unequalled at this time on the American, and unsurpassed on the English stage, it may with truth be said, that Mr. Forrest possesses within himself the 'elements of greatness;' and though

> '―――――――― hard it is to climb,
> The steep where Fame's proud temple shines afar,'

yet, if he judiciously husbands his resources, and tempers with discretion the exercise of his powers, he may select his own point of eminence, and, with an eagle's flight attain it."

Mr. Forrest, as early as 1829, made his first attempt to encourage native talent, by offering a prize of $500 for the best written tragedy founded on American History. The successful competitor was J. A. Stone, Esq., who produced "Metamora," which was first performed in New York, December 15, 1829. The success of the play was great, but it was not needed to give popularity to Mr. Forrest, who, previous to its production did an immense business, the houses averaging $1,000 per night, and on the night of his benefit there was $1,370 in. The play of "Metamora" was followed by Dr. Bird's "Gladiator," for which Mr. Forrest paid a remunerating price to the author. This piece was followed by "Oralloosa," etc. His generosity in recompensing dramatic authors, gave an impulse to that branch of literature, which had a beneficial effect for many years. In 1833, on the occasion of the Dulnap benefit in New York, Mr. Forrest played *Pierre* to Kemble's *Jaffier*, Fanny Kemble appearing as *Belvidera*. In the early part of the year 1834, Mr. Forrest signified his intention of visiting Europe, and soon afterwards sailed for Havre, the citizens of New York having given him a farewell dinner prior to his departure. He visited Italy, and extracts from his letters to private friends were frequently published. In 1836, Mr. Forrest paid his first professional visit to England, and made his first appearance on the London stage on the 17th of October, 1836.

It was during this visit that Mr. Forrest was married to Catherine Sinclair, daughter of John Sinclair.

Mr. Forrest's return to this country was a complete ovation. Everywhere he was received with the most flattering marks of approbation, and the receipts of the first three nights at the Park Theatre, New York, amounted to $4,200. For several years Mr. Forrest continued to perform in every city of the Union with the most marked success, and his advent was looked for with impatience by his many admirers and lovers of th drama. In 1845 Mr. Forrest paid a second visit to London, and while performing at the Princesses' Theatre, was hissed during the performance. This indignity Mr. F. attributed to Macready's influence. Mr. Forrest subsequently hissed Macready in Edinburgh, for what he considered a violation of good taste by the introduction of a *pas de mouchoir* in "Hamlet." These acts were the commencement of that sad tragedy in real life, which terminated in the riot at the Astor Place Opera House, New York, on the night of the 10th of May, 1849, when twenty-two were killed, and thirty-six wounded. On the 9th of February, 1852, Mr.

Forrest made his first appearance after the verdict in the divorce case of Forrest *v.* Forrest had been given, at the Broadway Theatre, New York. His success was immense, and the engagement continued till April 30th, a period embracing SIXTY-NINE NIGHTS; an engagement unparalleled in the annals of the American stage. At the conclusion of this triumph, the company presented him with a gold-headed cane, and he was serenaded at his hotel.

Mr. Forrest, considered as an actor, would occupy more room than we can afford at this time. A writer remarked of him nearly a quarter of a century ago:—

"An American by birth, education, and feeling, he has been the architect of his own reputation; with no adventitious aid, he has formed his style of acting from the study of nature, and the dictates of his own judgment. In addition to a fine natural genius for the stage, Mr. F. possesses, in an eminent degree, the physical requisites of a great actor—a person of fine proportions—carriage graceful and commanding—voice full and powerful—a face beaming with intellect, and capable of portraying the passions in their deepest energy; to which are superadded the advantages of a taste matured by study and observation, and a constitution which sustains him in uninterrupted exercise of his arduous profession. Nature having been thus bountiful to the subject of these remarks, he has shown that her benefits have not been unappreciated or misapplied."

We need add nothing farther, for what was then uttered will find a responsive approval from all who have witnessed Mr. Forrest's impersonations during the past year in Boston and New York.

Mr. Forrest has been frequently solicited to permit his name to be used as candidate for public office, by his democratic brethren. This he has refused, seeking no other honor than that he could legitimately lay hold on, in his arduous professional career.

CHAPTER XVII.

Macready's Reappearance. — Mrs. Knight. — The Washington Theatre. — The Mermaid. — The Project of a New Theatre. — Mr. William Pelby. — Act of Incorporation. — Departure of Mr. Finn for Europe. — Opening of the War between the Rival Houses. — Tom Flynn. — George Andrews. — Miss Rock. — Baron Hacket. — The Two Dromios. — Miss Clara Fisher. — Opening of the Tremont Theatre. — The Prize Address. — The First Struggle for Supremacy.

IMMEDIATELY after Forrest's engagement, Macready reappeared, announced as "positively the last visit he can ever have the honor of paying Boston;" a statement which, however true for the time being, has not been confirmed, as the gentleman has frequently appeared in this city since then. The engagement was very successful. Mrs. Knight, formerly Miss Povey, appeared at the Boston, but did not create the sensation she had in New York. As a vocalist, she was very good, and possessed considerable talents as an actress.

The benefit season came on, and on the occasion of Miss Pelby's benefit, her father and mother appeared with herself, in "William Tell."

The Washington Theatre, formerly the City Theatre, which, by the way, changed name with every manager, in the month of May was opened by Mr. Burroughs, who brought the company from the Lafayette and Albany theatres, which consisted of Mr. Thayer, (who made his debut in Boston as a member of the Philo Dramatic Society,) Mrs. Walstein, J. Mills Brown, Mr. Reed, Mrs. McBride, and others. The ring was converted into a pit, and attempts were made to do the legitimate, but Mr. Burroughs found in the course of a short time that he had attempted a fruitless task. He had during the summer, also, a very powerful competitor. A distinguished visitor from the Fejee Islands had arrived in town, and taken rooms at No. 3 Scollay's Buildings, where, surrounded by marine shells and a few of the native productions of her country, she held levees, day and evening, which proved very attractive. The same mermaid, after various travels, has finally settled down at the Boston Museum, where she can be seen in all her beauty.

Early in February, 1827, the project of a new theatre was broached. Notwithstanding the excellent management at the old house, a strong feeling of opposition to it was manifested, which dated from the Kean riot. The theatre had been but poorly supported, and this decline, which should have been attributed to the true causes, — the fickleness of the public, the commencement of lectures, etc., was alleged to be the result of feebleness on the part of the managers, to cater acceptably for the public taste. At this period, a difficulty occurred between the late William Pelby and the managers, Messrs. Finn and Kilner, of the old theatre; he demanding, as an actor, exorbitant terms and privileges, which being denied him as unusual and unjustifiable, caused him to seek out his friends, who rallied around him under the idea that William Pelby had been shut out from this theatre, and that he had been proscribed. The quarrels of actors and managers were then subjects of which the general public took cognizance, and oftentimes sided with or against, making a very small affair oftentimes a question for a party division. Mr. Pelby's friends were determined to see him righted, and the building of a new theatre was proposed. This was the origin of the Tremont Theatre, though its erection subsequently became a matter of private speculation. At a meeting of gentlemen of wealth and influence, holden at Concert Hall, in the early part of February, 1827, Mr. Pelby guaranteed to the shareholders eight per cent. per annum, for ten years, on the cost. The stock was taken up, and the stockholders numbered about six hundred, which, twenty-five years ago, comprised most of the leading theatre-goers of the city, whose influence was naturally in favor of the new theatre; and in March, 1827, the following organization took place:—

Trustees — Edward H. Robbins, Jr., Wm. P. Mason, Charles F. Kupfer, Sen., Willard Badger, and Augustus Peabody, Esqrs. *Secretary* — W. P. Gragg, Esq. *Treasurer* — W. H. Gardiner, Esq. *Building Committee* — E. H. Robbins, Jr., James Page, James McAllaster, Alpheus Carey, Joseph H. Thayer, John Redman, and Solomon Towne, Esqrs.

A site of land was the next step to be taken. It was proposed to buy the Washington Garden property, and erect there a first class theatrical temple, and some of the stockholders of the theatre in Federal street were disposed to sell the whole of their property, but the land in Tremont (then Common) street was finally agreed upon and purchased. It had been previously used for Gragg & Brigham's livery stables. The foundation walls were laid in May. There was some trouble in naming the theatre. It was proposed at first to call it the "Franklin," the "Columbia," etc. etc.; but in June, the trustees agreed that the edifice should be designated the TREMONT THEATRE, and the application made to the legislature for an act of incorporation was made in the name of the "Stockholders of the Tremont Theatre."

As a matter of record, we give below the act of incorporation. Only two of the gentlemen, who petitioned for it, survive: —

Commonwealth of Massachusetts, A. D. 1827.

AN ACT

TO INCORPORATE THE PROPRIETORS OF THE TREMONT THEATRE.

SEC. 1. *Be it enacted by the Senate and House of Representatives, in General Court assembled, and by the authority of the same,* That Thomas H. Perkins, Edward D. Clark, Charles F. Kupfer, Thomas Brewer, John Redman, and Oliver Mills, and all such persons as are or may be associated with them, for the purpose of erecting and keeping a theatre in Boston, and their successors, be, and they are hereby made a Corporation, by the name of the Proprietors of the Tremont Theatre; and by that name they may sue and be sued, have a Common Seal, and have and enjoy all the powers and privileges, and be subject to all the duties incident to Corporations; and they shall have power to make, and at their pleasure to alter, such by-laws, for the management and regulation of their corporate property and concerns, as to them may appear expedient; *provided,* the same be not repugnant to the Constitution or Laws of this Commonwealth.

SEC. 2. *Be it further enacted*, That said Corporation be authorized to purchase, take and hold, the land on which said Proprietors are now erecting a Theatre on Common street, in the city of Boston; and such other real and personal estate as may be the necessary and proper appendages of a Theatre, and manage and direct the operations of the same as a corporate body; *provided*, the whole real estate shall not exceed one hundred thousand dollars, and the personal estate shall not exceed fifty thousand dollars.

SEC. 3. *Be it further enacted*, That the said corporate property shall be divided into shares of equal value, and no transfer of a share shall be valid, until such transfer be recorded by the Clerk of the Corporation; and such shares may be attached on mesne process, and taken and sold on execution according to law.

SEC. 4. *Be it further enacted*, That any one or more of the persons named in the first section of this act, be authorized to call the first meeting of said Proprietors, for the purpose of organizing the Corporation, to be holden at such time and place as he or they shall appoint, by giving ten days notice thereof in an advertisement, to be published in one or more of the Boston newspapers.

SEC. 5. *Be it further enacted*, That this act may be altered, amended, or repealed, at the discretion of the Legislature.

[*Approved by the Governor*, *June* 16*th*, 1827.]

On the fourth of July, the same year, (1827,) the corner-stone was laid. It is at the north corner, fronting on Tremont street. No ceremony of any note took place. A few remarks were made by the chairman of the building committee. A box containing copies of the newspapers of the day, English and American coins, and a copy of the act of incorporation, was securely soldered by Edward D. Clark, Esq., the well known auctioneer, and placed beneath. Inside of the box was the following record engraved on a silver plate:—

COMMONWEALTH OF MASSACHUSETTS.

On the fourth day of July, in the year of our Lord one thousand eight hundred and twenty-seven, and the Independence of the

United States of America, the fifty second, this inscription was deposited by the Proprietors of the Tremont Theatre, in token of laying the *Corner Stone.*

Treasurer — W. H. Gardiner.

Secretary — Washington P. Gragg.

Building Committee — Edward H. Robbins, Jr., Oliver Mills, John Redman, Solomon Towne, James Page, James McAllaster, Charles F. Kupfer, Edward D. Clark, Alpheus Cary.

Architect — Isaiah Rogers.

Lessee — William Pelby.

President of the United States — John Quincy Adams.

Governor of Massachusetts — Levi Lincoln.

Mayor of the City of Boston — Josiah Quincy.

There is a slight change between the list first given of the first building committee and the last, which was made during the process of erection.

The theatre was erected in a very short time. Its heavy granite front at that time was the admiration of the people, and the papers of the day recorded its progress with pride. Mr. Pelby offered, early as May, 1827, a premium of *one hundred dollars* in money or plate to the author of the best poem, of not less than fifty or more than seventy lines, to be recited at the opening of the theatre, and a committee was appointed to award the prize.

The proprietors and managers of the old theatre were determined, however, not to allow the rival house an easy conquest, and Mr. Finn was despatched to England for recruits, and the interior of the theatre was thoroughly renovated. The excitement produced by this state of things was very great, equalling almost that which now precedes a local election. Many — and especially the older portion of the community — adhered to the "Old Drury." It was there that they had first beheld Hodgkinson, Fennel, Cooke, Cooper, and others, and their associations with the house were of too pleasant a nature to be broken off for any trivial cause, and their affections too permanently located to be won by any new beauty. There were others who were equally partial to the new house—they had either been instrumental in its erection, or were attracted by the novelty of the project; and, consequently, as the time approached for the opening of both houses, there was some little boasting about the relative merits of the two companies engaged, Finn, having arrived from England with strong reinforcements *per Coral* and *Brookline*, and Pelby, having scoured the American market, offering large salaries for any available talent.

The Federal Street commenced the campaign on the 17th of September, 1827, with the "Rivals" and the "Young Widow." The company consisted of several recruits from England.

Mr. Thomas Flynn, from the respectable provincial theatres and the Haymarket, was engaged as principal tragedian. Poor Tom died a few years since, poor as poverty. His career was a remarkable one, and his tomb-stone should bear the inscription, "He was his own worst enemy." Tom Walton, from the Theatre Royal, York, England, came out as principal singer. Mr. Geo. Andrews, who married Miss Woodward from the Liverpool "boards," as low comedian, Mr. King from Drury Lane, and Miss Rivers as leading actors. Miss Rock came out as a star. Mr. and Mrs. Bernard, (formerly Miss Tilden,) and Mrs. C. Young, were important additions from other theatres in the country.

The remains of the old stock corps were Messrs. Kilner, Finn, Clarke, Charnock, etc.; and among the ladies, Mrs. Finn, Mrs. Barnes, Mrs. Papanti, Miss Clarke, and Miss C. McBride.

With such a *corps dramatique* now, a manager could bid defiance to all rivalry. But these attractions were not the only ones, for Mr. and Mrs. Barnes appeared, the latter appearing as *Richard.* Miss Rock, an actress of uncommon versatility of talents, also came out, and for her benefit, performed in the "Bride of Lammermoor." Mr. and Mrs. Duff — always great favorites — and the best *Calanthe*, pronounced by many that ever trod the Boston "boards," with Maywood — excellent as *Sir Archy* in the "Man of the World" — were among the attractions. Mr. and Mrs. Blake appeared. Hacket made his first appearance in Boston, at this theatre, in October, and appeared in the "Comedy of Errors:" — *Dromio of Ephesus*, Hacket; *Dromio of Syracuse*, Barnes. Without any personal resemblance to Mr. Barnes, save a general conformity as to size, Mr. Hacket contrived by a perfect similarity of dress, and a wonderful imitation of Barnes' manner of speech and tone of voice, to render it sometimes doubtful whether Barnes — and not Hacket — was speaking. The town ran to see this performance, and filled the house nightly. Hacket, at that time, introduced imitations of Kean, Cooke, and others, which were very good.

Mr. Forrest also performed two engagements; the first, supported by Miss Rock, Mrs. Duff, Flynn, etc.; and the second, by Miss Placide. At the close of his first engagement, he had retired to his hotel, when the audience called for him. He was sent for, and returned, delivering a very neat speech.

The 19th of November, 1827, witnessed the first appearance, in this city, of Miss Clara Fisher, who opened in *Albina Mandeville*, in the "Will" — a part Miss Rock had performed in to the delight of all. She appeared also in *Goldfinch* — one of Mathews' favorite characters, and her success was complete. A Philadelphia newspaper, on the occasion of Mrs. Maeder's appearance in that city, recently remarked: — "It is now twenty-four years since Clara Fisher, then a girl of seventeen, trod these boards in the gay day of youth, triumphing by her hilarity of manner, and her brisk, lively style. Who that remembers her *Four Mowbrays* will not resuscitate agreeable reminiscences of her versatility and comic ability? How arch she was! how ingenious in her transformations! what taste she displayed in costume, and what a successful buoyancy of spirits she possessed, which, infectious in its good humor, caused her audiences to yield without resistance to the cheerful epidemic! Her singing was dashing, almost impudent in its style, but so bravely executed that admiration was the only emotion which it produced. Her *White Sergeant* was a bravura which was then sung as it has seldom been sung since. There was a glorious military *abandon* in her voice, a martial and bold carriage of her person, which was irresistibly delightful. Never was a song better *acted* than the piece in question, and its popularity was therefore unbounded. Even in male characters Clara Fisher was excellent. Her *Crack*, in the 'Turnpike Gate,' was a clever and amusing piece of acting, which was oddly illustrated by her gaiety of manner and general skill. Beautiful, vivacious, and precociously talented, she created a *furore* in this city which has rarely been equalled since."

Mr. Horn and Mrs. Knight gave the citizens the lyric drama. "Guy Mannering" and "Der Freischutz" were brought out. Mrs. Sloman, mother to Jane Sloman, the harpist, who is now in Charleston, S. C., made her first appearance as *Isabella*, on the 7th of January, 1828, and gained great fame as *Mrs. Haller* and *Belvidera.* Cooper, after his unsuccessful trip to London, performed in March, and on the 28th acted *Othello* to Forrest's *Iago*, and after Forrest's departure, played to good houses. A protege of Cooper's, Miss Hamilton, also appeared, and Monsieur Achille, and a troupe of French dancers, served to fill up the intervals between the comedy and farces.

With such attractions as these, one would suppose that full houses would have been the result, no matter what the attractions were elsewhere; but such was not invariably the case. Messrs. Finn and Kilner confined themselves exclusively to the stage management, a committee of the proprietors superintending the financial affairs, and the season closed in June.

The Tremont Theatre, though not finished, was announced to open on the 24th of September, 1827. The roof was on, but the granite façade was not completed. Great impatience was manifested among the play-going public to see the interior, and those privileged persons, "the members of the press," gave almost daily bulletins of the progress made. The Saturday previous to Monday, the opening night, the tickets were offered for sale, and such was the rush, that in less than twenty minutes every seat in the pit and first and second row of boxes was disposed of. The bill of entertainment was as follows:—

TREMONT THEATRE.

The Public is respectfully informed, that the *Tremont Theatre* will open

ON MONDAY EVENING, SEPTEMBER 24.

☞ The Orchestra will embrace the most distinguished musical talent in the country — Leader, . . . MR. OSTINELLI.

There will be presented Mrs. Inchbald's Comedy, called

Wives as they Were, and Maids as they Are.

Lord Priory, ... Mr. Herbert,
(of the New York and Philadelphia theatres,—first appearance in Boston).
Sir William Dorillon, ... Mr. Webb,
(of the Philadelphia Theatre,—first appearance in Boston).
Sir George Evelyn, ... Mr. Reed,
Mr. Bronzly, ... Mr. Blake,
(First appearance for two seasons).
Mr. Norberry, ... Mr. Forbes.
Oliver, ... Mr. J. Mills Brown.
Miss Dorillon, ... Mrs. Blake,
(of the New York Theatre).
Lady Mary Raffle, ... Mrs. Young,
(of the New York Theatre).
Lady Priory, ... Mrs. Pelby.

Previous to the Comedy, the *Prize Address* will be delivered by MR. BLAKE.

The Entertainment to conclude with the Farce of the

Lady and the Devil.

Wildlove, ... Mr. Reed,
Jeremy, ... Mr. J. Mills Brown,
Signor Rafael, ... Mr. Hart,

Claudian,	Mr. Field,
Landlord,	Mr. Martin,
Zephyrina,	Mrs. Young,
Negombo,	Mrs. Brewster.

In addition to the above, Messrs. Hyatt, W. Isherwood, Brewster Kelly, Collingbourne, and Smith, and Mrs. and Miss Riddle, Mrs. Smith, and Mrs. Forbes, and Mr. Keene, the Vocalist, are engaged for the season. Many ladies and gentlemen of distinguished talents, are engaged for limited periods.

☞ Boxes, $1; Third Tier, 75 cts.; Pit, 50 cts.; Centre Gallery, for people of color, 50 cts.; Side Gallery, 25 cts.

Days of Performance, Monday, Tuesday, Wednesday, Thursday, and Friday.

☞ Doors open at half-past 5; Performance to commence at half-past 6.

The prize address delivered on this occasion has been the subject of considerable remark, both at that time and since. When Mr. Pelby's intention of offering a prize was first announced, many who had before competed with Mr. Sprague, for other prizes, announced their intention of withdrawing from any farther contest, alleging, with great injustice, that it was the *name*, and not the *poem*, which had gained him his last honor; an assertion which subsequently proved to be false, for the next three prizes gained by Mr. Sprague — one in Philadelphia, one in Salem, and one in Portsmouth — were anonymously obtained, and only acknowledged by the author in later years. But shortly the names of the gentlemen composing the committee on the prize was announced, and Mr. Sprague was one, assisted by Franklin Dexter, Nathan Hale, Ebenezer Bailey, and John Ware, Esqrs. Mr. Sprague, by accepting a judgeship, signified his intention of allowing a clear field to others. A number of pieces were handed in, but none of them evincing any decided superiority as poetical compositions, and after repeated consultations the committee came to the conclusion that they would report to Mr. Pelby, that not one of the poems was worthy of the prize. Upon farther consideration, however, this report did not appear to be in accordance with the offer made, which was for *the best poem;* and however inferior it might be, still they were to single out *one* as better than the others. Accordingly they designated the poem by "Theron" as the least exceptionable, and the sealed paper accompanying the poem contained the name of "J. Jamieson, Hartford, Ct."

"Who is J. Jamieson?" was the question asked. Hartford was searched through and through; the postmaster, the ministers, and even the sexton, were consulted as to the individual, but no "J. Jamieson" was there to be found. The disappointed applicants for the prize then called upon the committee, through the public prints, to produce the man, and with a malevolence sometimes characteristic of disappointed second-rate geninuses, charged the committee with corruption, and accused several members with having awarded the prize to one of their own number. Mr. Sprague was singled out and pursued with great bitterness; and we cannot but think this unkind treatment may have been the cause of the allusion in Curiosity to "tenth-rate type-men."

> "That reptile race, with all that 's good at strife,
> Who trail their slime through every walk of life;
> Stain the white tablet where a great man's name
> Stands proudly chisell'd by the hand of Fame;
> Nor round the sacred fire-side fear to crawl,
> But drop their venom there, and poison all."

Some at that time discovered the style of this poet, who they pretended was ashamed to acknowledge the authorship. Others thought that it might have emanated from the study of a clergyman; but this was pronounced impossible, as no man in holy office would sanction the expression, which occurred in the poem: —

" Let pulpits fulminate, let presses groan,
Their woes and warnings — and what need they more
To cause the curse they piously deplore! "

The topic as to the identity of the author was long kept up, and at this day it is a matter of very little consequence who he is or may have been. The prize-money was paid to Mr. Buckingham, editor of the *Galaxy*, who has stated that Rev. John Pierpont was the gentleman who bespoke his agency in regard to the prologue, and that the prize-money was paid to him. Mr. Buckingham could not state that Mr. Pierpont was the author, and that gentleman "never either admitted or denied the accusation." At that time "J. Jamieson, of Hartford, Ct.," was the great Unknown.

The orchestra at the Tremont was very good. Mr. and Mrs. Barnes, after playing at the Boston, appeared at the Tremont, and Mr. and Mrs. Blake, owing to some trouble at the Tremont, went to the old house. The leading stars the first season were Mr. Holland, an excellent comic actor, Mr.* and Mrs. Hilson, (formerly Miss Johnson,) Mr. Adams, the tragedian, Mr. Horn

* At Louisville, Ky., of apoplexy, on the 23d of July, 1834, Mr. Thomas Hilson, long known in various parts of the United States as one of the best comedians of the day. He was apparently in perfect health till within fifteen minutes of his death.

and Mrs. Knight, Miss Rock, after her appearance at the old house, Mr. Cooper, after his appearance at the Federal Street, Miss Kelly, Mr. and Mrs. Wallack, etc. Mrs. Mestayer made her first appearance January 7, 1828, as *Mrs. Baalamb* in "Gambler's Fate." Mr. Pelby also engaged the French dancers, Mons. Barberre, Madame Hutin, and Md'lle. Celeste, at $300 per night, which brought the expenses up to $600 per night, and the scenic play of "Undine" was got up at a great expense, but proved a failure. A play called "Charlotte Temple," written by George Ward Glascott, was also produced, and "Timour the Tartar," with horse accompaniment, produced Jan. 21, '28. Up to the expiration of the 15th or 20th week, the season had proved profitable; and though the expenses were large, they had been promptly met. The season, however, closed on the 20th of May, leaving the manager deeply involved, and the proprietors without a dividend. The competition between the two houses had been carried on with unprecedented warmth. Pelby was accused of seducing stars from the Federal Street to the Tremont, and Finn was charged with equally grave misdemeanors. In the case of Miss George, she was announced to appear at both houses the same evening, and the charges of bribery and corruption were set afloat, and statements and counter-statements appeared in the papers. The old house, however, carried the day as regards the excellence of the stock company and stars, and the Tremont had superior advantages so far as a new house and a better location was concerned; but neither came out of this first struggle with any decided advantage to themselves.

CHAPTER XVIII.

Change of Management at the Tremont Theatre. — J. B. Booth as Acting-Manager. — The Company and Salaries. — Debut of John Gibbs Gilbert. — Forrest's First Appearance at the Tremont. — Der Freischutz. — Hyatt. — Madam Feron. — Tom Comer's First Benefit. — W. H. Smith's First Benefit. — Faults of the Theatre. — The Opera at the Old Theatre. — Commencement of the Regular Season. — Caldwell. — Finn's Unique Cards. — Debut of Mrs. Cramer, etc., etc.

Mr. Pelby became so embarrassed, that the directors of the corporation deemed it advisable to make some change. Mr. Pelby had also gained the enmity of the press, and members of his own company were not inclined to continue under his management. The idea, too, had exploded, that Boston had grown large enough to suport two first-class theatres. Mr. Pelby had hired the theatre for a term of ten years, agreeing to pay a rent of eight per cent. upon its cost, and, at the end of the third quarter of the first year, he was induced — as he thought, by unfair means — to sell out to an association of gentlemen, comprising F. W. Dana, Mitchell, John Rayner, B. C. Clark, H. H. Huggeford, Thomas Niles, John Fuller, Esq., and others. Mr. Francis W. Dana was at the head of this project, and the agreement on the part of the corporation was, that they might surrender the house at the end of the first year. They paid for the year the full rent of $9,000, and prepared to give the old house another trial. The company was strengthened, and J. B. Booth was engaged as acting-manager for the first two months, at a salary of $100 per week, and $100 a night for ten performances. The bill for the opening night, was as follows:—

TREMONT THEATRE.

☞ MR. BOOTH has the honor to acquaint the public, that the gentlemen composing the Committee of Arrangements for this theatre, have selected him to manage and direct the business of the stage. Mr. Booth is aware of the important and laborious task he has undertaken, but hopes that the desire felt by him and his constituents to reclaim the drama from approaching degeneracy, and a steady perseverence to *deserve* success by making the theatre a place of rational and improving amusement, will insure and receive the approbation of all.

On Monday Evening, September 1, 1828,
Will be performed, the Comedy of
SPEED THE PLOUGH.

Sir Philip Blandford, ... Mr. Webb.
Worrington, ... Mr. Collingbourne,
From the Bowery Theatre, New York.
Sir Abel Handy, ... Mr. Jones,
From the Park Theatre, New York.
Bob Handy, ... Mr. Thayer,
From the Lafayette Theatre, New York.
Henry, ... Mr. Field.
Farmer Ashfield, ... Mr. Hallam,
From the Philadelphia theatres.
Gerald, ... Mr. Jervis,
From the Park Theatre, New York.
Evergreen, ... Mr. Laws.
Postilion, ... Mr. Blaike.
Peter, ... Mr. Scott.
Valet, ... Mr. J. S. Jones.
Miss Blandford, ... Miss Hamilton,
Her first appearance at this theatre.
Lady Handy, ... Mrs. Lacombe,
From the New York theatres.
Susan Ashfield, ... Mrs. Roper,
From the Philadelphia theatres.
Dame Ashfield, ... Mrs. Jones,
From the Bowery Theatre, New York.

Previous to the Comedy,
AN ADDRESS,
Written by a Lady of this city, expressly for the occasion, will be spoken by Mr. Archer.

A New Act Drop, presenting a View of the Academic Grove, painted by Mr. Coyle, will be exhibited.

The evening's entertainment to conclude with
THE REVIEW.

Looney McTwolter, ... Mr. Comer,
From the Theatre Royal, Covent Garden.
John Lump, ... Mr. Simpson,
From the Chatham Theatre, New York.
Grace Gaylove, ... Mrs. Roper.

☞ The Box Office will be opened from 10 till 2 o'clock, (Saturdays from 10 to 12).

Boxes, $1; Third Tier of Boxes, 75 cents; Pit, 50 cents; Gallery, 25 cts.

The doors will be open at 6 o'clock. Performance to commence at 7 o'clock.

The address was the production of Mrs. Catherine A. Ware, a poetess of no ordinary ability.

Mr. Booth was assisted by Alexander Wilson, at a salary of $50 per week, as a kind of out-door manager, — Mr. Dana superintending the whole. The company was increased, and the following are the names of the leading actors who appeared during the season, with a few of the sums paid per week for their services: —

Thomas Comer, Musical Director, $40. Luigi Ostinelli, Leader of the Orchestra, $40. Mrs. Duff, $50. Mrs. Pelby and daughter, Mrs. George Barrett, Mrs. Papanti, Miss Riddle, Mrs. William Jones and husband, at an average of $50. Thomas Archer, $40. W. H. Smith, $30. Thayer, $28. Hyatt, $50. Lopez, as Prompter, (editor of Weymiss' and Lopez's Edition of Plays). Young Silas Field, Walker, C. Lehr, and R. Jones were in the paint-room, with Sam. Stockwell, as assistant. The Orchestra numbered twenty-eight musicians, averaging from $11 to $14 per week; and there was also a strong corps of chorus-singers, William B. Oliver, *Leader*. J. F. Barker, John Candy, David Whiting, George Birch, Phineas Glover, John Hall, Anselm Lothrop, at $10 per week. Under such systematic extravagance the season commenced.

During Booth's management Miss Rock, Miss Placide, Hamblin, Miss Louisa Lane, an infant prodigy, who afterwards played *Uncamunca*, to Major Stevens' *Tom Thumb*, in the "Extravaganza." Booth took leave, in order to fulfil his engagement at the South, in the character *Orestes*, a part done by him in French, when in New Orleans, to the admiration of many, who had seen the same impersonation by the great Talma. Mrs. Duff appeared with undiminished power this season. Joe Cowell succeeded Booth as manager; the latter, on his retirement, receiving from the lessees a beautiful cup and plate, valued at $100, as a mark of their appreciation of his services while manager. The theatre, during Booth's management, had done well. The Federal Street, shortly after its opening, reduced its prices of admission, which was considered as a triumph of the new theatre over the old. After this, a rapid succession of stars appeared, two or more often at the same time. Wallack, on the 3d of November, appeared, and on the 7th, Miss Clara Fisher commenced her first engagement at the Tremont, and a great one it was. On the occasion of Wallack's benefit,

"Much Ado About Nothing" was brought out:— *Benedict*, Wallack; *Beatrice*, Miss Clara Fisher. Cooper followed immediately after, supported by Mrs. Duff.

On the 28th of November, 1828, John Gibbs Gilbert, a resident of North End, made his *debut* in the character of *Jaffier*,—Mr. Wilson as *Pierre*, Mrs. Duff as *Belvidera*. The attempt was crowned with the greatest success. There was the awkward gait of the novice, and some crudities of expression, but his readings were correct, evincing a discriminating mind, and an originality which pleased the most critical, and gave the promise, which has been fully realized, of his becoming one of the most sterling actors of the day. His second appearance was as *Sir Edward Mortimer*, in which he made a hit.

Forrest's first appearance at the Tremont, was made in the character of *Hamlet*, on the 15th of November, 1828:— *Ghost*, Wilson; *Horatio*, W. H. Smith; *Queen*, Mrs. Pelby; *Ophelia*, Mrs. Cowell. During this engagement, in which Forrest evinced marked improvement in style over his earliest efforts in Boston, Shiel's play of "Evadne" was brought out— *Ludovico*, Forrest; *Colinna*, Wilson; *Vincento*, John G. Gilbert.

Thomas Comer, in the month of January, brought out "Der Freischutz," in an admirable manner. The "Barber of Seville" was also produced under the same direction during Mrs. Austin's engagement, the chief parts filled by Comer, Horn, Miss George, and Mrs. Papanti.

Hyatt was the life of the company, and adopted

many ingenious methods to draw a house, whenever his name was up for a benefit. On one occasion, he announced that twenty-five lottery tickets — wholes and halves — would be distributed from a balloon, in which Md'lle Scratchini Pasiamo would ascend. On another night, the following announcement was made: —

£100 NOTE.

Billy Black, (1st Act,) . . . . . Mr. Hyatt.
Billy Black, (2d ") . . . . . . Mr. Cowell.
Miss Arlington, ... Miss Riddle.
With the Song — "Buy a Broom."

☞ A dispute having arisen among the ladies, whether Mr. *Cowell* or Mr. *Hyatt* is the greater beauty — and, as some have declared Mr. *Cowell* to be the handsomest boy, and others "*wice wersa*" — Mr. Hyatt thinks it an incumbent duty to set this important dispute at rest; therefore, he will gratify the feelings of the ladies, by appearing with Mr. Cowell, (in the course of the farce,) and sing the comic duett of THE RIVAL BEAUTIES.

The joke of the above consists in the fact that neither of the gentlemen had any great claims to be considered an Apollo. Hyatt, at times, was a ready wit. In the farce of the "Rendezvous," the females were ordered to go to bed, by the old man, and they went out at the side door. One of them tried to slide back unperceived, but stumbled over the base of the column, and fell down, after which she vanished. "Go along to bed all of you," says the old man. "Yes, it's time for 'em to go to bed," says Hyatt, "for they're tumbling over their pillars already." The joke was cracked so instantly, that rounds of applause rewarded the ready wit. Hyatt enlisted in the United States Navy as a Marine, in 1832.

Madame Celeste also appeared and brought out the "Caliph of Bagdad."

The ballet was followed by the appearance of Madam Feron, who appeared in the "Barber of Seville," "Beggar's Opera," etc. She was born of French parents in London in 1797, and while yet a child, was brought forward at Vauxhall to execute music of a description similar to that then singing by Catalini at the Opera, and the wags of the day christened her the "little *Cat*," while her prototype received the elegant appellation of the great one. Madame Feron, subsequently visited Italy, where she pursued her studies, and afterwards achieved victories in all the principal European cities. Madame Feron belonged to the genus of astonishing vocalists. Her love of ornament was strong and sometimes ran away with her, but her cadenza were original and effective. As an actress, she was fascinating; and in private life, an elegant woman.

Miss Rock made a second engagement prior to her departure for Europe. Wallack reappeared, and put upon the stage "Rienzi."

The only scenic piece of any note this season was the "Enchanted Castle, or Knights of Old," in which Mr. W. H. Smith sustained the part of *Aldibert*, and probably first became initiated into the mysteries of that department of the profession, which he has so successfully improved upon, as shown in the style and magnificence of the Museum spectacles.

On the 6th of April, 1829, Thomas Comer, more familiarly known as "Honest Tom Comer," announced his first benefit in Boston. Many a time since then has that old familiar name been posted as the beneficiary of the evening. That it has not always attracted a crowded house, may be possible, but certainly it always deserved one, and so far as our own recollection extends has received it. Mr. Comer brought out Shakspeare's "Tempest," the part of *Ariel* by Miss Rock.

Mr. W. H. Smith's first benefit was on the 13th of April, a week following that of Mr. Comer's, both of whom, after nearly a quarter of a century, still hold prominent positions before the Boston public. Lest our readers might infer, by our allusion to fragments of centuries, that these gentlemen were very, very *old*, we will state that then they were very, very *young;* and occular demonstration can be had any evening that the hand of time has touched them lightly, and leaves them in the enjoyment of every faculty requisite to their laborious profession. On the night of Mr. Smith's first benefit, the entertainments consisted of "A Woman never Vexed, or The Rich Widow of Cornhill." *King Henry VI.*, Mr. Gilbert; *Robert Foster*, Mr. Field; *Clown*, Hyatt; *Agnes*, Mrs. Smith; and the play of the "Wandering Boys." *Paul*, W. H. Smith.

Towards the close of the season, "London and Paris" was brought out, and Mrs. George Barrett, then in the heyday of her beauty, possessing the same versatility of powers still evinced by this excellent actress, appeared, and Booth and Mrs. Duff performed an engagement; the house closing with M. M. Noah's play of "Marion and His Men," etc., on the Fourth of July.

That the season in point of attraction was brilliant, must be admitted; but the house was too small, or rather the dress circle would not contain those who would not take seats in the second tier; and as Mr. Barry and others afterwards found out, the expenses of any great attraction exceeded the receipts when the house was crammed, more especially after a reduction of prices took place. As has been seen, star succeeded star, with a rapidity since unknown, and the stock was kept up in every rank. The result was a loss of about *twenty-seven thousand dollars* to the committee of gentlemen. We will now take a look at the progress made at the old house.

On the 25th of August, Mr. Davis, the manager of the French Theatre, N. O., opened the Boston Theatre, for a short season, with his opera company, it being too early to risk a southern climate with his recent transatlantic importation. "La Dame Blanche," and a vaudeville entitled "Werther," were brought out.

The regular season, and the last at this house for many years, commenced on the 22d of September, with the "Heir at Law." *Dr. Pangloss*, Finn; *Steadfast*, Young; *Homespun*, Andrews; *Dorothy Douglass*, Mrs. Barnes; *Caroline Dormer*, Mrs. Finn; *Cicily Homespun*, Mrs. Young; and *Lord Dubberly*, Mr. Faulkner, his first appearance in Boston. The leading attraction was the Grand Corps of Parisian Dancers, who drew well. The only star of any note was Mr. Caldwell, manager of the New Orleans Theatre, who afforded a rich treat to those who fancied chaste acting. He afterwards appeared at the Tremont, the same season. Mr. A. Adams, the tragedian, appeared as *William Tell*, and in other parts, and the "Forty Thieves" was revived.

The attractions at the new house were so strong that

the Federal Street Theatre was almost deserted, notwithstanding the free tickets so lavishly circulated by the latter. The press also was loud in its complaints of the way things were conducted at the old house, and the stockholders were somewhat fatigued with carrying on the warfare. Mr. Finn took two benefits this season. On the 13th of December, '28, "One Hundred and Two, or The Veteran and his Prodigy," and "Thirty Years of the Life of a Gambler," were brought out, and a good house was attracted, mainly through the unique invitations published by Finn in the papers. Here is one :—

MORE DISCLOSURES.

FINN'S LETTERS TO THE PUBLIC.

Dear Public, pray permit H J
Finn, to address a D T
To U, and make a slight S A,
To influence the C T.

And N E faults you must X Qs,
Nor B my N M E;
If not instruct, I will M Us,
With all my N R G.

The grateful warmth which I O U,
X-ceeds T P D T;
I cannot, tho' I have my Q,
X-press my X T C.

From Q N's town to U T K,
From Mystic to P D,
There 's not a biped popin-J
That I would now N V.

On Monday night, my Public D R,
We shall X L, U C;
To every call, I will give E R,
And answer, "Here I B."

Need I say Y, 't would give me Es,
A full house should I C;
But O! for P T, do not Ts,
And make that house M T.

In the month of April, Mr. Finn, on the occasion of his second benefit, when "Peter Finn, or A Trip to see the Sea," and "Massachusetts Railroads," two pieces from the pen of the beneficiary, were produced, again addressed the public as follows:—

FINN'S BENEFIT AND HIS PACK OF CARDS.

"Keep a commanding card to bring in your strong suit when the trumps are out." — *Hoyle.*

Since *Benefit* cards are becoming the fashion,
And they now run in couples, like hounds on the track, —
In pursuit of a similar *game*, I shall dash on,
Hoping all *jolly dogs* will encourage my PACK.

That life is a game, needs not much illustration;
Many play for a robe — many more for a rag.
To play a good game 's the most safe *speculation;*
He who *is* the *best man* has the most reason to *brag.*

Old Industry's *spade* has *turn'd* up for our yeomen,
And turned out from our land some of Valor's best shrubs;
Our mechanics, too, yield in their courage to no men,
Who, our foes have found out, have a *strong hand* with clubs.

Little Cupid 's a *knave*, who plays *tricks* with his darts —
And the eyes of those ladies, who 've no wish to shun love,
Are the *diamonds* which win to the *altar* all *hearts;*
And the odds are, we finish the game with but "*one-love.*"

Tho' I often *make game* by a card with a *face,*
Yet judiciously *cutting* — a joke is of use.
As you *deal* with a *pun-ter* if *you* bate an *ace*
Of your favor, with me you 'll be playing the *deuce.*

Not in *kings* or in *queens*, but republican men,
That they 'll all come in numbers, my chief cônfidence is,
Three, four, five, and six, seven, eight, nine, or ten,
And I 'll take to myself all the worst con-*sequences.*

You shall have — and my promise I will not revoke,
On that night — as good *playing* as Boston affords;
For my *partners* will not need much *forcing* to joke, —
But, at all events, here you've a play, *upon words.*

My *suit* is to win from my friends all the *honors*
A player expects from their *hands* when addressing
Those regular *trumps*, who have been my best donors,
Who will pardon my many attempts at FINNESS-*ing.*

Miss Cramer made her debut at the theatre this season in the part of *Letitia Hardy*, (May 22, '29,) and on the occasion of Mr. Walton's benefit, his wife appeared, for the first time on any stage, in a dramatic version of Scott's Antiquary.

The after season of the Federal Street Theatre, though the rent was relinquished by the proprietors to Mr. Young, the acting manager, proved a losing concern; and, not having paid the performers, except a very few, they deserted the sinking ship, one by one, till at last they were able to make up a very scanty bill. The theatre closed on the night of Artillery Election, when Burk's play of "Bunker Hill" was performed.

CHAPTER XIX.

Contest between the Two Theatres. — The Old House Closed. — The Opera. — The Company. — Booth's Appearance. — His Strange Conduct, and Walk to Providence. — "Metamora." — The Production of English Dramas. — Richard Russell. — Charles Kean. — Master Burke. — Amphitheatre in Flagg Alley. — Ball of the Cadets at the Old Theatre. — Another of Finn's Cards, etc., etc.

THE contest between the two theatres had been carried on two years with unabated vigor, and, as we have stated, with a great loss to the Tremont. Mr. Dana and his friends concluded to give up the management, but it was agreed by the stockholders that they might hold it for another year, paying only the current expenses of the corporation with the interest on their mortgage debt. The rent on this second year amounted ed to only about $1,500, making an average for two years of something over $5,000 per annum. Negotiations were then entered into by the proprietors of the two houses, which resulted in the management of the Tremont leasing the old theatre, which they kept closed when the former was open, at a considerable expense.

After the regular season at the old house had closed, it was opened one night in August, for the benefit of George Andrews, when he was assisted by several of the leading actors from the new house.

On the 2d of September, the Italian Opera Company commenced a short season at the old house, and brought out "Tancredi," "Barber of Seville," etc.

This company was composed of Madame Feron, (who died in the month of May, 1853, in London,) Madame Brochta, Signor Rosich, Signor Angrisani, etc. Ostinelli led the orchestra, and Comer was musical director. This was the first regular attempt to present the lyric drama, with all the proper accompaniments, which proved successful. The same company, with the exception of Ostinelli, had been performing selections from different Italian operas at the Park Theatre, N. Y., with great success, which induced them to pay Boston a visit. Mr. Comer had left them and gone to Newport, when, to his surprise, Mr. J. Phalen, on the part of F. W. Dana, Esq., the manager, called on him and stated that the troupe would visit Boston, and that his services were required as musical director in the orchestra. He at once hastened to Boston, engaged his voices, and announced a rehearsal for the next day. The weather was intensely warm, and before proceeding to business, it was voted that shirt-sleeves were *en règle*. Mr. Comer commenced the drilling by giving the words of an opening chorus, "*Pare onare*, etc." Mr. W. B. Oliver, Captain Sam. Adams, and others, were quick at learning the music, but when it came to giving the words, the perspiration started from every pore. The book of "Italian in six easy lessons" had not then been compiled; but Mr. Comer found them apt scholars, and they found him an efficient teacher, and by hard work and perseverance the choristers were Italianized, and executed their part so well as that they received the compliments of Madame Feron, and troupe. The most fashionable houses were in attendance, and the boxes presented a magnificent array of Boston belles, many of whom are the stately matrons of the present day.

The union of the rival theatres, and the concentration upon one establishment of the interest hitherto divided between two, promised a most successful season for the Tremont. The interior of that house was greatly improved, and the company increased. Mr. Jones, of the New York theatres, had the direction of the scenic department. Mr. Comer had the management of the vocal department. Mr. Ostinelli conducted the orchestra, composed of Messrs. Granger, Peele, Eberle, Kendall, Hanna, Pierce, Warren, Schott, Geer, and others. Mr. Finn and Mr. Andrews, from the Federal Street, and Mr. Jones, from the English Opera House, with Mr. G. Jones, were engaged, and among the company of the previous season retained, were Messrs. Wilson, Smith, Thayer, Hyatt, Comer, Jones, Collingbourne, Scott, Blaike, J. S. Jones, Leman, Clements, Whiting, etc., etc.; Mrs. W. H. Smith, Mrs. Papanti, Mrs. Jones, Mrs. Campbell, Misses Eberle, McBride, etc. Mr. Wilson was the ostensible manager, and Mr. W. H. Smith, stage manager. The season commenced on the 14th of September with "Speed the Plough," the *Romaiker*, by Mad'lles Celeste and Constance, and "Touch and Take."

On the 16th of November Booth was engaged, and made his appearance. He performed for one or two nights with fine effect, when he was taken ill and obliged to keep his room. He recruited, however, and re-appeared as *Richard*, and on Monday, December 7, was announced to perform *Ludovico* in "Evadne," supported by Mr. Pelby as *Colonna*, and Mrs. Duff as *Evadne*. The after-piece, of "Amateurs and Actors," was to give occasion for Mr. Booth to play in a comic character. The house was crowded; not a nook or corner of the dress circle was unoccupied, and great numbers were refused admittance.

Mr. Booth's first entrance on the stage denoted something unusual. He was careless and hesitating in his delivery, and his countenance had none of its customary expression. He would falter in his discourse, jumble scraps of other plays into his dialogue, run to the prompter's side of the stage and lean against a side scene, while the prompter endeavored to help him forward in the play, by speaking out his part of the dialogue loud enough to be heard in the galleries. In this manner, he made a shift to get through the first two acts of the tragedy. Those familiar with the theatre saw very plainly that something was rotten in the State of Denmark; but a great proportion of the very crowded audience present, not knowing much of his manner of acting, did not comprehend the business, but only looked on, stared, gaped, and wondered, and protested that for an actor of so much celebrity, Mr. Booth played in a very spiritless and bungling fashion.

This *bizarrerie* soon came to a close. In the early part of the third act, while engaged in parlance with the king of Naples, the audience were surprised by his suddenly breaking off from the measured, heroical dignity of his stage tone, and with a comical simper, falling at once into a colloquial gossiping sort of chatter with his majesty, thus — "*Upon my word, sir, I don't know sir,*" etc. The audience were thrown into as much astonishment as the king of the two Sicilies at Signor Ludovico's sudden and anti-poetical downcome from his buskined height of declamation. For a moment all was silence; when Mr. Booth, turning round and facing the spectators, began to address them in this manner: — "*Ladies and gentlemen; I really don't know this part. I studied it only once before, much against my inclination. I will read the part, and the play shall go on. By your leave the play shall go on, and Mr. Wilson shall read the part for me.*" Here an overpowering burst of hissing and exclamations arose from all parts of the house, while Mr. Booth continued to face the audience with a grinning look, which at length broke out into an open laugh. Mr. Smith then rushed from behind the scenes upon the stage, and led him off, Mr. Booth exclaiming, "*I can't read, — I am a charity boy; — I can't read. Take me to the Lunatic Hospital!*" Here the drop curtain fell amid the murmurs and hisses of the house.

Presently appeared Mr. Smith from the stage door, and spoke in the following tenor: "Ladies and gentlemen, — it is obvious to you all, that Mr. Booth cannot appear again this evening, and that the play, therefore, cannot proceed. It is also well known that Mr. Booth has, for some time, been subject to partial insanity. It appears evident that he is not now what he has been. His reason has left him. With your indulgence we shall immediately proceed to consider what is to be done in this emergency." This temporary explanation appeared to satisfy the house, and Mr. Smith retired without any signs of disapprobation being manifested. After some minutes, he came forward again. "Ladies and gentlemen, — it is hoped that you will consider the circumstances which have caused the unlooked-for disappointment of this evening. Mr. Booth had been ill on Sat rday, but was to all appearance quite recovered. He would not have been announced to play this evening, had we not been assured by his physician that he had recovered his powers and was fully competent to fulfil his duties in the performance. As the pieces announced in the bills cannot be performed, it has been determined to make this substitution — the Interlude of "Is he Jealous?" will first be presented, after which, the comedy of "The Poor Gentleman."

Mr. Smith was retiring after this speech, when a loud hissing was set up, and voices began to call out, "*Booth, Booth. 'The Bride of Abydos,' 'The Master's Rival,*'" etc. Upon this, he appealed again to the politeness and good nature of the house to overlook their disappointment, lamenting that circumstances had obliged the managers to ask often for their forbearance. Some little disposition was shown to be riotous in the galleries, but the boxes were perfectly quiet, and there was but little commotion in the pit. The curtain rose, and there entered upon the stage Messrs. I. Jones, Comer, Scott, and Candy. They sung in a very spirited manner the glee of "Old King Cole," which had the effect of putting the refractory spirits into something like good humor. The singers were listened to in quiet, and encored.

There were, then, repeated calls made for Mr. Finn, when Mr. Smith came forward a third time. He stated that Mr. Finn would appear in five minutes, and went on to make some explanations of what he had said in a previous address on the subject of the cause of Mr. Booth's catastrophe. Having been informed that it was understood he had ascribed the cause of Booth's indisposition to liquor, he now declared that no such insinuation was intended, and that, on the contrary, Mr. Booth's attendants, who had been with him through the day, averred that he had drank nothing of the spirituous kind in that time."

Mr. Booth was immediately carried to his lodgings, and his disorder having increased, it was on Wednesday deemed advisable to obtain a consultation as to the propriety of placing him in the Lunatic Asylum, but on repairing to his room, the patient was *non est.* Search was made for him, and the only information that could be obtained was his application for a seat in the Providence stage, at the Marlboro' Hotel; but the stage having previously departed, he went off, and whither no one knew; and it was not till the arrival of a stage from Providence, that intelligence was conveyed by the driver, that on Wednesday he met Mr. Booth between Dedham and Walpole on foot, bearing towards Providence, without his outside garments, and without any extra clothing whatever. He reached Providence on Thursday, and, it was supposed, slept in the woods on Wednesday night. Kind friends at once took him in charge, and after a temporary retirement, he again appeared in this city.

Mrs. Austin appeared this season, and Forrest and Booth performed in "Venice Preserved," "Othello," etc. On the 15th of February, 1830, Mr. Forrest produced his prize tragedy of "Metamora," written by Dr. J. A. Stone, for the first time, supported by Scott, Jones,

Wilson, Mrs. Duff, and Mrs. Barrett; the original prologue was delivered by Mr. Thayer, the original epilogue by Mrs. Barrett. It proved in the highest degree attractive to the public, and crowds rushed to see this energetic impersonation of Mr. Forrest's. The mention of this piece reminds us of an anecdote of recent date. Mr. Forrest had performed the piece at the National Theatre, in this city, for five successive nights, to crowded houses. A gentleman remarked to Mr. Forrest, that he should feel flattered at this mark of approbation. "Mr. Stone, if he were alive," replied Mr. Forrest, "would undoubtedly feel proud." "But," continued the gentleman, "if other than a Forrest played it, the author might not have cause for self-congratulation." The tragedian was inclined to give all the credit to the author; but his friend placed it where it belonged, and rightly attributed the success of a very peculiar play to the eminent talent of the actor.

An original comedy, called "School for Courtship," was produced in February, in which Mr. Jones, the excellent scenic artist, produced a view of the Tremont House and Theatre, with Park Street Church in the distance, which was very fine. "Massaniello," which had been in rehearsal during the season, was brought out on the 5th of April with fine effect, and had a good run. Hacket also appeared.

This season was celebrated for the admirable manner in which the sterling old English comedies were acted by Finn, W. H. Smith, Kilner, (who joined the company with George Barrett, in January, and in passionate and hearty old men never has been equalled this side of the water). Andrews, Comer, Thayer, Hyatt,

Mrs. Duff, Mrs. Barrett, Mrs. Pelby, Mrs. Papanti, Mrs. Barnes, etc., Mr. Placide, also appeared this season. The expenses were kept within bounds, and the result was a clear profit of 18 or $20,000. The theatre closed on the 4th of July, and on the 7th Dinneford leased the Federal Street, and opened it as a summer house. J. M. Scott, Stone, Thayer, Miss McBride, Mrs. La Forest, were members of the company. El Hyder and other show pieces were brought out.

The season of 1830–1 commenced on the 6th of September. Richard Russell, formerly with Caldwell in New Orleans, was the manager; George H. Barrett, stage-manager; Mr. R. Jones, artist; Mr. J. Johnson, machinist. The company consisted of Messrs. Barrett, Finn, Andrews, Smith, Stone, Jones, Holden, Pearson, Johnson, Howard, Collingbourne, Scott, Adams, Leman, Stone, Russell, Master Russell, etc., etc., Mrs. Barrett, Mrs. Stone, Miss Eberle, Miss McBride, Mrs. Russell, Mrs. Smith, Mrs. Barnes, Mrs. Campbell, Miss Holden, and Miss Russell.

The opening performances were the "Soldier's Daughter," which introduced Mrs. Russell to a Boston audience as *Widow Cheerly*, Mr. Barrett reciting an opening address written by J. A Stone, Esq., of the theatre; and "Luke the Laborer" was performed.

Mr. Russell's intentions were good, and he intended to give the public attractive performances, but he did not meet with the support at first which he merited. To his credit be it recorded, he did accomplish a great deal towards the suppression of vice in and about the theatre. As an actor, he possessed considerable original and intrinsic merit, and his *Cosey* and *Sir Peter* were pronounced the best since Bernard.

The stars this season were Mrs. Sharpe, Miss George, Mad'lles Ravenot and Durissel, after an absence of two years:

> "—— mincing Ravenot sports tight pantalettes,
> And turns fop's head while turning pirouettes."

Hacket, who brought out "Rip Van Winkle," Forrest, Clara Fisher, Charles Kean, Madame Feron, Miss Kelly, Master Burke, Booth, Cooper, and Barton.

On the 17th of September, '30, was commemorated the great event of the first foundation of Boston, commenced by Gov. Winthrop two hundred years ago. It was a great holiday, in which all took part, the highest and the lowest. Speeches, songs, and feasts, were the order of the day. Dinners were given by different societies at the hotels. At the theatre, a prize address, written for the second centennial settlement of Boston, by Mrs. Sarah Josepha Hale, was spoken by Mrs. Russell, the manager's lady.

Charles Kean appeared for the first time as *Gloster*, in "Richard III.," on the 22d of November. He was at that time only twenty years of age. When he made his entrance on the stage, he was received with shouts of welcome; and, as if the people present were determined not to visit the sins of the father upon the child, they continued their applauses into three or four additional rounds, when the first had subsided. He appeared during this engagement as *Sir Giles Overreach*, *Hamlet*, *Shylock*, *Sir Edward Mortimer*, and *Reuben Glenroy*.

The celebrated Master Burke, announced as the "Irish Roscius," opened on Monday, January 31, as *Young Norval*, leading the orchestra between the plays. His engagement extended into March, and he appeared in the following characters: *Dr. Pangloss*, (to Mrs. W. H. Smith's *Cicely Homespun*,) *Whirligig Hall*, *Shylock*, *March of Intellect*, *Sir Abel Hardy*, *Richard III.*, *Terry O'Rourke*, *Dennis Bulgruddy*, *Hamlet*, (to Mrs. Barrett's *Ophelia*,) *Dr. Ollopod*, and *Romeo*, — a variety which indicates the versatility of his talents. His reception was *immense*. No other word can convey, to those who do not recollect the cordiality with which he was welcomed, any thing like an adequate idea. Balls and parties, sleigh rides and social gatherings, were dispensed with, the theatre was the centre of the fashionable and literary world of Boston, and the boxes were filled to their utmost capacity. A portion of the box tickets were sold at auction by Messrs. Coolidge & Haskell, and the second row was equally sought after with the first. The sum of $1344 was paid in premiums for the boxes for seven nights; and the amount of the advanced rates for nineteen nights was $2174.50, exclusive of the whole receipts, which did not fall far short of $20,000.

After Burke's engagement, the theatre was closed for nearly a month, Russell and a portion of the company visiting Salem and Providence with the great prodigy.

During the temporary close of the theatre, an amphitheatre in Flagg Alley, now Change Avenue, was opened for dramatic and equestrian performances, and was well patronized. It was in the rear of the Bite Tavern. Messrs. Vialle, Pallis, Williams, Miss Clarke,

Burns, Sands, Conway, appeared either in the ring, or on the stage. "Richard III." was got up, and Mr. and Mrs. Booth, the former only thirty-six inches in height and thirty-nine years of age, the latter thirty-two inches and twenty-five years of age, were trotted out to be admired by those who had run after prodigies; and as a more striking offset to Burke, "Master Baker" was produced, who did some parts with considerable cleverness.

It was this year that a grand birth-night ball, on the anniversary of Washington's birth day, was given at the old theatre by the Independent Corps of Cadets, Col. Baker, and it was considered (the De Joinville Ball and others not having come off) the most magnificent affair ever given in Boston. An entirely new flooring was laid over the stage and pit, and by partitioning off a portion, a *salon de danse* was formed one hundred feet in length, square at one extremity and semicircular at the other. The front of the lower boxes was covered with green drapery, the interior was lined with evergreens, and the rear was concealed by near two thousand stands of arms. The circular part was covered with an ornamented canopy resembling the cloth of a tent, from the centre of which was suspended an immense chandelier. The folds of the canopy wholly concealed the second range of boxes and all the house above it. The side scenes of the stage were removed as far back as possible, so as to admit the construction of an extensive oblong marquee richly decorated with sofas, pier tables, etc., and brilliantly illuminated. The theatrical effect of the house was thus entirely dissipated, and the whole of the visible interior was metamorphosed into two large marquees or pavillions opening into each other, which being surrounded with evergreen shrubbery mingled with stands of arms, produced the resemblance of an encampment prepared for a gala day, or such as the Soldan Saladin is represented to have made in honor of Richard, at the Diamond of the Desert. The floor of the saloon was tastefully painted by the bold and free pencil of Mr. Hubbard. The arms of the corps, its institution in 1741, the date of its organization, and its mottoes, were displayed with suitable blazonry in the marquee; and the national arms, the eagle surrounded by a circle of stars, was also blazoned under and around the central point of the pavillion. The general effect of the whole design, when the ball room became filled with beautiful and fashionable women and well-dressed men, was indescribably charming.

The Evening Gazette gave the following account:— "The company was estimated to consist of about six hundred individuals, of which perhaps the ladies were about three hundred and fifty. They were variously, elegantly, but most tastefully arrayed; and it was a theme of general remark that individual taste appeared to have been much consulted in the selection of their dresses and the display of their ornaments, rather than an appeal to a particular fashion, which, by creating an uniformity of appearance, has a mean effect in a dance.

"The Governor, whom the Cadets are attached as a body guard, was received with military music and conducted to a distinguished station at the farther extremity of the room; various other public characters were present.

"About half-past ten o'clock supper was announced; and part of the company were escorted to the saloon of the theatre, which is an elegant room, superbly decorated for the occasion with flowers, flags, and military emblems. Plates were laid for two hundred and twenty persons, and not more than that number could be accommodated at once; therefore the tables were replenished at different times in the course of the night. The viands were excellent, the confectionary display was rich and luxurious, and the wines were of such exquisite flavor as to gratify the most fastidious epicurian taste. The supper was furnished by Mr. Gallagher, keeper of the Exchange Coffee House, and was very creditable to his abilities as a caterer.

"Throughout the evening the managers were everywhere sedulous, attentive, and courteous to all their guests; and the members of the corps constantly distinguished for their uniform urbanity and politeness. The dancing room in the early part of the evening was much crowded, but as the departure of many of the elder guests, at an early hour, gave the dancing room to the juvenile portion of the company, their enjoyment appeared to rise into hilarity and delight.

"The repetition of suppers was continued through the whole night, as well as the dancing; and though the bulk of the company had departed by midnight, we believe the choice spirits remained, if not until the clock had given salutation to the morn, yet until the index of the watch admonished them that such a period would soon approach. We have seldom witnessed a scene of greater novelty, elegance, festivity, and social happiness than this Cadet Ball afforded on Washington's birthnight."

The above description, though it may not, strictly considered, form any part of a theatrical record, comes within our province as relating to the old theatre — the history of which we intended in the commencement to give from the day it first opened to its recent demolition. Other balls were subsequently held at the theatre, more or less brilliant.

The Tremont re-opened on the 4th of April. Mrs. Barrett took a benefit, and that favorite and oft repeated petit comedy of "Perfection" was played for the first time. "Zembuca" was got up, but did not prove attractive, and what the manager made by Burke was all dissipated ere the close of the season. The different benefits revived in a degree the falling fortunes of the house, but too frequently empty benches greeted the sight of the performers. Even Cooper, who appeared in May, and preserved his physical energies and performed with unabated vigor, found that the magic spell which he had so often thrown over the Boston public, was broken, and the manager hailed the closing day (June 20) with pleasure. He left the city a wiser and a poorer man. Among the benefits which proved most attractive was that of Mr. Finn's. His unique card on this occasion was as follows: —

PUBLIC ATTENTION

Is most respectfully solicited to Finn's Panoramic Pills, sold at the Tremont Theatre, wholesale and retail.

The celebrated Dr. Halstead has left the public a thumping legacy in his book on dyspepsia, but Doctor Logic would suggest that something more is *kneaded* to eradicate *lowness of spirits*, and eight years of successful practice have enabled him to test the remedy, and recommend it as the best *spring* medicine to free the system from *ill humor* — as from it, he has frequently experienced *great benefits;* and that he is no *quack*, will be seen from the moderate length of his *bill.* The following certificate is selected from many millions which may be inspected: —

"The subscriber had been for centuries afflicted with a total extinguishment of suspended animation, till, hearing of your never-to-be-too-highly-thought-of-panoramic-pills, I was induced to take a *box*, when I was near the last *stage*. I immediately discovered the *seat* of the complaint, and the *phiz*-ical effects were apparent, *prima facie*. The malady received a *check*, and in the course of a few hours I could sit up, stand upon my feet, and finally walk out without assistance. I think I am but doing justice to proclaim the many healing *acts* you have *performed;* and to recommend a numerous attendance on Wednesday evening, when I understand you intend administering a powerful dose of tincture of *Myrrth*, to be taken in *jam.*"

THE PUBLIC.

CHAPTER XX.

The Opening of the Tremont. — Appearance of Mr. Anderson. — The Anderson Troubles in New York and Boston. — "The Gladiator." — Mr. Sinclair. — The Opera. — Frederick S. Hill. — Miss Mary Duff. — The Social Condition of Actors — The Hermanns. — The Ravel Family. — Opening of the Federal Street. — First Performance of the "Hunchback." — Mrs. Barrymore. — Benefit of John Howard Payne. — The Kembles. — Expiration of Mr. Dana's Lease.

THE Tremont was opened on the 4th of July this year, when Mr. Holland appeared. Mr. Russell, having had quite enough of Boston, left it, and Mr. George H. Barrett was announced as the manager.

On the opening night, (August 29th, 1831,) "Wild Oats," and the "Highland Reel" were produced—both the comedy and the farce were by O'Keefe. There was very little alteration in the company from the preceding year. Mr. Kilner re-appeared. Charles Kean, Mr. and Mrs. Hackett, (formerly Miss Le Suggs,) Mrs. Hughes, J. Jones, Clara Fisher, Mr. and Mrs. Anderson, Forrest, Mons. Gouff, the Man Monkey, (who appeared at the old house one night, and then went to the Tremont,) Burke, J. J. Adams, tragedian, Pelby, Sinclair, F. S. Hill, Miss Mary Duff, Mrs. A. Drake, F. Brown, and Mr. E. C. Horn, were the most attractive.

The *prestige* of Clara Fisher's name departed this season, and Kean did only passably well. Burke attracted good houses, but he was not run after. His brother, Master W. Burke, performed a solo on the violin on the occasion of Burke's benefit.

Mr. Anderson and his lady, (formerly Miss Bartolozzi,) were announced to appear in "Guy Mannering" on the 3d of November:—*Henry Bertram*, Mr. Anderson; *Julia Mannering*, Mrs. Anderson; *Col. Mannering*, W. H. Smith, *Dominie Sampson*, Mr. Kilner; *Meg Merrilies*, Mrs. Hill.

Mr. Anderson had been the unfortunate cause of a theatrical row. On the passage to this country, he was indiscreet enough to utter certain disrespectful expressions in relation to Americans, the immediate consequence of which was trouble with the mate and passengers, and we believe that Jonathan and John came to blows, which resulted in the defeat of the latter. On the arrival of the vessel at New York, the mate and his friends took measures to form a party to prevent Mr. Anderson exercising his talents on the stage. Mr. Anderson, who was not without repute in his own country as a singer, had been engaged by Stephen Price to appear at the Park Theatre, and was accordingly announced in "Guy Mannering," on the 13th of October. Mr. A. was received on his entrance with hisses, shouts of "off!" "off!" etc., mingled with tokens of applause, which rendered it difficult to say whether the preponderance of the applause was for or against him. Mr. Thomas Barry, the stage-manager, endeavored to propitiate the audience, and obtain a hearing for the actor, but it was refused. After frequent fruitless attempts to obtain a truce, the play proceeded, mainly in dumb show. In the papers of the following day Mr. Anderson published the following:

TO THE PUBLIC.

Having been last evening denied an opportunity of addressing you, I am compelled to make an appeal through the public prints; a course I should have long since pursued, had I not felt unwilling, as a perfect stranger, to obtrude myself upon your notice, and thinking as I did that a personal explanation would be more appropriate and respectful. I am accused (as I have been informed) of speaking disrespectful of the American people. This I utterly disavow. On my passage to this country, I was unfortunate enough to have a disagreement with one of the passengers; but any observation that may have fallen from me on that occasion was altogether of a private nature, and alluded solely to the individual with whom the difficulty existed. I appeal to your good sense, whether it is likely, nay, whether it is not absolutely absurd, that I should have had the insane hardihood to make use of disrespectful expressions tending to prejudice me in the opinion of a public, upon whose patronage I was entirely dependent, and whose good will and approbation I was and am most anxious to receive? May I then trust, that on the next occasion I have the honor of appearing before you, you will not allow private consideration, or private pique, to weigh so heavily against me in my public capacity. I have only to add, that when under excitement, we are all liable to use (tho' I am not aware that I have) expressions, which in more deliberate moments we have occasion to deplore. If I have done any thing calculated to offend that pride of country in which I myself indulge as well as others, I deeply regret it; I would ask leave to make that apology which is unquestionably due on such an occasion.

J. R. Anderson.

The managers, deeming this card an ample apology, for any slight remarks which a foreigner might utter about America, announced Mr. Anderson for Saturday, the 15th Oct. The theatre was filled entirely with males, and it was made manifest long before the hour for the curtain to rise that there were two parties present, those in his favor and those opposed. The first act passed off without any disturbance, save an attempt made to hiss Thomas Barry, which was promptly quelled by the auditory, Mr. Barry making a brief speech. On the rising of the curtain at the second act, Mr. Simpson came forward, with a paper in his hand, which the audience rightly conjecturing to be the apology of Mr. Anderson, that we give above, refused to have it read. Mr. Simpson expressed the willingness of the management to abide by the decision of the public, and if it was the decided wish of the house that Mr. Anderson should be withdrawn, let it be distinctly manifested, and he pledged himself to comply. "Let him be withdrawn!" — "Send him home!" — "Yes, yes!" — were the replies which thundered from all parts of the house. Mr. Jones was immediately substituted, and the performances went on. The audience was a riotous one, but no attempt was made to injure property; and their wickedness was confined to throwing apples and oranges on to the stage. An immense multitude had assembled outside, who not only contrived to fight among themselves, but committed sundry disgraceful acts upon the theatre, by breaking the windows and lamps, alleging that the eagles which formerly adorned the latter had been removed by Mr. Price, who was hostile to American sentiment. This cause also led to the assembling of a crowd on the Sunday evening following, which broke a few panes of glass; but the removal of the eagles had been done by Mr. Simpson when the front of the house was repaired, during the previous season, unbeknown to Mr. Price. Mr. Anderson published statements and affidavits, which went to prove that the punishment was altogether unmerited; and several papers which had been opposed to Mr. A. pronounced him an injured man. Mr. Anderson, however, concluded not to contest the question before the bar of public opinion in New York, but accepted an engagement here, and, as we have stated, was announced to appear on the evening of November 3, '31.

The house was filled to overflowing. One or two ladies were in the boxes, but soon withdrew. Before the curtain went up, Mr. Barrett came forward, and stated that it was not the intention of the management to force Mr. Anderson upon the Boston public; that the statement he had published, which was substantiated by the oaths of himself and three others, had not been denied or questioned; and that the excitement in New York was unjustifiable. Mr. Barrett was warmly applauded, and the play proceeded. On Mr. Anderson's appearance he was received with the most uproarious applauses, which subsiding, a few who had the hardihood to oppose the overwhelming majority ventured a few faint hisses, which immediately produced a restoration of the applause, mingled with cries, — "Throw him over!" — "Put 'em out!" — "Out with the New Yorkers!" The house, after a lapse of some minutes, became orderly, and every thing passed on well until the third act was nearly through, when the crowd outside, instigated by a few New York Hotspurs, forced a way into the bars of the pit. The cry of fire was raised, and confusion prevailed. The musicians fled, and for a time the affair looked serious, rendered doubly so by the breaking of the windows and lamps in front, the newly laid Macadamised street furnishing ready materials for mischief. The actresses were so much alarmed that they left the theatre; and though after the intruders had been repulsed, and order restored, the audience called for the play to continue, the managers were obliged to pass to the farce, and no farther interruption was made. Several of the rioters were arrested and punished. Mr. Anderson published a card, thanking the public for their kindness, and completed his engagement successfully. He appeared as *Captain Malcolm* to Mrs. Anderson's *Stella Clifton*, in the "Slave, or Blessings of Freedom," *Tom Tug*, in the "Waterman," and gave a concert for the benefit of the poor, but the city government remitted the money to him.

On the 14th of November, Forrest brought out the "Gladiator," written for him by Dr. Bird, which was very successful. Mr. Pelby also produced "De Lara, or the Moorish Bride," written by Mrs. Caroline Lee Hentz, for Mr. Pelby. A very fine lithographic print by Pendleton is still extant of Mr. P. in this part. The "Water Witch," dramatized by Finn from Cooper's novel, had a good run.

Mr. Sinclair, father to Mrs. Sinclair, made his first appearance on the Boston boards February 6, as *Francis Osbaldiston*, in "Rob Roy," Mrs. Barrett as *Helen Mc Gregor.* He was pronounced, and undoubtedly was, the most accomplished male singer who then had appeared on the boards. After his engagement, he gave concerts with great success. On Monday, March 5th, "Cinderella" was produced the first time in this city, with the following cast: — *Felix*, Mr. Walton; *Pampolino*, Johnson; *Dandini*, Comer; *Alidon*, Collingborn; *Pedro*, G. H. Andrews; *Hunters*, Leman, Rice, etc.; *Cinderella*, Mrs. Austin; *Clorinda*, Miss Eberle; *Thisbe*, Mrs. W. H. Smith; *Fairy Queen*, Miss McBride. Music and choruses under the direction of Thomas Comer, Esq.; scenery by Mr. Jones, assisted by Sam. Stockwell.

As a spectacle, nothing equal to it had been witnessed in Boston. The orchestra, lead by Milon from Philadelphia, was full and effective, and the captivating Mrs. Austin sang with sweetness of tone and brilliancy of execution. It had a good run. Miss Hughes and Mr. Sinclair subsequently sustained the leading parts in this piece.

On the 22d of April, 1832, Mr. Frederick S. Hill, a Boston boy, opened in *Romeo*, Mrs. Barrett as *Juliet;* and subsequently performed *Charles Austencourt* in "Man and Wife," *Charles Surface* in "School for

Scandal," and *Henry Stanley* in "Paul Pry," in all of which he acquitted himself to the satisfaction of the public. Mr. Hill was for many years connected with the National Theatre, but subsequently retired from the profession, devoting his attention to literature, in which as a critic and essayist he possessed peculiar powers. He appeared once of late years at the Howard Athenæum, a few months prior to his death, which occurred in 1851.

Mr. Forrest and Mrs. Duff played an engagement, and in May 12, Miss Mary Duff, daughter of Mrs. Duff, appeared as *Helen Worrit,* a part in which she made her debut in Philadelphia, in the preceding year, where she also played *Cora* to Forrest's *Rolla.* In light, genteel comedy, she was quite good, and her mother's friends rallied around her and gave her handsome encouragement. This actresses' theatrical career was quite a remarkable one. She was married in the year 1835 to Augustus A. Addams, a young actor of merit, and Judge Conrad wrote the play of "Jack Cade" for him. He was a son of John S. Addams of Worcester county, Mass. The union between Miss Duff and Addams was any thing but a happy one, both being guilty of indiscretions, which finally led to a separation. Mrs. Addams then contracted an intimacy with Mr. Joseph Gilbert, and a second time Mrs. Addams dissolved the connection, and continued to play at the various southern and western theatres, till 1st of August, 1852, when she died at Memphis, Tenn. Addams died in Cincinnati, 1850.

We are happy to record that the profession in America, so far as the respectability of its members in private life is concerned, never stood higher; and the following, from the Westminster Review for January, 1853, is equally applicable both sides of the water.

We believe, says the Review, there never was a period when actors, as a class, were more thoroughly respectable. Provident views, and a passion for accumulation, have expelled the erratic and thriftless vice of by-gone generations. The old tavern propensities are gone out; the reckless dissipative and proverbial excesses have disappeared. * * * * The sins of the stage become notorious—its virtues are seldom heard of, and people are apt to conclude that it possesses none. A man may go through life strictly discharging all his moral and social responsibilities, without exciting the slightest notice; let him violate any of them, and his name is scandalized abroad at once. The same thing happens in reference to the stage. We are familiar, in a thousand exaggerated shapes, with its errors and lapses; but nobody ever tells us any thing about its quiet charities, its home fidelities, its heroic triumphs over those special and most dangerous opportunities and temptations by which it is beset. The evil that is done is always known; but "we know not what's resisted!" If we could trace these things to their source, we should discover that the stage is vitiated by contact with the great world, more than by any original taint in its own blood. The disgraces that have grown up in the theatre have been chiefly inflicted by the patronage of persons in power, who have introduced into the profession the individuals who have carried their shame into the green room. The theatre cannot escape the influence that forces these vicious grafts upon it. Men of fashion like to see their mistresses on the stage, and will make any sacrifice to get them there. It flatters their vanity, and procures them a sort of *eclat* they exult in. But the profession itself is not fairly chargeable with the discredit such circumstances have attached to it. Those who have been born and bred in it are not the persons who have degraded its reputation; and, with a reasonable allowance for their position, there is no class in the community more remarkable, for constancy and devotion in their domestic relations.

"Aladdin" was brought out this season at the Tremont. *Aladdin,* Mrs. Barrett; *Kassrac,* W. H. Smith. The latter part of the season was somewhat affected by the visit of the Hermanns, who gave their musical soireés at the Masonic Temple, and by the new amphitheatre at the North End, which was the commencement of the National Theatre. The season closed July 9th.

The season of 1832–3, commenced on the 27th of August, George H. Barrett as acting manager. The company included Messrs. Finn, Smith, Comer, and other favorites. The opening play was Goldsmith's comedy of "She Stoops to Conquer" with a fancy dance by Misses Eberle and McBride, followed by "My Master's Rival," a laughable farce. The stage was for the *first time lit with gas.*

The stars this season were Hackett, Miss Vincent, Wallack, (after an absence of three years,) Miss Hughes, C. E. Horn, Forrest, Charles Kean, Booth, Sinclair, Kembles, father and daughter, C. H. Eaton, and others of less note.

The season was not without incident worthy of note. Mr. Woodhull, a good melo-dramatic actor, and Miss Courtney, a fine looking woman, correct in her reading, graceful, lively and dashing, made their appearance.

Miss Vincent, quite a young actress, was exceedingly popular in such parts as *Letitia Hardy*, *Bertha*, *Clara*, *Miss Hardcastle*, *Kate O'Brien*, etc. She possessed a slight but beautiful figure, a face beaming with intelligence, and a most musical voice, which, without any great degree of cultivation, enabled her to execute the incidental songs in the pieces with good effect. The admirers of this lady were chiefly of the younger portion of the community. Mr. Wallack, during his engagement, brought out "The Brigand," in the second act of which he sang "Love's Ritonella," which was the air of the times. This engagement was successful. Mr. Forrest ran through his usual range of pieces, and brought out "Uralloosa, or the Son of the Incas," written by Dr. Bird.

On the 16th of November, that unequalled troupe of pantomimists, the *Ravel Family*, made their first appearance in Boston. The family then consisted of ten persons, and they attained at once that popularity which has continued until the present time. The "Carnival of Venice" and other pieces, drew crowds to the old Tremont.

On the 12th of November, the Federal Street Theatre was opened by the managers of the Tremont, and continued open for several weeks. Forrest appeared at the old house one night, and the Ravels the night following, and by thus appearing alternately the attraction was kept up. Charles Kean also appeared at the old theatre, supported by Hamblin and Miss Vincent, and then went to the Tremont. The object of keeping open both houses was to effect, if possible, the success of the little Warren Theatre. The box tickets at the Tremont were $1.00; at the Frederal Street, fifty cents; and purchasers of box tickets at the Tremont, had the privilege of entering the old house the same evening, without additional charge. On the 21st of November, J. Sheridan Knowles' popular play of the "Hunchback" was produced for the first time, at the Tremont Theatre; the play had been brought out on the evening previous, (20th inst.,) at the Warren, for the first time in Boston. At the Tremont, the cast was as follows:—*Master Walter*, Chas. Kean; *Sir Thos. Clifford*, Hamblin; *Modus*, George Barrett; *Lord Tinsel*, W. H. Smith; *Julia*, Miss Vincent; *Helen*, Mrs. Barrett. With such support it could not have failed of success. The fine display of talent witnessed in the concentrated efforts of Kean, Hamblin, and Miss Vincent, filled the house nightly, and the legitimate drama well presented, drew — as it invariably will — the fashion and talent of the city.

Mrs. Barrymore appeared at the Tremont, on the 17th of December. She had been playing at the Warren. This lady was among the first who introduced to the Boston stage a style of dancing attractive from grace alone, and entirely distinct from that school, the most important feature of which appears to consist in the zephyr-like drapery, and the immodest quantity worn at that. Mrs. Barrymore appeared as the *Wife and Widow* in the "Soldier's Wife and Soldier's Widow," and during the season, made a great hit as

Fenella, in the opera of "Masaniello," which was put on the stage in the most perfect manner, the vocalists consisting of Mr. Sinclair, Miss Hughes, Mrs. Austin, etc., and the chorus led by Mr. Oliver. "Artaxerxes," the "Tempest," "Guy Mannering," "Fra Diavolo" and "John of Paris," were also produced, and drew well.

On the 22d of February, Mr. Smith recited a poem, written by Mr. Stephen Bates, on the anniversary of Washington's birth-day.

In the month of April, 1833, a benefit was given by the citizens of Boston to John Howard Payne. This gentleman, after an absence of nearly twenty years, which had been passed in England and France, returned to the city of his early triumphs. Many kind friends resolved to imitate the example set in New York, and give Mr. Payne a benefit; for like many others, he returned from England and France not much enriched by his long sojourn abroad. A preparatory meeting was held at the Tremont House, and a committee of gentlemen appointed to carry out the object. The evening of the 3d of April was selected for this testimonial at the Tremont, and the pieces consisted entirely of selections from the various plays of Mr. Payne as follows—"Life in Humble Life," "Theresa," "The Lances," and "Charles II." Although the selection of the pieces was a graceful compliment to the beneficiary, and very appropriate to the occasion, it proved unfortunate, as they had been acted here a hundred times. The night selected was also unpropitious, preceding, as it did, the general Fast, when many families in this city unite in social gatherings. These and other causes rendered the attempt—so far as pecuniary reward was intended — a partial failure, but the *character* of the audience gave proof of the estimation in which Mr. Payne was held both as a man and an author. During the evening, Mrs. Barrett recited the following address, written for the occasion by Park Benjamin, Esq.: —

ADDRESS.

Could some enchantress, by her magic spell,
Fair as Love's Goddess from her ocean-shell,
Chase the dim vapors that conceal the past
And o'er Time's sea a tender radiance cast;
What various scenes, to gladden and surprise,
Would to your view, in bright succession, rise!
Alas! our age has unromantic grown,
And fancy is the sole enchantress known.
Invoke her aid, and from her starry bower,
She may descend to gild the passing hour.
Through the long vista of departed years,
What vision first, in Fancy light, appears?
See yonder group of happy playmates stand
Round one who seems the leader of the band!
His cheek is blushing with the rose's bloom,
Why o'er his forehead waves a crimson plume?
His form, for Cupid's, might well be adored,
Why is it girded with the glittering sword?
He speaks — the group disperse — now formed once more,
Behold on air a silken banner soar,
In seried ranks, with measured steps, they come.
Hark! the shrill fife and spirit-stirring drum.
What field is this? Who leads this gallant train?
'Tis Boston Common — Captain Howard Payne.
The scene is changed — lo! in the still midnight,
A lonely student, by his lamp's faint light.
Pale in his cheek — his eye all dim with tears;
Can such deep grief belong to childhood's years?
A son, his tribute affection pays —
To her whose smile had blest Life's early days.
Can this frail student be the radiant boy
Whose heart so late was redolent of joy?

Ah, yes! immured in Learning's cloistered shade,
Like a caged eagle's, does his spirit fade.
Once more a change of scene — and such a change!
A stage — a theatre — how brightly strange!
A simple lad, in cap and tartan dress,
Yet proud his bearing and suberb his crest —
"My name is Norval." Norval! can it be?
Transformed so quickly! that sweet voice — 'tis he!
That smile — lip half curled in high disdain,
That graceful form — nine cheers for Master Payne!
Let blushing honors gather round his fame —
This "happy deed shall gild his humble name;"
For the wide stage his youthful footsteps press,
To shield a much-loved father from distress;
And, greeted thus by richly-earned applause,
"Who shall resist him in a parent's cause?"
Loud were the praises that his welcome gave,
In that far land beyond th' Atlantic wave.
There, like a halo, on his young brow fell
The laurel-garland he has worn so well!
Another change — within so brief a span,
Has this fair boy become a serious man?
'Tis true — but sacred in his bosom glows
Are like that which burns mid Alpine snows.
Though tempests shatter the volcano's throne,
Though Winter belt him with an icy Zone,
Still do the splendors of his lofty head
On regions round a sunlike lustre shed.
So Genius, left to poverty and woe,
Whose rending thoughts the world can never know,
In its lone majesty, all coldly shrined,
Throws its broad gleam along the realms of mind.
A change of scene — the nearest and the last,
We need no spirit to reveal the past;
For, lo! 'tis present and before you now,
The warrior-child, with sword and plumed brow;
The student, bending o'er the written page;
The actor, proudly marching on the stage;
The author, bringing forms to life and light,
Which here reflected you may see to-night —
At length has come — Heaven grant no more to roam —
To his own native land, his "home, sweet home!"

At the close of the address, the orchestra struck up "Home, sweet Home," after which there arose a loud and general call for Mr. Payne, which was prolonged till the beneficiary made his appearance. He was, at first, greatly agitated, but soon recovering himself made a very appropriate address.

Mr. Payne's benefit was somewhat injured from the fact that the Kembles, who at first refused to visit Boston, on account of the management declining to accede to terms, which were equivalent to giving them the whole receipts and paying their expenses besides, were shortly announced to appear. On the 15th of April, Charles Kemble opened in "Hamlet;" *Laertes,* Smith; *Horatio,* Williamson; *Ophelia,* Mrs. Barrett; and on Tuesday, April 16, 1833, the celebrated Miss Fanny Kemble made her first appearance before a Boston audience in Rev. H. H. Milman's play of "Fazio, or the Italian Wife." *Fazio,* Kemble; *Bartolo,* Johnson; *Philario,* Williamson; BIANCA, Miss Kemble. During their engagement, they appeared together in the "Stranger," "School for Scandal," "Romeo and Juliet," "Provoked Husband," "Gamester," etc., creating an excitement in the dramatic world of Boston and vicinity. The tickets were sold at auction by Messrs. Coolidge & Haskell, and crowded houses, composed of the beauty and wealth of the city, assembled to honor Miss Kemble and her father.

During this engagement, C. H. Eaton played *Master Walter,* in the "Hunchback," with the Kembles, eliciting the greatest applause, for his masterly impersonation of a part upon which depends the success of the play.

The Federal Street was again opened on the 3d of June, by Barrett, when the "Cataract of the Ganges" was the principal attraction. Master Burke appeared at the Federal Street and then went to the Tremont, but his engagement was not very successful — the visit of General Jackson to this city monopolizing the attention of the public.

On the 8th of July, Mr. and Mrs. Barrett took a farewell benefit, the last night of the season. Mr. Barrett was called out, and bid his Boston friends farewell, stating that circumstances beyond his control compelled him to part from the Boston public.

With Mr. Barrett's engagement terminated the lease of three years, taken by Francis W. Dana. The terms of this lease were that the corporation should rent the bars for themselves, and that Mr. Dana should pay for the rent of the rest of the building a certain per centage on the receipts. The result was that by his arrangement with Russell and Barrett, Dana paid on an average a rent of about $2,200 a year, while the bars produced about $2,500, and the corporation derived in the aggregate from both sources a rent of something short of $5,000 a year. Mr. Dana refused to renew his lease upon any terms except part profits, or some other contingent contract depending upon receipts, which the directors declined. On his retirement from the lesseeship, Mr. Dana gave a dinner at Nahant to the leading actors and other gentlemen connected with the theatre. Mr. Dana was a shrewd business man. He was highly respected in the community, and at his death, which occurred in August, 1835, the public mourned the loss of an enterprising man.

CHAPTER XXI.

Biographical Sketch of Charles H. Eaton. — The Season of 1833–4. — Thomas Barry, Esq. — His First Season in Boston. — Tyrone Power. — The Visit of the Woods to Boston. — Dana *v.* Kemble. — Recollections and Reminiscences of the Woods, etc., etc.

To a majority of our readers, at all conversant with theatricals, the name of Charles H. Eaton will arouse melancholy yet pleasing memories. He was born in Poplar Street, Boston, June 10th, 1813, and died at the Exchange Hotel, Pittsburgh, June 4th, 1843, aged nearly 30 years. His father, though obliged to contend with adverse fortunes in his declining years, was an opulent merchant in the meridian of life; his son, Charles, therefore, received an excellent English education. After several years' tuition at the Fort Hill School, he was admitted to the English High School, where his academic course was completed; at one period he was a pupil of the Latin School, (then on School Street,) where he pursued the preparatory studies requisite for admission to college. The decided bent of Mr. Eaton's mind for the stage, early manifested itself. While a mere lad, he joined a private theatrical society, called the "*Siddonians.*" Never was there a more earnest and assiduous devotee of Thespis, than this youthful aspirant for Siddonian honors. The crude tyros who became constant patrons of the society, prided themselves upon appreciating and fostering native talent; C. H. Eaton, being greatly superior to his fellow amateurs, very assiduous and verbally accurate in all his parts, stood confessed to their admiring gaze, a "*star of the first magnitude!*" His first public appearance in the profession, to which he was eminently adapted, was in the winter of 1833, at the Warren Theatre; on this occasion, he played "*The Stranger*," in Kotzebue's tragedy of that name, for the *Benefit of Mr. Reuben Meer.* It was a most triumphant debut, as many of our readers well remember. Eaton's masterly delineations of character, immediately succeeding this his first professional effort, convinced all who were competent to judge, that his mind had the impress of genius. No actor of our day ever excited such universal interest as a debutant. A series of able personations of most arduous characters won for the youthful histrion, "golden opinions from all sorts of" journals. His second appearance was at the Tremont Theatre as *Richard III.*, a few months after his debut; it was a most effective and startling performance; the unexpected display of such excellence riveted the attention of his auditory. On the following morning, nearly every paper in Boston, that ever contained theatrical notices, lavished the highest encomiums upon the performance. Attached to the Commercial Gazette at the time was the most approved dramatic critic of Boston. His criticisms were received with implicit faith as oracular, "*ex cathedra*" announcements. He observed substantially of Mr. E.'s delineation of the Duke of Gloster, that he attended the theatre with the expectation of witnessing a laughable burlesque; he had anticipated that this new aspirant for Roscian immortality would follow in the footsteps of his illustrious predecessor, and his rash attempt prove a miserable abortion;

his astonishment was consequently great, upon witnessing, instead of the predicted caricature, a most masterly piece of acting. "In the last scene," said Mr. T., "Mr. Eaton (whom but for his '*big, manly voice*,' I should have called *Master* Eaton) seemed a very *fiend incarnate;* his look and mien constituted a thrilling picture of intensest rage." The next performance in order of time, was *Damon* on the same week. The house was crowded. At the close of the play, George Barrett, Esq., grasping his hand, exclaimed, "You young dog! how can you play so well? It is wonderful!" At the termination of this engagement, at the instance of his friends, Mr. E. retired to Burlington, (a small town near Boston,) to cultivate and improve his great natural powers. With treatises on elocution, an able work on gesticulation and posturing, (illustrated by plates,) and other requisites for the object in view, he there devoted several months with untiring industry to improvement in the vocation of his choice. Mr. Eaton paid great attention to his voice, acquiring a very great variety of intonation. The following fall, he returned to his native city. The Kembles were about appearing there for the first time. John O. Sargent, then assistant editor of the Atlas, and recently one of the editors of the Washington Republic, suggested that it would be a fine opportunity for him to give the *elite* of Boston a "*taste of his quality*." A large number of our citizens, prominent for talent, wealth, and station, had become Eaton's personal friends. A written request that he might appear with the renowned foreign artists, numerously signed, was sent to the management of the Tremont Theatre. The late Dr. Ingalls headed the list, and the signature of the lamented Lynde M. Walter followed. The wishes of so many gentlemen, eminent and influential, were readily complied with. Mr. Eaton enacted, as we have noted above, *Master Walter* to Miss Fanny Kemble's *Julia;* the house was crowded from floor to ceiling, but the young Bostonian, nothing abashed, armed with the confidence of true ability, proved himself fully equal to his task. He was received with deafening plaudits, and throughout the evening divided the applause with that lady, who had come among us an *adorable divinity*, with all the halo of her transatlantic triumphs. The play was repeated with the same cast and the same success. During the evening, Mr. Charles Kemble complimented Eaton highly, remarking that he was a fine reader, with a voice more powerful and melodious than any actor's within the scope of his experience. We well remember the attractive personal appearance of C. H. Eaton at this period. He was a decidedly handsome man; his head and face being strikingly intellectual. The features were what is understood as classical; a long, straight, Grecian nose, facial oval contour, chin rather long and rounded, a mouth made beautiful by a finely curved upper lip, combined with a clear, light, healthy complexion, will convey some idea of his pleasing exterior; his dark hazel eyes were full, large, and expressive, while a profusion of dark auburn hair, slightly curling, adorned his manly brow. Charles H. Eaton was not a large man, being but five feet six and a half inches in height; but he was very far from diminutive; his full, ample chest, the stately carriage of his head, and the great muscular development of his well-rounded limbs, made him seem above the medium size, though not "*ex pede Herculem*," in grace and dignity of mien he moved an Apollo. In 1835 he made his first theatrical tour. At his farewell benefit, he played *Brutus* in the "Fall of Tarquin." The Tremont was thronged. He was immediately engaged to play in Philadelphia, at the Arch Street Theatre. This was in October. After personating most successfully his principal characters, at the expiration of three weeks he went to Baltimore. While in Philadelphia, James Gordon Bennett, then a democratic editor, became his warm personal friend. In the "*monumental city*," he played a fortnight at the Holiday, and at the Front Street the same length of time. The most prominent parts were *Richard*, *Othello*, *Iago*, *Pescara*, *Damon*, *Brutus*, *Shylock*, *Sir Giles Overreach*, *Sir Edward Mortimer*, etc. The whole winter of '36 and a part of the ensuing spring were spent in Washington, where he had once more an opportunity to play with the Kembles and other *celebrities*. He here contracted a personal intimacy with some of the legislative magnates of our land. Some of the southern representatives who had not hitherto heard him, exclaimed, upon witnessing his *Master Walter*, with constitutional ardor, "Whom have we here? A resurrection of the elder Kean! A second Kean is among us!" etc. Upon his return to Boston the following autumn, the reception that awaited him was most enthusiastic. Mr. Pelby engaged him at the National. Every ticket was sold for several successive nights. This engagement was a most lucrative one for both manager and actor. Shortly after its termination, Mr. Eaton went to Bangor, where his success was unprecedentedly brilliant. That city was still enjoying the ephemeral prosperity consequent upon the eastern land speculations. He played to a full house each night, and on his benefit night more than a hundred paid for the privilege of being "*lobby members*." His two engagements here, and the one in Boston immediately preceding, yielded him several thousand dollars. About a month subsequent to this, Mr. E. effected another engagement at the National, for the purpose of playing the part of *Bernardo del Carpio*, in a tragedy of that name, written for him by Henry F. Harrington, Esq. Uncommon pains were taken to have it produced in a proper and effective manner; new and costly dresses were made for all the leading characters, and W. H. Smith, than whom no man living is more competent to the task, exerted himself strenuously to afford it a fair field. The author, Mr. Harrington, is a forcible writer, a man of decided talent, especially that peculiar talent essential to the success of a playwright. Unhappily, the author, who had within him the innate *materiel* of a first rate dramatist, did not, on this occasion, avoid the rock upon which novitiates of every description are so liable to founder. He attempted too much with his hero, and in reaching too high he *over*-reached, unobservant of the modesty and probabilities of nature. The part of *Bernardo* is a continuous, ever-increasing tornado of all the passions; — love, grief, hatred, despair, revenge, till piled-up horrors — Pelion upon Ossa — cap the stormy climax! An effective impersonation of *Bernardo* would require the strength of Alcides, and the Bull of Bashan's lungs! Mr. Eaton evinced his immense physical power by playing it five successive nights with unflagging energy. At this period he was in the prime of vigorous manhood, industrious and ambitious. The succeeding four or five years were passed by Mr. E. at the south-west, where he enjoyed great popularity, personal and professional. Upon his return to Boston in 1842, he played two engagements, evincing that refinement and chaste finish resulting from *experience* and *mind.* His last appearance in Boston was in the fall of 1842, at the Tremont Theatre, where he personated *Richard III.* to a house filled with his friends and admirers, who, alas! little thought that their eyes rested for the last time on him whom every one loved, and of whose genius all were proud; but such was the stern fiat of inexorable fate! At Pittsburgh he commenced an engagement, on the second night of which he played *William Tell* to a house filled to its utmost capacity. Being exhausted by the evening's exertions, he went to his hotel about eleven o'clock, and retired to his chamber. While an attendant was unlocking his door, he reclined upon the balustrade fronting it; while in that position he was seized with a dizziness, consequent upon a rush of blood to the head, a complaint to which he was subject. This sudden vertigo caused him to reel backwards; and the staircase being spiral, or what is termed a "*well*" stairway, he was precipitated the distance of *forty or fifty feet* to the *marble flags below!* It was found that his skull and one arm were fractured. Every possible attention was paid to him by the warm-hearted citizens, but he failed gradually, despite the best medical attendance, and died on June 4th, 1843, after five days of intense suffering. Soon after the untimely decease of the lamented tragedian, a committee was chosen by the citizens of Pittsburgh to collect funds for the erection of a monument to his memory. We have understood, and it is very painful to believe, that certain members of that committee were false to the sacred trust reposed in them. Before closing the compendium of C. H. Eaton's professional life, we wish to allude cursorily to his *style* of acting. It was peculiar,— strictly "*sui generis.*" With all the physical essentials of face, form, voice, and natural grace, he was enabled, thus richly endowed, to convey fully and forcibly his minutely accurate and scholarly conceptions. His performances all bore an intellectual impress. As a reader of Shakspeare, he was unsurpassed.

Mr. Dana, having refused to renew his lease, as we have stated, the directors were anxious to procure a manager, at once competent and able to take charge of the establishment. There were several applicants, but none who possessed the requisite talent. The name of Thos. Barry, then stage-manager at the Park Theatre, was suggested, and he was offered the house; and on his acceptation of it, there was universal regret in New York, universal rejoicing in Boston. "It will not be easy," said a New York editor at the time, "to make up the loss of Mr. Barry to our audience. He is the best stage-manager in America, and his gentlemanly deportment and estimable character have acquired for him universal respect here, and he carries with him the best wishes of a large number of warmly attached friends." Nearly twenty years have passed since this was written, and though Mr. Barry has experienced the vicissitudes of this life, and has passed through scenes calculated to render a man of less nerve and philosophy somewhat irritable, the same mildness of demeanor, the same frankness of manner, wins to him all with whom he comes in contact, and still entitles him to "universal respect." This remark does not apply merely to his friends in the outer world, but to members of his own profession, who respect him as one who is an ornament to it, and never disgraced his calling by any act which bore the slightest shade of meanness.

Mr. Barry's first move was to put the theatre in complete repair, which it greatly needed. This he did at an expense of $5,000, which came out of his own pocket. The interior was repainted, new drapery provided, and gas introduced into the body of the house, much to the satisfaction of the ladies, many of whom could trace a ruined dress to a visit to the theatre, owing to the dripping of the oil from the lamps. He secured the services of Messrs. Finn, Andrews, Smith, Johnson, Comer, Williamson, Colinbourne, Leman, etc., etc., Mrs. Hughes, Mrs. Smith, Miss McBride, Mrs. Barnes, Mrs. Campbell, Mrs. Holden, with Messrs. Forbes, Blake, Barry, Whiting, Miss Duff, Miss A. Fisher, and Mrs. Blake combined, made a strong stock company. Mr. Barrymore was director of spectacles, Mr. Comer musical director, and Mr. Ostinelli leader of the orchestra. The season commenced on the 2d of September with the "Honeymoon," in which Mr. Barry played *Duke Aranza*, and Miss Duff *Juliana*, followed by the farce of "Turn Out." Receipts, $482.75. The stars this season were Mr. Kemble, Fanny Kemble, Tyrone Power, Ravel Family, C. H. Eaton, Forrest, Hacket, Mr. and Mrs. Wood, Mr. Drake, etc.

On the 4th of September, Mr. Kemble and Fanny Kemble commenced an engagement and performed eighteen nights; the total receipts, with premiums, amounted to $11,671.75. The most productive night was that of "Isabella," and the "Chimney Piece." It was at this time that the case of Dana *v.* Kemble commenced. The facts in the case were briefly these. Mr. Dana was lessee of the Tremont Theatre, when Mr. Kemble and his daughter came to the United States and commenced playing at New York. After a vexatious and protracted negotiation, Mr. D. concluded, through Mr. George Barrett, then manager of the Tremont, an engagement with Mr. Kemble for the service of himself and daughter, on the terms demanded by him, and which were the same as those under which he played at the Park, and which he (Mr. K.) said, at the time of the negotiation, were "*one half the houses,*" that is to say, one half of the gross receipts during his engagement. Under this representation of Mr. Kemble, the engagement was concluded. He and his daughter came to Boston, played a number of nights, were paid, as per contract, and departed again to the South. Mr. Dana, as we have stated, relinquished the theatre, and Mr. Barry became lessee. Mr. Dana was in the habit of visiting the box-office, being on friendly terms with Mr. Barry, and happened in one day at the conclusion of the Kembles' engagement. Mr. Barry appeared to be troubled, and Mr. Dana asked the cause. "Why," said Barry, "the referees in the matter of premiums cannot agree." "What is the case?" inquired Mr. Dana. Mr. Barry then briefly explained, that he had sent to Mr. Kemble a check for the balance due on their engagement, and that Mr. Kemble refused to receive it, alleging that he should have a share of the premiums. The matter was left out. This led to some farther conversation, when Mr. Barry, alluding to the Kembles' engagement in New York, stated that their terms at the Park, where he was then stage-manager, instead of being a clear half of the house, as stated by Kemble, were, half after deducting £50 ($222.22) per night. Mr. Dana had based his engagement with the Kembles upon the ground that they had received a *clear* half; and having heard the story of the refusal of the money from Barry, walked quietly down to his lawyer, and Mr. Barry was shortly served with a trustee process, and Mr. Dana commenced a suit to recover that which had been paid, through the misrepresentation of Mr. Kemble. The case was finally decided in the Supreme Judicial Court in February, 1835, when the jury, having heard the evidence, awarded Mr. Dana all his demand, with interest, amounting to $2,560. W. H. Gardiner for the plaintiff, and S. D. Parker for the defendant.

Tyrone Power, known in the theatrical world as "Paddy Power," whose name is never mentioned without bringing to the mind his sad fate on board of the steamship President, made his first appearance in this city on the 30th of September, '33, as *Sir Patrick O'Plenipo*, in the "Irish Ambassador," and *McShane*, in the "Nervous Man." As a delineator of the genteel Irishman, Power was without a rival, and his equal is not now on the boards. Power has undoubtedly been surpassed in some pieces, those of a lower order, where the rough Irishman is portrayed, but never where the genuine humor of the part required a delicacy of coloring, and an almost intuitive conception, has he been equalled. He was among the first to render tolerable this class of plays; and though we have since had Collins, Williams, Greene, Brougham, all good, the true Paddy after all was Power.

The great ovation of the season was the appearance of Mr. and Mrs. Wood, (formerly Miss Paton,) who created as great an excitement almost as the more recent arrival of Jenny Lind.

The Woods made their first appearance in Boston on the 4th of December, 1833, in Rossini's opera "Cinderella," or rather the English version of it, which differs materially from "Cenerentola." Very great expectations had been excited in reference to Mrs. Wood, and the highest perfection any one dared to imagine was attained in her performance. Endowed with a voice of extraordinary compass, excellent quality and great power, she brought to the execution of her music remarkable cultivation and scientific attainment, with that command of feeling and expression which touches and moves the mass. Her articulation was distinct, and her execution, however rapid, always clear. The nicest gradations of light and shade had a lovely example in her treatment of the music, and from "Once a king" to "Now with grief," she held the audience spellbound with the enchantment of her voice and its astonishing capability. The silvery tones of that wonderful voice had full display in the duet, "Whence this soft and pleasing flame," the entire consent and blending of her softest zephyr-like tones, with the mellow voice of Mr. Wood, having a magical effect. In the *finale*, her wondrous execution and sweep of voice, absolutely electrified the audience, united as this traversing of the scale was, to power and richness, never before observed in a *soprano* of such agility and flexibility. Mr. Wood agreeably surprised, nay even astonished his public by the grace and fluency of his execution, the sweet mellow and full tones of a voice ranging from the upper bass to high tenor, and the manly elegance of his person. From the opening air "Morning its sweets is flinging" to his introduced solo in the ball scene, all bespoke him such a tenor as Boston had never looked upon before. The recollection of his exceeding grace and beauty in the softer passages, and the thrilling force and passion of "Can I my love resign," will never be effaced from the grateful remembrance of those who heard Mr. Wood in "Cinderella." With all the power and rich tone of the best Italian singer who has since visited this city, he also possessed a facility and exquisite grace in the *piano* and *pianissimo* none of them have united in the same person. In a word he brought to his execution of music the rich and glowing strength of Bettini, and the soft delicate beauty of Salvi, with the flexibility and truth of Perelli. The subordinate characters were admirably presented at this time, Comer being the Dandini, Johnson the Baron, and the envious sisters were done to the life by Mrs. Blake and Mrs. Smith.

After this opera, came "Guy Mannering," "The Barber of Seville," "Love in a Village," "The Waterman," "Der Freischutz," "The Devil's Bridge," "The Quaker," "Massaniello," "The Marriage of Figaro," "Clara and the Slave," in all of which the Woods sustained that enthusiasm and unequivocal public favor their first appearance had produced. In all this wide range of music they were found to be accomplished to a degree unimagined in any experience at that period. Every style they attempted brought them new triumphs, and their concert performances increased the list until new record of pieces executed became synonymous with perfect success. Nothing like their duets has ever been heard in this city since, excepting perhaps the occasional hit of Madame Bishop, and Reeves in Linda, and the exquisite blending of voice by Tedesco and Perelli. With the Woods, however, this fusion and blending of voice and soul in song, was the rule and constant practice. After playing in opera about one month they left for the South. In October, and December, 1835, they had two engagements here, when. "The Maid of Judah," "Fra Diavolo," "Robert the Devil," and "La Sonnambula," were brought out. In the two former Mr. Wood made a great sensation, by his singing of "When the Trump of Fame," "Young Agnes," and "Proudly and Wide," and lead of the chorus in "Under the Shady Greenwood Tree." In both the characters of *Ivanhoe* and the *Brigand*, he looked as admirably as he sang. Pending the production of "Robert the Devil," Mrs. Wood chanced to be indisposed, and Mr. W. chose to be offended by a notice of it in the Post. He wrote the editor a peppery note which received a severe reply, and Mr. Barry, the manager, in a pet, stopped his paper, advertisements, etc. The Post gave the opera a hard run for this, and followed Mr. Barry with slaps. When "La Sonnambula" appeared, however, all came round again; the public and the Post were alike delighted, and both the Woods recovered their former popularity. The opera took Boston literally by storm, and the superb acting of Mrs. Wood, in close of act second, with her brilliant, electrifying rush over their senses in "Ah, don't mingle," made her again the popular idol. Wood's presentment of "Still so gently," has seldom been surpassed even by Italian singers of the highest grade, and in the concerted pieces, the Woods moved in perfect harmony. Madame Otto did good service in "Lisa," and Mr. Brough made his only hit in the *Count.* "La Sonnambula" had a great run, that opera and "Cinderella" being the prime favorites of Boston in those days.

Mrs. Wood made *Amina* difficult for all her successors, both her acting and singing in that character satisfying the most fastidious. She made the *rondo finale* to carry a vast amount of most brilliant execution, and tasked her invention for new difficulties and truly wonderful vocal feats.

In March, 1836, another engagement was played at the Tremont, with a farewell benefit, on the 17th, in "La Sonnambula."

Some years afterwards the Woods revisited Boston, when it was found that his voice had gained in volume and certainty during the interval, and hers, on the contrary, had fallen off in both particulars. Their popularity had been affected by absence, the intervention of many other wonders, and his quarrels with the press. Musicians generally and singers especially are by nature and the force of habit, very sensitive, and the Woods should not suffer in public estimation for this foible beyond their due proportion of popular indignation. A reference to our list of operas, in which they were distinguished, is sufficient to appease their incensed accusers, leaving their gems of concert performance as most delightful remembrance. Who that ever heard Mrs. Wood in "We Met," "Savourneen Deelish," "I've been Roaming," "Should he Upbraid," "Bid me Discourse," "Come where aspens quiver," or Mr. Wood in "The Soldier's Tear," "The Sea," "The Maid of Langoellen," "My Love is like the red red Rose," "The Angel's Whisper," will ever forget them?

In 1840, the Woods revisited this country, but he did not appear on the first night of the opera at the Park Theatre, being indisposed to encounter hisses and uproar, on account of his feud with the Courier and Enquirer critic. Mrs. Wood had a good reception, and with her introduction to popularity, Mr. Wood finally overcame the hostility his folly had provoked. On the 7th of December, 1840, the Woods re-appeared in this city at Tremont Theatre, in the favorite "La Sonnambula," with Brough, Andrews, and Mrs. Smith, for aids. They had a warm greeting from old friends and enthusiastic admirers. For the first week good houses were attracted by the old spell, and the charm of Mrs. Wood's "While this heart," and "Ah, do n't mingle," with his "Still so gently," appeared to have lost none of its power. Brough, however, gave a chill to his friends, by the falling off in "As I view now." During this engagement, which terminated December 28th, "The Beggars' Opera," "The Maid of Judah," "Guy Mannering," "Clari," "The Waterman," "Love in a Village," "The Quaker," and "Cinderella" were presented, the latter having a good run. In the music of "Ivanhoe," Mr. Wood gave convincing proof that his voice had wonderfully improved both in power and firm attack of those notes above the staff, which formerly gave him not a little annoyance to seize upon and hold, as might have been expected from an organ partaking of the baritone and tenor. It has been made a serious complaint against this singer that he strained too evidently upon B flat in alt, especially in the great solo from "La Sonnambula." A reference to subsequent examples of pure or high tenor voices even contraltino, would, however, find the same defect, and too frequent resort to falsetto on such ticklish passages. In the song, "When the trump of fame," made Ivanhoe's great solo, Mr. Wood's improvement was brilliantly manifested as the sudden rise upon the words "Red with gore," had at his former visit not unfrequently baulked him. Now that and other difficulties were taken with electrical power and gracing ease, bringing down the house in shouts of applause for such feats of skill and thrilling force in alt. The concert performances of this gifted pair did not renew that excitement of the old time when the Masonic Temple was crowded every Saturday evening with the elite of Boston and its suburbs, and four encores for one song attested the hold of his public Joseph Wood then enjoyed. But two concerts were attempted during his last visit — both given after the close of the operatic engagement.

The Boston Post says of the last, that some two hundred persons only attended. The entertainment was better than the first, and Mr. Wood did not appear so poorly. It concludes a list of causes for this small attendance by saying, "This is a fickle world." Two causes beside the want of novelty, and Mr. Wood's quarrelling with critics had a powerful influence against them. Caradori had many determined advocates, who, in 1834, were sorely grieved with opposition by the Wood *clique*, and now repaid their debt of injury. The other, and perhaps the most potent of all, was found in the distress which prevailed during 1840, the year of hard cider and log cabins, retrenchment of expenditure, and violent absorbing political excitement.

CHAPTER XXII.

Joseph Wood. — His Sudden Rise and the Cause. — James G. Maeder. — Anecdotes. — Receipts of the First Boston Engagement. — The Kembles. — Mr. Barry's Second Season. — Park Benjamin's Address. — The Appearance of J. Sheridan Knowles. — Charles Mathews, etc.

THE sudden rise of Joseph Wood, to whom we alluded in the last chapter, to a firm position among tenor singers of the first rank in English opera and ballads, surprised all his cotemporaries in the musical world, and fairly astonished the public. With the English version of Rossini's "Cenerentola," he bounded into fame, and the certainty of that wealth he speedily realized. In connection with the performance of "Cinderella" in English, and the commencement of Mr.

Wood's career, this narration of facts came from one intimately acquainted with its hero.

While the adaptation yet remained in the hands of its getters up, and expectation was highly excited for a new proof that Mrs. Wood's voice and brilliant execution of the most difficult music had close affinity to perfection; a difficulty in regard to a tenor fit to enact the Prince and execute the music in a style worthy a comparison with the heroine, threatened ruin to a hopeful speculation.

Mr. Wood had no place in the list of candidates, and no one was deemed available by those interested. The sagacity and keen appreciation of J. G. Maeder made the operatic spectacle a harvest of gold, and crowned Joseph Wood in the Prince with laurels fresh and fair. While conversing in the green room about the all important tenor, Meader informed Mr. Wood that he possessed a fine voice and might accomplish the part if he would but try. Wood laughed heartily at the joke, but Meader insisted upon a trial and finally got Wood to work, he being the accompanist with the piano-forte. With so good a teacher, rapid progress in the art of singing was obtained, and ere many days had elapsed, Wood himself began to think Maeder's jest and quiz might prove a most pleasant reality. After drilling his pupil in the music allotted the Prince, Mr. Maeder determined to introduce a song, which could not fail to excite a sensation when given by such a voice as Mr. Wood's rehearsals proved him possessed of. "Can I my love resign," gave *eclat* to "Cinderella" and from the first hearing to its last, that *bravura* invariably thrilled and delighted the audience. The opera was decidedly successful on the opening night, and Mr. Wood amply justified his training. He was enthusiastically applauded throughout, and the introduced song brought down the house. It was encored with frantic shouts of joy over a new found treasure, and from that moment Joseph Wood became a celebrity. Previously she alone engrossed popular regard, now their united attention swept all before it, and when to America they came, all other musical stars were at once eclipsed, if not extinguished.

Unfortunately for Wood, he was unable to sustain this unexpected success with dignity and quiet self-possession, but undermined his popularity by frequent squabbles with editors and critics, and damaged the "Woods," by apparently sharp dealings, with those who assisted in their great triumphs. His shrewdness and promptitude in money matters were, it is said, fully exemplified at the moment of his departure from this country. Like many other Englishmen, the strong temptation of eight per cent. annual dividend enticed Wood into United States Bank investments, and entire belief in the solvency of that institution. He became a large stockholder, and deposited his surplus earnings there for safe keeping. Just before it failed he obtained some knowledge of coming events, withdrew his deposit and embarked for England in the first packet which sailed after the bank stopped payment. The ship was detained in the Irish Channel by adverse winds, and Mr. Wood hired a boat to put himself and family on shore at Milford, Haven. From thence he took post to London, and, being a day or two in advance of the disastrous intelligence, succeeded in running off all his United States

Bank stock at saving prices. When the news transpired a great fall immediately ensued, and some newspapers assailed Wood for this Yankee trick, done by a keen Yorkshireman. A denial was somewhat feebly made by his friends, but the world believed the whole story and laughed heartily at Wood's activity in the preservation of property accumulated with so much ease.

The Woods soon after returned to England, and, in 1843, she went into a convent, he to a farm near York. A year or two since she emerged from obscurity to astonish Dublin with the brilliancy of her execution in the old list of operas, but Mr. Wood held fast to his new profession and the enjoyment of a hard-earned competence.

The receipts of the Woods' first engagement in Boston were as follows: —

1833.	Dec.	4th,	Cinderella, ...	$687 25
"	"	6th,	"	590 75
"	"	9th,	Guy Mannering, ...	608 25
"	"	10th,	Cinderella, ...	558 50
"	"	12th,	Barber of Seville, . . .	564 50
"	"	13th,	Love in a Village, ...	330 25
"	"	16th,	Barber of Seville, and Waterman,	823 50
"	"	17th,	Barber of Seville, and Waterman,	439 50
"	"	19th,	Der Freischutz, ...	623 00
"	"	20th,	Barber of Seville, and Waterman,	414 75
"	"	23d,	Der Freischutz, ...	657 25
"	"	24th,	The Devil's Bridge, ...	739 75
"	"	26th,	Masaniello, ...	511 25
"	"	27th,	The Devil's Bridge, . . .	452 50
"	"	30th,	Massaniello, ...	492 50
"	"	31st,	Cinderella, ...	355 25
1834.	Jan.	2d,	Barber of Seville, ...	379 50
"	"	3d,	Drama and 2d Act Masaniello, .	354 50
"	"	4th,	Marriage of Figaro, and Clari, .	811 75
				$10,394 50

We have heard many anecdotes of Mrs. Wood, and the following we find floating round the newspapers. We do not vouch for its accuracy:—

"A general, living in the neighborhood of Philadelphia, who had become suddenly rich, furnished a house in a costly manner, and gave gay parties. He had little else but his wealth, however, to render them attractive; his wife, being especially untutored and unpolished, as he had married before he became rich, and both were elevated to their present importance without the requisite personal qualifications to sustain it. To render one of their parties more than usually popular, they invited Mr. and Mrs. Wood among their guests. These at first respectfully declined, on the ground of fatigue; but they were pressed with so much earnestness, that they at length were subdued into consent. When the entertainments of the evening were fairly commenced, and several ladies among the visitors had sung, the hostess invited Mrs. Wood to seat herself at the piano, as the company would be delighted to hear her beautiful voice; but Mrs. Wood begged, with a very serious countenance, to be excused. At first, the astonishment created by this refusal was evinced by a dead silence, and a fixed stare; but at length, the disappointed hostess broke forth:

"'What! not sing! Mrs. Wood; why, it was for this that I invited you to my party. I should not have thought of asking you but for this; and I told all my guests that you were coming, and that they would hear you sing!'

"'Oh!' replied Mrs. Wood, with great readiness, 'that quite alters the case; I was not at all aware of this, or I should not have refused; but since you have invited me professionally, I shall of course sing immediately!'

"'That's a *good* creature!' rejoined the hostess, 'I thought you could not persist in refusing me.'

"So Mrs. Wood seated herself at the piano, sang delightfully, and, to the entire gratification of hostess and guests, gave, without hesitation, every song she was asked for, and some were encored. On the following day, however, when the host and hostess were counting up the cost of their entertainment, (for, rich as they were, they had not lost their former regard for economy,) to their utter consternation there came in from Mr. Wood a bill of two hundred dollars for Mrs. Wood's 'professional services' at the party of the preceding evening, accompanied by a note, couched in terms which made it quite certain that the demand would be legally enforced if attempted to be resisted; and, however much the 'general' and his 'lady' were mortified by this unexpected demand, they deemed it most prudent to pay it and hold their tongues."

There is a reminiscence connected with the first production of La Sonnambula in this city, on the 28th of December, 1835, which is amusing. On their return the Woods did not make that immediate sensation in Boston that they anticipated from their previous success. The New York papers had been extremely laudatory of "La Sonnambula," and for that the Bostonians were reserving their dollars. Its production was not intended by the management, and it was only the result of circumstances, that it was brought out at all. The houses were very poor, considering the attraction, and Mr. Barry was at a loss to account for it, while the Woods were chagrined at their lack of popularity. The matter was discussed on the stage one day, when Mr. Comer suggested the propriety of bringing out "La Sonnambula." Mr. Barry listened to the proposition; but Mr. Wood declared that it could not be done under four or five weeks, and about twenty rehearsals would be required. "I will guarantee," continued Mr. Comer, "to produce it in a fortnight from Monday." "Impossible," said Jo Wood, "for this is Friday." Mr. Barry looked upon Mr. Comer as if he doubted the possibility of bringing out an opera, which was entirely new to chorus and orchestra, while Brough appeared to consider it impracticable. After dinner that day, the Woods and Barry talked the matter over. Those troublesome members of society, yclept editors, were asking, "When are we to have 'La Sonnambula?'" and the public re-echoed the query. "I wish," said Wood, looking at his glass of rich burgundy, as he held it up, "that Comer could accomplish what he proposes." "I have no doubt," rejoined Barry, "that if he undertakes it, it will be done within the time specified." "Do you really think it possible?" asked Mrs. Wood; — "it would be a great feat to bring it out in that time." Mr. Barry confessed he was startled when Mr. Comer first proposed it, but since he gave it thought he believed it might be done. "Let us send for Comer, then," said Mr. Wood, who rung the bell, and despatched the servant with a note. Mr. Comer was soon in the presence of the trio, who inundated him with interrogatories, and presented to him an entire chaos of objections. "All I ask," said Mr. Comer, "to carry this to a successful termination, is entire liberty to do just as I please, without dictation or interference; on Monday fortnight I guarantee a performance of La Sonnambula which shall be creditable to all concerned."

"What say, Barry?" asked Wood.

"I think it is best to let Mr. Comer proceed."

"Well then, Comer, we are all of one opinion; go ahead, you have *carte blanche*."

Comer declined remaining, and on taking the pianoforte score observed that it would have to be separated, and given to copyists, to which they gave consent; and before the next morning at 10 o'clock, the scriveners, by aid of the midnight lamp, had six copies made. The chorus were summoned, and informed of what had been undertaken. Mr. Oliver thought it a hazardous job, but joined heart and voice in the attempt, and was supported by Capt. Sam. Adams and the other choristers. The saloon of the theatre was occupied by Mr. Comer, drilling the chorus; the greenroom by Ostinelli, with the orchestra, and the progress was wonderful. The chorus in six days had acquired a knowledge of several choruses, and they were finally approaching perfection, when Brough and Wood came in, and the former was very desirous to try his songs with the chorus. This Mr. Comer declined doing, alleging that the time occupied in going over his role might enable the choruses to rehearse their parts at least half a dozen times. The gentlemen took the hint, and did not again interfere. The time approached, and Mr. Comer redoubled his efforts; and when ready for a full rehearsal, Mrs. Wood for the first time made her appearance, and was astonished at the perfection of the whole. The last rehearsal was had, when Mrs. Wood suggested that so long as

Mr. Comer was there to direct and lead, it might do, but expressed a fear that on the night of performance the chorus might not be so *au fait* in taking up the answers. Mr. Comer, however, had foreseen this difficulty; and to guard against it, he appeared on the first night of "La Sonnambula" as a peasant, and by constant action and attention, he brought the chorus up to the work, and contributed materially to the success of the piece.

The receipts previous to the production of this piece had fallen as low as two hundred dollars per night, the week but one preceding netting only $1,626.75. The receipts of La Sonnambula were as follows:—

1835.	Dec. 28,	La Sonnambula, ...	$648 25
	29,	" "	685 25
	30,	" "	720 50
	" 31,	" "	699 00
1836.	Jan. 1,	" "	814 25
	" 4,	" "	740 75
	" 5,	" "	666 50
	" 6,	" "	654 00
	" 7,	" "	716 25
	" 8,	" "	782 25
	" 11,	" " Tickets at auction,	820 00
			$7,947 00

One might suppose that such energy on Mr. Comer's part would have met with some appreciating mark of respect; and so it did, for the next day Mrs. Wood pressed his hand, and left in the palm a small package. On opening it a small silver snuffbox was found, bearing a suitable inscription. Of the real value of the box some idea may be gleaned, when we state that the recipient at once regaled the orchestra and choristers;

and on affording them an opportunity to drink the health, prosperity, and *generosity* of the donors, in a temperate manner, expended about four times its value. In justice to the manager, Mr. Thomas Barry, be it said, he fully appreciated the efforts of Mr. Comer, and presented him with a very handsome and appropriate silver goblet. The first production of "Fra Diavolo" by the Woods in this city, in 1834, was also noted by a miniature row. Previous to the arrival of the Woods, Mr. Barry intimated to Mr. Comer, that he had just received the piano forte score from them of the opera of "Fra Diavolo," and that the part of *Lorenzo* must be assigned to Mr. Thomas Walton, who had been singing with the Woods in New York, giving as their reason that Mr. Thomas Williamson, then a popular vocalist, and a member of the Tremont company, was incompetent to sustain the part. Mrs. Wood also hinted that the facial features of Mr. Williamson, who unfortunately had damaged his nose, were objectionable. Mr. Barry asked Mr. Comer his opinion of Mr. Williamson's ability to do justice to the part, and having received assurance of his qualifications, gave him orders to rehearse the songs. The Woods came, and with them Mr. Walton, who rehearsed *Lorenzo*, the Woods having made up their minds to have him in the opera at any rate; but they found, on the rising of the curtain, that *vox populi* is more potent than the arbitrary will of vocalists, for Mr. Williamson's friends had assembled in great numbers. The overture was played, and the curtain rose; but no sooner did the multitude behold Walton as *Lorenzo*, than shouts of disapprobation commenced. He attempted to speak, but it was useless.

Mrs. Wood appeared, but the uproar continued. Mr. Barry came forward to explain, and was heard, but not to the satisfaction of the audience, and many were anticipating a riot, when Williamson was discovered in the second tier of boxes. The uproar increased, when an " unknown voice " shouted, — " *Tom, go and put on your flannels!* " Mr. Williamson retired, and in a few minutes it was announced that the part of *Lorenzo* would be sustained by Mr. Williamson. The opera recommenced, Mr. W. appeared as *Lorenzo,* and the performances closed amid great applause.

The Kembles appeared several times this season. Mr. Barry aimed at making the drama attractive, and to lift it to a moral standard; and with these views he procured all the available stars of the day, and at the close of his first season, received from the press and the public the greatest praise for his efforts. Aside from the stars enumerated, Mr. and Mrs. Barrett returned, and appeared in "School for Scandal," etc.

The second season of Mr. Barry's management, that of 1834–5, commenced on the 1st of September, with but little change in the company. Mr. John Gilbert, Mr. and Mrs. Barrett were added to it.

The stars were Clara Fisher, C. H. Eaton, J. Sheridan Knowles, Booth, Yankee Hill, Cooper, Mrs. Austin, Miss Phillips, Mr. J. Wallack, Fanny Jarman, Celeste, Miss Watson, Emma Wheatley, A. A. Adams, — a galaxy indeed!

The opening plays were, " Every one has his Fault," and the " Bold Dragoons ; " the receipts were $515.50. A poetical address, written by Park Benjamin, was spoken by Mrs. Barrett. If we except Mr. Sprague

Mr. Benjamin's productions, on such occasions, are pre-eminently worthy of attention. Though written for a special purpose, and consequently limited somewhat in their interest, they possess merit sufficient to command the attention of every lover of poetry. There is in the following several excellent ideas clothed in words which are most musical to the ear:—

ADDRESS,

Spoken by Mrs. Barrett, on the opening of the Tremont Theatre, on the night of her return to the Boston Stage.

BY PARK BENJAMIN, ESQ.

When o'er the waste of waves some wanderer roams
From his own country's free and happy homes—
His native land just blending with the sky—
What tears of sorrow dim his straining eye!
But when returned, these happy homes appear,
And every prospect, to his bosom dear,
Unchanged in beauty, rises to his sight,
How, like a fountain, springs his new delight!
So, for awhile, when forced to bid adieu
To much-loved scenes, and, ah! sweet friends to you,
Sad were my thoughts—but now, when I behold
Your welcome smiles and hear your welcome told
In language long familiar to my heart,—
The woman, not the actress, plays her part.

To-night, the drama from her brief repose
Wakes into life, with purer radiance glows,
And, onward led by your approving hands,
Like some bright Goddess in her temple stands.
Here is her shrine and here her votaries throng,
To tell her glories in their choral song.
Here Painting, Music, Poetry combine
Their votive wreaths to make her half divine.
Lo! where dark Tragedy sweeps proudly by,
Darts the swift lightning from her clouded eye,
Shows the red dagger and the poisoned bowl
And turns to ice the currents of the soul.

Ha! ha! see where old Comedy derides
His solemn sister — how he shakes his sides!
A different knife and bowl he loves to keep,
Calls other spirits from the vasty deep,
And slyly beckons, with a knowing glance,
Mirth-making music to lead her out the dance.
Music! ah, who of all I see around
Loves not the enchanting harmony of sound?
Last in the train comes Painting, clothed in light,
To show the beauty of the world at night.
When darkness rests on all external forms
Her mimic splendor every object warms,
In our own land to our delighted eyes
Gleam the soft colors of Italian skies:
Mountains and rivers, palaces and towers,
All, at her magic summons, all are ours!

Cheered by her smiles, each lovely art attends,
On you it calls its best and kindest friends.
For you the Drama, on her favorite stage,
Holds up her faithful mirror to the age.
Oh! keep it bright! that here, reflected true,
Her hideous features Vice may shrink to view;
And, Heaven-born Virtue here may ever trace
The mild reflection of her angel face.
Your voices, then! the Drama's power proclaim,
And with new laurels crown the Drama's fame.

On the 13th of October, 1834, J. Sheridan Knowles, the author of many of our popular plays, appeared for the first time in Boston as *Master Walter*, in his own play of the "Hunchback." Mr. Knowles was received in New York most cordially; in Philadelphia he had been tendered a public dinner, and these facts, with the novelty of an author bodily delineating the creatures of his imagination, gave a zest to the public appetite. Few authors, we may remark *en passant*, have taken leading parts in their own dramas. Garrick performed his own *Lying Varlet*, Macklin was great as *Sir Perti-*

nax and *Sir Archy*, and Colley Cibber was remarkable for his performances in the "Careless Husband" and some other of his plays. They had passed from the stage before Knowles appeared. Since his day, there are but few who have combined the qualities of playwright and actor. Miss Kemble, Miss Vandenhoff, and Mrs. Mowatt, are the only ones of modern date, who has succeeded in this duplicate and difficult task.

Mr. Knowles appeared as *Master Walter*, in the "Hunchback," to George Barrett's *Sir Thomas Clifford*, Mrs. Barrett's *Julia*, and Mrs. W. H. Smith's *Helen;* also, in "William Tell," "Virginius," "The Wife, or a Tale of Mantua," all his own productions, and in "Macbeth." Mr. Knowles, (and we mention this for the benefit of some actors, who differ in their conception,) communicated a very different impression of *Master Walter*, from what the younger Kean had done. Instead of the gruff, morose old man, Mr. Knowles make him out a very amiable man, plotting nothing but the happiness of those whom he best loved. *Virginius* was deemed his best impersonation, but in all his plays he developed new beauties, and brought out points which had escaped the notice of others. Mr. Knowles possessed a pleasant voice, dashed, however, with a little of the "brogue" of his native land. On his opening night he was called out, and made a brief speech, returning thanks for his enthusiastic reception, and closing thus — "The least said, my friends, soonest mended; if I try to say any thing more I know I shall make some blunder — so God bless you!" Cheer after cheer was given for *Paddy* Knowles, as the warm-hearted Irish dramatist loved to write himself.

The receipts of Knowles' nights, Mr. Booth playing on his occasional off nights, were: —

1834.	October	13th,	Hunchback,	$690 50
"	"	14th,	William Tell,	381 50
"	"	15th,	Virginius,	357 50
"	"	16th,	Hunchback,	287 75
"	"	17th,	The Wife,	307 50
"	"	20th,	Macbeth,	327 00
"	"	22d,	Wm. Tell, (Benefit,)	663 00
				$2,923 25

Mr. Knowles has, of late years, abandoned his old path in the walks of literature, and having joined the Baptist church, is now devoting all his energies to the propagation of the gospel. The English papers lately recorded his delivering an address on religion, and defying any Roman Catholic to meet him in open debate. In a late number of the Home Journal, the following paragraph appeared: —

"A letter received by the last steamer, from our distinguished and deeply-valued friend Knowles, brought freshly to mind the delightful hours which we enjoyed in his company when, fifteen years ago, he was a temporary resident among us. Mr. Knowles is now in the sixty-eighth year of his age, the fifty-fourth of his authorship — he wrote a play in his fourteenth year — and the thirty-second of his fame; for it was the triumphant success of "Virginius," in 1820, that established his position as the dramatist of his time. We regret to learn that Mr. Knowles has not escaped the infirmities to which his advanced age exposes him. For the last three months he has been a severe sufferer from an attack of bronchitis, and has, three times in the same period, had to encounter his old enemy, the gout. At the date of his letter, however, he was slowly, but he hoped, surely recovering. Our friend speaks warmly of the happy period of his residence in this country, and expresses a strong desire to renew the friendships which he then formed. We need not say how cordially this desire is reciprocated by ourselves, and by all who had the singular happiness of an acquaintance with him. Two hemispheres admire his genius; but only those who have sat with him at the fireside and the convivial board, in unrestrained and oft-repeated converse, know what a kindly, generous, and noble heart beats in the bosom of James Sheridan Knowles. May he live long to enjoy the honors which he has won, and the leisure which his country has bestowed upon him!"

To his credit be it said that Mr. SHERIDAN KNOWLES, on his return from the United States, was offered £2,000 by a London bookseller, for an abusive book upon America. Mr. Knowles promptly declined the offer.

Miss Phillips, from London, then only twenty-two years of age, made her appearance in Boston as *Juliet*, to J. Wallack's *Romeo*, on the 10th of November. Her impersonation of this character was pronounced in New York fully equal to any thing that had been seen, but the Boston critics were of a different opinion. The characters represented by her were *Belvidera*, *Julia*, *Mrs. Haller*, etc.

Mr. Cooper also appeared this season, and Charles Mathews arrived in town and commenced an engagement on the 10th of December, but was taken sick and for many days confined to his room. He was able finally to re-appear, and took his farewell benefit — a long farewell it proved, for he never returned; on the 5th of January, 1835, when he gave "The Youthful Days of Mr. Mathews," and "The Lone House." The engagement of Mr. Mathews would have proved, if he had not been taken ill, one of the most profitable of the season. As it was the receipts were large: —

1834.	Dec.	10th,	"At Home," and Monsieur Tonson, .	$584 00
"	"	22d,	2d Vol. Comic Almanac, and Lone House,	810 50
"	"	24th,	Sketch Book, Before Breakfast, . .	415 00
"	"	26th,	Memorandum Book, Monsieur Tonson,	308 75
"	"	29th,	Poor Gentleman, ...	361 75
"	"	31st,	Comic Annual, ...	204 50
1835.	Jan.	1st,	Before Breakfast, etc., ...	305 75
"	"	5th,	Youthful Day, and Lone House, . .	553 75
				$3,544 00

CHAPTER XXIII.

Fanny Jarman. — F. S. Hill's Prize Poem. — Miss Charlotte Cushman's First Appearance. — Miss Watson. — Her Intrigue with Paganini. — Mr. Harrington, Professor of Ventriloquism. — The Old Theatre. — The Season of 1835-36. — The Veteran Dowton. — James Murdock. — First Appearance of Miss Clifton. — Mr. and Mrs. Keeley. — Epes Sargent's "Bride of Genoa." — First Appearance of Ellen Tree. — Lines by John Q. Adams. — Receipts. — Leman, Charlotte Cushman, etc.

Miss Fanny Jarman appeared this season, (1834–5). She had been very well received at New York, and chose the character of *Julia*, in the "Hunchback," for her first appearance in Boston, on the 9th of January, 1835. Her husband, (for *Miss* Jarman was married,) Mr. Tiernan played *Master Walter* with considerable discrimination, though the chief attraction was his wife. With a person tall and commanding, Miss Jarman possessed a voice of much sweetness in its tones, and considerable power. Her face was comely without being striking, and with actions and motions graceful and interesting, she proved a very attractive actress. The houses rarely during this engagement fell below $500, and on the occasion of a benefit, when the "Jealous Wife" and "Perfection" were performed, there was $910.25 in. Mr. and Mrs. Tiernan subsequently played several engagements in this city, and she is at present in London.

Mr. Smith, at his benefit this year, recited F. S. Hill's prize poem, dedicated to the Boston Fire Department, for which the beneficiary awarded the premium of $50. It proved very attractive, drawing $646.50, and has frequently been recited since. Celeste, during her engagement, brought out February 2, 1835, the "Wept of the Wish Ton Wish!" which drew great houses. On the occasion of her benefit, ($1,126,) she delivered an address to her Boston friends. At the annual benefit ($716) of Mrs. Smith, her sister, Miss Eliza Riddle played *Julia*, in the "Hunchback," to Mrs. Smith's *Helen*, with marked success.

Towards the close of the season, Mrs. Maeder, formerly Miss Clara Fisher, appeared as *Paul* in Buckstone's "Pet of the Petticoats," and on April 8th Miss Charlotte Cushman, now the eminent tragedienne, made her first appearance on any stage as the *Countess* in the opera of "Marriage of Figaro," to a house of $363.75, Mrs. Maeder appearing as *Susanna*. Miss Cushman was born in Boston, and her first appearance in public was at a social concert given in this city, at the hall No. 1 Franklin Avenue, on the 25th of March, 1830. Mr. Farmer presided at the piano-forte, and Messrs.

John F. Pray, Stedman, Morris, Chase, White, Coupa, were the instrumental performers. During Mrs. Wood's engagement in this city, Miss Cushman sang at one of her concerts. Mrs. Wood, pleased with her voice, which was a fine contralto, advised her to turn her attention to singing on the stage, and Mr. Maeder, the husband of Clara Fisher, who came out with the Woods, brought her out in the *Countess.*

On the 13th of April, Miss Charlotte Watson made her appearance as *Mary Copp*, in "Charles II.," and as *Cherubina* in the "Marriage of Figaro," supported by Miss Cushman and Mrs. Maeder, ($865). Miss Watson had been "puffed" to a very extraordinary height in New York, but she proved to be an actress in miniature, and very pretty singer of simple music. Her engagement was quite brief. The desire to see the lady was considerably increased, from the fact that she had been the heroine of a runaway affair, with no less a personage than the celebrated Paganini, the first violinist in the world, who had given concerts in connection with Miss Watson at various places in England and Scotland, and finally made overtures of marriage, which she accepted, upon the conditions imposed, that they were to proceed to Paris, and there unbeknown to her father the marriage was to take place, Paganini stating it was important that this should be done in order to secure her a settlement at his banker's. Paganini's plan being matured, he, under pretence of ill health, set off for France, accompanied by his valet. Miss Watson, in accordance with previous arrangements, the following morning repaired to Paganini's attorney, who with his wife accompanied her to Boulogne, where she arrived, and found her—*father!* who it appears anticipating that Paganini's motives were not honorable, had, on finding his daughter absent, immediately started in search. Miss Watson flew into the arms of her father, and returned to London. What Paganini's intentions were, was a matter of considerable comment in the *beau monde.* It is said that after her arrival in this country, he sent out a special messenger, who stated that he was authorized to assure Miss Watson of his master's honorable intentions, and his readiness to espouse her, offering at the same time to compensate Mr. Watson for the loss of his daughter's services, and to indemnify him for his own professional claims, and the expenses he would incur in removing with his family and accompanying her to Italy. Mr. Watson would not treat with the ambassador of the violinist, and declined all farther negotiation.

Mr. Knowles played a second engagement this season with the support of Miss Emma Wheatley.

Mr. A. A. Adams, who married Miss Mary Duff, after an absence of five years returned, and appeared at the Tremont. He was an actor of great merit, but his folly led him to indulge in dissipation, and he lost the position he had within his grasp. Mr. and Mrs. W. H. Smith took their benefit towards the close of the season, when Miss Charlotte Cushman sang "Trifler Forbear." Miss Cushman took her benefit to a house containing only $258.00.

In the summer of 1834, the Federal Street was opened by Mr. Harrington, professor of ventriloquism and natural magic, the same gentleman who still continues to appear at different periods of the year in this and the surrounding cities, making short excursions, returning to his snug and quiet home at North Chelsea, to enjoy the fruits of his campaigns. He was the last, we believe, who appeared at the old theatre, to give public entertainments prior to its being converted into the Odeon, under which name it was inaugurated on the 5th of August, 1835, when Hon. S. A. Eliot delivered an address, and the pupils of the Boston Academy of Music furnished the music.

The season of 1835–6 commenced on the 17th of August. The house had been entirely refitted, a new stage built, with other improvements. The artist, Sam. Stockwell, had exerted himself to render the interior at once chaste and beautiful, and so well did he succeed that Mr. Barry presented him with a silver pitcher, as a token of his appreciation of the artist's services. The opening plays were, "Much Ado about Nothing," and "My Neighbor's Wife," ($499.25). The stars this season were Celeste, the Woods, Fanny Jarman, J. H. Wallack, John Reeve, J. S. Ball, and Dowton. Mrs. Lewis also appeared and played *Richard*, *Othello*, *Shylock*, etc. Mr. John Reeve, the "Rascal Jack," who loved a joke to such an extent, that in washing them down his throat, he finally caused his death, appeared and performed a good engagement. On the night of the performance of "Tom and Jerry," and the "Unfinished Gentleman," there was $1064.50 in the house.

The great feature of the season, however, was the appearance of the veteran Dowton, who made his first bow to a Boston audience on the 23d of June, 1836, and during his engagement played *Sir Robert Bramble*, *Sir Anthony Absolute*, *Old Dornton* in the "Road to

Ruin," *Sir John Falstaff, Sir George Thunder* in "Wild Oats," *Dr. Cantwell* in the "Hypocrite," *Sir Peter Teazle, Peter Simpson* in "Simpson & Co.," and *Sir Matthew Scraggs* in the "Englishman in India."

"Old Dowton" was at this time seventy-one years of age. He was born in Exeter, England, in 1765, and first appeared at Drury Lane as *Sheva*, in the "Jew," Oct. 10, 1793. He had been manager of several theatres, and, though quite advanced in years, was still a great actor. His representations of choleric humanity were carried to the summit of perfection. A critic observed as follows of Dowton:—"The greatest living comedian out of the direct pale of gentility, though we by no means mean to insinuate that he is vulgar, is Mr. Dowton. He can smooth over a natural vehemence, indulge himself in the most delightful cordiality, and be carried away into the uttermost transports of rage, with equal felicity." Dowton had his faults on the stage, the most prominent being his inclination to profanity, which he regretted himself, but carried away in a part, and being a person of impulse, a loud oath frequently escaped his lips. Mr. Dowton did not draw very well. His benefit, however, was honored, and the treasurer received $1040.25; but his houses averaged below $250.

The season of 1836–7 commenced on the 8th of August. Kilner, Mr. and Mrs. Barrett, Mr. and Mrs. Gilbert, were the leading actors; Smith, Comer, Johnson, etc., having very injudiciously been allowed to leave for the National Theatre. The opening play was, "Speed the Plough," and Mr. James Murdock, now the star tragedian and excellent elocutionist, made his first appearance in Boston as *Henry*. The public soon discovered the merits of this excellent actor, and he became at once very popular.

The stars this season included Celeste, Finn, Mr. and Mrs. Watson, Mrs. Bailey, J. S. Balls, Josephine Clifton, Dowton, Mr. Plummer, Fanny Jarman, Ellen Tree, Mr. and Mrs. Keeley, Power, Hacket, Mr. and Mrs. Barnes, etc.

Miss Clifton appeared on the 3d of October, 1836, as *Bianca*, in Fazio, for the first time in Boston. She had appeared in New York, and had made a trip across the water before the Bostonians had an opportunity of judging of her merits. She came, therefore, with a great reputation. Fanny Kemble, it was supposed, had monopolized the parts in which Miss Clifton appeared, but the Bostonians, while admitting the superiority of the former, paid homage to their countrywoman. With a majesty of mien, unsurpassed by any actress, she presented the varied passions of the tragic scene in a manner which commanded respect and challenged admiration. Her *Bianca* many recall with great pleasure, as one of those theatrical portraitures which hang upon memory's walls, as vivid to the mental eye as when first beholden. Miss Clifton married Mr. Place, of New Orleans, and died several years ago.

Mr. and Mrs. Keeley commenced their first Boston engagement on the 7th of November, in the drama of "Lucille, or the Story of a Heart." We need not allude to their merits, or to their position in the profession. Their light has shone in two hemispheres, and still burns brightly in London.

Mr. Barry brought out this year, at a great expense,

"The Massacre, or the Malay's Revenge," a spectacle, or rather a historical drama, from the pen of George Colman, the younger. Messrs. Gilbert, Hield, Murdock, Leman, Muzzy, Andrews, Bayne, Addams, Curtis, Sarzedas, Houpt, with Mrs. Barrett, Mrs. Hield, Miss A. Fisher, and Miss McBride, sustained the different parts. It did not prove very attractive, though its performance on Thanksgiving evening attracted a $978.25 house.

On the occasion of Miss Clifton's second engagement, she brought out, February 13, 1837, Epes Sargent's five act play called "The Bride of Genoa," ($772.25). Miss Clifton played *Montaldo*, a young Genevese, and Mrs. Richardson *Laura*. The play proved attractive, and reflected great credit not only upon Miss Clifton, but upon the author. This, we believe, was among the earliest dramatic productions of Mr. Sargent, who in this piece and in "Velasco," gave promise of becoming one of the first dramatic poets of the age. Had he continued to pursue this branch of literature, we should not now be so dependent upon foreign productions. The "Bride of Genoa" was played four nights, and was pronounced by competent critics "a signal dramatic triumph."

On the 20th of February, 1837, Miss Ellen Tree, now Mrs. Charles Kean, appeared for the first time in this city as *Julia*, in the "Hunchback." *Sir Thomas Clifford*, Mr. Barry; *Master Walter*, Mr. Hield; *Modus*, Murdock, (the best *Modus* we ever saw); *Helen*, Mrs. Richardson. Miss Tree's fame had preceded her. Every admirer of histrionic art had awaited with impatience her arrival from New York and Philadelphia, where her praises had been sung in prose and poetry. Fame, however, had done no more for her than justice, for she was then at the head of living actresses, and though at present *un peu passé*, as Mrs. Charles Kean, she remains unrivalled in many characters. Her acting was classical and finished. Her performance did not astound the audience by its energetic boldness, or draw forth tumultuous applause by any forced fervor of its passion. It was, on the contrary, that style, at times seen in Mrs. Mowatt's acting, gentle, subdued, and polished; not startling, but winning upon the judgment as the play advanced. In every action, in every point there was *mind.* Her triumphant success in this country, was unequalled. She delighted every one. John Quincy Adams was so pleased with her impersonations that he paid her the following compliment: —

"'Tis Nature's witchery attracts the smile;
'Tis *her soft sorrows* that our tears beguile;
Nature to thee her fairest gifts imparts;
She bids thee fascinate, to win all hearts —
The wife, the queen, the wayward child we see,
And fair perfection, all abide in thee."

Washington, June 22nd, 1838.

The receipts of this engagement were as follows: —

1837.	Feb.	20th,	Hunchback, ...	$751 25
"	"	21st,	As You Like It, . . .	521 00
"	"	22d,	The Wife, ...	790 00
"	"	23d,	Belle's Stratagem, . . .	680 25
"	"	24th,	The Hunchback, ...	674 25
"	"	27th,	The Wonder, ...	759 75
"	"	28th,	Romeo and Juliet, ...	451 50
"	March	1st,	As You Like It. Ransom, .	648 25
"	"	2d,	School for Scandal. Ransom, .	667 25

1837.	March 3d,	Provoked Husband, and Perfection, (Benefit,)	730 75
"	" 6th,	Wrecker's Daughter, . .	794 75
"	" 7th,	Much Ado About Nothing, and Perfection, ...	647 75
"	" 8th,	Wrecker's Daughter, . .	594 00
"	" 9th,	The Wife, and Youthful Queen, .	500 75
"	" 10th,	The Wonder. Ransom, . .	528 00
"	" 13th,	Twelfth Night. Youthful Queen,	656 25
"	" 14th,	The Wife. Youthful Queen, .	612 50
"	" 15th,	Ion, ...	722 50
"	" 16th,	Ion, ...	688 25
"	" 17th,	Honey Moon. A Roland for an Oliver, (Benefit,)	858 50
"	" 20th,	Ion, ...	506 50
"	" 21st,	Twelfth Night. Youthful Queen,	601 25
"	" 22d,	Belle's Stratagem. Ransom, .	627 50
"	" 23d,	Provoked Husband, Perfection,	487 50
"	" 24th,	Honey Moon. Ransom, . .	754 25
"	" 27th,	Hunchback. Youthful Queen, (Benefit,)	1003 00

"Albimonti," a play by Mr. Charles Hayward, was brought out this season. Master William Hield, on the occasion of his mother's benefit, made his debut as *Young Norval,* (April 10th, 1837,) and Mr. Joseph A. Heman made his debut on the occasion of Mr. Leman's benefit. Mr. Leman played *Sir Giles Overreach* for the first time. Mr. Leman was, in 1852–3, a member of the stock company at the National Theatre. After the Tremont had declined, Mr. Leman visited the western part of the country, where he remained several years. He is a sure and steady actor, accomplished as a poet, and highly valued in private life.

Mrs. Watson, Mr. Bailey, and Mr. Plummer appeared in the opera of the "Pirate Boy," on the 17th of April, 1837. They gave a popularity to one song at least during their brief engagement — which for months afterwards was sung by every young lady, who possessed any vocal accomplishment, hummed over by every amateur, and whistled in every alley. Go where you would it was "Lightly may the boat row," and frequently during their engagement this trio were called out six times to repeat this popular piece. In the months of May and June, in 1837, Miss Charlotte Cushman gave the earliest taste of that dramatic spirit, which she has since cultivated to so much advantage. On the 30th of May she appeared as *Lady Macbeth*, to Barry's *Macbeth*, and astonished every one. She followed up her first triumph by playing *Portia* to C. H. Eaton's *Shylock*, and also performed *Fortunato Falconi*, *Elvira Morgianna*, and announced thus early her predilections for male parts by a performance of *Henry*, in "Speed the Plough." Although she had given up, by her assumption of these, all hopes of attaining eminence in the lyric drama, she sung "Hail Columbia" on Murdock's benefit night, and was rapturously applauded.

Thus closed the third season of Mr. Barry's management.

CHAPTER XXIV.

Continuation of Mr. Barry's Management. — Bianca Viscounti. — Forrest's Great Engagement. — Velasco. — Vandenhoff. — Mrs. Shaw. — Miss Hildreth. — Miss Missouri. — Her Romantic History. — Lady of Lyons. — Mr. Barry's Last Season. — Edward Shales. — His Dramatic Career. — A Review of Mr. Barry's Management.

THE next season of Mr. Barry's management, that of 1837–8, commenced on the 7th of August. Mr. and Mrs. Barrett were engaged at the opening for a few weeks, having then just returned from Europe, where Mr. Barrett, we believe, performed, but not with any marked success. The stars this year were Yankee Hill, Booth, Mr. Lathane, Miss Melton, Ellen Tree, Miss Clifton, Forrest, Vandenhoff, Finn, Mrs. Shaw, Madame Augusta, Mr. Hamblin, Miss Missouri, Rice, Murdock, Johnson, Huntonville, and Davenport, now starring it in England, were members of the stock company. Miss Clifton brought out (September 29th) Willis's play of "Bianca Viscounti," ($593.50,) which was well received. On the 16th of October, 1837, Mr. Forrest appeared as *Othello*, the first appearance on his return from England, after an absence of four years. Mr. Forrest played twenty nights, and the receipts were $11,400. His two benefits yielded him $1,725.

Miss Tree followed Forrest, and on the 20th of November, brought out, for the first time, Mr. Sargent's tragedy of "Velasco." Mr. Barry was liberal in getting it up, and the cast was a strong one: — *Velasco,*

Murdoch; *Julio*, Barry; *Izidora*, Miss Tree; *Carlos*, Miss McBride. The piece was well received ($431.50,) but is now seldom performed. Miss Davenport revived it in late years, but it did not prove attractive, on account of the miserable manner in which it was put on the stage.

Mrs. Barry, wife of the manager, made her first appearance before a Boston audience on the 1st of December, 1837, as *Mrs. Rackett*, in "Belle's Stratagem," to Ellen Tree's *Letitia Hardy*. On the 4th of December, Mr. Vandenhoff made his first appearance in this city as *Coriolanus*, and during his engagement he played *Macbeth*, *Cato*, *Brutus*, *Virginius*, *Othello*, and *Hamlet*. Mrs. Barry played the leading female parts, Mr. Gilbert and Mr. Murdoch performing second. Words were wanting to express the admiration of the critics of this gentleman's transcendent talents. Many who remembered Cooke, pronounced Vandenhoff his superior, and his *Cato* — a part in which even Garrick failed — and his *Hamlet*, are remembered by many as perfect master-pieces. Though appreciated by the few his engagement was not what it should have been, what it would be were he again to cross the Atlantic, though in a subsequent visit he did very well. The only excuse we can offer was the financial difficulties of the country, which engrossed public attention. Mrs. Shaw's (Mrs. Hamblin) first appearance in this city was as *Julia*, in the "Hunchback," on the 28th of January, 1838. This lady, in sprightly comedy, has been unequalled. Her performance, of late years, has lost that vivacity and *abandon* which were the chief charms of her style. Her engagement was quite brief, during which, however, she played *Hamlet*, and Md'lle Augusta and her corps de ballet followed. "La Bayadere," an operatic ballet, was produced on the 29th of January, 1838, and was put on the stage in the most admirable style. Mr. Horncastle, the first tenor singer appeared, and the leading characters were sustained by Md'lle Augusta, Miss Kerr, and Madame Otto. Many recollect undoubtedly the scenery of this piece, which exceeded, especially the closing scene, any thing ever seen in this city, doing infinite credit to the skill and genius of Mr. Stockwell. The piece had a good run, and crowds rushed to see the "Indian Paradise" to which Zoleo ascended. Among the novelties this season, was the debut of Miss Hildreth, daughter of Dr. Hildreth, of Dracut, who appeared *Marianna* in the "Wife," *Bianca*, *Lady Teazle*, etc. She played occasionally for one or two seasons, and then retired from the profession.

On the 9th of May, 1838, Ernest Maltravers, dramatized by Miss Louisa H. Medina, and then first presented, introduced to a Boston audience Miss Missouri in the character of *Alice*. Mr. Hamblin, of whom the young lady was a protegé, appearing after the absence of six years as *Richard Darvil* to a house containing $457.75. Miss Missouri performed only ten nights in this city, and for one so young gave great satisfaction. This was her first and only engagement in Boston. She was by birth the sister of Josephine Clifton. She received her education at Mrs. Willard's celebrated Seminary at Troy, and two years prior to her first appearance in New York, received tuition from Mr. Horn the vocalist, Mr. Trust the pianist, Mr. Jones of the

Park Theatre, Dr. Barker elocutionist, and Mr. Hamblin. She was quite young, scarcely seventeen, just ripening into womanhood, with a rounded, elegant figure, a complexion exquisitely fair, and a pair of most radiant eyes. To these personal attractions she united a mind well trained and a rare intellect, and gave every promise of future eminence in her profession. The story of her life is an affecting narration, bordering strongly upon romance. Early in life she had a passionate attachment to the stage, and after completing her education placed herself under the tuition of Mr. Hamblin, becoming a member of his family. This step was taken contrary to the wishes of her mother, a woman of doubtful respectability, who from some cause or other evinced a determination to prevent her making her appearance. Her brother, a young man by the name of Miller, espoused the mother's side, and published in a paper called the Polyanthus, edited by G. W. Dixon, a most violent attack on Mr. Hamblin, charging him with abducting the girl, and accusing him of the very worst intentions towards her. On reading this article Miss Missouri swooned; she had borne the persecutions of a set of villains, but this blow, revealing as it did to the world who she was, and whence she sprung, wounded her deeply. A feminine sensibility of soul, a refinement of mind, and a nice sense of decorum, with a corresponding delicacy of constitution, ever awakened the sympathies and pity of all who knew her. She was mortified beyond measure, and her brain reeled beneath her load of sorrow. She saw around her a selfish circle of persons contesting for the control of her talents, and the emoluments from their exercise — and unable to stem the tide which set against her, she yielded and died of inflammation of the brain. A thousand rumors were current. A thorough *post mortem* examination, by the most eminent physicians, bore record to the unsullied purity of a fair girl. Her death was universally regretted. The parties implicated were arrested — Miller for threatening Hamblin's life, and Dixon for some other cause — but a few months only passed by, and this sad episode in every-day life was forgotten.

Forrest played an engagement in May, and on the 24th the play of the "Lady of Lyons," since so popular, was first produced at the Tremont to a house containing only $210. This play, however, had been produced on the 16th of May at the National Theatre, *the first time* in Boston. The cast at the Tremont was as follows: *Claude*, Forrest; *Col. Damas*, Gilbert; *Beauseant*, Cline; *Glavis*, Muzzy; *Mons. Deschappelles*, Davenport; *Gaspar*, Cunningham; *Pauline*, Mrs. Barrett; *Widow Melnotte*, Mrs. Muzzy. At the National, the cast was, *Claude*, George Jones; *Beauseant*, Ayling; *Glavis*, J. S. Jones; *Col. Damas*, Spear; *Gaspar*, Saunders; *Mons. Deschappelles*, Marshall; *Pauline*, Mrs. Geo. Jones; *Madame Deschappelles*, Mrs. Pelby; *Janet*, Mrs. Parker. This piece has proved one of the most popular ever written. The ladies are peculiarly partial to it, and with a decent cast always draws a good house. Mr. Murdoch left the theatre in the month of May, when he took a farewell benefit. His departure was regretted by the public.

The sixth and last season of Mr. Barry's management

commenced on the 27th of August, 1838, with the "School for Scandal," ($569.75). Miss Rock, Mr. Finn, and Mr. Kilner, were engaged for a limited number of nights. The stock company included Comer, Barry, Gilbert, Whiting, Muzzy, Benson, Adams, Mrs. Gilbert, Mrs. Barry, Miss A. Fisher, Mrs. Smith, etc., and Miss Fanny Jones as principal danseuse.

"Masaniello" was revived, the leading parts sustained by Person, Brough, Morgan, and Mrs. Barrymore. The Bedouin Arabs astonished the public with their prodigious leaps and evolutions, trials of strength, pyramids of men, etc. The leading stars were Forrest, Mdlle. Augusta, Wallack, Miss Shirreff, and Miss Seguin, Hacket, the Woods, Celeste, Mr. Bailey, Mr. and Mrs. Sloman, etc. etc. Tom Kilner, in October, '38, left the theatre, announcing his intention to settle out west, where he is still living.

The season of 1838–9 was almost devoid of interest. The fortunes of the drama were so desperate, that the curtains went up some nights to less than $90 in the house. Mr. Barry, under this state of affairs, allowed the No-haired Horse to appear, and also permitted one Shales, an amateur, to astonish the modern Athenians with his impersonation of *Richard III.* With these exceptions, Mr. Barry never deserted the legitimate province of the stage, but such trivial deviations in so long a career should be passed over lightly.

We should not allow the name of Edward Shales to pass without some brief tribute. His story is a brief one. Possessing a love of the drama, he conceived an idea that he was amply qualified to represent the leading heroes of tragedy, with fine effect; and our stage-struck hero soon made known his aspirations, which were ably seconded by a party of the maddest wags that ever resided in Boston at one time. They encouraged him in the idea that nature had done every thing for him, and he gave his friends a touch of his quality in the loft of a stable. Never did a tyro receive such flattering encomiums as he received from these critics, who advised him, by all means, to perfect himself in *Richard III.*, and astonish Boston by a display of talent. He at once consented, and during the time of preparation, sundry oyster and champaigne suppers were partaken of at his expense. The regular drama being on the decline, Mr. Barry consented, and Shales appeared. We need not say that the hit was great. A benefit was announced for Mr. Shales, to take place at the Tremont on the 11th of June, 1839, when Shales was to appear in two acts of "Richard III." At an early hour, the house was densely packed, by all the lovers of fun in Boston, who had been privately notified that a rich dramatic treat might be expected, the ladies with becoming good taste absenting themselves, save one or two, who were not to be excluded from the entertainment. Mr. Shales appeared, and the most rapturous applause burst forth from every part of the house, and for many moments he was occupied in making due acknowledgments to the audience. He soon commenced his part, and never before had Shakspeare had such an interpreter. His pronunciation was equally faulty with his conception, and his carriage still worse. A few missiles were thrown upon the stage at the commencement, and Shales began to have an idea that he had put his foot into it, but he resolved to go on. Proceeding a little farther, he was saluted by a thin paper bag of flour, which transmogrified *Richard* into a miller, and the curtain went down till the actor had time to cleanse himself. Other acts of disorder were committed; and the friends so far forgot themselves, as to throw small copper coin, while a lady was on the stage. The manager at once came forward, and offered a reward of fifty dollars for the discovery of the person, intimating that whatever they might be pleased to do while Mr. Shales was on the stage, they must respect the presence of a lady. This they strictly obeyed, and *Lady Anne* was held sacred. The act in which Shales figured was finally drawing to a close, when an immense wreath, composed of cabbage leaves and other products of the kitchen garden, was thrown to him, amid the most tremendous cheering. He received it with all due courtesy, and the curtain went down, for the tenth time during the evening. Loud calls were now made for "Shales!" "Shales!" "Shales!" and he finally appeared, when some of his friends, most fantastically dressed, rose in the proscenium box, and offered for his acceptance a service of plate — made of *tin!* He approached, and a few remarks were made; he accepted the waiter, and was bearing it off in triumph, when a perfect tornado of flour balls reached him, not to mention a watery stream from a syringe. He held fast hold of his present, however, and made his exit. The service of plate disappeared that night in a most mysterious manner. Mr. Shales was kind enough to allow it to be placed on the table of the greenroom, from whence it was conveyed to the paint room. Here it was found by another person, who had it put in a box, directed and sent it to the landlord of one of the leading hotels in a suburban town, with the intention of notifying a few choice spirits to there convene and enjoy a social hour; but the landlord took umbrage at the plate, and when he next visited Boston, made a circuitous route over Cambridge bridge, and consigned the box and plate to the water. The wreath was sent to New York, where it was much admired. The scribblers of the day alluded to this affair in various ways. One, through the columns of the Post, wrote:—

"And know you not your enemy,
Your greatest foe in town?
'T was William Pelby who did send
The knaves to put you down.

"You spoil his houses when you play.
All his attraction fails,
When on the Tremont bills appears
Richard, by Mr. Shales."

"Straws," of the N. O. Picayune, had his verses, one of which was as follows:—

"Great Shales! ve does n't touch thy hump,
Nor dare ve reach thy crown;
Ve stops short at the eye-brows, quite
Dumfounded by thy frown!
Vainly shall rivals claim the wreath —
Thy genius doth secure it;—
The test of tragic genius is,
That muscles can't endure it!"

Mr. Shales, we must do him the credit to say, attracted the largest house of the season, ($1,129.50,) and bore the joke with great good humor, concluding, "let him laugh who wins;" and after all, he possessed more shrewdness than he had credit for;

> "His after fate untold in Thespian strain,
> His *Richard* ne'er astonished a crowded house again."

"Nicholas Nickleby" was brought out, and *Squeers* (John Gilbert) and his better half as *Mrs. Squeers*, dealt out the brimstone and treacle to about forty boys to the admiration of crowded houses. Smith as *Nicholas* shouted "Wretch!" and Muzzy as *Mantalini* threatened to break his "dimnition head," while Miss Rock as *Smike* picked up the crumbs with becoming gravity. The piece proved successful. It was the delight of the juveniles. Another piece called "Trudge, Fudge, and Drudge," was brought out on the occasion of Mr. Charles Craft's benefit, the popular box-office keeper, who for many years was chief of this department. On that occasion, Mr. Crafts appeared on the stage, — his first, and we believe his last appearance on the boards. Mr. Barry brought the season to a close in June, and terminated his labors after six years' campaign as manager of the Tremont Theatre.

If the reader will cast his eye back and glance at the array of talent brought out under Mr. Barry's management, and if he will recall the various productions, the novelty and necessary expenses incurred to make the theatre what it should be, he will certainly admit that Mr. Barry deserved a rich reward. He had exerted himself to make the drama attractive, and to lift it to a moral standard. He studied to meet the approbation of the respectable classes of the community, and he toiled hard to keep himself a "man of his word." But the result of all this was most disastrous to Mr. Barry, for his loss during the six years exceeded *twenty-six thousand dollars*. His most fortunate season, that of 1834–5, produced the unprecedented sum for Boston of $94,000; the expenses amounted to $97,000. During his lease, the country passed through scenes of pecuniary disasters almost unparalleled; yet had the building held that number of persons which every first class theatre must hold to pay the necessary expenses, we doubt not he would have fought the fight with success, and come out of the struggle with full pockets. The theatre, unfortunately, was deficient in accommodation. The first and second tier of boxes had seats for 264 persons only, and the average receipts of one of the greatest engagements, that of the Woods in "La Sonnambula," amounted to $675 per night, while the expenses amounted to $700. In New York, the Woods averaged for sixteen nights, with the same opera, $1,467, but the Park held 411 persons in the lower tier of boxes, the Tremont only 132. The rent paid by Mr. Barry was $9,500 a year for the whole of the Tremont Theatre, including the bars, which, owing to the action of the city authorities during his engagement, so limited the use of the bars, that the rent fell in his hands from $2,500 to $1000. The directors in their report of 1839, made to the stockholders, admitted that the corporation netted 50 per cent. more than had been realized from any preceding lessee, stating, "Mr. Barry is the only tenant we have yet had who has both satisfied the public, and paid a fair remunerating rent to the proprietors, and the fact that the theatrical business in Boston for the last two or three years has been, and still is, in a state of extraordinary depression."

At this time Mr. Barry was somewhat in arrears for rent, and notwithstanding this favorable report, and the fact that he had paid $16,000 in repairs, gas fittings, etc., they demanded and obtained the full payment of the bond. His books, wardrobe, every thing came under the auctioneer's hammer, and Mr. Barry left Boston as poor as Lazarus.

Such a termination to his many trials was a hard recompense for his six years of toil. He had not only been obliged to contend against the crises in the money market, but Mr. Pelby proved an inveterate enemy through life to the Tremont Theatre, and sought its overthrow by every means in his power, as a retaliation for the treatment he had experienced from the first board of directors. No star came to this country of any note after Mr. Pelby opened the Warren, but received at once liberal offers to appear at his theatre. Mr. Barry was of course in the field, and to obtain them was obliged to outbid Mr. Pelby's offers, which he never wished to be accepted. We attach no blame to the latter gentleman for this piece of diplomacy, and merely mention it to give an idea of a not unimportant agent in the decline of the Tremont. This fact, coupled with the more important one that the theatre was too small, explains the question sometimes asked, Why did Boston not sustain the Tremont Theatre?

CHAPTER XXV.

The Tremont under J. S. Jones. — Season '39-40. — The Company. — Mr. Ranger. — Charles Kean. — Death of Mr. Stimpson. — Mrs. Fitzwilliam. — Jack Falstaff, by George Andrews. — The Finn and Eberle Benefit. — Attempt to reduce the Prices. — Tyrone Power. — Fanny Elssler. — The Woods. — John Braham, etc. etc.

After the departure of Mr. Barry, the proprietors of the theatre had numerous applications for the lease, but our townsman, J. S. Jones, Esq., was deemed the best qualified for the post, and it was rented to him for four years, with the right to terminate in two or three years. The rent was $8000 the first year, and $8,500 the subsequent years.

The season of 1839–40, under Mr. Jones, commenced on the 2d of September, with the "Poor Gentleman," and the farce of the "Little Adopted." Mr. Gilbert, the stage-manager, delivered an opening address, in the course of which the following allusion was made to Mr. Barry: —

"Ay! look around — above — it is the same
Old Shakspeare's temple, as when erst you came.
There you have often sat, and *here* have seen
The buffoon peasant and the tragic queen.
Here have you heard the lover plead his cause,
And seen the hero fight for liberty and laws.
'T is *not* the same! for ONE has left the shrine
Who loved with flowers its hundred gates to 'twine,
He who directed, he who led our band,
Has gone to labor in a sister land.
Our hearts are with him for his good success;
Here 's to his health, his home, his happiness."

The company included Mr. and Mrs. Gilbert, Mr. and Mrs. W. H. Smith, Mr. and Mrs. Muzzy, Mr. and Mrs. Ayling, Mrs. Sheridan, Mrs. Anderson, Miss Boquet, Fanny Jones, Messrs. George H. Andrews, J. F. Williamson, D. Whiting, A. W. Fenno, D. A. Sarzedas, W. H. Curtis, J. H. Ring. Leader of the orchestra, Holloway; James Kendall, clarionet; Edward Kendall, bugle; Geer, Warren, Woodhouse, etc.

The theatre was decorated throughout, and a splendid drop act was painted by W. M. Bayne, who has of late years acquired a fortune, by his Panorama of a Voyage to Europe.

Mrs. Anderson made a hit this season as *Jane Lomax*, and ably supported Mr. Forrest during his engagement, performing *Julie de Mortimar* to Mr. F.'s *Richelieu*, with an effect since unequalled.

On the 4th of November, Mr. Ranger appeared for the first time as *Marquis St. Croix*, in the comedy written by himself, entitled the "Romantic Widow." Many will remember this gentleman for his excellent impersonation of the French gentlemen, in which he excelled. This gentleman was more successful in New York than here. He belonged to the class of actors whose peculiarities may be summed up in the single word — *beautiful*. His every movement was symmetry and grace; but, notwithstanding these qualifications, he played to poor houses.

Charles Kean followed, and attracted good houses. His *Hamlet* was pronounced excellent throughout; his *King Lear*, beautiful and almost unrivalled; but as the "crook-backed tyrant," he was not so successful. Mr. Kean also appeared as *Claude Melnotte*, and performed

Pizarro to Mrs. Anderson's *Elvira* on Thanksgiving evening, when Mr. Stimpson, the captain of the supernumeraries, was killed by the curtain weight falling upon him and fracturing his skull.

On the 16th of December, Mrs. Fitzwilliam, the same who still delights a London audience, appeared. The play of "Widow Wiggins," in which she sustained six characters, was very attractive. Her appearance on the boards, at a time when there was a depression in business, and consequently many long faces, was deemed a public benefit, for her faultless acting chased away the clouds of despondency, and smoothed the furrows of care. Her vocal as well as histrionic powers were, at that time, exceedingly versatile, and her "Music Mad" called forth repeated rounds of applause. "Foreign and Native Graces" was one of Mrs. Fitzwilliams's most popular pieces; and this lady, although not remarkable for her beauty, won, by force of real talent, the suffrages of all theatre-goers. She played *Rosalind* to W. H. Smith's *Orlando*, and Frederick's *Jacques*, on the night of her benefit, which was honored by a full house.

After the departure of this lady, a series of stock benefits took place. Mr. George H. Andrews appeared as *Sir John Falstaff*. A wicked critic was bold enough to remark, that "he played Jack Falstaff to kill; that is, he killed off Falstaff to begin with — murdered him absolutely — and then played Jack *Andrews* very well during the rest of the performance;" a very just opinion of this effort. Mrs. Anderson's benefit was a good one. She was aided by Ranger, and her father, William Pelby, appeared in the 5th act of "Brutus," his first appearance on the Tremont boards for eight years.

On the 27th of January, 1840, a benefit was given at the Tremont to the widow and children of Henry J. Finn, whose recent loss in the Lexington (Jan. 13, 1840) then excited the greatest sympathy. A meeting of gentlemen was holden at the Exchange Coffee House, at which Josiah Bradlee, Esq., presided, and William Hayden was secretary, when a committee was appointed to superintend the benefit. Mr. and Mrs. Seguin, Mr. and Mrs. Wallack, Mr. Knight the vocalist, Mr. Ranger, and the stock company, volunteered their services, and the price was raised to $2 boxes, and $1 pit and second circle. The result was a house containing $1175. A benefit was also given to Mrs. Eberle, whose husband, an actor, was also lost on board the Lexington, which attracted at the regular prices $1116. These benefits were honorable alike to the brother artists who so generously contributed their services, and to the finer feelings and sympathies that cluster around the heart. The public responded to the calls, and the truckmen turned out strong. At the Eberle benefit, a uniform band of marines from the Navy Yard came over. The families, after deducting a few expenses, received about $900 each.

Mr. Ranger's benefit was during this engagement fashionably attended. On that occasion a medal of splendid embossed gold, the free gift of a large number of his friends and admirers, was presented to him. It bore a suitable inscription, and Mr. Ranger in accepting it responded in a most courteous and appropriate manner.

On the 21st of February, Mr. Jones finding it up hill work, closed the house, which he had a right to do by a restriction in the lease. He had done all that could be expected of him to sustain this popular play-house; but the public were not disposed to pay $1 per ticket, and, aware of this fact, the manager desired to reduce the prices, but the proprietors of the theatre would not listen to a proposal, which might, if adopted when first suggested, have tended to contribute to its popularity, and preserved it even to this day as a dramatic temple. It is true, however, that the season of 1839–40 was a most disastrous one to theatrical entertainments throughout the country, for in New York and Philadelphia they were equally unsuccessful.

Mr. Jones reopened the theatre on the 30th of March. Forrest, Mr. and Mrs. H. Wallack, and Hacket, appeared. On the 11th of May, 1840, Signor Hervio Nano opened as the "Gnome King."

The theatre was subsequently closed a few days, to afford time for the preparation of F. S. Hill's "Six Degrees of Crime," which was partially successful, and finally closed on the 4th of July.

The loss of the season was considerable, and the receipts for thirty-seven weeks were little rising of $48,000. Among other stars not particularized above, who appeared this season, were Dan Marble, Finn, whose last performance in this city was October 4, 1839, as *Logic* and *Mawworm*, Miss Hildreth, Celeste, Murdoch, Lecompte, and Ballet, and L. F. Tasistro, formerly editor of the *London Athenæum*.

The season of 1840–1 was commenced by Mr. Jones on the 24th of August. The plays were, "John Bull," in which Tyrone Power, the eminent delineator of Irish character, played *Dennis Brulgruddery*, and the "Irish Lion," the leading part also sustained by Mr. Power, who had then just arrived from Liverpool, and was induced to play three nights prior to his New York engagement. The name of Power will forever be associated with the fate of the steamship President, in which he was a passenger. He was born in the county of Waterford, Ireland, on the 2d of November, 1797. Power's account of his travels in America is still extant.

To return to the record of local affairs. The company consisted of Mr. and Mrs. Gilbert, Mr. and Mrs. Creswick, Mr. and Mrs. Muzzy, Mr. and Mrs. Ayling, Mrs. W. H. Smith, Mrs. H. Cramer, Fanny Jones, G. H. Andrews, S. D. Johnson, Hill, Curtis, Spear, Ring, etc. Scenic artist, Bartholomew. Dan Marble appeared this season, and pleased those partial to his peculiar style. He was good in his line of Yankee parts, and has had no equal on the boards since his death.

Fanny Elssler, the first theatrical celebrity who came from France to salute the United States, made her first appearance in Boston on the evening of the 7th of September, 1840. Her great reputation as a danseuse, surpassed only by Taglioni, and by many preferred even to her, had preceded her arrival, and her success in New York had so bewildered the editors and critics, that the language was deficient in words to express their admiration. "All that we had imagined of poetry," said one, "of music, of sculpture, of refinement, elegance, and beauty, were realized. The colors of the rainbow, the delicacy of the flowers, the purity of the crystal waters, have nothing more radiant, exquisite, or transparent, than the gossamer floatings of this glorious creature. For the first time in our lives we *felt* what the poet meant by the 'airy gems,' the 'spoken flowers,' and the 'oracular songs,' of his enraptured fancy." Such language, as we read it, long after the "divine Fanny" has disappeared from public notice, strikes us as the ravings of some crack-brained fop, but at that time so enraptured were the public, that it fell upon the ear as the very moderate sentiments of a very cool admirer. Fanny Elssler carried America by her exquisite grace, even as Jenny Lind conquered all hearts by her beautiful voice; and as she may be considered the best danseuse we have ever seen in this country, we quote the following very accurate description of her, from the "Beauties of the Opera and Ballet:"—"La Fanny is tall, beautifully formed, with limbs that strongly resemble those of the hunting Diana, combining strength with the most delicate and graceful style; her small and classically shaped head is placed on her shoulders in a singularly elegant manner; the pure fairness of her skin requires no artificial whiteness, while her eyes beam with a species of playful malice, well suited to the half-ironical expression at times visible in the corners of her finely-curved lips; her rich, glossy hair, of bright chesnut hue, is usually braided over a forehead formed to wear, with equal grace and dignity, the diadem of a queen, or the floral wreath of a nymph.

The announcement of her advent was hailed with joy, and our usually staid citizens indulged in various bursts of enthusiasm, and many actually walked before the Tremont House for hours, in hopes that the divinity would show herself at the window. Twenty-one boxes were sold on the Saturday previous, and on the morning of Monday, the remainder were sold at auction. The first week of her appearance was a most notable one, aside from her great attraction, assisted as she was by Mons. Sylvan. On the 10th of September, the great Bunker Hill Convention was holden, and a fair was held by the ladies to complete the Bunker Hill Monument. It was an exciting week, but "Nathalie" and "La Sylphide" were not lost amidst these political and patriotic scenes. It was "Elssler" on every side. She was dreamed of, talked of, and idolized; and some wag having circulated a report that "Fanny" would take an airing in her barouche, quite a gathering took place on Tremont street. Boston was not alone in this ovation, for the ladies from Boston to Philadelphia, all wore Elssler cuffs, made of velvet with bright buttons. In every store window articles were displayed flavoring of the mania. Elssler boot-jacks, Elssler bread, etc. etc., were to be seen, showing how violent was the attack of *Fannyelsslermaniaphobia.* It was during this visit that Fanny contributed her share of a benefit to completing Bunker Hill Monument, which amounted to $569.50. Boston was somewhat laughed at for accepting this gift, and the scribblers had their jokes; but after all it was Boston money.

Fanny's last appearance at this engagement was on the 2d of October, to a crowded house. She was called out; and being led forward by Mons. Sylvan, she pressed her hand upon her heart, and said:

"*Ladies and Gentlemen:* This is the first time I have appeared before you with pain. Am I to leave you forever? No, it shall not be. I will not say adieu, but hope to see you again."

The once angelic Fanny Elssler is still living, according to late accounts, a sturdy matron, whose present embonpoint would never indicate her former grace and loveliness. The Chevalier Wyckoff, who figured with this lady while in this country, has recently been imprisoned in Genoa, for attempting to abduct a Miss Gamble. He is now at liberty, and we could forgive him his sins, were he to bring another Elssler to this country.

The receipts of this engagement were very great. Mr. Jones paid Fanny Elssler $500 per night, and the following was the result. Fanny did not dance on the memorable 10th of September. Mr. Creswick, now in London, appeared in the "Sea Captain," and a better melo-dramatic actor we have never seen. The receipts below include the premiums obtained at auction by the sale of tickets, Messrs. Coolidge and Haskell, auctioneers:—

1840.	Sept.	7,	$1242
	"	9,	1726
	"	11,	1537
	"	14,	1184 25
	"	16,	1118
	"	18,	959
	"	21,	909
	"	23,	816 75
	"	25,	1160 75
	"	28,	620 75
	"	29,	624 75
	Oct.	1,	969 50
	"	2,	1391 75

Mr. Forrest succeeded Elssler, and was followed by

Mr. Vandenhoff, the elder, and Miss Vandenhoff, their second appearance in Boston. Mr. V.'s *Hamlet* is remembered by our critics as *the Hamlet* of the stage. Miss Josephine Clifton, Mr. Buckstone, now in London, appeared. Mr. and Mrs. Wood, and Mr. Brough, appeared on the 7th of December in "La Sonnambula," and during their engagement, full, fashionable, and musical audiences graced the boxes. On the 11th of January, 1841, John Braham made his first appearance in a Boston theatre at the Tremont, in the character of *Henry Bertram*, (Guy Mannering,) without, however, any vocalist to sustain him, the only show of opera being his own unaided efforts. He subsequently appeared in *Count Belino*, (the Devil's Bridge,) and the operetta "The Cabinet." For his benefit and farewell to a Boston stage, he took the second and third acts of "Massaniello" and "The Waterman."

Having previously appeared in concerts under the patronage of the Handel and Haydn Society, there was slight curiosity to hear the veteran English tenor in opera travestie, and the experiment of substituting one singer, however brilliant, for an opera company, met a cold reception from the public accustomed to "the Woods" and the Seguine troupe. Mr. Braham was, unfortunately for his stage popularity, no actor, but on the contrary marred every character by excessive awkwardness. He never pretended to embody the graceful lover or hero for which the bills announced him. Added to these drawbacks, the want of a good stage presence destroyed all the illusions of the scene, and brought his audience back to a cold reality of John Braham, the great tenor, singing like a machine, and giving not the least idea of *Harry Bertram*, *Count Belino*, or *Tom Tug*. A few performances, to wretched houses, closed this unfortunate exhibition, and Braham returned to his appropriate field of action, the concert room, where he continued to reap a golden harvest, and by his superb vocalization soon effaced all recollection of his failure in opera. England's greatest tenor, as we have already stated, was introduced to Boston audiences by the Handel and Haydn Society. The announcement of his debut was a *chef d'œuvre* of the enthusiastic secretary, who, for so many years, managed the affairs of that association. On the 20th and 22d of November, 1840, two entertainments were promised, so affording Bostonians the only opportunity of listening to the dulcet notes of Europe's most celebrated songster. Crowds rushed to pay their dollar for this only opportunity, and the vast majority were fully satisfied that John Braham's reputation had a solid foundation in the great feats he accomplished. His remarkable power, compass, and good quality of voice, fairly astonished, in their remarkable union, all listeners. They could not credit the existence of their own senses, when they witnessed such daring and brilliant performance of the greatest difficulties, by a man acknowledged to be very near threescore and ten. The sensation produced by his wonderful command of the most extensive tenor *repertoire*, and the thrilling energy and delightful *verve* and expression, that gave all his music grace and color, was increased to a positive *furore* by the *fracas* between the Handel and Haydn Society and a critic. A flaming card appeared in the journals of that day, signed by several prominent members of the Handel and Haydn, in which the critic was denounced as unworthy of credit and public confidence in his vocation of critic.

So unusual a procedure stirred up a mighty commotion here, and the amount of discussion and excitement produced, almost equalled hard cider and log cabin uproar through which the country had then passed.

Mr. Braham, after his failure at the Tremont, went into the concert-giving business on his own account, besides singing for the Handel and Haydn in oratorios and selections from sacred music. Toward the close of his somewhat protracted concert season, he invoked Russell and the Rainers to his aid. His farewell concert took place Feb. 16, 1841, and his last appearance on the 20th of that month, for Mr. Hayter's benefit.

In sacred music, his most popular and effective performances were, "Sound an Alarm," from Judas Maccabaeus; "Comfort Ye," and "Every Valley;." "Thy Rebuke," and "Behold and See;" "He that Dwelleth," and "Thou shalt Dash Them;" "Deeper and Deeper Still," and "I 'll Waft her Angels;" "Total Eclipse," and "Why doth the God of Israel Sleep," and "The Judgment Hymn." He was also pleasing in the "David" of Neukom, (though in that he fell short of Coburn in his best days,) and in the tenor songs from "The Creation."

In "Sound an Alarm," "Thou shalt Dash Them," the great tests of a tenor in "Samson," and "The Judgment Hymn," he has never been approached here, and the most daring are confounded in their attempt to imitate his surpassing excellence.

In music of a secular character, he shone most brilliantly when delivering "Scots wha hae wi' Wallace bled," "All the Blue Bonnets are over the Border," "The Bay of Biscay," "The Death of Nelson," and "The Marseilles Hymn." His fire and outpouring of soul in these moved and swayed his audience to a degree few tenors ever attained with our cold public. "Rocked in the Cradle of the Deep," "The Soldier's Dream," "Robin Adair," "The Last Words of Marmion," "The Evening Gun," and "Kelvin Grove," never failed to bring out his wondrous union of feeling and expression with just the amount of execution which should meet the demands of the music, and yet not smother and conceal the sentiment. John Braham was a marvel, and those who missed the opportunity to hear that greatest musical wonder of this or any other age, must have deeply regretted their inadvertence. He retained his energy and command of the tenor scale longer than any other man has ever done. Donzelli, the celebrated Italian *primo tenore*, who flourished some twenty years since, came the nearest to Braham in this respect, having acquitted himself well in *Otello* at Naples when sixty years old; but John Braham made the Birmingham town hall ring with his clarion voice at the age of eighty, and last winter filled Exeter Hall with admiring throngs, when some years past that extreme limit of human life.

The theatre was kept opened at full prices until Feb. 10th, a period of twenty-five weeks, the receipts of which were $45,504.75. It was then closed, but reopened on the 15th at reduced prices, with "The Cataract of the Ganges," a fine equestrian troupe having been engaged. "Napoleon," "Amalek, the Arab," and "Mazeppa," were brought out. Mr. Creswick was the hero of these pieces, and he delighted not only the juveniles, but the entire public. Mr. and Mrs. Vandenhoff, Hill, and others, appeared.

The first half-price night brought $603.13 to the house, and the average receipts for many weeks at the half price were equal to the average of full prices. The Woods, at full prices, averaged for three weeks $2,886.50; the equestrian corps for a similar length of time, at half price, $2,033; and the Vandenhoffs, $1,800. Thus the half price, with less attraction and less expense than the Woods, produced an attendance greater in proportion, and the receipt of nearly as much money. The gross receipts of the season for forty-two weeks were $70,250.67, of which $18,531.14 were paid to stars.

CHAPTER XXVI.

The Last Years of the Tremont Theatre. — Messrs. Andrews and Preston. — The Seguins. — Visit of the Prince de Joinville. — Samuel Butler. — Boz. — Season of 1842-3. — George Vandenhoff. — The Broughams. — Josh. Silsby. — Closing Scenes at the Tremont. — The Last Night. — First Appearance of the Learned Blacksmith. — Destruction of the Temple by Fire, etc. etc.

MR. JONES relinquished his connection with the theatre at the close of the season of 1840-1, when Mr. Geo. H. Andrews and John Preston, Esq., undertook its management. The season under their auspices commenced on the 23d of August, when the "Heir at Law," "33 John Street," and "Lottery Ticket," were performed, and a new drop act from the pencil of Mr. Samuel Stockwell, fell for the first time. The company embraced Mr. and Mrs. John G. Gilbert, Mr. and Mrs. J. M. Field, Mrs. W. H. Smith, Miss Fisher, Mrs. Cramer, W. F. Johnson, S. Johnson, Fenno, Mr. and Mrs. Creswick, etc. Mr. Comer was musical director, Signor Ostinelli led the orchestra, and Miss Fanny Jones was principal danseuse. The leading stars were Hacket, Forrest, Mr. and Mrs. Seguin, Mr. Manners, Elssler, and Sam. Butler.

The Seguins were very successful, and occupied a large share of public attention, even from the date of their first appearance in this city, Nov. 5, 1838, to May, 1847, when Marti's Operatic Company eclipsed in their admirable presentment of Italian Opera, all the glories of former dramatic vocalists, and consigned English opera to neglect. When Mr. Seguin first appeared here in Rooker's opera, "Anidie, or the Love Test," he produced a marked sensation. A critic upon that opera as then presented at Tremont Theatre for the first time, says of him: "The moment Seguin opened his mouth, one universal gape of astonishment infected all, such was the wonder produced by his magnificent organ. At the first close of his recitative, the most enthusiastic applause appreciated that pure, legitimate, and ponderous bass; of large and even quality, his distinct enunciation, perfect intonation, and such a body of tone, that Lablache alone will be placed above him. 'My boyhood's Home' caused an immense sensation." Mrs. Seguin appeared in opera a year or two after this, and by her remarkable versatility, tact in management, and intense devotion to getting up the operas, frequently rehearsing and directing all day and singing in the evening, pecuniary success for a long time crowned the Seguins with laurels. Her best character was undoubtedly the *Bohemian Girl*, and his *Devilshoof*, in that opera. Both were clever, and taking in a wide range of characters by a pleasing union of good singing with appropriate action and excellent by-play. He was probably the best actor that ever appeared on the operatic stage, when the character suited him, and he was in the vein. In the opera just alluded to, "The Postillion," and "Massaniello," he was exactly suited with a role to bring out the humor and vivacity so profusely given by nature. Just before his death, Mr. Seguin became the low comedian at Wallack's Lyceum in New York, but made no sensation there, and his friends regretted that close of a brilliant life, especially when it was found that no pecuniary distress induced the mistake.

Fanny Elssler, supported by Mons. Sylvain, appeared on the 13th of October, and attracted, as on her former visit, crowded houses. Her last appearance in this city was on the 17th of November, when she gave the 2d act from "La Sylphide," 2d scenes of "La Gipsey," and "Jalleo de Xeres."

On the 22d of November, James Sheridan Knowles' comedy of "Old Maids" was brought out, and run for one week, when it was shelved, and since then has rarely if ever been performed. It did not do well at the Tremont, but this was not entirely owing to the want of merit in the play, but to the great outside attraction of the Prince de Joinville, and that never-to-be-forgotten ball, given in his honor at Faneuil Hall, which had more powerful attractions than the theatre. Mr. Sam. Butler from London next essayed to attract an audience, and Mr. T. C. Grattan's "Ben Nazir" was brought out, for the first time in America, Dec. 6th. The author was at the time British Consul in this city. The play was originally written for Edmund Kean, and with it he hoped to regain his position in the theatrical world of London, but he was unable to commit even the words to memory, and it proved a most signal failure. Kean being convinced that he had lost the power of study, never afterwards attempted a new part. Mr. Butler did what Kean could not, he was perfect in the text, but his talents were not of that stamp to present a new part in the most favorable light, though he gained applause for his *Hamlet* and other characters. He was a man of commanding figure, and after his return to England, became unsuccessful both as an actor and manager, and finally resorted to drinking, which hastened his death.

The theatre in December was closed. The full prices, that is $1 to the boxes, had been in force, and it proved almost ruinous. On the 20th of December, the theatre after a temporary close, was re-opened at half prices, with "London Assurance," which was given with the following cast: —

Sir Harcourt Courtly, ... John Gilbert,
Charles Courtly, ... Creswick,
Dazzle, ... Field,
Meddle, ... Johnson,
Cool, ... Fenno,
Mr. Spanker, ... S. D. Johnson,

Lady Gay Spanker, . .	Miss Charlotte Cushman,
Grace Harkway, . . .	Mrs. Field,
Pert, ...	Miss Fisher.

Mr. Gilbert's *Sir Harcourt* was not generally admired; and though he has since frequently performed it, has never given satisfaction to the critical. At this time, in fact, Mr. W. R. Blake, the best *Sir Harcourt* ever probably on the American stage, was announced to succeed Mr. Gilbert in this part, and the latter taking umbrage, retired from the company. Mr. Field's *Dazzle* has only been equalled by John Brougham, who is the only rival that ever approached the original presentation by Mr. Field in this city. The play of "Nicholas Nickleby" was revived, and on Monday, Jan. 24th, Mr. Field brought out his Masque Phrenologic, entitled "Boz," on which occasion Charles Dickens, Esq., was present. Mr. Field did *Boz*, and a most correct counterpart he was. The masque was an introduction of Dickens' leading characters upon the stage.

The result of twenty-five weeks' management found Messrs. Andrews & Preston about ten thousand dollars worse off than at the commencement, and they tendered the lease of the house to the proprietors, which was accepted. The theatre had not been managed in all its departments as it should have been, and the Boston Museum performances, at twenty-five cents, were commencing to be somewhat attractive. A commonwealth was then formed among the actors, who made a joint interest. Under this system, Mr. Forrest and Miss Clifton, Miss Mary Ann Lee, Miss Julia Turnbull, Herr Driesbach and his lions, appeared. A paying business was done at first; but before the season closed, trouble broke out in the company, relative to the appearance of Mrs. Cramer, who had previously left the company, and Johnson and Field indulged in a set-to in the box-office. This matter was called up on a night of performance, and Mr. Child, the treasurer, came out and explained matters. The theatre closed in June, to the regret of no one.

The season of 1842–3, and the last at this theatre, was opened by J. S. Jones. It commenced on the 5th of September, with "Poor Gentleman," and "A Roland for an Oliver." Messrs. Chapman, J. C. Howard, and Mr. and Mrs. Greene, were members of the company.

On the 15th of November, Mr. George Vandenhoff appeared at the Tremont, as *Hamlet*, a part of which his father stands pre-eminently *the* representative, in the memory of all theatre-goers. The success of the son, however, was commensurate with his abilities. Mr. Jones brought out this season "The Braziers of Naples," which had a good run. In the month of January, 1843, Mr. Thomas Barry played a short engagement, and in the same month Mr. and Mrs. John Brougham, then lately from England, though they had visited New York and Philadelphia, just previous to their Boston visit, played a good engagement. They opened in the "Love Chase." Mr. Brougham appeared as *Dazzle*, and, though it was very acceptible, was objected to by some as being too much of an Irishman. Mr. Gilbert played *Sir Harcourt*, Mrs. Brougham *Lady Gay*, and Mrs. W. H. Smith *Grace Harkway*. Mr. Ayling and Mr. Leman were also in the play. Josh. Silsbee, who has since acquired considerable reputation abroad, Mr. Forrest, Miss Clifton, Professor Risley, and his son, the Olympic Circus, H. P. Grattan, and the Ravel Family, were the leading attractions. The performances of Risley and his son have since been imitated, but never equalled. He was Magnus Apollo in comeliness, a Hercules in strength, and the son a Cupid in beauty. Of all exhibitions of physical grace in classical posturing they surpassed any we have ever seen. The throwing of the boy into the air, who turned a somerset and alighted safely on his father's feet, invariably drew forth the loudest applause. Risley, previous to his arrival here, narrowly escaped death by the earthquake at Port-au-Petre. He subsequently visited England, where his little boy became the pet of the nobility.

The closing scenes at the old Tremont may be briefly related. In the month of June, 1843, on the 17th, President Tyler visited Boston, to attend the ceremonies attending the completion of Bunker Hill Monument, when WEBSTER delivered the oration. The theatre that week was thronged with strangers, and a performance was given on Saturday evening to accommodate the hundreds that were here from the country. The proprietors, having concluded the sale of the theatre to Rev. Mr. Colver's Baptist Society, the last night's performances were announced for the benefit of the manager, J. S. Jones, June 23, 1843, when "The Poor Gentleman, two dances by Fanny Jones, and "A Lover by Proxy," filled up the bill of entertainment.

At the close of the acting, the entire *dramatis personæ*, consisting of nearly twenty individuals, male and female, advanced towards the foot-lights arranged in crescent form, and executed a charming Scotch air with much effect, accompanied with obvious strong emotions in their parting adieus to the community who had bestowed on their efforts its long sustaining rays of patronage. Loud and repeated huzzas, with constant waving of hats and handkerchiefs, followed the piece, which was succeeded by a spontaneous call from the whole audience for Mr. Jones. In compliance with it, in a moment or two he appeared before his patrons, and addressed them in a very appropriate manner. During its delivery his manner indicated deep feeling, oppressed with heartfelt regret, in contemplating the change that was about to take place in that temple of the muses. The edifice was raised and dedicated to illustrate the histrionic art. It was adapted to such purpose, and to no other properly. It could have been conducted in that manner which would have fully carried out its tasteful and public spirited founders. It had been the resort of the *elite*, the refined, the respectable, and the moral of both sexes and of all ranks. He thanked these classes for their support during his management. The doctrine had been industriously circulated, that the drama was on the decline; but this was not so, as when he had engaged considerable attraction, the house was not near large enough to admit the throng that endeavored to press within its walls. It could have been altered to have answered this object, and then it would have been profitable to all parties interested. If ever there was a time for a manager to make a speech, this was the hour. But he was unused to public speaking, though if it were otherwise, he should not enlarge on the causes which will transform the theatre into another institution. He could do so, and show that they did not originate so much in a desire for private and public good, as the unworthy motives to subserve the base designs of aversion and bigotry. Yet he forbore. The truth would hereafter appear. In conclusion, he thanked the audience for their uniform kindness, and respectfully and sincerely bade them farewell. His remarks were continually interrupted by enthusiastic applause.

The next speaker called for was Boston's favorite son, Mr. John Gilbert. He came forward and spoke some minutes, expressing the same views as those of Mr. Jones, with reference to the drama and the alterations soon to take place on that stage. The house was the appropriate place for his profession, and for nothing else. It was built at great expense for that object, and should be devoted to it. There were defects in the drama, but they could be removed by judicious management, and all its objectionable traits effaced, whereby the most scrupulously fastidious might be satisfied that it was a good institution, and be induced to patronize it. He was a Boston boy, and he felt for the honor of the place of his nativity, in the prospect of his fellow-citizens permitting the drama, which was one of the instruments of social refinement and mental cultivation, to go down in darkness. No one regretted the aspect of gloom that hung round its destiny more than Mr. Gilbert, who had been associated in this city with this house from the moment it was built. Yet he would not despair. There was a redeeming spirit in his fellow-citizens. He could not bring himself to believe they would allow such a result; and, therefore, he would not take his last leave of them, but merely bid them good night. He bowed and retired amidst constant cheering.

A call was then made on Mr. J. M. Field, but he did not appear. Mr. Blake, of another establishment, here rose in the proscenium box, and stated, that sixteen years ago, on the opening of the Tremont Theatre, he delivered the introductory poetical address upon its boards; and now, by a singular novel occurrence, he found himself placed in a position where, perhaps, he might utter the last words within its walls in its behalf. He would embrace that fortunate opportunity. He then went into a defence of the drama, considered and answered the principal objections to it in an able manner; showed they were unsound, and the offspring of ignorance and prejudice, combined with the cant of the day. He proved that this institution had been in ancient days, and is, and will continue to be in coming generations, the handmaid of mental and moral improvement. It always had been attacked by fanaticism, without sound reason. Its use was one thing; its abuse another, and a very different thing. For that, it should not be condemned. Religion itself had been abused. He respected true piety, but not that assumed sanctity which had assailed the drama, and to which this institution might be sacrificed. The test of virtue was found in acts, not words. By this rule, he was perfectly willing to institute a comparison between the lives of actors and actresses and those religious zealots who believed themselves to be alone righteous, and despised others, the members of his profession. In the hour of affliction, at the bedside of the sick and the dying, he had often witnessed the conduct of the two parties. He had seen the actress smooth the pillow, administer the medical drug, and speak words of consolation to the expiring patient, when the assumed pious fled from the contagion of the fatal disease; he had witnessed the burial by actors when even ministers shrunk from the performance of their duty. Such scenes were frequent among his profession, and he submitted which had the best claim to be called Christians. The sketches of benevolence the speaker drew were touching, and listened to with silent attention, and at the end applauded with hearty feeling. Previous to leaving the house, the audience gave nine enthusiastic cheers, and separated with manifest regret that this cherished institution, the work of their fathers, an ornament and a boast of the metropolis, should be converted from the original intention of its builders.

The theatre had been opened forty-two weeks. The expenses of the stock company for thirty weeks were $900 per week, and a reduction was then made for the remaining twelve weeks, which averaged $700, making, with the amount paid to stars, $15,095.02, the gross sum of $50,495.02. The largest receipt any one night was $734.37, and the gross receipts for the season were $47,525.25, leaving the deficiency of about three thousand dollars. Such was the result of the last theatrical season at the Tremont Theatre.

On the evening of June 26th, the learned blacksmith, Elihu Burritt, delivered a lecture in the theatre, the nett proceeds of which went towards defraying the cost of the alteration of it into a church, which was done at an expense of about $25,000. A portion of the building was arranged for stores, offices; and the large hall, used on Sunday as a place of worship, was, on week days and evenings, let for miscellaneous meetings, political caucuses, concerts, lectures, etc., and the name of the "TREMONT TEMPLE" was given to the edifice. The Mercantile Library Association here held their popular series of lectures, and Webster, Choate, and Everett, poured forth their eloquence to delighted audiences within its walls. It was here that Jenny Lind, Kate Hayes, and others, charmed enthusiastic auditories; and it was here also that Gliddon discovered the sex of Anch-pa-mach, to the astonishment of those who witnessed the unrolling of the mummy.

In 1849, the edifice narrowly escaped destruction by fire, which originated in the basement; and it was finally destroyed by fire on the morning of Wednesday, March 31, 1852. At this conflagration, Mr. John Hall, a carpenter, lost his life, and George Estee, a fireman, was injured for life. The total loss of property was very large, as the building was occupied by artists, dentists, etc., whose actual loss could not be ascertained. Mr. Thomas Thompson, a gentleman of this city, had in the attic a large number of valuable paintings and statues, all of which were destroyed. The fire likewise communicated to Chapman Hall and other adjacent buildings, which were destroyed.

The proprietors soon determined to rebuild the Temple, and a large and beautiful edifice, containing a fine music hall, now occupies the site where formerly stood the Tremont Theatre. The architect, Mr. Wm. Washburn, has combined economy of room with elegance of accommodation, and the greatest ingenuity is exhibited in the introduction of light into the passage ways and rooms.

CHAPTER XXVII.

The re-opening of the Boston Theatre. — O. C. Wyman, Esq. — The Seguins. — The Howard Athenæum. — Mr. and Mrs. Charles Kean. — Edwin Forrest. — Mr. Fleming. — The Museum. — King John. — The Viennoise Children. — Titus A. Peep, Esq. — C. R. Thorne. — The last Season. — Messrs. Wright, Fenno & Co., etc. etc.

THE re-opening of the Boston Theatre, in 1846, for theatrical representations, brings us once more to chronicle the progress of the drama under its time-honoured roof. For many years it had been used as a lecture room, or occupied by musical and religious societies for their exercises. Mr. Oliver C. Wyman, by the advice of many friends, in 1846, leased the building, and at once restored the interior to its original adaptation. It was a hazardous undertaking, but the lessee being amply qualified for his post, nothing was wanting to ensure its success on the score of managerial ability, but unforeseen circumstances prevented the accomplishment of that end, which, under more favourable auspices, would have resulted from this attempt to render Old Drury once more, *the* theatre of Boston. The interior arrangements were somewhat faulty in design, and alterations were subsequently made. The company engaged was numerous and effective, embracing Mr. and Mrs. Gilbert, Mr. and Mrs. Bland, (formerly Miss Faucet,) Mrs. W. H. Smith, Mr. Phillips, Mrs. Cramer, Mrs. Mueller, Miss Wagstaff, Miss Bouquet, etc., with Brougham, Fleming,

T. Placide, Whitney, Stevens, etc. The managerial corps was organized as follows:—

Lessee, ...	Mr. O. C. Wyman.
Stage Manager, ...	John G. Gilbert.
Treasurer, ...	Charles Craft.
Prompter, ...	H. J. Conway.
Leader of Orchestra, and Musical Director,	C. H. Mueller.
Principal Scenic Artist, ...	S. B. Stockwell.
Machinist, ...	D. P. Elsworth.
Costumer, ...	S. D. Johnson.
Property Maker, ...	Andrew Spence.

The opening night was August 24, 1846. The plays were, "Speed the Plough," a d the "Irish Lion," cast to the entire strength of the company, and the house was filled in every corner by not only those who in years previous had here received their choicest theatrical entertainments, but by many who hailed with pleasure the dawn of a new era in the production of the legitimate drama in this city.

A Prize Address, written by Mrs. Frances S. Osgood, was spoken by Mr. Gil ert. As a composition, it is meritorious, but it was not adapted to the occasion. Many anticipated that the poet would recall the scenes of the past, in which Old Drury was so richly endowed, but the Muse was content with recalling to recollection the leading characters of the drama, closing with the following lines:—

"Here the lithe spirit of the dance shall spring,
Like an embodied zephyr on the wing.
Here, too, the soul of song shall float in air,
And on its wings your hearts, enchanted, bear;
Ah! yield to them, to us, the meed we claim,—
Your smiles to light the path that leads to fame.

So shall this life of mockery seem more sweet,
And flowers shall rise to rest our pilgrim feet,
While from our lips, inspired by hope divine,
Like fire shall flow the bard's melodious line."

The act drop, by Stockwell, was a well designed and spiritedly finished picture of "Athens as it is," representing the modern city and the ancient ruins in one comprehensive view. Mr. George Barrett appeared. Mr. Henry Placide played two engagements this season, one of which was very good. His *Sir Peter Teazle* was a finished performance, and his *Haversack* in "Napoleon's Old Guard," will long be remembered. The "Comedy of Errors" was brought out during his engagement, and the *Two Dromios* were played by Messrs. H. and T. Placide. Mr. J. W. Wallack made his first appearance, after an absence of two years, on the 14th September, 1846, when he played *Benedict* and *Dick Dashall.* His share of a fortnight's engagement was about $1200, and the most popular piece was "Don Cæsar de Bazan," which drew upwards of $600 nightly.

The Seguin Operatic Troupe succeeded Wallack. It was composed of Mr. and Mrs. Seguin, Mr. Frazer and Mr. Meyer; and the operas of the "Postillion of Lonjumeau," "La Sonnambula," "Don Pasquale," "Brewer of Preston," "Bohemian Girl," and "Norma," were brought out. Balfe's "Bohemian Girl" drew the largest house, $712, and the Seguin Troupe, for a three weeks' engagement, received about $2,500.

It was during the Seguins' engagement at the Old Theatre, that the present Howard Athenæum was opened (Oct. 5, 1846) by James H. Hackett & Co., which had some effect upon the close of their engagement.

Boston was again possessed of two first-class theatres, after an interval of several years, and the struggle for superiority was strong. On the 19th of October, Mr. and Mrs. Charles Kean commenced an engagement at the Boston Theatre, with the "Gamester." The remembrance of Ellen Tree drew forth the fashionable, and a brilliant audience was in attendance, though the receipts were only $505.80. "Ion" drew $622.65, and two benefits averaged $700. The opposition at the Howard Athenæum, during the Keans' engagement, would have seriously affected less brilliant stars. On one evening at the Howard, Mrs. Mowatt, Madame Augusta, Md'lle Dernier, George Vandenhoff, and Davenport, all appeared; a combination that would, if presented now, attract a thousand dollar house. Mr. Wallack succeeded the Keans, but the engagement was "poor business," all round; but on the 16th of November, that never-failing attractive star, Edwin Forrest, came to the relief of the management, and brought to the house good and paying audiences, as the reader will see by the following receipts of the first six nights: —

1846.	November	16,	King Lear,	$518 44
"	"	17,	Othello,	694 50
"	"	18,	Metamora,	872 31
"	"	19,	Macbeth,	585 00
"	"	20,	Damon and Pythias,	563 45
"	"	23,	Metamora,	719 75
				$3,953 45

The engagement continued through three weeks,

(Booth at the Howard,) and Mr. Forrest's share was upwards of $4,000. On the night of his benefit, he played *Claude Melnotte* to Mrs. Bland's *Pauline*, and to an audience of $722.14. It was during this engagement that Mr. W. M. Fleming, the present acting manager at the National, first received from the Boston public that meed of praise, which he merited by his very able support of the great American tragedian. It gives us pleasure to record that Mr. Fleming has never forfeited the good opinion then so warmly expressed by the press and the people, and still continues one of Boston's favorites in his line of business. For correctness in the text, he is noted, and his undivided attention is invariably given to whatever he attempts.

After Forrest, Mr. James Murdoch came, but the attractions at the Howard (Miss Mary Taylor, Hackett, Vandenhoff, Crisp, Warren) were too powerful, and the receipts rarely exceeded $100. The same may be said of Mr. Placide's second engagement, though there was a temporary revival of the interest in the performances at this theatre, when Mrs. George Barrett was called on to sustain Mr. Placide, in the leading female parts. The receipts, when entirely dependent upon the stock company, did not on some nights exceed $50, and the weekly expenses averaged about $800.

The Museum at this time was coming into notice, and assuming a position among the theatrical entertainments of the day. Messrs. Smith, Mestayer, Hunt, Mrs. Knight, were there, and plays were presented with that care and attention which has since brought this place so favorably into public notice. The National, under Pelby, was also doing a good business, by catering to the "blood-and-thunder" taste of the lower half million; and, as we have stated, Hacket, at the Howard, was straining every nerve to produce attractions. Under these disadvantageous circumstances, none of the managers were reaping a very great harvest. Mr. Wyman commenced at this time a correspondence with Kean, to bring out "King John" with his splendid dresses, etc., as produced at the Park Theatre in New York, very generously offering to expend a large sum in getting it up, provided Mr. Kean would divide after one hundred per night, but he insisted upon half the gross receipts. This Mr. Wyman refused to give, unwilling to run so great a risk. It was unfortunate for both, that some arrangement was not entered into. The Viennoise Children arriving in New York, Mr. Simpson cut Mr. Kean short at the Park, and for eight weeks he was idle, at a loss to him of several thousand dollars. Had Mr. Kean accepted Mr. Wyman's proposals, he would have been at the Boston when the Viennoise were at the Howard, and their immense attraction would in a great measure have been equalled by "King John." Failing in this, the "Forty Thieves," and "Beauty and the Beast," were the chief attractions at the Boston, to offset the forty-two Viennoise children, till the Seguin Troupe arrived. The result was disastrous to the fortunes of the Boston Theatre. The *novelty* of the Viennoise attracted for many weeks, while the Boston was doing but little. An occasional benefit, of a member of the stock, drew a good house. John Brougham's extravaganza of "Titus a Peep," attracted $359.88. This was a local farce, founded upon the following incident. On an evening when Mr.

Forrest was performing, some gentlemen who had indulged in rather more than their heads could conveniently bear, occupied the stage box, and were so boisterous in their talk as to interrupt Mr. Forrest, who coming down from the stage, met "Acorn" behind the scenes, and at once remonstrated. "Never mind them," said Acorn; "they have been requested to keep more quiet, but the truth is — they are *tight as peeps.*" Mr. Forrest, misunderstanding the reply, remarked, that he did n't know who Titus A. Peep was, but he was bound to have him put out, if he made any farther disturbance. The season closed on the 15th of March, when Mr. Crafts took a benefit, and Mr. Wyman, who had fitted up the house at a great expense of $20,000, retired from the lesseeship much poorer than when he commenced.

Mr. Charles R. Thorne became the next manager of the Boston, opening that house on the 21st of June, 1847, for the purpose of presenting the Viennoise Children, who continued till the 4th of July. Under Mr. Thorne's management, the dramatic season of 1847–8 was commenced on the 16th of August, his stock company embracing Mr. and Mrs. Thorne, Mrs. Cramer, Miss Mestayer, Mrs. Mueller, Messrs. Neaffie, McFarland, Spear, W. F. Johnson, all of whom appeared on the opening night in the comedy of the "Honeymoon." Mr. J. B. Booth, Jr., was also a member, and in some part gave promises of future eminence, which promises, we regret, have never been realized. The star engagements were with Mr. C. Webb, French Ballet Company, Wallack, Booth, (who played *Othello* to his son's *Iago*,) Forrest, Anderson,

E. S. Conner, Madame Anna Bishop's Opera Company, Jim Crow Rice, etc. etc.

The leading stock pieces brought out were the "Last Days of Pompeii," and "Mazeppa."

In the fall of 1848, (Nov. 6,) Messrs. Welch, Delvan & Nathans, gave their equestrian pantomimic and dramatic performances at the Boston, and had a very prosperous season. From this time it was opened by various adventurers, and for many purposes. Miss Cushman played an engagement here after her return from Europe. In 1850, the Ravels leased it, and did an immense business, and in 1851, Macallister the magician attracted full and fashionable houses for a period of ten weeks. Still later, Parodi, under the auspices of Mr. Walker, appeared at this theatre.

On the 13th of April, 1852, the theatre and land were offered at public sale. On the front lot in Federal St., $4.25 was bid; but the sale was postponed, and in a few days was sold at private sale, to Messrs. Merriam, Brewer & Co.

On the night of the 22d of April, 1852, the National Theatre was destroyed by fire. Messrs. Wright, Fenno & Co., the lessees, at once applied to Messrs. Merriam, Brewer & Co., for the use of the old theatre. The property was not then in their possession, and the stockholders of the Boston Theatre, having concluded the sale, were fearful that some accident might cause a fire, and the sale would be vitiated. Messrs. Merriam, Brewer & Co., with great generosity, and from sympathy with the managers of the National in their distress, at once agreed to take the theatre, at the time agreed upon, taking all risk upon themselves. This decision gave Messrs. Wright, Fenno & Co. a field to operate in, and the bills were out the same day for the opening of the Boston, with "Love's Sacrifice," and "Caught in his own Trap;" thus enabling Mrs. Sinclair and Mr. Vandenhoff to complete the engagement they had commenced at the National. The receipts of this brief and last theatrical season at the Boston Theatre were as follows: —

1852.			
April	22,	Love's Sacrifice, Caught in his own Trap,	$406 87
"	23,	" " Sketches in India,	370 75
"	26,	Lady of Lyons, and Highway Rob.,	436 00
"	27,	Much Ado, and Two Queens,	385 25
"	"	" Auction Sales,	28 00
"	28,	Lady of Lyons, and Sketches in India,	322 25
		Vandenhoff's Benefit, Auction Sales,	15 87
"	29,	Much Ado, and Rough Diamonds,	254 37
"	"	Auction Sales,	9 12
"	30,	Patrician's Daughter, and Queen's Husband,	280 87
May	3,	Ingomar, and Swiss Swains,	227 37
"	4,	" King and Carpenter,	162 50
"	5,	School for Scandal, Governor's Wife,	252 37
"	6,	Benefit of the National Company, Mrs. Sinclair and Mr. Vandenhoff volunteer,	167 12
"	7,	Lady of Lyons, 2d act, and School for Scandal, Mrs. Sinclair's Benefit and last appearance,	350 00
"	8,	Afternoon Miscellaneous Performance by Stock Company,	17 87

On the closing night of this house, by the National company, William Shimmin, Esq., of this city, was present, and witnessed the last fall of the curtain, having been one of the audience that hailed the opening of the Boston Theatre on the 3d of February, 1794.

On Saturday evening, the Aurora Dramatic Club played for the benefit of the sufferers, giving "Speed the Plough," and "A Nabob for an Hour," the last performance given at the Boston Theatre. The house was bad.

The enterprise of Messrs. Wright, Fenno & Co., in thus opening the theatre, was a dramatic triumph; for though the old theatre was stocked with scenery, the wardrobe was lacking, and many members of the company had lost their all by the fire of the night previous. The opening exclamation of *St. Loo* in the play performed, where he says, —

> "Drained to the bottom, and my pocket made
> What prudent Nature loathes, a vacuum!
> I am an empty bag," etc. —

was too true of many an actor, who played that night in borrowed clothes, of some fellow-actor at the Howard or the Museum. As the purchasers had made preparations to build, they could only allow performances until Friday, the 7th of May. On Monday, May 10th, Messrs. Clark & Son sold at auction the properties and fixtures of the theatre. Hundreds were attracted to the sale, to take a farewell view of a theatre so rich in historical associations, many of which we have endeavored to chronicle in this Record. A beautiful block of stores now occupy the site of the former BOSTON THEATRE.

CHAPTER XXVIII.

The National Theatre. — Its Origin. — Mr. Pelby. — The Warren Theatre. — The National Theatre. — J. B. Wright. — Thomas A. Cooper. — Miss Davenport. — Josh. Silsbee. — Miss Julia Dean. — McKean Buchanan. — F. S. Hill. — J. S. Jones. — Hamilton. — Wright, Fenno & Co., etc. etc.

It is not our intention to give a detailed account of the National Theatre. The performances at times have been of that order in which the reader would feel little interest, and its history presents very few features of striking originality.

In 1832, an amphitheatre was built on the site of the present National Theatre, by Jeremiah and Theodore Washburn, for William & Thomas L. Stewart, who were the owners, and it was opened by them as the "American Amphitheatre," on the 27th of February, in that year, for equestrian purposes. Performances were also given on a small stage, and "Victorine, or the Orphan of Paris," was performed, for the first time in this city, at that place. The Messrs. Stewarts were the proprietors of an equestrian company, and they desired a place in the city at which they might perform during three or four months, when the inclemency of the weather prevented them from making their customary country circuit.

In the spring of 1832, Mr. Pelby returned from the South, cherishing the most hostile feelings against the

Tremont Theatre, its proprietors, and lessee, by whom, from causes already recorded, he deemed himself injured. His feelings were so worked up by some remarks made by Mr. Dana, that, accompanied by a friend, he called on Mr. Dana, for the purpose of demanding an apology, or inflicting personal chastisement. Mr. Dana was fortunately not at home, and Mr. Pelby's friend then remonstrated with him upon his course of conduct, arguing that little good would be the result. "I'll tell you what to do," said he; "hire the American Amphitheatre, and run the Tremont." The suggestion struck Mr. Pelby favorably, and he adopted it.

Mr. Pelby was soon engaged in contracting for the lease of the Amphitheatre, and on the 12th day of May, 1832, the articles of agreement were signed between William Pelby and Wm. & Thos. L. Stewart, for the lease of it for five years. The understanding was, that three months during the winter, the Stewarts should perform equestrian spectacles, and give performances in the ring; but this part of the contract was never fulfilled by Mr. Pelby, who, after the departure of the Stewarts, converted the place into a regular theatre, adapted exclusively for dramatic performances. The Stewarts were subsequently unfortunate in business, and the establishment passed into Mr. Pelby's hands; but had the Amphitheatre not been erected, it is more than probable that Mr. P. would have made his "fling for fame" in some other locality.

We have anticipated, thus briefly, the commencement of Mr. Pelby's managerial career at the North End.

The Amphitheatre once leased to him, he changed the name to the Warren Theatre, and on the 3d of July, 1832, opened it to the public, with "Victorine," and "The Spoiled Child," to an audience of $60.75. Mr. F. S. Hill was stage-manager till 1838. The company embraced Pelby, Wallace, F. S. Hill, J. S. Jones, J. Mills Brown, (who reappeared after an absence of four years,) Meer, Kent, and a host of others; while in the female department were Miss Ophelia Pelby, (afterwards Mrs. Anderson, who died on the 25th of January, 1852,) Mrs. Meer, Mrs. Nelson, Miss Bouquet, and others. Under the name of the Warren, Mr. Pelby conducted this house till 1836. During the four seasons, Messrs. T. D. Rice, (Jim Crow,) G. H. Hill, C. H. Eaton, John Barnes, J. B. Booth, W. R. Blake, J. R. Scott, W. G. Jones, (died June 20, 1853,) Coney and Blanchard, Mons. Gouffe, appeared as stars. In 1836, Mr. Pelby re-constructed the theatre, enlarged and otherwise improved it, and opened it on the 15th of August as the National Theatre, to an audience of $866. The theatre had, in fact, been rebuilt; though, to avoid some difficulty with the city, the little Warren was only taken down little at a time, but very little of the original structure was left. Mr. W. H. Smith continued as stage-manager, and Mr. J. B. Wright filled the important post of prompter. Mr. Wright commenced his career as call-boy at the Tremont, and by his industry and attention to business rendered himself at the National one of the most useful members of that establishment. In his department, he has no superior in any theatre, and he has since, as stage-manager, evinced the most excellent tact and taste, by the very superior manner in which plays have been produced at this theatre. For many years, the National, under Pelby, maintained a firm position, and gained the public suffrage to such an extent, that Mr. Pelby could have retired at one time in the possession of a large fortune. His companies were invariably good, and those popular favorites throughout the United States, Messrs. W. F. Johnson, T. P. Cunningham, Wyseman Marshall, Saunders, W. M. Leman, Mr. and Mrs. C. R. Thorne, O. C. Durivage, Spear, Murdoch, Hunt, Gilbert, Andrews, and hosts of others, were constantly on the boards, and plays were frequently produced in a superior manner even to their production at the Tremont. It would be tedious to record the progress made at this house, season after season, and we will therefore allude to some of the star engagements of note.

On the 10th of September, 1838, Thomas A. Cooper, the veteran actor, after an absence of nearly six years, appeared at the National as *Sir William Dorillon,* to his daughter's *Miss Dorillon,* in Mrs. Inchbald's comedy of "Wives as They Were." He had for many years been living in retirement at Bristol, Penn., and visited Boston for the purpose of taking a final leave of the Boston boards, and introducing his daughter. The engagement was not remarkable, and Cooper received but slight sympathy, for the many troubles brought upon himself by indulgence. His last night of performance was on the 21st of September. The receipts of this engagement were as follows: —

1838.	Sept. 10,	Wives as They Were, etc.	$131 00
	" 11,	Hunchback,	224 88
	" 12,	Much Ado About Nothing,	65 00
	" 13,	Damon and Pythias,	125 37
	" 14,	Othello,	144 88
	" 17,	Rule a Wife and Have a Wife,	165 38
	" 18,	Much Ado About Nothing,	115 38
	" 19,	Rule a Wife and Have a Wife,	91 87
	" 20,	Damon and Pythias,	142 62
	" 21,	Gamester,	161 62
			$1,368 00

Cooper in former years had, in a single night, attracted to the old house $1,100.

On the 1st of October, 1838, Miss Jean Margaret Davenport made her first appearance before a Boston audience, as *Richard III.*, and sustained three parts in a piece called "The Manager's Daughter," written by Edward Lancaster, in which both Mr. and Mrs. Davenport appeared. Miss Davenport was at that time stated to be "only eleven years of age," and was regarded, and justly too, as an infant phenomenon. She had already created a furore in England and in New York by her acting. By many she was deemed fully equal to Master Betty, in the best days of that prodigy, and far surpassed Burke. Her conception of *Richard*, *Shylock*, and other characters in the higher walks of the drama, was certainly astonishing, while her delivery was not the mere repetition of a parrot, but was sensible, and evinced the talent of an artist. Her success was fair; and inducements being held out by the public, after the termination of her engagement at the National, her father leased the Lion Theatre, and for a few nights did wonders. We need not say, that Miss Davenport, then the prodigy, is now the talented actress, who of late years has delighted thousands in this city by her admirable style of acting, and who, as the *Countess*, in "Love," *Julia*, in the "Hunchback," and *Adrienne Lecouvre*, has left a lasting impression upon the minds of all patrons of the drama. Her father died in Cincinnati a few years since. He was a gentleman of education, and proved invaluable to his daughter's success, by his tact and discrimination.

The receipts of Miss Davenport's first engagement in Boston, in 1838, were as follows: —

Oct. 1,	Richard III. Manager's Daughter, .	$402 50
" 2,	Merchant of Venice, "	172 37 1-2
" 3,	School for Scandal, ...	146 12 1-2
" 4,	" " Four Mowbrays, . .	170 12 1-2
" 5,	Douglass. Spoiled Child, . . .	145 50
" 8,	Dumb Boy of Manchester. Old and Young,	287 62 1-2
" 9,	Dumb Boy, &c. Actress of all Work, .	148 62 1-2
" 10,	" " Spoiled Child, . .	111 00
" 11,	" " " " . .	163 00
" 12,	Matteo Falcone, " "	204 50
		$1,591 37 1-2

Miss Davenport was then about thirteen years of age, and in the above plays performed *Richard*, *Shylock*, *Sir Peter Teazle* to Mrs. Davenport's *Lady Teazle*, *Young Norval*, and *Little Pickle*, in which she made her *debut* on the stage, and thus exhibited in a short time the versatility of her talent.

Mrs. Fitzwilliam, J. B. Buckstone, W. C. Macready, (in 1843,) Hackett, J. S. Silsbee, who has since acquired a great reputation abroad for his delineations of Yankee characters, and who first appeared on the stage in Cincinnati, in 1840, as *Deuteronomy Dutiful*, in a farce called the "Wool Dealer," Mr. Anderson, an actor of the greatest merit, and the best *Claude Melnotte* we ever saw, Mrs. Hunt, afterwards Mrs. Mossop, whose *espieglerie* has turned the heads of more than one young man, and a host of others appeared, under the auspices of Manager Pelby — many of whom have already been alluded to in this record. On the 26th of October, 1846, Miss Julia Dean made her first appearance as *Juliet*. This young lady, a grand-daughter of Samuel Drake, one of the pioneers of the drama in the West, was born at Louisville, Kentucky, and her circuit has since been chiefly confined to the western theatres, though within two years past, she has appeared in New York and Philadelphia, with the most decided success. At the time she visited this city, her name was unknown in theatrical annals, and she was obliged to contend against the overpowering attractions of Mrs. Mowatt, Madame Augusta, George Vandenhoff and Davenport, at the Howard Athenæum, and Mr. and Mrs. Kean at the Boston Theatre. Miss Dean is undoubtedly the most promising young American actress on the stage, and a brilliant career awaits her. In many characters she is already unrivalled, and so well appreciated has she been wherever she appears, that a handsome fortune has been accumulated by her.

Miss Kimberly made her debut at the National in 1850, and McKean Buchanan first gave Bostonians a taste of his talent at this theatre. Graham, an English tragedian, who subsequently died in St. Louis, also made his appearance here, and, lastly, Mrs. Sinclair attracted very fair houses, by her performances at this theatre.

Mr. Pelby was very successful in his choice of stage-managers. F. S. Hill was not only competent to the discharge of his duties, but his literary qualifications were very respectable. He wrote the "Six Degrees of Crime," and other pieces which drew money into Mr. Pelby's treasury. Mr. W. H. Smith, by his thorough knowledge of stage business, gave effect to every piece that was produced. Mr. Smith, in making his arrangements with Mr. Pelby, was so strict in his articles of agreement, that not even the manager was allowed to cross the stage, unless by his permission. J. S. Jones was another invaluable man to Mr. Pelby, both on account of the talent he possessed as a playwright, and the sound advice he was able to impart in regard to business matters. His plays, too numerous to mention, were very popular. The "Surgeon," from his pen, drew crowded houses. Mr. Cartlitch was also valuable in this capacity, and was succeeded by J. E. Murdoch, who was followed by Messrs. W. R. Blake, Robert Hamilton, (a gentleman of fine literary attainments,) and by Thomas Barry, Esq.

During an engagement at the National, Mr. James E. Murdoch brought out "Witchcraft," a tragedy in five acts, by Cornelius Mathews, which has been published in London, and translated into French; an honor never before extended to any American work of the kind. It has received from the highest critical authority, in both countries, the warmest commendation. It was acted in Philadelphia, on its first presentation to the public, for four successive nights. Mr. Murdoch afterwards carried his manuscript play to Cincinnati, where it was received with unbounded applause. The press of that city spoke of it in unequivocal terms, and in this city it was received with flattering marks of approbation by the press and the public.

Mr. Barry, after an absence of many years, took the management in 1848, and from that time till the present, the National has increased in the favor of the more respectable portion of the community. Mr. Barry's reputation at once attracted to the theatre hundreds who for years had absented themselves from its door. Mr. Barry continued with Mr. Pelby during the season of 1849; and Mr. Pelby having died, he assumed the acting and stage management for Mrs. Pelby till the expiration of the season of 1850–1, when he returned to New York, where he still lives, the accomplished and much respected manager of the Broadway. The season of 1851–2, Mr. John B. Wright was acting and stage manager, and also joint lessee, under the title of Wright, Fenno & Bird. The house was in every respect worthy of patronage, while in charge of the firm; and the public appreciated the efforts made to cater for an enlightened community. Mr. Fenno, as treasurer and box-keeper, made many friends by his proverbial politeness and constant attention to business, and every thing promised well; but on the night of April 22, 1852, a fire broke out in the theatre, whether the result of accident, or the work of an incendiary, was never discovered, and in a few hours the entire building with all its contents was in flames. Mrs. C. N. Sinclair and Mr. Vandenhoff performed on the evening of the 21st in the "School for Scandal," and the "Rough Diamond" was the after-piece. The play announced for the 22d was "Love's Sacrifice," which was performed, as we have stated, at the Boston Theatre.

Thus briefly we have sketched the history of the National, the favorite resort of residents of the North End, who take considerable pride in "their theatre," as they term it. It proved, under Mr. Pelby's management, a formidable competitor to the Tremont, and its influence has otherwise been felt. The standard of the theatre has been that of the second class, but it has occasionally aspired above "blue fire and mysterious music," and at times has been *the* theatre of Boston. Mr. Pelby both made and lost large sums in it during his career.

CHAPTER XXIX.

Proposals for a New Theatre. — The New National Theatre. — Laying of the Corner Stone. — Mr. G. V. Brooke. — The Theatre lighted up. — The Opening Night. — Douglass Stewart. — Md'lle Palser. — New Fares. — Receipts. — Edwin Forrest's Engagement. — The Spanish Dancers. — The Company Reduced. — Leonard's Complimentary Benefit. — Presentation of Plate to Brooke, etc. etc.

Immediately after the destruction of the National Theatre by fire, (22d April, 1852,) Mr. Joseph Leonard, the well-known auctioneer, published in the papers a notice, requesting gentlemen who were in favor of the erection of a new theatre, to walk into the hotels and subscribe for the stock, papers having been circulated for that purpose. The want of a capacious theatre had long been talked of; and as it was given out that the National would not be rebuilt, the time was deemed appropriate for agitating the subject. In this enterprise Mr. Leonard was joined by several of our leading citizens, and on the 28th of April, 1852, a meeting was called at the Revere House. From this meeting originated the new theatre and opera house, now building on Mason Street. An unavoidable delay having taken place in the choice of a site of land, Mr. Leonard directed his attention to the new National Theatre, which was then talked of as among the things that were to be. On the 10th of May, 1852, he received the lease, contracts were made for building a theatre worth $45,000, exclusive of the land, which was taken on a lease, with the privilege of purchasing at an agreed price within a certain number of years. Messrs. Page & Jepson, master carpenters, with some few others, were principally interested in this project. The work was at once commenced, and on the 6th of July the corner stone was laid with appropriate ceremonies, William Dehon, Esq., delivering a most excellent address. A metallic box was deposited under the stone, containing rare coins, a specimen of California gold, theatre bills, a piece of the foundation of the Federal Street Theatre, copies of the newspapers of the day, and a parchment containing this record:—

NATIONAL THEATRE:

Erected, August, 1836.
Destroyed by fire, April 22, 1852.
Corner Stone laid July 6th: Address by Wm. Dehon, Esq.
Architects: Joseph F. Billings, Fred. C. Sleeper.
Builders: { John A. Page, T. F. Whidden, Samuel Jepson, } Masons, Carpenters.
Lessee: Joseph Leonard.
Acting and Stage Manager: John B. Wright.
Assistant Stage Manager and Prompter: Henry Lewis.
Treasurer: William Ellison.
Box Keeper: Henry W. Fenno.

It was the understanding that the theatre was to be ready for occupancy on the 1st of September, and with this impression Mr. Leonard at once went to work to secure a company. The qualifications of Mr. Leonard for managerial duties were but few. His associations with members of the theatrical profession, and his natural taste for dramatic entertainments, had imbued him with the belief that he should make a successful manager, and, with confidence in his own judgment, and a liberality entirely characteristic, he organized a corps for his new theatre, dating his engagements from the 6th of September. As that time approached, it was evident that the theatre would not be ready for occupancy, and Mr. Leonard, in self-defence, was obliged to assist in finishing it. Many of the actors were receiving their salaries; and an engagement having been made with G. V. Brooke for October, he came, and announced his readiness to fulfil his part of the engagement, but as the theatre was not finished, Mr. Leonard was obliged to compromise, and paid Mr. Brooke *six hundred dollars* forfeiture, and gave a new engagement for four weeks. This, with other sums paid out prior to the opening, reached the large sum of $4,100,—enough to cripple a man of greater means than Mr. Leonard, and a man with less heart would have yielded to this combination of disastrous circumstances. Mr. James W. Wallack was also engaged to appear, and when the time came the theatre was not opened. With that courtesy which has ever distinguished him, he wrote to the management, regretting that circumstances were as they were, and concluded by saying, "when you want me, let me know."

Although not finished, the theatre was announced to open on the 1st of November. The interior may be briefly described as containing a parquette, first tier of boxes on a level with the rear of the parquette, a second tier of boxes called the dress circle, and a gallery, with six private boxes. The first tier will hold 440 persons, the parquette 390, the second tier 600, and the gallery about 1000, making sitting room for 2,430. This is exclusive of room in the lobby. The stage is 76 feet wide and 66 feet deep, and 29 feet between the wings or side scenes. The curtain is 40 feet wide and 38 feet high, and the whole theatre is 151 feet deep by 80 feet in width. A building, containing a large scene-room, and nearly all the dressing-rooms and green-rooms, is connected, being 50 feet in length and 17 feet in width. The conveniences behind the curtain are excellent and commodious.

On Saturday evening, October 30, the theatre was lighted up, and a few of the personal friends of the manager were present, who partook of a collation, and witnessed Md'lle Palser's "first fling for fame." It seemed an impossibility to open the theatre on the Monday following, but by dint of constant labor, the interior was so far perfected that it was opened on Monday, the 1st of November, 1852, though some six weeks elapsed before the theatre was finished, or rather patched up, — as, in our opinion, it is not finished yet.

The opening bill was the "Heir at Law," an Original Address, by W. O. Eaton, spoken by W. M. Leman; Polish Dance by Md'lle Palser and John Dobbs. A new act drop, called "Byron's Dream," was painted by Hayes, and the company embraced W. M. Fleming and wife, W. H. Curtis, Douglass Stewart, Mr. and Mrs. J. J. Prior, J. Munroe, Mr. and Mrs. Buxton, S. D. Johnson, Aiken, Mrs. W. H. Smith, Mrs. Archbold, W. F. Johnson, Fanny Howard, Cornelia Jefferson, Bertha Lewis, Julia Pelby, Mrs. Vickery, (who made her first appearance as *Bianca* on the 5th of November,) R. Stilt, ballet master, and others. Of these a portion had been engaged by Mr. Leonard, and a few by Mr. Wright, stage-manager. Mr. Leonard was extremely liberal in his engagements, and paid a few most extravagant salaries. Md'lle Palser and Douglass Stewart were of foreign importation. It was anticipated that Douglass Stewart, who came highly recommended to Mr. Leonard, would prove a card. Some even predicted that William Warren, of the Museum, was to have a rival. His debut was as *Dr. Pangloss*, and poor enough it proved, but his apologists attributed the failure to the "natural embarrassment of the occasion." Unfortunately, Mr. Stewart never got over this embarrassment; and Mr. Leonard, finding that the article was not up to "invoice value," a mutual agreement to separate, after a few weeks, took place. Md'lle Palser, from the English theatres, was well received, and proved quite popular, but was not of that value to the theatre which bore any proportion to her large salary. In person she was quite prepossessing, having youth, beauty, and a healthy development of form, while her style was modest, graceful, and fascinating. Not called upon to make any great exertion, she evinced very little originality, and when she left for home, was far from being improved in her profession. Mrs. Archbold, once a great favorite in London, and subsequently popular at Dublin, was far indeed above mediocrity, and as the tart old women, or ladies of a doubtful age, she is truly excellent. Mrs. Vickery assumed a position as a tragic actress, which she has since fully sustained. She has her peculiarities of pronunciation; but where we can find one better actress, we can single out twenty far inferior. Mr. Fleming made his first appearance on the third night of the season as *Richelieu,* and during the star engagements has rendered very efficient service by his able support. Mrs. George Barrett commenced an engagement as *Lady Teazle,* and continued through J. W. Wallack's engagement, which commenced on the 22d of November. Mr. Wallack attracted to the theatre the most fashionable houses, and astonished his oldest friends, those who recollected him thirty years ago, by his acting, which, in its artistic finish, seemed but little impaired by time. His benefit was attended by the fashion of the city, and being called out, he acquitted himself in a handsome manner, by speaking a good word for the management, a flattering notice of Brooke, and extended an invitation to all to visit him at Wallack's Theatre, in New York.

Mr. G. V. Brooke, supported by Mrs. Barrett, commenced on the 6th of December. The receipts during his engagement were as follows: —

1852.	Dec. 6,	Othello,	$687 25
	" 7,	The Wife,	317 25
	" 8,	Othello,	405 00
	" 9,	Merchant of Venice,	335 50
	" 10,	New Way to Pay Old Debts,	350 25
	" 13,	Corsican Brothers,	594 00
	" 14,	" "	492 50
	" 15,	" "	370 00
	" 16,	" "	443 75
	" 17,	" "	357 75
	" 20,	" "	465 25
	" 21,	" "	289 00
	" 22,	" "	305 25
	" 23,	" "	246 25
	" 24,	Richelieu, Mrs. Barrett's Benefit,	317 00
	" 25,	Medley, — Afternoon, Christmas,	157 75
	" "	Corsican Brothers, evening,	400 00
			$6,526 75

Christmas fell on Saturday, and an afternoon performance was given, and also an evening performance, which was, strictly speaking, contrary to law, though not without a precedent, though a single one, performances having been given at the Tremont Theatre on a Saturday evening in 1840, to accommodate a large number of strangers then in town to attend the Bunker Hill Convention. Mr. Leonard made an effort about this time to have the law against dramatic performances on Saturday evening repealed, but after some discussion in the legislature, he and other petitioners had leave to withdraw. Mr. Brooke continued another week, and received the support of the Misses Denins. The receipts were : —

1852.	Dec. 27,	Hunchback, ...	$335 50
	" 28,	The Wife, ...	237 50
	" 29,	Richard III., ...	449 00
	" 30,	Stranger, ...	342 00
	" 31,	Othello, ...	620 25
			$1,984 25

On the occasion of the last representation of Othello, which drew a good house, Mr. Fleming played *Othello*, Mr. Brooke *Iago*, Mrs. Barrett *Desdemona*, and Mrs. Vickery *Emelia*. Brooke was better as "Mine Ancient" than in the impersonation of the Moor, and the other characters being so efficiently sustained that the performance was truly a splendid piece of acting throughout.

At the termination of Brooke's engagement, the theatre had been opened two months, at an expense of $9,200 per month, or $2,300 per week, which includes current expenses, new properties, scenery, etc. The gross receipts during the two months averaged $9,100 per month, which, though apparently a loss of $100 per month, cannot be so considered, as a portion of the receipts went to stock the theatre. Had the theatre been properly stocked at the commencement, the receipts would have far exceeded the running expenses of the theatre.

The next star engagement was with Edwin Forrest, the American tragedian, who received a clear half of the receipts. A man's talents are certainly worth all they will bring; and we cannot blame Mr. Forrest for placing a high estimate on his own abilities, especially when we know that he is the most attractive star on the American stage, and can, by his own individual powers, attract more people to a theatre than any living actor. Mr. Forrest but recently closed at the Broadway Theatre, New York, owing to spraining his ancle, after *seventy-two consecutive performances.* There are, however, but few managers who can afford to pay these terms, for many of Mr. Forrest's pieces require a strong stock company. The receipts were very large:—

1853.	Jan. 10,	Damon and Pythias, .	$750 50	
	" 11,	Richelieu, ...	574 50	
	" 12,	Othello, ...	618 00	
	" 13,	Virginius, ...	844 25	
	" 14,	Hamlet, ...	501 00	2,788 25
	" 17,	Metamora, ...	877 00	
	" 18,	"	686 25	
	" 19,	"	651 75	
	" 20,	"	620 75	
	" 21,	"	617 00	3,452 75
	" 24,	Gladiator, ...	670 00	
	" 25,	"	698 00	
	" 26,	"	485 50	
	" 27,	"	480 25	
	" 28,	Othello, ...	445 75	2,780 75
	" 31,	Macbeth, ...	580 75	
	Feb. 1,	Jack Cade, ...	568 00	
	" 2,	" "	542 50	
	" 3,	" "	387 75	
	" 4,	Metamora, ...	477 00	2,556 00
	" 7,	Hamlet, Benefit, . .		587 75
				$12,165 50

On the second night of this engagement, a curtain on the stage, in sight of the audience, took fire, and a regular stampede occurred. Mr. Forrest remained perfectly quiet, and, the fire being extinguished, the play continued. The great week of the engagement was that of Metamora, which, it will be observed, drew very nearly an average of *seven hundred dollars* nightly. The gross receipts were $12,165.50, which being divided, left for the manager, as his portion of twenty-one nights, $6,082.75. The expenses of the company, too large and too expensive, were certainly $300 per night, by which it will be seen that Mr. Forrest's engagement put no money in the treasury. It would have done so, however, if the theatre had been managed with more tact, and an efficient working company had been engaged.

In the month of February, the Spanish dancers came, This troupe was selected by James H. Hackett in Paris, and brought out to this country on speculation. Soto was the leading danseuse, and was by birth a Spanish woman, and in several of her dances evinced the natural vigor characteristic of Spain. Pougead ranked first in popular favor on the score of personal beauty, but Melisse was far the best danseuse of the troupe, possessing a muscular strength which enabled her to execute the *tours de force* with astonishing power; but unfortunately she lacked beauty of facial feature. Lavigne was quite a pleasing dancer, and Drouet and Leeder answered very well to give numerical importance to the troupe. Mons. Mege, the male dancer, was very good, and more noted as a posturer than a dancer. There was real artistic talent in this troupe, but not enough to give them powers of attraction in cities where better dances had often been seen; and aware probably of this fact, and unwilling to "carry weight," their drapery was exceedingly scant and light, not sufficient to merit the charge of immodesty, but enough to pique the curiosity of the susceptible. It was during this month, about the 18th, that the guillotine was put in operation, and some fifteen of the company were discharged. They who were thus turned out without warning, very naturally uttered protestations against the management; and though a lack of means to pay so heavy a company seemed to compel recourse to some such step, a more conciliatory method of reducing the expenses might have been resorted to. On the 14th of March, James E. Murdoch and Miss Heron commenced an engagement; and on the 21st, Miles' play of "De Soto" was brought out, in which Mr. Murdoch and Miss Heron received the support of Messrs. Fleming, Leman, Curtis, Prior, and Mrs. Prior. The last scene represented a tableau of Powell's Burial of De Soto, which had a fine effect.

Early in March, a few personal friends of Mr. Leonard determined upon tendering him a grand complimentary benefit, and at once held meetings to make preparations. A large number of gentlemen loaned the use of names, and others, who sympathized with Mr. Leonard in his losses, came forward, and on the 16th the house was crowded by his friends. The performances consisted of "Wine Works Wonders," in which Murdoch played *Young Mirable;* the trial scene from the "Merchant of Venice," *Shylock*, Fleming, *Portia*, Mrs. Melinda Jones; the "Virginia Mummy," with T. D. Rice; and the screen scene from the "School for Scandal, — *Charles Surface*, Murdoch; *Joseph Surface*, Fleming; *Sir Peter Teazle*, W. F. Johnson; *Lady Teazle*, Mrs. George Barrett. The performances were excellent, especially the last scene from Sheridan's inimitable comedy. We doubt if the Boston public ever witnessed it in greater perfection. As a testimonial of personal friendship, this benefit was very proper; as a complimentary benefit, it was simply ridiculous, for a complimentary benefit is generally tendered as a mark of respect to one who has achieved a triumph, and certainly Mr. Leonard had no laurels to boast of at that time. The actual amount of tickets sold, the prices having been raised, was about $900 worth.

Another complimentary benefit followed this, which was tendered to Mrs. Pelby. Mrs. Pelby played *Elvira*, and Mrs. Thorne, who came on expressly from New York, *Cora*, in "Pizzaro," to a very excellent house. The "Princess and the Peacock," an operatic serio-tragic extravaganza, local in its hits, which was originally performed at Mrs. W. H. Smith's benefit, was also given, and received with shouts of applause. It was the production of a couple of young gentlemen of this city, and proved very acceptable to the public. Palser also made her last appearance in America on this occasion. Messrs. Coney and Taylor and their dogs were the next attractions. They had exhausted their attractive powers at the Howard Athenæum previous to this. On the 11th of April, Mr. Lysander Thompson appeared, but the season had so far advanced that his claims were not acknowledged. Mr. Thompson made his first appearance in America at Burton's in New York. In his particular walk of the drama, that of impersonating the Yorkshireman and countryman, he is confessedly without an equal. The London Times once remarked of him: —

"Nothing can surpass the excellence both of his *Tyke* and his *Zekiel Homespun*. They belong to that class of exquisite personation which criticism can scarcely do more than record. He comes on to the stage with a *naïveté* so inimitable, and in effect so irresistibly ludicrous, as to immediately take possession of, and establish himself with the audience.

> 'With steady face, and sober, humorous mien,
> He trod the outline of the comic scene,
> The VERY MAN, in LOOK, in VOICE, and AIR,
> And though upon the stage, appeared no PLAYER.'

The manner in which Mr. Thompson makes up the personages he represents is almost sufficient to stamp him a man of genius. Throughout the whole of his performance there is not the least appearance of art — no straining after effect, no mannerism or stage trickery — but all is natural, and kept within the bounds of moderation. His dialect, action, and good-humored grin, are all in strict keeping with the character of the unsophisticated, artless countryman. In scenes of pathos and tenderness, he is equally as successful as in the comic and more bustling portion of his performance; and he never offends by approaching to any thing like buffoonery or extravagance."

The business was very bad, and an afternoon performance was given on the 16th, when the theatre was closed for the season. A few benefits were taken by the stock after this, and Mrs. Warner received "a complimentary." The entire company was discharged, including Mr. Wright, the stage-manager, and Mr. Fenno, the treasurer. On the 2d of May, the theatre was re-opened, with Mr. J. W. Wallack, Jr., Mr.

Fredericks, Mr. Dickinson, Miss Wyette, were engaged at the south, as members of the stock. Mr. Wallack brought out " Civilization," but it did not draw.

On the 16th of May, G. V. Brooke again visited Boston, and performed an engagement at the National, taking a farewell of a Boston audience on the 27th, when, we see by the papers, that a service of plate was presented to Mr. Brooke by Mr. Fleming, in behalf of "a few of his many friends in Boston and Providence." Mr. Brooke is really too good an actor to resort to any means not strictly legitimate to advance his position.

The result of the season has not been so successful as one could wish; but the error lies with Mr. Leonard, who undertook what few men are capable of performing, though no manager with years of experience could have stood up better under the accumulated load of troubles than he. His mistake was made at the outset, in omitting to have a time specified for the theatre to be finished, and his capital was partially used up in fitting up the theatre. The company was a most extravagant one, and worked badly together; but as the darkest hour is just before daybreak, so we are inclined to believe that another season will redeem the past. Messrs. Leonard & Fleming have formed a partnership, and, properly conducted, the theatre will prove, as it has heretofore been considered, the best investment of capital for dramatic purposes in the United States.

CHAPTER XXX.

The Lion Theatre. — The Opening. — Mr. Barrymore. — The Jewess — The Golden Farmer. — Cooke's Company. — The Davenports at the Lion. — Mechanics' Institute. — The Melodeon, etc. etc.

In the latter part of the year 1835, Mr. James Raymond and associates, of New York, purchased the estate in Washington street known as the Lion Tavern, and at once commenced the erection of an amphitheatre, for equestrian and dramatic purposes. A large number of workmen were engaged, and so rapid was the progress made, that, as one of the papers of that day remarked, "within a little month, or in about the same space of time that Hamlet's mother was married to his uncle, the edifice was completed and the bills were out for the opening of the Lion Theatre." The management, in December, 1835, offered a prize of $50, for the best opening address, and no fewer than forty-three poems were submitted. A competent committee, consisting of Grenville Mellen, Esq., Dr. J. V. C. Smith, and Isaac McLellen, Jr., Esq., were the umpires. The interior of the house was neatly arranged. A circle, for equestrian performances, occupied the usual place of the pit, directly in front of the stage, the pit extending under the boxes, of which there were three tiers. The decorations, by Reinagle, were very neat. The opening night was Jan. 11, 1836, when Buckstone's "Open House," and "Law and the Lions," were the dramatic entertainments, with scenes in the circle, in which Buckley, T. Nathans, Robinson, Perez, Roine, Bryant, Wilmott, Dickinson, and J. Nathans, were the most prominent. Mr. E. C. Weeks was at the head of the establishment. Mr. Buckley was director of the equestrian department, and Mr. Barrymore of the corps dramatique, which comprised Messrs. Houpt, Herbert, Mestayer, Knapp, Durivage, and Mesdames Kent, Barrett, Mestayer, Eberle, Misses Monier, Hurley, Whittemore.

The drop curtain, representing the passage of the Alps by Bonaparte, was painted by Mr. R. Jones. The address, written by T. M. Devon, as the author signed himself, was spoken by Miss Monier, a young lady of no remarkable force, but equal to any then at the Lion, which as a whole was a poor company. The first tragedian who trod the boards was Mr. Ingersoll, a native of Charlestown, then about twenty-two years of age, who created some sensation in *Damon* and *Virginius*. Mrs. Hamblin appeared, and "Zante," and the "Secret Mine," an equestrian melo-dramatic piece, was brought out, and to Mr. Barrymore's superior skill as a manager it was indebted for its popularity. The grand spectacle drama of "The Jewess," was produced at a great expense. Every attention was paid to scenic effect; the costumes were made by that prince of costumers, Andrew Jackson Allen. The entire stud of horses, elephants, camels, and dromedaries, gave great effect to the procession. The leading parts were sustained as follows: *Mordecai*, Mr. Ingersoll; *Esther*, Mrs. Hamblin; *Vashiti*, Mrs. Ingersoll. This play was not "The Jewess" which had been produced at the South with such effect, but the Book of Esther dramatized. It was very popular. Mrs. Barrymore introduced a dance of children, who in their drilling gave us a foretaste of the Viennoise Children, while as an instructor Mrs. B. was fully equal to Madame Wiess. "Tekeli," "Ivan," and other equestrian pieces, were got up, and Mr. Barrymore wrote and produced a two-act melo-drama, called "Lorvina of Tobolski," which was popular. Johnson, the clown, invariably kept the children in good humor, and the theatre was well patronized. John Sefton brought out the "Golden Farmer," which had a great run. The first season closed in April, 1836, when the equestrians started on their summer excursions, through the country, commencing at Weymouth, and Messrs. Ingersoll and Hunt took a portion of the properties, scenery, etc., to Providence, and there opened the Lion Theatre.

The Lion Theatre was shortly after re-opened by Mr. Barrymore, and on Monday evening, May 16, '36, Mr. J. B. Booth appeared. It closed after Mr. Booth's engagement. In the summer of 1836, the old building in front of the theatre was pulled down, and the present stores erected. Alterations were also made in the interior. Mr. Smith superintended the decorations. Mr. Harrison, formerly of the Bowery, then just destroyed by fire, came on to take the acting management for the next season, which commenced Nov. 7, 1836. Mr. Colingbourn was stage-manager, and the whole was under the superintendence of Welch. The same style of entertainments was continued till April, when the theatre was closed, and the house and land were offered for sale or to let. In the month of June, Cooke's equestrian company leased the Lion, and gave entertainments, the best of the kind we ever had in this city. The stud of horses was never surpassed, and many of them were unfortunately burnt at a fire in Philadelphia. Messrs. Houpt & Thorne next tried their hands at managing the Lion, and C. H. Eaton appeared, supported by Mr. and Mrs. Hield, but it was a brief season.

The theatre was repeatedly offered for sale, and was closed for several months. The monetary panic had, in 1837, a most disastrous effect upon the drama, and theatrical performances of all descriptions. Mr. Davenport, father of Miss J. M. Davenport, leased the theatre in October, 1838. Miss Davenport had already appeared at the National, and she succeeded in attracting full and very select audiences to the Lion, during a brief season. Mr. John Redman finally became the purchaser of the theatre, and at once converted it into a concert and lecture hall. According to Dr. J. V. C. Smith, he christened his purchase the "Mechanics' Institute," and caused it to be cut in granite over the front door; but when the Handel and Haydn Society leased it for their sacred oratorios, they covered this over with a sign, which designated it the Melodeon, by which name it was known. The first performance given by the Handel and Haydn Society was December 29, 1839, when the "Messiah" was produced. Miscellaneous concerts had previously been held there. On Sundays, the hall was occupied by a religious society, and week days was let to entertainments of a promiscuous character.

In 1844, a Mr. Leander Rodney leased the Melodeon for a brief season, and converted it into a temporary theatre, when Mr. Macready and Miss Cushman appeared, and attracted the most fashionable audiences. Since then it has been enlarged in the interior, and subsequently became the property of Mr. Eliphalet Baker; and on account of the fine acoustic qualities it possessed, was selected by Jenny Lind, Sontag, Alboni, and other musical celebrities, for their entertainments. It has now passed, by purchase, into the hands of the "Boston Theatre and New Opera House Company."

CHAPTER XXXI.

The Howard Athenæum. — W. F. Johnson. — The Opening Company. — Jas. H. Hackett. — A Sketch of the Baron. — His Youthful Days. — The Seguins. — Mrs. Anna Cora Mowatt. — A Sketch of Mrs. Mowatt. — Her Career as an Actress. — Edward Davenport, etc. etc.

THE Millerite excitement of 1843–4 reached its climax in the following year. The venerable Father Miller, finding that the day set apart by him for the closing up of all earthly affairs, did not result as he anticipated, entered into another calculation, and discovered a slight mistake of a few hundred or a few thousand years, we forget which. This announcement saddened the hearts of those who had given up all, and made preparation for immediate departure, and their place of worship in Howard Street, called the Tabernacle, was soon afterwards deserted, and remained for a short time a miserable wooden monument, one story high, to the folly of Millerism.

The want of a leading theatre, in a city where strangers were thrown upon their resources in the evening, was severely felt, for in the spring of 1845 the Boston Museum, and the National Theatre, were the only prominent places of public amusement. A small saloon, called Graham's Olympic, had a location in Court St., but three hundred persons would have given a "packed house," and the Boston Theatre had not then been reopened. The Tabernacle, from its central position, seemed to offer a very excellent site for a theatre, and W. F. Johnson, W. L. Ayling, Thos. Ford, and Leonard Brayley, thought that it might with profit be converted into a temporary residence for Thespis and Melpomene. The Millerites were not particularly partial to theatrical representations, and it was evident that some shrewdness must be exhibited in procuring the lease, lest they might think that De Foe's couplet,

> "Wherever God erects a house of prayer,
> The devil always builds a chapel there,"

was about to have a permanent realization. They were at first opposed to leasing it, on any account, but finally concluded a bargain and signed the lease; and the mechanic's hammer, the artist's brush, and decorator's skill, were soon brought into requisition, and the exterior and interior soon underwent an important change. A handsome front was erected, painted to resemble free stone, with neat and convenient entrances. The floor descended from the entrance to the orchestra, with a pitch which secured an uninterrupted view of the foot-lights to the most distant seats, which were cushioned. The scenic artists, Messrs. Jones and Curtis, gave to the scenic appointments a pleasant aspect, while the former exhibited his talent in an act drop, illustrative of the passage in "As You Like It,"

> "Run, run, Orlando, carve on every tree
> The fair, the chaste, the unexpressive she."

The new theatre was called the Howard Athenæum, and the following ladies and gentlemen were members of the regular stock company: — Mesdames Maeder, H. Cramer, W. L. Ayling, W. H. Chippendale, C. W. Hunt, Walcott, Judah, G. Howard, Wm. Jones, W. H. Smith, Misses Drake, Booth, Mace, De Luce, Messrs. W. F. Johnson, W. L. Ayling, G. W. Jamieson, J. A. J. Neafie, A. J. Phillips, D. Whiting, C. H. Walcott, G. Howard, Sullivan, Booth, Parker, Munroe, Russell, Binnie, Taylor, Davis, Jones, Adams, Resor, Gilbert, and Master Fox. Mr. Meyrer was leader of the orchestra.

The performances on the opening night, (Oct. 13, 1845,) under the stage-management of Messrs. Johnson and Ayling, Messrs. Ford and Brayley attending to the business, consisted of an Opening Address, written by F. S. Hill, Esq., spoken by Mrs. Cramer, the "School for Scandal," and the "Day After the Wedding." The admittance to all parts of the house was 50 cents, and a numerous auditory gave the enterprise a substantial token of support on the first night. On the third night Mr. James H. Hackett appeared. As we have omitted any sketch of this gentleman, we will here supply the deficiency.

James Henry Hackett was born in the city of New York on the 15th of March, 1800. His father, Thos. G. Hackett, was a native of Holland, and emigrated to America in 1794, and died in 1803. The widow, with her only son, James Henry, retired to Jamaica, L. I., and in the Academy there young James acquired the rudiments of his education, and sufficient knowledge of the classics to obtain an entrance at Columbia College in New York, in 1812. He remained in college about two years, when he renounced his original intention of studying law, and entered the counting-house of one of his relatives. In 1819, Mr. Hackett married Miss Lee Sugg, then a popular actress at the Park Theatre, New York, and retired to Utica, where he was engaged successfully in trade. In 1825, a desire to enter upon a wider field of speculation induced him to visit New York, where in a short time he found himself so embarrassed, that he determined to accept the stage as a profession, having in early life had strong dramatic predilections, coupled with great cleverness as a mimic, and in March, 1826, he made his first appearance on any stage at the Park Theatre, N. Y., as *Justice Woodcock*, in "Love in a Village." His success was equivocal for some time, but he finally made a hit as one of the *Dromios*, in the "Comedy of Errors." In 1826, he visited England, and in April, 1827, he was induced to try an experiment at Covent Garden, by introducing Yankee stories, and imitations of Kean, Macready, etc., which was partially successful. In 1829, Mr. Hackett became lessee and manager of the Chatham and Bowery Theatres, but soon gave them up, and devoted his time to his profession, and to the production of his original plays, "Rip Van Winkle," "Nimrod Wildfire," etc.

Mr. Hackett had the honor of holding a correspondence with Hon. John Quincy Adams on the character of Hamlet, in 1839. He differed somewhat from the "Sage of Quincy," and thus concluded his letter, which was written in London:—"The only excuse I can offer you, for permitting my love of the subject to render me so diffuse, is, that I, too, 'from boyhood,' have been 'enthusiastic' in relation to this character, and have habituated myself for years to ponder over its points, as a miser would pore over his gold, collecting the earliest editions of this play, and searching the accumulated annotations of its numerous critics, many of whom, in attempting to explain, have often only mystified the meaning of a clear original text, by alterations, omissions, and substitutions, and shown themselves 'ignorant as vain,' and as wide of the author's design, and as vexatious to every true lover of the bard, as must be some of the actors of our time, who exhibit to audiences seemingly 'capable of nothing but inexplicable dumb show and noise,' 'a sort of conventional, stage-beau-ideal, destitute of that meditative and philosophic repose, which Shakspeare has made the leading feature of the character."

Mr. Hackett has performed in London on many occasions, and, being the first Yankee comedian, attracted very good houses. His acting has considerable originality. It is related that he was performing *Nimrod Wildfire* at the Park Theatre, in New York, which piece he concludes by a dance, and kicking over the tea things. He was applauded most vociferously, and repeated the dance, giving the tea set another shaking, with such effect that the insatiate monsters in the gallery wanted more crockery demolished, continuing their applause till *Nimrod* approached the footlights and said: "I should be most happy to repeat the dance, but I am out of breath, and, what is worse, the manager is *out of cups and saucers!*" Of his right to the title of Baron, there can be no doubt; for in the London Court Journal of October 12th, 1839, we find the following: —

> HACKETT. — Died, at New Orleans, U. S., on the 22d of August last, of yellow fever, Baron Hackett of Hackett's Town, a native of Holland, whose ancestor emigrated from Ireland. He was an aid-de-camp to the Prince of Orange, and served with distinction in the French Army, particularly at the Battle of Waterloo, and at the siege of Antwerp. The Baron of Hackett's Town was originally one of the Irish peerages that have become dormant, and the dignity devolves upon the cousin-german of the late Baron — Mr. Hackett, the American comedian, at present in London.

The Baron, however, had the honor of the title. Mr. Hackett was manager with Niblo, of the Astor Place Opera House, at the time of the riots, caused by the troubles of Forrest and Macready. His last speculation was the bringing over of the French and Spanish dancers, who have recently appeared at the National and Howard. He was also the first manager of the Howard Athenæum, in this city, after it was re-built, and his late performances at that house of *Sir John Falstaff*, *Monsieur Mallett*, etc., are evidences of his talent as an actor.

Mr. Hackett was succeeded by the Seguins, who

brought out "Norma" for the first time, which we shall allude to more at length.

On the 30th of November, Mrs. Anna Cora Mowatt, supported by Mr. Crisp, made her first appearance in this city on the stage, having read in public previous to this. She was supported by Mr. W. H. Crisp, and commenced her honorable career in this city as *Pauline*, in the "Lady of Lyons;" Mrs. Judah, her first appearance, as *Madame Deschappelles*. Mrs. Mowatt subsequently appeared in the "Honey Moon," "The Wife," "School for Scandal," "Romeo and Juliet," and on the 11th inst., brought out her own comedy of "Fashion," which had had a run of three weeks in New York.

The career of Mrs. Mowatt has been one of the most remarkable that the annals of the stage bears record of, and we will briefly give an outline sketch of her biography. Anna Cora Ogden was born in Bordeaux, France, whither her father had removed from the United States for business purposes. Her mother was the grand-daughter of Francis Lewis, one of the signers of the Declaration of Independence. Anna was the tenth of fourteen children, and in an old chateau, where they resided, near Bordeaux, she first gave promise of the possession of histrionic talent, while performing on fête days and anniversaries, little plays which were cast to the strength of this numerous family. Unfortunate in business, Mr. Ogden returned to America, Anna being then six years of age, and the voyage was one of great severity. The vessel became a wreck, and one of her brothers was lost. The passengers and crew clung to the wreck, and were rescued by a vessel bound to

Havre. From that port a second departure was taken, and the family arrived in New York, where Anna received a most excellent education. Although the parents possessed no decided predilections for the stage, all the members had a taste and love of the stage, and private theatricals was the principal amusement of this very happy family, in which Anna took the lead, not only playing the heroines, but adapting pieces for the mimic stage. When Anna was but fourteen, Mr. Mowatt, a lawyer of wealth, became quite attached to her, and, after some years of attention, they were married, without the knowledge of her parents, who did not object to the match, but thought her youth a barrier to present marriage. Mrs. Mowatt subsequently visited Europe for the benefit of her health, accompanying a married sister, and while in Paris wrote a five-act play called the "Persian Slave," which was performed on her return home. Misfortune overtook her husband, and the fond wife resolved at once to exert herself for his advantage. She determined to give public readings. "For reasons," says an article in Howitt's Journal, published when Mrs. Mowatt appeared in England, "which every reader will perfectly appreciate, she felt she could not commence this new and public life in New York, where she had been known under circumstances so totally different: she therefore selected Boston, the most intellectual city of the Union, as the place of debut. Mrs. Mowatt's name was already known to the press, by a number of fugitive poems and tales contributed to magazines of the day, and she was warmly welcomed by the Boston public. The hall was filled to repletion, and when the delicate form of the debutante appeared on the platform, there was a murmur of surprise, that so fragile a bud had attempted so arduous a mission." Her first reading was given at the Masonic Temple, on Thursday evening, October 28, 1841. She carried with her the heart of every listener, for she exhibited the most beautiful moral spectacle of which human nature is capable, that of a wife turning her accomplishments to account, to relieve the necessities of her husband. Her youth and beauty, though sufficient of themselves to command attention, were lost sight of when she began to speak, and one had leisure only to regard the exquisite tones of her voice, as it gave utterance to her admirable conceptions of poetical genius. Her stay in this city was brief, but the judgment then pronounced upon her abilities was final, for having passed through the ordeal of Boston criticism, and met with approval, she fearlessly went forth to fascinate by the loveliness of her person, and to captivate by the genuineness of her talent. Mrs. Mowatt had been induced to enter upon this career, in the hopes of saving her husband's estate from being sold, but the anxiety and the labor self-imposed proved too much for her feeble frame, and she was for some time seriously ill, and the homestead she cherished was sold. On her recovery, her husband became the principal partner in the publishing business, and Mrs. Mowatt exerted the strength of her intellect to assist him. Under the name of Mrs. Helen Berkley, she wrote a series of very popular articles, and also brought out a novel called the Fortune Hunter, and collated and revised many books for her husband to publish, from which much money was made. Her husband was again unfortunate, when she turned her hand to another department of literature, and wrote "Fashion," a five-act play, the intention of which was to satirize the life of the parvenues of America. It was brought out at the Park in New York, and was well received, though a difference of opinion was entertained as to its merits. Edgar A. Poe remarked that its general tone was adopted from the "School for Scandal," to which it bore just such an affinity as the shell of a locust to the locust that tenants it, "as the spectrum of a Congreve Rocket to the Congreve Rocket itself." It possessed considerable merit as a composition, and was played in several theatres in the Union. Mrs. Mowatt finally concluded to adopt the profession, and made her debut at the Park Theatre in the fall of 1845, as *Pauline* in the "Lady of Lyons," and from that moment to the present her success has been brilliant. "The great charm of her acting," remarked Poe at that time, "is its naturalness. She looks, speaks, and moves, with a well-controlled impulsiveness, as different as can be conceived from the customary rant and cant, the harsh conventionality of the stage." This is true of present style, which possesses in an eminent degree an ever varying freshness. She had made but little preparation for her new career. Mr. W. H. Crisp imparted to her some general ideas, but the rest was nature's dictation. She shortly after her debut came to Boston, and, as we have stated, appeared at the Howard Athenæum under the management of W. F. Johnson. To follow Mrs. Mowatt in her subsequent wanderings, would occupy more space than we can devote. Her tour at the South was a dramatic triumph, which a veteran might have been proud of; and in every city she left such a favorable impression, that her more recent visits have invariably attracted good houses, and rendered her, excepting Forrest, the most attractive star of the day. In 1847, Mrs. Mowatt brought out her most popular play of "Armand, or the Child of the People," — which was produced in New York and Boston, just prior to her departure for Europe, which took place on the 1st of November from Boston. Her career in Europe was every way successful, and she gained not only the applause due to talent, but the friendship and esteem of many who bestowed their admiration upon one who was so justly entitled to it. She was accompanied by Mr. Edward Davenport, a Boston boy, who has reflected credit upon the city of his birth, by his theatrical success.

Mrs. Mowatt, while in England, had the misfortune to lose her husband, and passed the early months of widowhood in retirement, and after an absence of four years returned to America, in improved health, once more to delight her friends, whose name is legion. Report now has it, that Mrs. Mowatt is shortly to be married to Mr. Ritchie, of Richmond, and will leave the stage. However much we might rejoice at this union, the public will regret it, for it removes from them an actress whose presence is ever welcome, and who had, when an accident befell her in the month of March, 1852, by being thrown from her horse in this city, an opportunity of knowing in what esteem she is held by our residents.

CHAPTER XXXII.

The Seguins in Norma. — First Production of that Piece. — Mr. and Mrs. Charles Kean. — Mr. Stark, Dyott, Mr. Murdoch, Miss Fanny Jones, Miss Mary Ann Lee. — The Seguins, and the "Bohemian Girl," etc. etc.

WE have already noticed the career of the Seguins in our city from its commencement in November, 1838, to its *de facto* termination in 1847. Under the skilful management of Mrs. Seguin and her indefatigable exertions, the popularity acquired for English versions of Italian, French, and German opera by "The Woods," Mrs. Austin, Miss Hughes, Phillips, and other brilliant singers, remained intact, until mock turtle went out of fashion, as the genuine article became known by Marti's excellent company. The most successful and brilliant English opera season in this city after the days of "The Woods," commenced at the old Tabernacle, or Howard Athenæum, by grace of a lively imagination, on the 27th of October, 1845, when the since world famous opera "Norma" was for the first time performed here in English version. Seguin was the *Oroveso;* his wife, the *Druid Priestess;* Fraser, the *Roman Proconsul;* and Mrs. Maeder, the gentle *Adalgisa.* The opera took well, and was given five times to full houses. For the closing night of this brief engagement, selections were given from the "Bohemian Girl," "La Sonnambula," "Cinderella," "Fra Diavolo," "Amilie," "The Mountain Sylph," "Niobe," and "Guy Mannering." It was estimated that 1300 or 1500 persons attended each night that "Norma" was performed, and the principals satisfied expectation well in that most trying opera. Engagements at the South enforced a close of this brief and prosperous season, but a promise to return for a long sojourn here relieved opera-goers from a great weight of sorrow when the Seguin company left Boston that winter.

Mr. and Mrs. Charles Kean appeared in November, and during their engagement the company was strengthened by the appearance of Mr. Dyott, and Mr. Stark, who came to Boston from the Provinces. He was a member of the elocution class of the Lyceum, and distinguished himself by his impersonations of *Shylock*, and under Mr. Murdoch made great progress. He subsequently appeared at the National, and then visited Europe. It was on his return that he joined the Howard company, and supported Mrs. Mowatt and the Keans. Of late years he has been in California, and at the present writing is on his way to Australia.

There was some little feeling manifested at the raising of prices from 50 cts. to $1.00 during the Keans' engagement, but the Boston public wisely concluded not to raise any row, but to allow those who were willing to pay the dollar to visit the theatre, and those "contrary minded" to remain at home, the only wise plan in this enlightened age. The managers gave the Keans a clear half, and were obliged to take this course. The Keans at first did not do well, but the houses gradually improved, as many desired to take a farewell of the once charming Ellen Tree, and others to behold one of whom report had told so flattering a tale. The poorest house they played to was on Thanksgiving evening, but Mr. Kean very generously gave up to the management his share of the receipts.

Mr. Murdoch succeeded the Keans, and was followed by Miss Mary Ann Lee, the danseuse, who was supported by George W. Smyth. A more graceful danseuse than Miss Lee has rarely been on our boards. Her style was similar to that of Blangy, and, possessing a beautiful face, she captivated many susceptible young Bostonians. On the night of a complimentary benefit, she appeared in "One Hour, or the Carnival Ball," and gave evidence of the possession of vocal talent. During Miss Lee's engagement, a complimentary benefit was given to Miss Fanny Jones, (Jan. 7, 1846,) who danced a ball-room polka with Mrs. Hunt, and several fancy dances, her last appearance on the stage.

On the 12th of January, 1846, the Seguins according to contract returned, and commenced with Balfe's popular "Bohemian Girl;" a run which no other company ever attained, the engagement being extended by renewals to February 16th. Operatic performances were given in this long interval five times a week, and generally a concert in which the principals were engaged was given Saturday evening.

The "Bohemian Girl" took well, as in that Mrs. Seguin had a part suited to develop her best talent, Seguin ample scope for drollery, and Frazer his best songs. Delavanti was rather stiff in action, but his voice has rarely been equalled upon our lyric stage, and he still occupies, in English opera, where it finds its last abiding place, the provincial towns of old England, a good position. The gems of this opera were soon the rage in saloons, and ground upon organs, or hummed in the streets. "I dreamt that I dwelt in marble halls," absolutely possessed, as with an enchanter's spell, the female population of this vicinity, and that was *the* all-engrossing idea of amateur singers. In a large party given during this excitement, request was made for a song, and the ladies present being interrogated as to their repertoire, each and all responded "I dreamt."

That excess of popularity did not, however, long endure, and Mrs. Seguin found it at last voted *de trop*, both in the concert room and in character. "Come with the Gipsey Bride," "The fair land of Poland," and "You'll remember me," yet retain a good measure of popular regard, and would even now find a response in the general pulse. "La Sonnambula," "Fra Diavolo," "The Elixir of Love," "The Postillion of Lonjumeau," "Cinderella," "Masaniello," "Norma," "The Marriage of Figaro," "Rob Roy," and "Olympic Revels," were afterwards presented. "Fra Diavolo" and "The Postillion" gave Seguin fine opportunity to show off his redundant *vis-comica*, and most thoroughly did he improve the chance. In the former his mimicry and spirited action gave color and life to the opera, and in the "Postillion" he was essential to a successful performance, as the song "A Primo Basso, Sir, am I," never failed to bring down the house, though he did not *always* get down to double G, as pretended.

Beside the versatility and clever singing of Mrs. Seguin, who seemed competent to every style of music, and united to good action a pleasing voice and prepossessing appearance to please the public, the sweet and mellow tenor of Frazer had, despite his habit of singing false, and never reaching quite up to pitch, attraction for the masses. Without her aid he was nothing, but sustained and kept up by a well trained and instructed director, he was not the worst tenor who has taken first business here. The aid given by Mrs. Maeder was material in good execution of her music, and W. F. Johnson supplied a good Marquis for the Postillion, so far as the action and by-play were concerned.

Supported by a good chorus and fair orchestra, the Seguins brought out their operas in so taking a style, that for six weeks crowds were attracted into a crazy old building which leaked at every thaw or hard shower, and was deemed by many liable to fall upon the multitude at any moment from very weakness of construction.

So potent was the spell that bound old Boston to English opera then, that almost every performance had a good house, and many were honored with overflows. Two benefits were awarded to Mrs. Seguin, and both had 1400 auditors within the walls, beside many hundreds unable to obtain admission, that remained upon the side-walks content with catching a strain at intervals.

Mrs. Maeder's benefit closed this long season, and witnessed the last honors paid to English opera and the Seguins. They came again, and tried to overcome the attraction of Italian opera, but Marti's company made all lesser lights dim, and now that genuine opera was known and its charm felt, all farther struggle to a competition only aggravated damaging contrast, and gave poignancy to regret over lost attraction by severe pecuniary inflictions in reminder of an unpleasant fact.

Mr. Johnson, towards the close of the Seguins' engagement, sold out his interest, and it is a little singular that the notes received, while in possession of a third party, were stolen on the re-opening of the new Athenæum, from the pocket, and a law suit in consequence resulted in both parties being allowed to pay their own costs, and retire in disgust.

John Brougham played a brief engagement, when the benefits of the members of the stock commenced. The name of A. J. Phillips, one of the members, was up for a benefit on the evening of February 25, 1846, and "Pizarro" was performed, the part of *Rolla* by John Sheridan, the well-known professor of the art of self-defence, who volunteered for the occasion. The performances closed without any incident worthy of note, and the building had been vacated about twenty minutes, when a fire broke out in the rear of the stage, and so combustible was the tenement, that in less than ten minutes it was enveloped in flames, and in half an hour, scenery, wardrobe, properties, every thing was consumed.

The property had just previous to this been purchased of Dr. Walker, in the name of Ford & Brayley, and the former had, previous to the closing of the theatre, visited every part and left all apparently safe. The cause of the fire was never satisfactorily known, but we remember while looking at the ruins the following morning, to have heard one of the supernumeraries observe to another, that say what they might, about its being the work of an incendiary, he believed that if it had n't have been for that fire from heaven in "Pizarro," the place would still be standing. It is possible that a spark may have concealed itself in the scenery, which afterwards burst out into a flame. The actors lost their wardrobes, which were suddenly discovered to be of very great value; but their losses were made good, by benefits given subsequently at the Melodeon and elsewhere. The orchestra lost their instruments, and a concert for their relief was given by the Boston Academy of Music.

The fire communicated to the stable of Mr. Read, in the rear, and to the houses of Dr. Jackson and Mr. Peabody on Somerset Street, all of which sustained damage, and but for the activity of the firemen, must have fallen in the flames.

CHAPTER XXXIII.

The Howard Athenæum. — Opening Night. —Introduction of William Warren. — Blangy. — The Viennoise Children. — Marti's celebrated Havana Opera Company. — Tedesco. — Incident in her Life. — Signor Perelli, etc. etc.

After the destruction of the Tabernacle by fire, the land remained unimproved for some time, various projects being agitated. The want of a first-class theatre was talked of, but capitalists had learned, from past experience, that if one was to be built, it must be on a larger scale than the dimensions of the lot would allow. Messrs. Boyd & Beard, however, required at that time a central and spacious depot for the manufacture and sale of their beers, ales, and mineral water, and with the assistance of others, the land was purchased, and it was determined to build a theatre, Messrs. Boyd & Beard reserving the basement as a manufactory.

On the 4th of July, 1846, the corner stone of the present Howard Athenæum was laid, on which occasion Hon. I. H. Wright delivered a short address, and a collation was partaken of at the Pemberton House. Isaiah Rogers, Esq., was the architect, and the front of granite was erected by Messrs. Standish & Woodbury in thirty-two days after the corner-stone was laid, and on the 5th of October the interior was sufficiently advanced to permit its opening, under the direction of James H. Hackett & Co., and the stage management of W. H. Chippendale. The performances on the opening night brought to the footlights the entire strength of the company, consisting of an Opening Address, delivered by George Vandenhoff, the "Rivals," with the following effective support:—

Sir Anthony Absolute,	Mr. Chippendale.
Captain Absolute,	Mr. J. H. Hall.
Sir Lucius O'Trigger,	Mr. Wm. Warren.
Bob Acres,	Mr. Crisp.
Falkland,	Mr. Ayling.
Fag,	Mr. Bradshaw.
David,	Mr. Saunders.
Lydia Languish,	Miss Mary Taylor.
Julia.	Miss Maywood.
Mrs. Malaprop,	Mrs. Maywood.
Lucy,	Miss Hildreth.
Maid,	Mrs. Stone.

This was followed by the musical burletta of the "Chaste Salute:"—

Darville,	Mr. H. Hunt.
Thibaut,	Mr. Chippendale.
Philippe,	Mr. Saunders.
Baroness,	Mrs. Maywood.
Madame Thibaut,	Miss M. Taylor.
Sophia,	Miss Phillips.

The prices of admission were, parquette boxes, $1; parquette and dress circle, 75 cents; boxes, 50 cents; second circle, 25 cents. These prices were subsequently changed, and the tariff now used adopted.

It was on this occasion that Mr. William Warren, now of the Boston Museum, first made his appearance in this city, as *Sir Lucius O'Trigger.* No actor ever won the approbation of a Boston audience more rapidly than Mr. Warren, and no actor is held in higher estimation at the present day than he. The season continued until the 27th of February, and was marked by the appearance of Md'lle Blangy, (who brought out "La Giselle" in good style, assisted by Mons. Hazard,) Mrs. Mowatt, Davenport, Madame Augusta, Mr. Collins, the Irish comedian, Camilla Sivori, Booth, and Ciocca. "Guy Mannering" was brought out in December with fine effect. *Abel Sampson,* Chippendale; *Dandie Dinmont,* Warren; *Julia Mannering,* Miss Mary Taylor; *Lucy Bertram,* Miss Phillips, now Mrs. Conover; *Meg Merrilies,* Mrs. Crisp. Hackett appeared, and George Vandenhoff introduced a recitation of Collins' Ode to the Passions, with orchestral accompaniment, which was very effective. The crowning achievement of the season, however, was the visit of the Viennoise Dancers, who made their first appearance on the 11th of January, 1847, and continued till the close, filling the treasury beyond any attraction since offered.

Mr. Hackett left with the Viennoise Children, and the theatre passed into the hands of his partner, Thos. Ford, who leased it for a brief season to Sands, Lent & Co., for circus performances, who were succeeded on the 23d of April, 1847, by the opera company.

It was on this occasion that Boston first recognized genuine Italian Opera in the performance of Verdi's "Ernani," by a complete, fully organized company, known to fame as the Havana Opera Troupe, formed by Marti, purveyor of fish, and proprietor of the great Tacon Theatre.

A superb orchestra led by Arditi and the superlative contrabassist Botesini, with a good chorus and principals of extraordinary merit, presented Verdi's best opera in a style that absolutely electrified the audience. All the recollections of English opera were effaced by this life-breathing, passionate, and effective performance, and from that hour a new ideal of excellence in operatic affairs became fixed and irrevocable. Such a combination of brilliancy, effect, and vigor, with the sentimental and tender, had never before revealed itself upon the Boston lyric stage, and the excitement produced by this new sensation was commensurate with the marvels that produced it.

The opera itself was interesting from a wild and romantic plot, worked up in a good libretto, and that innate beauty had been most effectively treated by the composer.

So masterly was the orchestration and the introduction of novel, yet most pleasing combinations, modulations, and octaves, with an exquisite skill in use of solo talent in aid of a masterly conceived partition, that, strong as prejudice had been against its composer, this opera instantly commanded admiration, disarmed prejudice, and gave Verdi universal popularity.

In this debut of a new composer and first hearing of Italian Opera, all the essentials to a great success were found, and it would be difficult to decide whether Verdi, the orchestra and chorus, or the principal singers, received the majority of votes from a public well-nigh frenzied with delight.

The remarkable personal beauty of Tedesco, and her rich, voluptuous, and easily produced volume of voice, probably excited more enthusiasm than any other item of this grand tableau. That vocalist, strange as it might seem to American gallantry, commenced her operatic career with a terrible experience of Italian rudeness. Her father being of that hated race who hold Lombardy in bitter subjection, the fair debutante found the audience of La Scala quite willing to make her the scapegoat for an unpopular composer, and hissed, brayed, and hooted at Fortunata for a mortal hour, on the night of her debut in "Saul." The agent of Marti, on the *qui vive* for novelty, engaged and shipped to Havana the rejected of Milan, with confident expectation that she would attract the gallant Habanese in crowds to Marti's operatic temple. She did move Havana as if by the lever of Archimedes, her person and voice both possessing a potent spell. Her benefit realized $8,000, and ingenuity was tasked for new floral or poetic honors to such a ravishing prima donna.

Boston scarcely equalled Havana in those respects, but the delicious quality of her voice, its graceful production, and the flood of melody she could pour out in all the ease and freedom of a mocking-bird, overcame even Puritan reserve. The admiration she excited on her first appearance was intense, and not until a trifling unladylike deportment became a habit, did the hold upon a Boston public then acquired lose its power, and finally become aversion.

The character of *Ernani* was sustained by a tenor not then celebrated, but his pure, flexible, and expressive voice made Perelli famous after the first proof that he possessed in rare abundance perfection of voice, style, and method.

His unisons with the soprano were exquisite, and in the duet, "Ah! morirr," enchantment held the audience breathless in delight. The wonderful unison finale, "O! Carlo Magno," brought Tedesco and Perelli fully out in their clear and pure sustenance of the climax, giving a zest and charm to its full, rich harmony, which never failed to excite a furore. Novelli and Vita, the basso and baritono, were also excellent, giving a full support to all the concerted pieces in which they participated, and in solo their good quality of tone, purity of intonation, and finished school, were remarked with satisfaction. The vocalization of Tedesco, Perelli, Novelli, and Vita, left no room for any other feeling than delighted admiration, the natural beauty of voice and finished elegance of a good school, with true Italian warmth, appearing in graceful perfection. They were not, however, actors, or competent to a faithful impersonation of character, and but very few vocalists ever pretend to be. In the blaze of enthusiasm, and nearly frantic delight that "Ernani" awakened here, this defect had but slight consideration, and the run then commenced had, with occasional relapses, a continuance until June 6th, when the first season closed with a performance of "Moses in Egypt," at the Melodeon, before the largest audience ever assembled there, 1637 tickets being taken. In this long interval several phases of popular feeling were observed, as the opera and principal singers chanced to be more or less attractive. "Linda di Chamouni" introduced Caranti Vita, a pure soprano of little timbre and unpleasantly tremulous, but endowed with a most prepossessing person. It did not take well, and gave place to Pacini's "Saffo," which, by the popularity of Tedesco and the lovely contralto of Sofie Marini, convulsed the city as "Ernani" had done. The duet for soprano and contralto is charming in itself, but given as they gave it, with a perfect blending and fusion of voice and soul, few could resist the potent spell. "I due Foscari" was brought forward next for Rainieri, a soprano sfogato of exquisite finish and smoothness in execution. She had a gratifying reception, and her vocalization excited applause in almost Tedescan abundance. The opera was, however, too horrible, and the music too sombre, for general audiences, so it failed of sensation. "Romeo and Juliet," as the operatic version of two composers, next attracted crowds, the fair Tedesco appearing in martial dress, with a preposterous long tunic and sword of immense length, to fulminate "La tremenda ultrice spade," and make love to gentle *Juliet* in the person of Caranti Vita. The representative of *Romeo* was evidently hampered with her virile habiliments, and obtained less favor than in either of her two preceding operas. In the bravura and duet with Caranti, she gained hearty applause.

The admirers of Caranti now took courage as she gained confidence and developed the beauty of a fine soprano, and even ventured to question the supremacy of Tedesco.

Great things had been said of the primo tenore in advance of his debut, and extravagant anticipations formed. When Severi appeared, however, it was evident that his voice was nearly gone, and though he got, by spasmodic and fitful effort, a chance note or two fraught with expression and good tune, he never could sustain the high rank of first tenor in such a company. He made a hit in the death scene of "I Lombardi," but Perelli's throne remained unshaken, and the masses paid him allegiance.

Rossini's great opera, "Moses in Egypt," was performed first as a concert, and with immense effect upon a crowded house, as the choral execution surpassed all ideas of excellence suggested by our sacred music associations. Tedesco and Perelli were enchanting in their soul-fraught and voice-blending duet, and Rainieri gave the queen's solo, "Ah, d' un afflita," with such perfection as to eclipse any previous union here of perfect execution with feeling and expression of the deepest emotion.

"Norma," with Tedesco and Rainieri, revived the furore, and raised premiums to a high pitch, the receipts on each night of its performance exceeding $1,300.

The auctioneer was early invoked to aid in distributing chances for the rich musical lottery, presented by the Havana company, and premiums frequently ran to a ridiculous excess. Parquette seats in the "Ernani" soon went up to $1.50 and $1.75 advance on the original

50 cents; and in some other instances, when Tedesco appeared, the seats commanded $4 to $5 premium. Two great public houses were then intrusted with orders for boxes and seats, and their competition in trade gave an impetus to the bidding. The concerts given on Saturday nights were not fully attended, custom indicating the Melodeon or Tremont Temple for such performances. Botesini, however, astonished the musicians by his converting a three stringed double bass into a violin, and the prodigies of execution he brought from an instrument so unwieldy to others. In the orchestra he bore up and sustained the whole mass of harmony, and proved himself a match for any four players in the body of tone and effect produced; but in the exhibition of his solo talent, those who marvelled at his orchestral exploits, were obliged to confess Paganini had one equal.

The pecuniary result of this first season was a net profit of $12,000, and the honors paid to Fortunata Tedesco attained their greatest excess in the casting at her feet of a warm admirer's hat and cane, in token of his own entire prostration.

This company returned in September, but their reception lacked much of the warmth and intensity so remarkable in the first visit.

Novelty no longer attracted the curious and those eager for a new sensation, while the confidence of control over their audience betrayed the singers into levity and indifferent treatment of the music intrusted to them.

CHAPTER XXXIV.

Continuation of the Howard Athenæum. — Madame Anna Bishop. — Elize Biscaccianti. — Truffi. — Fancy Balls. — W. C. Macready. — Maurice Power. — Bateman Children. — Charles R. Thorne. — Jean Margaret Davenport. — H. W. Finn. — Operas. — Baker & English. C. D. Pitt. — Mrs. Mowatt. — Forrest. — Miss Laura Addison. — Mrs. Warner. — Madame Thillon. — Lola Montes. — The Season of 1852–3. — Henry Willard. — Miss Fitzpatrick. — Alboni. — Sontag, etc. etc.

On the 8th of June, 1847, the Howard Athenæum was re-opened for a short season by Thomas Ford, W. L. Ayling as stage-manager. Mr. George H. Andrews and Mrs. Abbott, with Blangy and Vallee, appeared, and in July the Ravels came.

The season of 1847–8 commenced August 16th, with Mr. Ford as lessee, W. H. Chippendale acting manager, and W. L. Ayling as stage-manager. Several new faces appeared among the stock, but none who proved permanent favorites. The stars consisted of Mr. Harvey Tuckett, who appeared as *Don Cæsar de Bazan*, *Falstaff*, etc.; Madame Anna Bishop, Booth, Ciocca, Italian Opera Company in September; Anderson, who was supported by Mrs. George Jones, and appeared in "Lady of Lyons," "King of the Commons," etc.; Mrs. Mowatt and Davenport, just prior to her departure for Europe; Seguin Operatic Troupe, Dan Marble and Professor Risley & Sons, Rice, H. P. Grattan, the Monplaisers, Signora Biscaccianti, the Heron Family, and the Bedouin Arabs.

Madame Bishop made her first appearance in Opera

before a Boston audience August 26, 1847, at this house, in scenes from Balfe's "Maid of Artois," and followed up that success by scenes from "The Barber of Seville," "Linda of Chamounix," "Tancredi," "La Sonnambula," "The Love Spell," and "Anna Bolena."

Her greatest success then was undoubtedly in the recitative and aria from "Tancredi," which, in her noble bearing, heroic stage presence, and superb delivery of either recitation or air, commanded universal admiration. Such breadth and freedom of phrasing and perfection of recitative was a rarity, and the liquid flow of melody in the song charmed every cultivated ear. In the death scene of "Anna Bolena," this versatile vocalist and finished actress found ample response to her fidelity of presentment and the chaste style which pervaded the performance. In the rondo finale of "La Sonnambula," her brilliant execution almost overcame the embarrassment of voice, extremely limited in compass, and caused many regrets that nature had not been more generous to one so able to make good use of her vocal and personal gifts. The familiar "Una voce" was made by her to assume fresh interest by rapid execution in staccato, which rivalled the best violin player's utmost facility in that difficult trait.

No woman has ever been able to personate heroes of the Othello and Tancredi stamp with that absolute embodiment Madame Bishop invariably presented. Form, gait, and action were assimilated to the character represented. Coming so close upon the Havana Opera company, her audiences were not large, though highly appreciative and enthusiastic.

At a subsequent period she appeared in costume at

the Melodeon and Tremont Temple, exciting both wonder and enthusiastic applause by her admirable personation of *Othello* and *Desdemona*, on the same evening, in the former place, and the freedom of a Mexican girl's manner at the latter. The music of each role was presented with appropriate style, giving her embodiments of characters a lifelike semblance, at once rare and deeply interesting.

In the concert-room, Madame Bishop proved herself mistress of every style, and the most remarkable linguist that has yet been noticed in musical annals. Twenty different tongues were by her married to music with a purity and grace of delivery that satisfied the most exacting native.

Like the song which gave her so great and well-deserved a celebrity, she made the union of melody and language "delightful to the ravished sense;" and whether it were Russian, French, or Hottentot, their roughness became smooth and liquid flow of rhythm.

In the English opera which her company gave at the Boston Theatre, a duet between Linda and her lover as given by Madame Bishop and Reeves, (a brother of Sims Reeves,) fairly intoxicated the city in their soft and perfect blending of voices, to make English at once expressive and melodious.

In September, 1847, the Havana Opera Company again visited Boston, performing for a short time at the Howard, and then removing their scene of dramatic concerts to Tremont Temple. Of this season the most taking performance was "Corrado d' Altamura," in which Sofie Marini had a fine part. It was given but once, and that once nearly occasioned at rehearsal a disrupture of the company, as Tedesco, jealous of Marini, insisted upon a transposition to suit her own voice, or whim, that destroyed the effect of a finale and the contralto's great point. Signor Villarino found it difficult to quell Tedesco's rage at being refused this concession, and for a time confusion worse confounded bore unrestricted sway.

In the Howard Athenæum "La Sonnambula," with Caranti Vita, Perelli, Rainieri, in the principal characters, led off, followed by "Norma," with Severi, Tedesco, and Rainieri, as principals, "Ernani," with its original cast, "The Barber of Seville," with Tedesco, Vita, and Lormi, were presented with a fair ensemble to a moderate audience. Their dramatic concerts were failures in almost every point of view. The public resented Villarino's economy in quitting the Howard, and thus depriving them of genuine opera.

The first appearance of Elize Ostinelli upon the Boston stage took place at the Howard Athenæum, January 5th, 1848, "La Sonnambula" being the opera, Vietti the *Elvino*, and Avignone the *Rodolfo*. She was extremely agitated during the whole performance, and, not being able to control her voice, disappointed expectations wrought to a high pitch by New York eulogiums. Nature had been prodigal in gifts of voice, but a slight and extremely nervous frame often refused to sustain her through an opera. She then betrayed an impurity of intonation which, in contrast with the Italian vocalists so recently here, chilled enthusiasm, and required all the efforts of her especial friends to excuse and cover up by applause. This friendly reception as the American prima donna and Boston's first show upon the

Italian lyric stage, gave her confidence, and her second appearance was a genuine triumph, so far as a very petite figure could be converted into a good stage presence by the charm of a fine voice under good control, and its capability of wonders in vocalization as exhibited in the rondo finale. After "La Sonnambula" had exhausted its attraction, she appeared in "Lucia di Lammermoor," with great success, her flexibility and beauty of voice having free scope in the cavatina and rondo, and her union of good acting with a brilliancy and ease of vocalization rarely equalled in the mad scene, taking captive even the most exacting dillettanti, who freshly remembered Persiani and Jenny Lind in that character.

She accomplished this mastery of all difficulties with indifferent support; and not until the last night of the opera, when Benedetti and Beneventano appeared in aid, was her full display of extraordinary vocal and histrionic powers manifested here. A furore in anticipation of a great performance, and Benedetti's first appearance, raised $400 of premiums from the sale of tickets for that night, and the excitement of their audience brought out an enthusiasm in the performers seldom witnessed upon the lyric stage. On the 26th of January, a truly grand complimentary benefit was given her by a public so enthusiastic that $760 were paid in premiums for the choice of seats, and the net proceeds of that substantial compliment were $1,600. Biscaccianti was, at various subsequent periods, highly successful in concerts at the Melodeon and Tremont Temple, with Perelli and Henri Herz. She then visited Europe for improvement of style and method, returning to give concerts in New York and Boston. Opera at low prices had then destroyed the attraction of concerts, and she went to California to achieve great concert success; after that she visited Lima to give operatic performances.

Sands, Lent & Co. again took the theatre, and at the expiration of their season a series of masquerade balls were given, which reflected any thing but credit upon this temple of the drama! In May, 1848, the Astor Place Opera Company leased the theatre, and on the 31st of May, Signora Truffi made her first appearance before a Boston audience. The opera was "Lucrezia Borgia," and she assumed the *Dutchess*, Benedetti being the *Genaro*, Rosi the *Duke*, and Signora Lieti Rossi the *Orsini*. Truffi captivated by the charms of an elegant person, a graceful, expressive action, and a rich, well-managed mezzo soprano. Benedetti's then glorious tenor swept away the remembrance of all other tenors. Rosi made a good *Duke*, for that day when Badiali was unknown; and the representative of *Orsini* made a great hit. Verdi's "Nabucco," with Truffi, Benedetti, Rosi, and Beneventano followed, but produced no sensation. Truffi excited a furore by her *Elvira*, ("Ernani,") but Arnoldi made a poor hero, and Beneventano a ridiculous king. In Mercadante's "Il Guiramento," a great triumph was obtained by Benedetti and Truffi. The season did not prove lucrative, and to relieve distressed singers, musicians, etc., a complimentary benefit was given at the last performance, June 26, in which Truffi appeared in *Lucrezia*, with Benedetti as *Genaro*, sang the cavatina from "Ernani," in which she introduced a fine trill, and with Benedetti gave the last act of "Il Guiramento." Truffi retained her great popularity here until after she became Signora Benedetti, when her voice appeared to have lost its remarkable purity and flexibility, and her acting had become very tame and indifferent.

The season of 1848–9 was commenced under Ford, and during his reign the Viennoise Children and the Moravian Singers appeared, followed by the Lehmann Family, who subsequently joined the Ravels. Miss Lehmann, whose death was caused in consequence of her dress taking fire, while performing at Niblo's, was a member of this corps.

In the latter part of October, Mr. John Brougham leased the theatre, ostensibly for the production of one of his own pieces, but after the papers were signed, Mr. Ford discovered that Mr. W. E. Burton and Mr. Brougham had secured Mr. Macready, who, under the joint management of the two B.'s, made his re-appearance, on the evening of October 30th, in *Macbeth*, supported by Mrs. J. Wallack. This engagement was profitable to the speculating B.'s. Mr. Burton, after Macready's departure, was announced to appear, but he left for New York, without fulfilling his intention. The theatre was, for the remainder of the season, in Mr. Ayling's charge, and the business was most disastrous. Isabel Dickson appeared — J. P. Addams, Mrs. Dinneford, and Maurice Power, son of Tyrone Power, made his first appearance here as *McShane*, in the "Nervous Man." He was a gentleman, but no actor.

The management at one time reduced the prices to 25 cents, and Addams and Locke appeared. Complimentary benefits were given to Robert Hamilton and to George E. Campbell, then reporter for the Times, now a judge in California, who wrote a local play, in which a scene representing the interior of the police court was introduced. On the 15th of January, Madame Laborde appeared as *Lucia*, which was followed by the management of Mr. Fry, who introduced his opera, which proved a failure. After their departure, there was a temporary revival with Blangy, Durand, Chippendale, Johnson, Skerrett; and in June the Bateman Children, since celebrated as prodigies by their success in England, under Le Grand Smith, Esq., made their appearance, and the Viennoise Children in July wound up a very checkered season.

Mr. Charles R. Thorne leased the theatre and opened it on the 27th of August, for the season 1849–50. Mr. E. Eddy was stage-manager, and the company included Mr. and Mrs. Thorne, Mrs. Skerrett, Miss Wagstaff, Miss Fanny Wheeler, Mrs. Muzzy, Miss Mace, Messrs. Eddy, C. Webb, G. Jordan, Skerrett, Saunders, Bellamy, Ward, Watkins, etc., etc.; and on the opening night "Macbeth" and "Perfection" were performed. Between the plays, Miss Anna Walters (Mrs. Jordan) made her first appearance in Boston as a danseuse, and proved a very pleasing acquisition to the theatre. During the season Mr. Hackett, Mrs. Mossop, Collins, Chanfrau, Mr. Bass, Hudson, the Seguin Troupe, with Rosa Jaques and Mrs. Farren, appeared.

The season, however, in addition to the above attractions, was marked by the re-appearance in Boston of Miss Jean Margaret Davenport, who, on the 15th of October, 1849, appeared as *Julia* in the "Hunchback." She had left our shores, a prodigy of youthful genius, a mere phenomenon, who, like Burke and Batty, Clara Fisher, and others, it was anticipated would prove a forced plant, whose fragrance had been exhausted ere it reached its growth. They who judged by these precedents were pleasantly disappointed, when they beheld in Miss Davenport an actress of no ordinary merit, and her success was brilliant. She played a brief but excellent engagement, won many friends, and returned in the following December to renew the delight of all theatre-goers, by her performance of the *Countess* in "Love," a part which she played to overflowing houses. She was supported by Mr. Neaffie, who, as *Huon*, gained deserved applause.

On the 21st of January, 1850, Mr. H. W. Finn, who had made his debut at Providence a short time previous, appeared for the first time in this city as *Dr. Pangloss*, in the "Heir at Law," and subsequently as *Billy Lackaday* in "Sweethearts and Wives," and *Mons. Jaques*. The reputation of the father, the inimitable comedian, attracted for the son on the opening night a good house, and for a tyro he acquitted himself remarkably well. His best performance was *Mons. Jaques*. After a temporary absence from the stage, Mr. Finn resumed his professional duties in California in 1853. In March, Max Maretzek brought his Opera Company here, and was followed in May by the troupe comprising Badiali, Marini, Bosio, Salvi, etc. The Negro Opera concluded the season, and Mr. Thorne retired from the management of the Howard.

The dramatic season of 1850–1 at the Howard Athenæum was commenced by Messrs. Baker & English, and on the opening night, August 19, 1850, "The

Rivals, or A Trip to Bath," and "The Three Cuckoos," were perf rmed. Of the stock company, Mr. and Mrs. John Gilbert, Mr. John Brougham, Mrs. W. H. Smith, were the most prominent. Mrs. English, Mrs. H. M. Stephens, Mr. G. Arnold, S. Johnson, Raymond, and E. Warden, were also attached to the theatre, with Miss Ince as danseuse. Mr. Brougham brought out his comedy of "Romance and Reality," and the principal star engagements were those of Miss Mary Taylor, Miss Charlotte Cushman, assisted by Neaffie in September, Miss Davenport, supported by A. W. Fenno, who on the 25th of October, brought out "Adrienne the Actress," and on the 4th of November revived Mr. Sargent's play of "Velasco." On a second engagement, Miss Davenport, supported by Charles D. Pitt, brought out "Charlotte Corday," which did not materially add to her reputation as an actress. Blangy, with Durand, appeared during the season.

Mr. C. D. Pitt made a favorable impression in this city, and his acting subsequently at the Museum was warmly praised.

Mr. and Mrs. Thorne, Mrs. Hamblin, (Mrs. Shaw,) and Wyseman Marshall, also appeared. Before the close of the regular dramatic season, Mr. Ayling assumed the management, and "Alfred Ellton," a play written by a clergyman, was produced, and early in May the theatre closed, the star of the evening refusing to appear unless arrearages were paid. A circus company filled up the usual dramatic summer vacation.

The season of 1851–2, under the management of Wyseman Marshall, commenced on the 8th of September with "Love's Sacrifice." The preliminary announcement of the lessee said: — "The manager hopes, by a straight-forward course, to merit the patronage and approbation of all lovers of the legitimate drama." It was late in the season when Mr. Marshall concluded to take the theatre, and it was difficult to procure a very strong stock company, but he secured the services of Mrs. Melinda Jones, Mr. and Mrs. Sloane, Mrs. Cramer, Miss Cramer, (now Mrs. Neagle,) Meeker, Hamblin, Mrs. Groves, Whitman, Brand, and subsequently Mrs. W. H. Smith and W. F. Johnson. On the second night, September 9th, Mrs. Mowatt made her re-appearance, for the first time after her European tour, as *Julianna*, in the "Honey Moon." She was most cordially received, and her engagement, which continued through the "Three Days' Jubilee," proved eminently successful. She was succeeded by Baron Hackett, and on the 13th of October Miss Davenport brought out O. C. Wyman, Esq.'s translation of "Valeria." The translation did full justice to the original, and improved it in many particulars, but the play had not the merit requisite for a successful piece. The Seguins and Julia Turnbull next essayed to attract the public, with a fair result, but the theatrical firmament was looking hazy, when Mr. Edwin Forrest re-appeared, after an absence of several years, on the 3d of November. His engagement brought more money into the house, length of time considered, than any other of the season.

The next star was Miss Laura Addison. Her father, Mr. Wilmhurst, was a tradesman in Colchester, England, where Miss Addison was born, in November, 1822. She made her debut at Norwich, England, in 1842, as *Elvira* in "Pizarro," and first appeared on the London boards at Saddler's Wells in 1847, and remained for some years a popular member of the excellent histrionic company. She subsequently performed with success at the Haymarket and at Drury Lane, and made her first appearance in America at the Broadway Theatre, New York, and then visited Boston. Her success here was not what she anticipated, and her visit to this country did not create that sensation which many anticipated, who knew of her popularity in London. In August, Miss Addison visited Niagara Falls, and while returning to New York from Albany she died, after a few days' illness, on board the steamboat Oregon, Sept. 2, 1852, of congestion of the brain.

Mrs. Warner, the celebrated English actress, now somewhat advanced in years, appeared in November, and during her engagement performed *Mrs. Beverley*, *Lady Macbeth*, *Julia*, *Mrs. Haller*, *Queen Katharine*, and *Hermione* in the "Winter's Tale." Her *Lady Macbeth* was excellent, but her great hit was in *Hermione*, in the statue scene, which will long remain indelibly fixed on the minds of those who witnessed it, as a fine artistical bit of stage effect.

Madame Thillon and Mr. Hudson appeared in December, and did an immense business with the "Crown Diamonds." The lady was indebted for her success mainly to a pretty face, which attracted the admirers of personal beauty, more than to her vocal powers, which were limited and of no very high order. On one night of her engagement, the tickets and premiums amounted to $1,400. During Madame Thillon's engagement, Mr. George Barrett and his daughter, Miss Georgianna

Barrett, now Mrs. Philip Warren, appeared on the off-nights. Mr. McKean Buchanan also played a short engagement. On the 14th of February, Mrs. Mowatt commenced her second engagement, closing on the 12th of March. She made a great hit in *Parthenia* to Marshall's *Ingomar*, and after her recovery from the effects of an accident received by being thrown from her horse, she received a complimentary benefit, tendered to her by his honor Mayor Seaver, Robert G. Shaw, Esq., and others.

Lola Montes succeeded Mrs. Mowatt. Her appearance on the stage, as a danseuse, was a mockery of that art which has been cultivated by Taglioni, Cerito, Elssler, and Grisi, while her attempts at acting have rendered her ludicrous in the extreme. Miss Davenport commenced a farewell engagement, prior to her return to England, on the 5th of April, and attracted large audiences. Mr. John Brougham subsequently appeared, and during his engagement Mr. Rice's most excellent travestie of Hamlet was brought out. Mrs. Pelby played one night for her daughter's benefit, and in June Mr. Marshall let the house to the Ravel Family, who did a fair business.

The season was one of the very few at this house that have proved remunerative to the manager. Mr. Marshall was fortunate in obtaining a succession of "stars," and with a very meagre company, and an economical system, he arrived at the termination of the season with a surplus of some $10,000. The house, he was well aware, was not sufficiently capacious to warrant any very heavy expenses; and though he was sometimes severely handled, he adopted the only course, that of silence, and proved himself the winner in the end.

The season of 1852–3 was commenced on the 31st of August, 1852, by Henry Willard, as "lessee and sole manager." Mr. Anderson, the "Wizard of the North," gave his exhibition there for a short time, and having closed on Friday evening, the 17th of September, Mr. Willard announced the opening of the theatre for the dramatic season on the 20th, and it was duly opened, with the notorious Lola Montes. The interior had been entirely repainted and improved. To give the interior a drawing-room appearance, Mr. Willard displayed on the walls, in the rear of the private boxes, a number of prints, beautifully framed, representing the removal of the remains of the great Napoleon from St. Helena and the interment at the Hospital of the Invalides at Paris. This selection of subjects looked ominous of the future, and has proved so, for the Athenæum under Mr. Willard's management has worn a funeral aspect. In fact, it required very little imagination at times to fancy Thespis and Melpomene weeping over the tomb of the legitimate drama, and sighing to see actors devoid of talent, and actresses whose voices denoted speedy dissolution of body and soul, impersonating the heroes and heroines of Shakspeare, and of Bulwer, Knowles, and other leading dramatists Miss Kimberly, Madame Thillon, Mr. Hudson, Mrs. Warner, and the Rousset family, appeared in succession, and did indifferently well.

On the 3d of January, Mrs. Anna Cora Mowatt commenced an engagement, opening as *Parthenia*, a character in which she has no equal, and during her engagement she attracted very excellent houses. Mrs. Sinclair was announced to appear, but did not make her appearance in Boston, but sent on a plea of illness, from which she recovered in a very short time. Mr. Forrest was at that time performing at the National. Miss Kimberly played another brief engagement, and the first portion of the dramatic season was brought to a close in January, when Le Grand Smith leased the theatre, and brought out the opera troupe, of which Marietta Alboni was the prima donna. The pieces produced were "Cenerentola," "La Figlia del Regimento," "La Sonnambula," "Norma," "Il Barbieri de Seviglie." Nine performances were given by the opera company, Messrs. Cony and Taylor, with their dogs, performing on the off-nights. Madame Alboni had her greatest triumph in La Figlia, an impersonation which has seldom been compassed in this city. This operatic spectacle did not prove very remunerative to Mr. Marshall, of New York, and Le Grand Smith, more on account of the feeble surport given to Alboni by her assistants, than from any other cause. It was stated that the nightly expenses were $1,500. Mr. Neaffie and Miss Heron succeeded the opera in February. In the month of March, Mr. Willard announced a new season, with a company of great ability and talent, but unfortunately many could not discover the improvement. Mr. Jefferson and Mr. Palmer were certainly acquisitions, and with Mr. Goodall formed the only trio of actors who rose above mediocrity, that have been attached to the corps during the season. On the 14th of March, the Spanish Dancers, comprising Soto, Melisse, Pougaud,

Drouet, Lavigne, Leeder, and Monsieur Mege, having terminated an engagement at the National, commenced at the Howard. It was on this night that Miss Emma Fitzpatrick made her first appearance in Boston, as *Letitia Hardy*, supported by D. S. Palmer as *Doricourt*, and Mr. Martin as *Hardy*. Miss Fitzpatrick was born in Clifton, near the city of Bristol, England. Her father was from the county of Kilkenny in Ireland, and at one time was in affluent circumstances, but the vicissitudes of life left the family after his death, dependent upon their own exertions, and Miss Fitzpatrick adopted the profession, *con amore*, making her debut as *Lydia Languish*, to Mrs. Glover's *Mrs. Malaprop*, at Newcastle (Potteries). To Mrs. Glover she was indebted for what stage education she received, and with this eminent actress she was a great favorite. After performing at several of the provincial theatres, she played at the Dublin Theatre, where she gained repute, and was thence summoned to London, where at the Haymarket she made her debut as *Helen* in the "Hunchback," and shortly after appeared at Drury Lane, then managed by Bunn, in the same character to Miss Helen Faucit's *Julia*. It is a bit of green-room gossip, that Miss Faucit, who is *the* actress of the present era, although somewhat envious of any youthful debutante, on account of her own age, was asked her opinion of Miss Fitzpatrick. The lady gave a celestial direction to her nose, a few whiffs with her fan, and replied, "She is a good dresser." This was marked envy; but the compliment bestowed was just, for in her make up she displays the greatest taste, and is always well dressed, without the slightest approach to tawdry. She performed for some time in London, and was engaged by Hackett to visit America, which offer she accepted, and appeared at Niblo's in New York, in August, 1852. Her connection with the dancers was unfortunate for her dramatic reputation. The dancers before she came were regarded as inferior in merit, and Miss Fitzpatrick was apparently second to them, which placed her in a false position. Her acting, as a light comedienne, has a vigor and style, which renders her, especially in dashing comedy, one of the best actresses of the day; and her *Helen*, *Mrs. Chillington*, *Lady Teazle*, etc., were performances with which the critical could find no fault. Her health at times deprives her of that force requisite for many impersonations, but when in good spirits and well supported, she is truly a charming actress. On the first night of her appearance in Boston, a little incident occurred worthy of note, if only to show how trivial a dereliction from custom will serve to break the ice for a new performer. The audience did not appear to enter into Miss Fitzpatrick's vein, and with their proverbial coldness were inclined to hold back their applause, perhaps inclined to think the *Letitia* a very bold girl, to hazard what appeared to them an unwarranted freedom, inasmuch as the personation differed from stereotyped performances of that part. The play proceeded till *Letitia*, approaching *Doricourt*, asks: "Do you know what the lamb says?" An instantaneous reply came from the gallery of—bah! ha! ha! which afforded an opportunity for the lady to give a specimen of a silvery laugh, to which the audience added a chorus. This served as an introduction, and her performances were always well received. Mr. Hackett played during the engagement.

The next claimant for popular favor at the Howard was Mrs. McCready, a pupil of Peter Richings of Philadelphia, and wife of Dr. McCready. She had performed only a week on the stage, before her appearance at the Howard. Her best impersonation was that of *Julia* in the "Hunchback," (Miss Fitzpatrick, whose stay was prolonged a week after the departure of the dancers, performing *Helen*,) Mr. J. H. Oxley as *Master Walter*, Goodall as *Sir Thomas Clifford*. Mrs. McCready, in other parts, gave signs of careful study, and, though a novice, there is, we think, a promise in her present acting which leads us to believe that time and study alone are required to perfect her as an actress, there being no lack of natural mental vigor.

On Tuesday evening, April 19th, 1853, Madame Sontag's Opera Troupe commenced their season at the Howard, and gave three operas each week till May 20th, the houses varying in receipts from $1,300 to $800; a difference partially to be attributed to the fact that Count Rosi interfered with Mr. Ullman, the agent, and reduced the number of tickets sent to the press, on one occasion. We did not allude to the fact at the time, as we are indifferent to these minor matters, nor do we believe that the public are much interested in such episodes; but the almost universal howl sent forth by the afflicted had its effect in destroying that harmony which should exist in the public mind, especially when the lyrical drama is the object of patronage. The Sontag troupe did well here, and made money; but had they come earlier, when the Bostonians were ripe for

Madame Sontag, the harvest would be one of gold, instead of silver. Of the style in which operas were produced, we need not allude, for the public will long remember the captivating prima donna, Badiali, Pozzolino, Vietti, Gasparoni, Biondi, Signora Mora, Signora Rosina Pico, Vietti, etc., and the popular leader, Carl Eckert. The recollection of this operatic troupe will long remain a pleasant memory, to which the mind will often recur, renewing in imagination the pleasure experienced by the reality. The arrest of Palmer and Philbrick marks this engagement; but it is a blemish which we willingly pass over in silence.

Performances were given on the off-nights by Mr. Willard's stock company; and on the nights of the opera, the Eagle, or, as it was called after Messrs. Olwine & Goodall tried their hand at it, the "American" Theatre, was opened by the manager of the Howard, but with little success. Mrs. Warner played an engagement at the Howard. She came to Boston to play at the National, but that house had closed the season, and she was out of employment. On the 17th of May, Mrs. Warner took a benefit at the Howard, when Mrs. Mowatt appeared as *Desdemona*, and Wyseman Marshall as *Othello;* Mrs. Warner was to appear as *Emelia*, but severe indisposition prevented, and Mrs. Melinda Jones assumed the role. On the 5th of May, H. W. Fenno, late of the National, took a benefit at this house, and on the 19th J. B. Wright, also a graduate of the National, was the beneficiary, when Mr. Henry Sedley made his re-appearance, and Mrs. Pelby, Miss Julia Pelby, and Miss Anna Cruise volunteered. The result was not such a reward as Mr. Wright deserved. He has been a hard-working, industrious stage-manager, and we hope soon to see him in a position for which he is eminently qualified.

The last star engagement of the season was that of Mr. James W. Wallack, Jr., who had been playing at the National. The Howard closed its doors for the dramatic season in June.

CHAPTER XXXV.

The Boston Museum. — The Patrons of the Museum. — The Drunkard. — Opening Night at the New Museum. — Mrs. Barrett. — The Vaudeville Saloon at Boylston Hall. — The Eagle Theatre. — Mr. Pelby's coup d'etat. — The Olympic Saloon. — The Boston Adelphi. — The Lyceum Theatre. — The Dramatic Museum. — Beach Street Museum. — The Predictions of a Veteran. — Closing Remarks.

We have alluded incidentally in previous chapters to the Boston Museum. This popular place of amusement is now a feature of this city. From a very humble beginning, it has increased and strengthened, till it has attained a name which is as enviable as it is well-deserved.

On the 14th of June, 1841, the "Boston Museum and Gallery of Fine Arts," was opened by Mr. Moses Kimball and associates, in the building erected for the purpose at the corner of Tremont and Bromfield streets.

The collection of natural curiosities was the same that formerly belonged to the New England Museum, but many additions were made, and several valuable curiosities were added. There had been several museums in Boston, but this new place differed from all others, from the fact that it had a spacious music saloon over the Museum, capable of holding 1200 persons. The walls of the saloon were hung with pictures, and the stage was sufficiently capacious for the performance of vaudevilles, etc. The drop scene was very neat and appropriate, and the place was quite comfortable and cosey. The hall was dedicated on the 14th by a grand concert, in which Mr. Sinclair, (father to Mrs. E. Forrest,) and Miss Melton, were the attractions. These entertainments proved very acceptable to the public, and in course of the first twenty months, Yankee Hill, Dr. Valentine, Mr. Walcott, Miss Rock, Dempster, Mr. Young, Mr. and Mrs. Maeder, S. C. Massett, Miss Moss, Mrs. Seymour, Edward Kendall, Miss Sarah, Knight, the Indian Warriors and Squaws, Mr. Love, the polyphonist, the Rainer Family, Signor Blitz, the Mysterious Gipsey Girl, Major Stevens' Diorama of the Battle of Bunker Hill, the Miss Shaws, were at different times exhibiting at the Museum.

In February, 1843, Mr. Kimball engaged John Sefton and Mrs. Maeder to bring out "Operattas," and on the 6th inst., the "Masque Ball" was brought out. This was the commencement of dramatic representations at the Museum, and in the fall of the same year an efficient *corps dramatique*, under W. H. Smith, was organized, and performances were given. On the 25th of September, 1843, Miss Adelaide Phillips ("only ten years old") made her first appearance as *Little Pickle*, and gave promise of that advancement which she has since made. Miss Phillips, by the kindness of her friends and Jenny Lind, is now in Europe perfecting her vocal acquirements under competent masters, and a brilliant future is in store for her. The Museum attracted all classes, and it was the resort not only of the middling and lower classes, but of the more wealthy residents, for the pieces were well put on the stage, and the actors above mediocrity. The Museum was then and is now patronized by a large class who do not frequent theatres, but who have a nice perception of the difference between tweedle-*dum* and tweedle-*dee*. We have noticed, however, that many who make a first attempt at countenancing theatricals at the Museum, may shortly after be found at the regular theatres, and the Museum has thus done much towards increasing the lovers of the drama. The production of the moral play called "The Drunkard," written by W. H. Smith, decided the fate of the Museum, for it attracted to the house an unprecedented number of visitors, and established permanently the popularity of Boston Museum. In the year 1846 the present Museum was built by Mr. Kimball and his associates, and on the 2d of November of that year the first entertainment was given. The building, designed by H. & J. E. Billings, and erected under the superintendence of Anthony Hanson, is admirably adapted for the purposes for which it was built. It was during the season of 1846–7 that "Aladdin" was brought out, which had a run of eight weeks, and was performed ninety-one times to crowded houses. Mrs. George Barrett also appeared, and has attracted since then a very large amount of money to that house. To record in detail the various performances or the novelties that have been offered, would, at this time, be a repetition of what is still fresh in the memory of our readers. Mr. Kimball is one of the shrewdest managers in this country, and has at all times in reserve sufficient attractions to render him independent of stars, though of late years this place has been the scene of Mr. Booth's performances, when in Boston. Mr. W. H. Smith, as stage-director, has no equal in this city, and to his efforts may be attributed a large portion of the success of the Museum. Mr. Comer, as leader of the orchestra and musical director, rendered the most efficient services, while Mr. Warren is a host in himself, and Mrs. Thoman, Mrs. Vincent, Mr. J. A. Smith, G. H. Finn, and others, are highly esteemed. There is not a theatre in this country which is more agreeable for an actor than this. Behind the scenes all is harmony, and a degree of etiquette is observed, which should be introduced into every theatre.

During the season of 1852–3 at the Museum, Miss Julia Bennet (Mrs. Barrow) performed an engagement of ten successive weeks, to good houses.

That Boston has ever contained a goodly number of persons who were patrons of the drama, we have evidence in the number of entertainments supported, and the numerous localities where Thespis or Melpomene have had temporary sway. Boylston Hall, so long occupied by the Handel and Haydn Society, was in 1840 leased by Wyseman Marshall, and on the 15th of July opened under his auspices, as a summer theatre, the National and Tremont being closed. The hall was well ventilated, and the place was called the Vaudeville Saloon. A constant succession of novelties, during a brief season, served to attract very excellent audiences, composed chiefly of strangers. The leading attractions were Mrs. W. H. Smith, Leman, O. Marshall, W. G. Jones, Miss Fanny Jones, G. Haynes, who appeared as *William Tell*, E. Jones, J. Salmon, G. H. Wyatt, J. P. Adams, Mrs. Hildreth, and the Fox Children. This dramatic saloon continued in "full tide of successful experiment" till the vacation at the other theatres closed, when the manager and actors were obliged to leave, to fill engagements at the regular theatres.

In 1841, an amphitheatre was erected on the corner of Haverhill and Traverse streets, where performances were given by various equestrian corps. In 1842, it was fitted up, and called the Eagle Theatre, and was opened June 27, 1842, by Wyseman Marshall, when an address was delivered by Mrs. Charles Hill. The prices of admission were, private boxes, 50 cts.; boxes, 25 cts.; pit, 12 1-2 cts. On the 20th of August, Mr. W. H. Smith, after a temporary absence from Boston, returned and took the stage management. Melodramas and comedies were given here, and with such effect that the Little Eagle, as it was called, threatened to ruin the National Theatre. Mr. Pelby had been obliged, in order to compete, to reduce his prices to 25 cents. Although the Eagle was not coining money, it was gradually killing the National, when Mr. Pelby bought a quarter interest in the theatre, and one night visited the premises and cut away a portion of the building which supported the roof; and thus, after a season of a few months' duration, brought the season at the Eagle to a close. A law suit was threatened, but the case never came to trial. Mr. Marshall lost the little he was worth in this enterprise, but it gave him that experience which has since been worth more than the money lost.

In 1841, Mr. Lee fitted up his saloon on Washington street, for the purpose of giving concerts. It was subsequently leased by J. W. Appleton, Ostinelli, Sarsedas, and others, who called it the Olympic Saloon, and with a company comprising A. W. Fenno, Curtis, and others, farces and light comedies were given. It was here that Miss Mary Ann Lee appeared, and fascinated the students of Cambridge, and the young men of Boston, by her dancing. It passed through several hands, and Miss Turnbull, the Maeders, F. S. Hill, Miss Fisher, and others, were connected with it. It had a brief existence.

On the 5th of April, 1847, the Boston Adelphi Theatre was opened by Messrs. Brougham and Bland, (located in Court street, over Waterman's House Furnishing Store,) with "Faint Heart Never Won Fair Lady," the burlesque of "Cher Ryan Dfairs Tar," and the "Widow's Victim." The company consisted of Mrs. Brougham, Miss Wagstaff, Mrs. A. W. Benson, Mrs. Bland, Messrs. John Brougham, Bland, Whiting, Graham, Parker, Stephens, Williams, etc. On the opening night, Mr. Brougham delivered one of his facetious addresses, which is worth preserving:—

OPENING ADDRESS.

DELIVERED BY MR. BROUGHAM AT THE ADELPHI ON MONDAY NIGHT.

[*After some altercation behind the Scene.*]

PROMPTER.

But, Mr. Brougham, pray don't; what will they say?
Just what they please; be sure they 'll have their way;
There, Sir, I told you they 'd expect no less.
Begin without an opening address!
Why, 't is in fact the "open sesame"—
Once spoken, our good friend, the public, may
Come freely, though not altogether free,
But just as Casim Baba did before,
By leaving their own *quarters* at the door.
Our house, methinks, though not exactly white,
Has just as constitutional a right
To greet its auditors with opening speech,
Are there not representatives in each?
There, of this age, this country's population;
Here, of all ages, and of every nation;
With them delay or dulness is no crime;
Here, there is no trifling with the public time;
There, acts take weeks before they see the light;
Here, we produce some five or six a night:
For our acts, wit and humor we invoke;
In theirs, 't would puzzle you to find a joke;
Here we' ve a couple, on each side the door.
Grave wisdom there presides without a smile;
Here she takes folly's sprightly mask awhile;
Both houses, therefore, have this end and aim,
The right to vindicate, the wrong to shame;
In each, with you, the gravest duty lies,
To oil the wheels, by granting the supplies.
But now, for what we are about to do,
A word in secret, listen — *entre nous ;*
I can 't exactly say; of this I 'm certain,
There are some plots in train behind that curtain.
I don 't much like to treat such matters lightly;
But my advice is, you should watch them nightly.

Lose not a moment, and, beyond a doubt,
You 'll find by and by that *something* will come out.
Some schemes, I dare not whisper if I would;
Some scenes I cannot paint—I wish I could.
Let me implore you not to join the movers
In any way, except to be *approvers*.
We 've heard and breathed the recent martial air
Played by the "public instruments," and swear,
That to a man, we 're ready one and all,
To do our duty at the prompter's call.
'Tis not the first time we have so appeared,
For oft before we 've "kindly volunteered."
You 'll find some new enlistments in our corps,
And some old soldiers whom you 've seen before;
With one ambition animating all,
By the Adelphi's flag to stand or fall,
Just as the scene requires. Our marshal tact
Must not be spoken of; you 'll see us act.
Manœuvres various, but not quite the same,
Makes gallant Taylor's an historic name;
By Parthian prowess are our laurels won—
Our greatest glory a successful *run.*
Let us then hope, in this all iron age,
When universal raildom is the rage,
You 'll not forget this new established "stage."
To gain your suffrages we toil like Turks,
Even our painter at the canvas works;
His views are yours, for zeal he's not surpassed,
But nails his (water) colors to the mast;
The envied victory your voice commands,
To give the *palm* rests solely in your hands.
You can each doubt remove; be pleased to do it—
Go for "THE ADELPHI"—pshaw, I mean *come to it.*

The Adelphi was a favorite resort of the lovers of fun, and John Brougham was the life of the place. The burlesques which were brought out were very good, and attracted well. "Metamora" was burlesqued, Mrs. Brougham performing *Tapiokee,* and "Tom and Jerry, or Life in Boston," from its local hits, did well. Miss

Anna Cruise and Mrs. W. H. Smith were attached to the company. The house was very small, and even when crowded would not admit of sufficient receipts to afford a very remunerating business to the managers.

The Lyceum Theatre, in Sudbury street, afterwards the Eagle, and lately christened the American, was opened in 1849 by Mr. H. Bland, and was managed by Bland and Skerrett. Messrs. Crouta and Mestayer subsequently tried their hands at it, and others have since indulged their managerial propensities by short seasons. It has never benefited the management for any length of time.

On the 16th of October, 1848, Messrs. Robert Hamilton and C. L. Stone opened the Dramatic Museum, in Beach street, near the United States Hotel. The performances embraced "As You Like It," *Rosalind*, Miss Clara Ellis; *Touchstone*, C. W. Hunt; an Opening Address, written by Frederick S. Hill, and the farce of "The Lady and the Devil." The business was not remarkable, and the projectors of the enterprise burnt their fingers. It was subsequently called the Beach Street Museum, and the "Female Forty Thieves," in which Miss Mestayer figured, drew tremendous houses. It was opened by several adventurers, at intervals, for a year or more, and is now occupied by the Catholics, the basement being used as a market house.

There have been several other places of amusement, more or less public, of which we make no note, as they present no marked feature, though from them have emanated several actors who have become ornaments to their profession.

Having alluded to the various places where the drama

has been presented to the Boston public, we may with propriety drop the curtain, and close this record of the stage in Boston. We would at this time return our thanks to all who have assisted us in its preparation. One gentleman, however, has passed away since its commencement, from whom we received the most generous aid, and who, previous to his death, was kind enough to suggest the propriety of its appearing in book form, and made notes for our use of some mis-statements in the earlier chapters. To enumerate those who have given us information would occupy too much space, and, if we should attempt it, would be a task which would require days to complete. We are under great obligations, also, to our contemporaries of the press, both in Boston and in other cities, for their kindly notices of the Record.

The reader who has perused these chapters, must have been impressed with the fact, that the drama is the amusement most favored by the people, and the most enduring in its hold upon the public. For nearly sixty years Boston has sustained one or more theatres, and the New Opera House and Theatre, now in process of erection, will receive from the public a most generous support. In closing, we will quote from a letter written by Thomas Barry, Esq., a short extract, which, though not intended for publicity, is appropriate to the times. It was written a year ago: —

"The drama is firmly planted in New England for good or for evil; you cannot crush it by prejudice, or destroy it by misplaced religious enthusiasm. The public can make a theatre a blessing or a curse. In all ages and in all lands, history fully proves that the stage has flourished most, and been most generally upheld, where taste is most refined, and manners softened by the influence of civilization. Where liberty breathes, there the drama exists; and it is worthy of remark, that it flourishes only in those States that are not cursed by despotism. Much of the hostility to the drama at present existing in the Eastern States, is doubtless inherited by the people from their ancestors, who looked with horror on the profligacy of Charles the Second, when, imitating the contagious example of the monarch, the English nation became abandoned to gross sensuality. The arts were prostrated in the cause of licentiousness, and the drama did not escape the contamination. You will have, sooner or later, a first-class theatre in Boston, and if properly built and properly conducted, it will prove A BOON TO THE PUBLIC, AND A FORTUNE TO THE MANAGER."

These are the prophetic words of a veteran actor and manager; may we live to see them historical facts in some future Record of the Stage in Boston.

www.ingramcontent.com/pod-product-compliance
Lightning Source LLC
LaVergne TN
LVHW020917110826
845150LV00004B/702

9781425555207